Borders, Nationalism, and the African State

BORDERS, NATIONALISM, AND THE AFRICAN STATE

edited by

Ricardo René Larémont

LYNNE
RIENNER
PUBLISHERS

BOULDER
LONDON

Published in the United States of America in 2005 by
Lynne Rienner Publishers, Inc.
1800 30th Street, Boulder, Colorado 80301
www.rienner.com

and in the United Kingdom by
Lynne Rienner Publishers, Inc.
3 Henrietta Street, Covent Garden, London WC2E 8LU

Library of Congress Cataloging-in-Publication Data
Borders, nationalism, and the African state / edited by Ricardo René
Larémont.
    Includes bibliographical references and index.
    ISBN 1-58826-340-1 (hardcover : alk. paper)
    1. Africa—Boundaries. 2. Africa—Colonial influence. 3.
Africa—Ethnic relations—Political aspects. 4. Africa—Politics and
Government—1960– I. Larémont, Ricardo René.
    DT31.B725 2005
    960.3'2—dc22

                                                    2004026083

British Cataloguing in Publication Data
A Cataloguing in Publication record for this book
is available from the British Library.

Printed and bound in the United States of America

The paper used in this publication meets the requirements
of the American National Standard for Permanence of
Paper for Printed Library Materials Z39.48-1992.

5   4   3   2   1

To

Ana Maria Larémont

Contents

Illustrations

Acknowledgments

This book would not have been possible without the generous financial support of the Carnegie Corporation. Within the Carnegie Corporation, its president, Vartan Gregorian, provided visionary leadership in supporting the project, and Stephen Del Rosso and Lynn DiMartino gave steadfast support and guidance. Special thanks must be given to Stephen Del Rosso for having confidence in our Binghamton University research team, for his unwavering support at moments of research difficulties, and for his delightful sense of good humor. When I became worried, Stephen always found a way to make me smile. I thank him so much for that.

Along the road to completing the book, extraordinary and talented collaborators accompanied me: Francis Deng with his elegant writing, clear thinking, and unstinting gracefulness; Edmond Keller with his sage advice, good humor, and great insight; Herbert Weiss with his encyclopedic knowledge of central Africa, loving counsel, and true friendship. Dr. Weiss's collaborator, Tatiana Caryannis, provided prescient analyses at an early stage of her career. Jimmy Kandeh is a professional and a true friend. My collaborators here at Binghamton, William Martin, Robert Ostergard, and Ali Mazrui, provided critical advice and support at various stages of the project. And lastly, my longtime editor, Grace Houghton, as always helped me clarify and simplify my academic prose.

In addition to these principal contributors, numerous undergraduate and graduate students here at the State University of New York at Binghamton assisted with the project. They include Rodwan Abouharb, Amitabha Bhoumik, Richard Burger, Rachel Cremona, Sarah Dreisinger, Christine Finn, Ryan Fitzpatrick, Uri Foox, Nischit Hegde, Myung-Hee Kim, Nicole Miller, Jennifer Piñales, and Maria Elena Sandovici. I would also like to acknowledge the support and advice of Mark Bromley, SIPRI; Donna Devoist, Fernand Braudel Center; John Frazier, chair of Binghamton's Department of Geography; Michael Grillot of the International Energy Statistics Team, U.S. Department of Energy; Abdullah Ibrahim, University of the Western Cape; Juan Linz, Yale University; Richard Rehberg, Binghamton University; and Ian Smillie of Partnership Africa Canada.

Librarians at Binghamton University and Columbia University helped me to obtain data and other materials for this research, particularly Carol Clemente here at Binghamton. Her management of the interlibrary loan system made it seem as though I was working within a much larger research library. At Columbia University, Joseph Caruso graciously provided access to university materials at a critical moment during this research. His intervention helped me enormously.

Finalement, je remercie la source de ma joie, Li Shen Yun. Avant toi, j'étais perdu. Avec toi, je suis ancré.

1

Borders, States, and Nationalism

Ricardo René Larémont

By the end of the twentieth century, most Western European and North American states enjoyed effective governments and mostly stable societies. In contrast, European states—especially in the Balkans—and many African states experienced substantial political instability and mass racial and ethnic violence. Why?

To answer this question, a study was undertaken, culminating in this book. The study focused on four African states. Three factors were identified as being essential for building stable states and societies: the consolidation of borders, the building of state institutions, and the creation of national consciousness. In order to understand how these three factors constitute the essential elements for stable states and societies, this chapter provides a broad historical background. Subsequent chapters then offer in-depth analyses of border consolidation, state formation, and national identity formation in Sudan, Ethiopia, the Democratic Republic of Congo (hereinafter DRC), and Sierra Leone. Two additional chapters analyze economic contexts for civil warfare and the position of African states in the world economy, bringing the important perspective of political economy into the mix. We chose Sudan, Ethiopia, the DRC, and Sierra Leone partly because they give us varying views of the partial accomplishment of these critical state objectives in the African context, and partly because of the constraints of financing. Our original research design also included Nigeria, Algeria, Angola, and South Africa among our cases. When we failed to obtain adequate funding, we reduced our cases to the four contained herein.

What becomes clear from our review of border consolidation, state formation, and nationalism in Western Europe, Eastern Europe, and Africa is that state development is neither linear nor predictable. Furthermore, what is most instructive from a review of history is that almost all Western European states developed over several centuries. To expect Eastern European and African countries to accomplish these objectives in decades when centuries were required in Western Europe may be overly optimistic. This chapter contends that the processes of border consolidation, state formation, and nationalism in Eastern Europe (especially in the Balkans) and in Africa are substantially similar. Comprehending this similarity helps us understand how to proceed not only with questions of borders, state formation, and nationalism, but also with issues of establishing more stable and peaceful societies in the developing world.

When borders are not consolidated, when effective political institutions have not been created, and when nationalist projects remain incomplete, the result is instability and a tendency toward either civil conflict or warfare. This combination of phenomena has been observed often in Africa, particularly in our four case studies: Sudan, Ethiopia, the DRC, and Sierra Leone.

The long-term and comparative review of history provided in this chapter reveals that stable governments are most often built after more or less stable boundaries have been established. The challenge for most of Africa and the Balkans has been that the territorial boundaries of most extant states were demarcated by colonial powers during the nineteenth and early twentieth centuries. In Africa, these borders were accepted by newly decolonized governments in the early 1960s, yet despite formal recognition, these borders have remained porous and often undefended. The fluidity and irrelevance of African borders has been in large part due to their haphazard demarcation by European colonialists who ignored locally existing societies. African borders were designed to meet colonial objectives. After their acceptance in the postcolonial period, these unconsolidated borders have inhibited the extension of state jurisdiction, and have thwarted the formation of needed state institutions. Moreover, the state's weakened capacity has engendered social instability and conditions that lead to irredentist revolt.

The borders of African states were fixed by European colonialists during a narrow window of time (essentially from 1878 to 1914). In the immediate postcolonial period (beginning in the early 1960s), these borders were reified by independence leaders. From the 1960s until today the most ardent supporters of colonially inherited borders have been urbanized political elites who have the most to gain by their maintenance. People in rural areas (where the majority of Africans still reside) consider borders—and often the state—irrelevant.

After this initial theoretical chapter, the study of borders, states, and nationalism examines whether the constraints of colonially inherited borders has inhibited state formation and national consolidation in Sudan, Ethiopia, the DRC, and Sierra Leone. In Chapters 2 through 5 we engage in in-depth analyses of the four cases. The researchers used two methodological approaches. First, in our four countries public opinion surveys were used to ascertain mass views with regard to borders, the state, and nationalism. This body of information was then set within a historical analysis. By doing so, we hope readers can develop an understanding of the transformation of the state and nation over time. Chapters 6 and 7 add the dimension of a political economy analysis, analyzing economic factors that determine state effectiveness.

Throughout these analyses, we had to examine the issues of border consolidation, state formation, and nationalism both separately and as a whole. Although these three issues are related, they can also be examined as discrete processes. When analyzing the critical relationship between colonially inherited borders and the creation and maintenance of state institutions, we focused on how the inheritance of colonial borders and the decision not to alter them affected or inhibited the formation of viable state institutions. We then examined the transformation, reformation, or disintegration of state institutions during the postcolonial period. In our final analyses of Sudan, Ethiopia, the DRC, and Sierra Leone we wanted to discern whether the "states" in our four cases were successful in creating a set of institutions of rule in both urban areas and the countryside that was meaningful to the general populace.

When examining the question of nationalism, we tried to assess whether possibilities and strategies existed for creating cohesive multiethnic, multireligious nations in the African context, which is one in which nationalism has been attempted to be formed in what is usually an inchoate state (in other words, where the territorial notion of the state is often contested or being renegotiated). Throughout our analyses we were very concerned about the theoretical and practical aspects. Can multiethnic nationalism and the development of state institutions be possible in such contexts (i.e., where the borders of the state are unstable)? Is it possible to analyze the "state" and the "nation" in these circumstances? While engaged in our research we faced rather serious obstacles, but nevertheless proceeded. We had to examine borders, states, nationalism, war, and conflict resolution in real, rather than ideal, circumstances.

Borders, States, Nationalism, and Our Perspectives

At this juncture, we want to reveal our points of view. Because of our sensitivity to and awareness of the devastating consequences of warfare, and despite our long-standing commitment to inclusive democratic politics, in this study we tend to stress the principle that state capacity is more important than incorporative political processes. In our view inclusive politics become important only after the establishment of the state's essential capacity to defend itself from external aggressors and to protect its citizens from violence. From our perspective, state capacity is essential—and often missing in developing, multiethnic states. Where there is sufficient state capacity, multiethnic states can be created even by force—albeit at considerable social and political cost as in Tito's Yugoslavia. While we recognize that force can create unity, we at the same time are sensitive to the ethical, political, and social costs of a strong, authoritarian state. Throughout we have been aware of the necessity to strike a balance between addressing the need for adequate state capacity while avoiding authoritarianism. In the African context, we hope to discuss the possibilities for building multiethnic and multireligious states and nations—despite their formidable difficulty in formation—because, in an increasingly globalized world, multiethnic and multilinguistic states seem inevitable. Throughout, however, we have tried to maintain an ethical sensitivity. This ethical imperative requires our discussion of the possible creation of states within environments of minimal political coercion. This combination of objectives makes this project important not only for Africa, but also for world affairs.

In our discussions of borders, states, and nationalism, we treat the state as an important category for analysis because we believe that capable states are necessary for the protection of citizens and for the economic development of society. When examining relationships among border consolidation, state formation, nationalism, and their chronological implementation, our review of European and African history discerned five possible sequences:

1. Border consolidation followed by state formation followed by questionable attempts at nationalism (England)
2. State formation followed by border consolidation followed by multiethnic, multilinguistic nationalism followed by multiethnic, unilinguistic nationalism (France)
3. Uniethnic, unilinguistic nationalism followed by state formation followed by border consolidation (Prussia/Germany)
4. Border consolidation followed by linguistic nationalism followed by state formation (Italy) and,
5. Unsuccessful attempts at border consolidation, state formation, and nationalism in colonial and postcolonial contexts (the Balkans and many states in Africa)

Borders and the Analysis of the State

> Tell a man today to go and build a state and he will try to establish a definite and defensible territorial boundary and compel those who live inside it to obey him.
>
> —S. E. Finer[1]

As we review the European processes of state and nation formation in this chapter, the critical questions for us are the following: Does the state and its institutions have to be constructed and stabilized before the nation is built? Can the nation be imagined and built before the creation of the state? Are stable borders connected to these two processes? If various sequences are possible in Europe, wouldn't it be logical that various sequences would be possible in Africa?[2]

Regarding the state and its capacity, we use modes of analysis espoused by various authorities including Max Weber, Perry Anderson,

Charles Tilly, Ali A. Mazrui, and Crawford Young.[3] We focus on categories of state function to analyze state effectiveness. We believe that effective states discharge the following functions:

- Defend their nationals or citizens from external enemies through the use of an effective army
- Regulate crime and disorder through the use of a police force
- Develop an effective civilian bureaucracy to administer the functions of the state
- Raise revenue and create an economic infrastructure to pay its army, its police force, and its civilian bureaucracy
- Resolve disputes through a system of law and a judiciary that enforces the law
- Create laws through a legislative process
- Provide public services such as safety, education, health care, transportation and roads, and postal service
- Acquire and sustain political legitimacy (legitimacy enables the state to govern with lower attendant social costs)

Beyond these essential functions, in order for a state to be a true state, according to Weber (and others), it must claim "the monopoly of legitimate use of physical force within a territory."[4] This often means that the state must be able to define and defend its borders so that it can assert this monopoly. Beyond this question of border control, many scholars of the Western European nation-state add an additional factor: unilinguistic or uniethnic nationalism.[5] What makes this study both challenging and important is that we are examining the possibilities for creating multiethnic and multilinguistic polities in a context where borders are either unstable or contested.

The four African states in this study (Sudan, Ethiopia, the DRC, and Sierra Leone) are like many other African states. They are multiethnic or multiracial, they are multireligious, and they most often include distinct social groupings that have been assembled within the confines of artificial colonial borders.[6] In the Sudan we find a society that was racially divided first between mostly Arab and mostly Negroid sub-Saharan African peoples and then religiously divided among Muslims, Christians, and practitioners of African traditional religions. In Ethiopia we find a multiethnic society that was never completely colonized by Europeans but that nevertheless suffers from attempts to create a cohesive nation. The DRC is also a multiethnic society that tends to be difficult to unite. Moreover, the challenges of unity are complicated by substantial mineral resources; those interested in making profits, rather than fostering national unity, prefer to play the politics and economics of division. Sierra Leone, like the Congo, is also multiethnic and has experienced (on a smaller but still bloody scale) the divisions that result when ethnic politics merge with profit politics.

Political leaders of newly independent African states built their states and governments upon territories with borders that were for the most part drawn arbitrarily by European colonialists. In 1963 the Organization of African States recognized these borders as legally valid and inviolable. As a result, the borders of African states were defined and states were created juridically without reference to the assemblage of ethnic groups, religious groups, and peoples residing within those borders. Fixing and accepting these borders outside the normal processes of military conquest or voluntary affiliation has merged disparate social groups into nation-states that tend to be very unstable.

The territorial boundaries of newly independent African states were ratified by political leaders in the early 1960s because they believed at that time that accepting these borders would reduce warfare both in the short term and the long term, but in many critical cases, four of which are the subject of this study, this decision has engendered greater conflict. Since independence, many African states, both in terms of governmental efficacy and in terms of nationalism, have not been as effective or as successful as originally envisioned. Borders, or more specifically colonial borders, have been a contributing factor.

Borders and the Analysis of Nationalism

To understand how borders, states, and nationalism fit together we will examine six historical cases: France, England, Prussia/Germany, Italy, the Balkan state of Yugoslavia, and several African states. By looking closely at the interrelationships of these three variables in six different situations we begin to understand the complexity and variability of how states, nations, and borders interact.

Regarding nationalism in our four African cases, we specifically delineate the ethnic, religious, or racial groups that reside within each of these states. We then describe how these different groups interact, collaborate, or conflict. To understand the interactions of different social groups we used survey analysis in addition to synthesis of other data to assess whether multiethnic, multiracial, or multireligious nations could be configured within the constraints of colonially inherited borders. If our assessment determined that cooperative nationalism is not a possibility within these borders, alternate policies were recommended.

Borders simultaneously lack meaning and have great meaning. From the perspective of ordinary African citizens, territorial boundaries have little meaning because these boundaries need to be crossed for trade and commercial reasons or because of family ties. From the viewpoint of the state, however, boundaries are geopolitically and sociopolitically necessary, especially for building state institutions such as the military and the police. Ordinarily, legitimate governmental objectives can not be clarified or implemented unless the territory where governmental authority is to be extended can be defined and understood. Weak states working to become more effective states are eventually concerned with borders in their task of extending governmental authority over specific territory.

When examining nationalism without reference to borders, we look at two alternatives. Would Africa have to go the nativist, atavistic route, opting for a nationalism based on ethnic or linguistic uniformity? Or would multiethnic, multiracial, and multireligious states be possible in the African context?

Nationalism, whether configured upon heterogeneous or homogeneous grounds, has obvious political value. As Rupert Anderson noted, when effective nationalism is achieved, it creates a

> community of people who feel they belong together in the double sense that they share deeply significant elements of a common heritage and that they have a common destiny for the future. In the contemporary world the nation is for the great portions of mankind the community with which men most intensely and most unconditionally identify themselves, even to the extent of being able to lay down their lives for it, however deeply they may differ among themselves on other issues.
>
> The nation today is the largest community which, when the chips are down, effectively commands men's loyalty, overriding the claims both of the lesser communities within it and those which cut across it or potentially enfold it within a still greater society, reaching ultimately to mankind as a whole. In this sense a nation can be called a "terminal" community.[7]

Within our present options for nationalism, the choices seem to be between defining nationalism upon homogeneous or heterogeneous grounds. In the future we believe that nationalism will be heterogeneously defined, given the scale and speed of mass migration—both voluntary and involuntary—that is evident globally. When these migratory patterns are linked to new definitions of transnational identity and citizenship, we observe global forces at work demanding redefinitions of the meanings of the state, borders, identity, and citizenship.

Considering the interaction of these factors from a historical perspective, in Western Europe, especially in England and France, border consolidation occurred and state institutions were developed before nationalism became important. The states of Great Britain and France pursued their nationalist projects after first establishing and stabilizing the borders of their states and developing effective state institutions. State institutions in England and France stabilized during the seventeenth century, before these countries initiated their nationalist projects. Given the demographic dominance of the English, the incorporation of Scotland and Wales were more pacific affairs—in contrast, for example, to the violent incorporation of Burgundy into France—and multiethnic nationalism was never expressed as a significant part of England's political and ideological agendas. France, however, because of its entrenched ethnic and linguistic heterogeneity, opted first for multiethnic, multilinguistic nationalism at the end of the eighteenth century and then shifted to multiethnic, unilinguistic nationalism in the nineteenth and twentieth centuries. This effort to form a nation in France was a conscious and conscientious state project that endured for at least 140 years.[8] At the end of the twentieth century, the nationalist projects in Great Britain and France underwent new stresses, principally caused by new immigration from North Africa, West Africa, South Asia, and the Caribbean. These new immigrants are forcing the states of Great Britain and France to confront their definitions and formulations of nationalism, moving from the ambiguous nationalism of Britain and the centralizing nationalism of France to new forms that are still unclear.

The discussion of the need and plausibility of multiethnic and multilinguistic polities is needed at this moment in history because one clear and disturbing trend during the twentieth century was the expression of extremist uniethnic and unilinguistic nationalism. In most analyses of nationalism, it has most often been assumed that nationalism must have a uniethnic or unilinguistic basis. Can stable nationalism be built instead upon polyethnicity or polylinguistics? During the twentieth century most forms of nationalism that arose were premised upon exclusivity and persecution of outgroups. In Africa, Eastern Europe, South Asia, and Southeast Asia (notably Indonesia), and also in economically developed regions of the world (note such movements among the Bretons, the Flemings, the French Canadians, the Scots, and the Welsh), we have observed uniethnic and unilinguistic forms of nationalism based upon exclusion. These trends pose ethical questions. They also present questions about unrestrained population splintering and economic inefficiency. Charles Tilly observed that "if all the peoples on behalf of whom someone has recently made a claim to separate statehood were actually to acquire their own territories, the world would splinter from the present 160-odd recognized states to thousands of satellite entities, most of them tiny and economically nonviable."[9]

Our view is that the future lies in efforts toward transethnic, transreligious, and translinguistic nationalism because such entities lead to greater economic power and efficiency. Second, in many contexts the important ancillary benefit of effectively creating heterogeneous nations is that they lead not only to economic efficiency but they also lead to lower costs of coercion for the state. The state's longer-term stability requires the loyalty of its citizens, whether the state is constructed upon homogeneous or heterogeneous lines. We believe that our analysis of the possibilities of nationalism in our four African cases will help us venture into new studies of nationalism in complex, heterogeneous societies.

France: Borders, the State, and Nationalism

By the late tenth century A.D., France as a state and nation did not exist. What would eventually become France was territorially undefined, it was linguistically diverse, and state institutions were nonexistent. During a sustained period that required almost three centuries, France's monarchs developed capable administrative systems for taxing the populace. This capacity to tax and obtain revenue financed needed state institutions. Before the eventual creation of these sophisticated state institutions, what was in place in France was a shadowy judicial entity known as the *regnum Francorum*. This regnum Francorum lacked clear territorial boundaries, had weak political leadership, and was divided into seven linguistic subsystems: Celtic, Teutonic, Basque, Catalan, Provençal, and Francien or French.[10] This linguistic diversity provided challenges to national unification. France's efforts to consolidate its borders required three centuries, involving the gradual expansion of state power from the Île-de-France region surrounding Paris to the consequent incorporation of peripheral regions including Normandy, Guyenne, Brittany, Burgundy, and Provence. During the thirteenth century these peripheral regions were all semiautonomous. The territorial incorporation of these regions (including Languedoc) into the political center began during the fifteenth century and was mostly complete by the seventeenth century.[11]

If a comparative snapshot of the status of borders, states, and nations in the tenth century were taken, England and France would provide notable contrasts. While France was not defined territorially, England was (with the exception of Northumberland, Cumberland, and Durham).[12] In contrast to France where six languages were in use, England employed only three (Norman French, Celtic, and Anglo-Saxon). France, therefore, provided a greater challenge regarding the consolidation of borders, the building of the state, and the formation of the nation. These challenges to build a state and nation under conditions that were territorially difficult and linguistically and ethnically complex spurred monarchs from Phillip II onwards to construct a strong, centralized state to unify a society with fissiparous tendencies.

The processes of border consolidation and the building of state institutions in France were interrelated. Borders were established and expanded by monarchs in Île-de-France/Paris who had the military capability to enforce their will upon subjugated peoples. This territorial incorporation was made possible mainly by military conquest and sometimes by luck (in some cases, the French monarchs' political rivals in outlying provinces simply died).

The most important aspect of building the French state involved the critical relationship between raising revenue through taxes and paying armies and police forces to defend the interests of the state. Rulers both in France and England understood early that the first demands of a state required developing taxation systems that would enable them to finance what they understood as the two prerequisites for the survival of the state: the creation of an army to defend against external aggressors and the creation of police forces to establish internal order and eliminate banditry. The development of systems of taxation and the creation of armies and police forces in France (and in England) helped them consolidate their borders. The successful levy of taxes in France (and England) enabled these states to finance other institutions of government in addition to the army and police, including judiciaries, road maintenance, postal services, et cetera.

The connection between a state's ability to raise revenue and its institutional capabilities is critical. By being able to raise revenue via taxation, France was able to create its first institution for its survival: an army. With revenues in hand, France's monarch established first an ad hoc army and then the first standing army in Europe (the *compagnies d'ordonnance* that were established in 1445).[13] This standing army was then enlarged and modernized during subsequent centuries. Efforts at taxation began in the fourteenth century and continued through the twentieth century. During the critical seventeenth century, however, France developed its more systematic methods for the collection of tax revenue. By collecting taxes capably, the state survived until the revolution.

The first French king to impose taxes was Phillip II, who levied the first set of ad hoc, intermittent taxes in 1190.[14] These first taxes were temporary war subsidies levied on an emergency basis. Phillip IV, one of his successors, expanded the use of these ad hoc war subsidies in 1302.[15] Regular rather than ad hoc attempts at taxation began in France with the imposition of the *gabelle* in 1340s.[16] The *gabelle* was an indirect tax on the consumption of salt. At about the same time that the *gabelle* was imposed, other taxes, including the *aides*, were created. These *aides* were also indirect taxes imposed on the consumption of important items including wine, beer, cider, et cetera.[17] The *gabelle* and the *aides* comprised the essential elements of French taxation during this early period. Approximately twenty years later, in 1360, the Crown made the *aides* and the *gabelle* permanent.[18] Shortly thereafter, in 1363, the Crown added another tax called the *fouage*. Like the later *taille* and the *aides*, the revenue from the *fouage* financed state institutions, principally the army.[19]

After the imposition of the *fouage*, Charles VII modified the taxation system in 1439. In that year, he imposed the *taille*. The inhabitants of an area that fell under his direct royal control (known as the *pays d'éléction* or Languedoïl) paid what was called the *taille personelle* (assessed on personal net worth or wealth). Inhabitants in an area just adjacent to royal control (in the *pays d'état* of Normandy, Guyenne, Burgundy, Brittany, and Languedoc) paid the *taille réelle* (which was assessed on the value and productivity of land). This difference in taxation revealed the partial incorporation of Normandy, Guyenne, Burgundy, Brittany, and Languedoc into

France. In 1446 Charles VII imposed yet another *taille* called the *taille des gens d'armes*.[20] This combination of taxes (the *gabelle*, the *aides*, the *fouage*, the *taille*, and the *taille des gens d'armes*) became the core of a taxation system that financed state institutions.

The nexus between raising taxes and financing an army during the fourteenth and fifteenth centuries in France was clear. Because of the more stable provision of state revenues, France's standing army, created in 1445, grew eventually to approximately 5,200 soldiers. France's army continued to grow after this initial period. With its standing army, France's monarchs were able to police and consolidate borders.

France's taxation systems were made more effective during the critical seventeenth century. Major improvements in the effectiveness of tax administration were undertaken by Ministers Sully (1598–1611), Richelieu (1624–1642), Mazarin (1643–1661), and Colbert (1661–1683). By improving the state's ability to collect taxes, they also significantly enhanced the French state's administrative infrastructure. Due to their tax collection innovations, the French state raised more revenue during the seventeenth century which, in turn, strengthened the state's capabilities.

Other important governmental innovations in France involved the enhancement of the state's methods of governance. Beginning in 1642, Louis XIII and Minister Richelieu created the political offices of the *intendants de la justice, police, et finance*.[21] In these *intendants* the king centralized the offices of taxation, defense, and judicial administration, making the *intendants* the most important political personages within the kingdom, ranking immediately after the king in importance.[22] The office of *intendant* strengthened France's political infrastructure significantly, enabling the monarch to enforce his rule on the grass-roots level even more effectively. Louis XIV (who succeeded Louis XIII) and Ministers Mazarin and Colbert (who succeeded Richelieu) further strengthened these systems of tax collection and governance. Except for the brief five-year anti-tax Fronde revolt that lasted from 1648 to 1653, this system of governance served France until the French Revolution in 1789.

After the reign of Louis XIII, Louis XIV with Ministers Mazarin and Colbert created other relevant state institutions by diversifying state bureaucracy and making it more effective. They created three bodies to manage the French state. The most important was the Conseil d'État or Conseil d'en Haut, a policy council established in 1654. This council was composed of the secretaries of state for foreign affairs, the army and the navy, and the *contrôleur general* of finances. It dealt with the most important matters of state and frequently focused on foreign affairs. Besides the Conseil d'État, Louis created the Conseil des Dépêches (1661) that supervised the machinery of government and was responsible for the internal administration of the state. Also in 1661, he created a Conseil des Finances to maintain and organize the collection of taxes and finance.

Returning to the question of the military, Louis XIV continued to expand France's army. Under his rule the army eventually grew to three hundred thousand soldiers. The expansion of the army became possible because Louis XIV could rely upon a very stable tax system. Included by this time was collection of the *taille*, the *aides*, the *gabelle* (salt taxes), and receipts from royal taxes, the royal domain, and the sale of public offices. He also had a stable governmental structure, overseen by the *conseils* and implemented by the *intendants*.[23]

While France did create effective state institutions and while it did develop a formidable ability to tax, it did not, in contrast to England, create an effective legislature that served as a countervailing power to the monarch. France's monarchs were able to raise funds almost unilaterally without serious consultation with a legislature because early on France's kings developed a redoubtable capacity to coerce tax collection by using the military. In contrast, England's military forces were much smaller and decentralized; they were also more directly controlled by local lords than by the monarch. This decentralization of military forces along with the English historical tradition of consultation regarding taxation (which had roots in the thirteenth century) led to an early brokerage of power between nobility and monarch, and facilitated the creation of a more active and powerful parliament. By contrast, the Estates-General, France's attempt at a parliament, tried to exert parliamentary prerogatives in the seventeenth century when it criticized regent Marie de Medici's management of the state's finances (in 1614). When it failed either to criticize or limit the regent's power effectively, regent Marie and Louis XIII dismissed the Parlement. It was stripped of its emerging political authority, relegated solely to judicial affairs, and not convened to deliberate on legislative matters until 1789, in the midst of the French Revolution.[24] Thus, the Parlements in France were limited principally to judicial rather than legislative affairs.[25]

When examining the growth of the state in France during the fourteenth through the seventeenth centuries, it is important to recognize that France for much of this period was actually split into two geographic zones. The first zone under centralized royal control was called the *pays d'élection* or Languedoïl. Because of this centralized control the residents of the *pays d'élection* or Languedoïl paid different taxes than those paid by the inhabitants of the *pays d'état*, a somewhat more autonomous zone adjacent to Languedoïl. This second zone included Normandy, Guyenne, Burgundy, Brittany, and Languedoc. The residents of this second zone not only paid different taxes, but also often resisted paying those taxes. Their successful tax resistance plus the different taxation system indicated that this zone was not completely incorporated into France. Royal incorporation of the *pays d'état* took place gradually during the seventeenth century. Authorities in Paris slowly expanded governmental control from the center to the periphery of what became known geographically as France. As its military, bureaucratic, taxation, and fiscal capabilities became more effective, the French state gradually expanded and centralized, as revealed in the more effective taxation in peripheral regions.

The ability to tax successfully enabled the French state to establish critical state institutions, especially a military (to defend the state against external enemies) and a police force (to maintain internal security). Furthermore, the creation of the office of the *intendants* enabled the monarch to extend his rule and deliver governmental services to the local level. Once installed and regularized, the *intendants* levied taxes, sustained armies and police forces, maintained order, and supervised the administration of justice for the monarch. This led to greater state effectiveness, but it was the creation of an effective tax system that sustained the effectiveness of the state. The imposition of taxes was clearly resented and even resisted. In the final analysis, however, taxpayers finally acceded to paying taxes because maintenance of minimum levels of public order consequently made economic development possible. When one reviews the processes of state formation in general, all effective states eventually must collect taxes, glean rents, or borrow money to raise the necessary funds to sustain state institutions. Taxation is the most effective form of raising revenue while at the same time assuring the penetration of the state into the society. The architects of the French state, unlike many twentieth-century developing states, understood the relationship between taxation and governmental efficacy early in the state's development. This system of taxation and governance required nearly four centuries to develop fully, with initiatives beginning in the fourteenth century and becoming systematized during the seventeenth century.

France developed a strong, effective state and consolidated most of its territorial borders before focusing on questions of nationalism and national unification. France's nationalist project began during the French Revolution and continued to evolve into the twentieth century. Over time the nationalist project changed, shifting from a radically egalitarian program at the end of the eighteenth century that focused on abolishing social differences based on race and ethnicity to a nationalist program that sought to create a new citizen who would be molded via recruitment into the schools and the army.[26] This new *citoyen* would be a French-speaking supporter of republicanism. This nationalist project was a formidable political and cultural undertaking because France at the end of the eighteenth century was linguistically and ethnically diverse. Its people clung to regional identities and spoke diverse languages, including French, Basque, Catalan, Breton, Flemish, German, Italian, and Provençal.[27] Using first the schools and primary-school education, the leaders of the French state expanded the teaching and use of French in a specific attempt to incorporate these non-French-speaking regions into France. Second, as increasing numbers of Frenchmen were conscripted into first the revolutionary and then

Napoleon's armies, the use of French in the ranks of the soldiers was extended and became standardized. By using public elementary schooling and army life, the French state formed a French-speaking nation in a land that had been marked by profound ethnic and linguistic diversity.[28]

It is important to underscore that France's effort at border consolidation, state formation, and effective nationalism required about five centuries. This longer period for state and national development, without significant interference from other imperial powers, distinguishes the French case from the Eastern European and African cases.

England: Borders, the State, and Nationalism

England was territorially defined by 975 A.D.[29] The territorial definition of England at such an early stage in the development of the state facilitated and stabilized subsequent processes for the building of state institutions. Only three regions of what came to be known as England remained unincorporated during the tenth century (Northumberland, Cumberland, and Durham). These three regions were merged into England by 1327.[30] The Welsh, an ethnically distinct people who spoke a different language from the Norman French and from the Anglo-Saxons of England, were politically incorporated into England during the thirteenth century. Scotland, yet another distinct region, merged with Great Britain by the Act of Union of 1707.

As mentioned in the previous section, one of the critical tasks of government has involved the development of financial systems to underwrite operation of state institutions. In the cases of England and France, this involved primary reliance upon systems of taxation rather than sale of primary commodities (rents) or debt financing. (Debt financing became important later in the development of these states but it remained secondary in importance to taxation.) In the case of France, taxes were often levied by monarchs in negotiations with local lords within the feudal system, but these negotiations were frequently formal and the power relationship in these negotiations favored the monarch. In England, the situation was quite different. Early on, to levy taxes in England, the monarch had to negotiate with nobility, clergy, and burghers in the forum of Parliament. This tradition and process had roots in the thirteenth century when in 1295 Edward I (1273–1307) assembled Parliament for the first time for the express purpose of collecting taxes to raise an army.[31] This consultation process, begun in 1295, became fully formalized by the 1640s, despite a period of monarchical resistance by so-called "strong kings" like Henry II (1154–1189), John (1199–1216), and Henry III (1216–1272) who challenged parliamentary participation in the government's tax-raising ventures. Brokered political power in English governance and consent from Parliament began in the mid-thirteenth century and became more well-established by the mid-fourteenth century.[32] This tendency toward brokered political power between monarch and parliament was so pronounced that Sir John Fortescue could remark that "in France, . . . the minority could impose taxes at will, whereas in England it had to seek consent."[33] This process of parliamentary consultation to raise taxes was reinforced further during the fifteenth century and afterwards. Beginning in the fifteenth century and clearly by the seventeenth century, England developed a state that was capable of raising taxes, maintaining the peace, and waging warfare very effectively. Most important for the purposes of this analysis is the fact that in England the monarch could levy taxes only in consultation with Parliament. In France, by contrast, such consultations were neither required nor expected.

State financing in England became more stable and accountable in the middle of the fifteenth century when royal spending came under the scrutiny of the Exchequer to the Crown. The Exchequer developed the authority to review independently the monarch's receipts and expenses, thus curbing the power of the Crown. This process contrasted notably to France's financial system where accounting was both suspect and inflated. The capacity to review royal accounts helped assure the integrity of England's financial system.[34] Later, in 1660, the Exchequer expanded its authority, undertaking the "complete responsibility for funding expenditures for the defence of the kingdom."[35] The Exchequer's expanded power also helped the government to improve the collection of taxes and the administration of revenue, making the English state more effective.

In the history of British taxation, the first direct taxes were imposed upon land. This tax burden fell directly upon landowners and the nobility. After imposing direct land taxes, indirect taxes were imposed, taking the form of excise taxes, tariffs, stamp duties, and commodity taxes on consumable items including beer, salt, saffron, hops, lead, tin, iron, glass, oil, soap, starch, gold, silver, copperware, spirits, cider, vinegar, refined sugar, candles, leather, paper, housing, and housebuilding. These indirect taxes began in 1685[36] and created important sources of revenue for the state while also shifting the tax burden from the landed classes, who had paid the direct taxes on land, to the newly emergent merchant and working classes who—as consumers of taxed consumables—were added to the tax rolls. (Of these new commodity taxes, the taxes on liquor were most profitable.)[37] Also imposed was the hearth tax, a twice-yearly tax on each fire-hearth and stove.[38]

Over time, first indirect taxation of these goods and then debt financing increasingly replaced direct taxation as the principal source of finance for the English state.[39] The emergence of debt financing (borrowing) was the third development that was important to England's capacity as a state. By being able to borrow in credit markets, the English state was able to raise funds for government outside of the typical realm of taxation. This third source of financing began in earnest in 1694.[40] These multiple sources of revenue financed state institutions, especially such critical institutions as

England's first standing army (the New Model Army) which was established in 1645 and then disbanded in 1660. After the forty-thousand-man New Model Army was disbanded, it was replaced by a smaller eight-thousand-man militia. These defense forces—and other governmental institutions—would not have existed without the taxes that were authorized by Parliament and administered by the Exchequer.[41]

While England developed effective taxation systems to finance governmental institutions, it is uncertain whether England ever really developed a clear nationalist project.[42] The island of Britain had (and still has) a multiethnic character, being first peopled by the English, Welsh, and Scots. England incorporated Wales territorially in 1536 and Scotland in 1707, with the Act of Union. After World War II, the ethnic and racial composition of Britain became more complex with the arrival of Caribbean and South Asian peoples. If England has experienced nationalism, its nationalism seems rather different from other forms of European nationalism. Linda Colley has argued that England became Britain (incorporating the Welsh and Scots socially rather than just territorially) by incorporating this "Celtic fringe" consciously and in reaction to the revolutionary movements in the British North American colonies and in France. As revolutionaries in America began succeeding militarily and after revolutionaries in France began espousing egalitarianism across classes, leaders in England began their own nationalist project of incorporating the "Celtic fringe" by increasing peerages in the House of Lords for Scots and Welsh and by encouraging intermarriage among English, Scot, and Welsh elite families.[43] This integration took place on an elite level and trickled down somewhat to the Scottish and Welsh working classes because as they learned English, their employment prospects improved.[44]

Consolidation and protection of borders in England was easier than in France, and Great Britain was also less diverse linguistically, in part due to the demographic preponderance of the English over the Welsh and the Scots, making the nationalist project less important. This combination of factors accelerated the development of a state that was less centralized and less militarized than France and less prone to the creation of coercive state institutions.

Germany and Italy: Borders, the State, and Nationalism

German and Italian processes of border consolidation, state formation, and nationalism differed from those in France and England. In the case of Germany, borders were quite fluid. The German state had to be built upon the constituent elements of the Holy Roman Empire, a political entity comprising 294 statelets, territories, and jurisdictions.[45] The very idea, therefore, of uniting Germany was quite daunting, while that of a geographical Italy was ancient, dating from at least the time of Cicero in the third century B.C.[46]

In Germany and Italy, linguistic-based nationalism preceded border consolidation and the building of state institutions. In Germany, the type of nationalism that drove the building of the state and the consolidation of borders was altogether different from the leveling, radical, heterogeneous nationalism of early revolutionary France and England's half-measured, ambiguous nationalism. Germany's nationalism was more conservative and was a political and linguistic reaction to the French nationalism that was imposed upon Germany by France's invading revolutionary army in 1807. That first version of French nationalism was radical, egalitarian, and heterogeneously constructed. It was based upon ideas of citizenship that emphasized the elimination of racial, ethnic, and linguistic differences.[47] By contrast to this early version of French nationalism, Germany's reaction was atavistic and rooted in profound reverence for the use and regeneration of the German language. This language-based nationalism later took a genetic turn, especially under twentieth-century Nazism. Nevertheless, most nineteenth-century German nationalism was based upon a dichotomous in-group/out-group separation of those persons who deserved German identity and citizenship and those who did not. Those who spoke German (and later those who could be defined as genetically German) were citizens and Germans. They comprised the in-group. Those who did not speak German (and later those who were not genetically German) comprised the out-group. This second group of persons was not eligible to become German and could be excluded from citizenship. They could also be subjected to discrimination. What is similar in the German and Italian processes of nationalism and state formation is that in both processes language and literature became the primary cultural variables in the definition of nationalism. Also, in Germany and Italy nationalism was articulated before the resolution of the question of borders and the building of state institutions.[48] This difference in sequencing distinguishes the German and the Italian cases from the British and French examples previously discussed, and makes our discussion of the German and Italian cases more similar to our next set of cases involving Yugoslavia and Africa.

Language-based German nationalism began with Germaine Necker (1766–1817) and Johann Gottfried von Herder (1744–1803), intellectuals who argued that German nationalism should be premised upon the expanded use and glorification of the German language. Their view was that language provided the natural basis for social and political associations.[49] Their views concerning nationalism began taking a more racist orientation with the writings of Johann Gottlieb Fichte (1762–1814). In his *Addresses to the German Nation* he took Necker's and von Herder's ideas concerning language-based nationalism and argued that Germans were superior to non-Germans.[50] Building upon Fichte's initiatives, Friedrich Schlegel and Ernst Moritz Arndt went further, arguing for the creation of a state that would be purely German and and continued arguing for the explicit superiority of

Germans to non-Germans.[51] This line of thought easily led to twentieth-century Nazism. Arndt said that "it is much more appropriate to nature that the human races be strictly separated [*strenge abgesondert*] into nations than that several nations should be fused as has happened in recent times. . . . Each state is an independent individual existing for itself; it is unconditionally its own master, has its peculiar character and governs itself by its own peculiar laws, habits, and customs."[52]

Within this push for German unification, the ideological movement aimed to build first the *Volk* (the people) through *Volkwille* (the will of the people) before the formation of the *Nation* (the nation) and then the *Staat* (the state).[53] For these German nationalists, and for Herder, Fichte, and Arndt in particular, the nation and the state were to be based upon ethnic or racial exclusivity because, as Herder said, "the happiness of one nationality cannot be forced upon, thrust upon, or loaded upon another or all others."[54] After German nationalism was established, the German state was created and German borders were consolidated. This work was undertaken during the nineteenth century by German political activists such as Wilhelm I and Otto von Bismarck.

Like Germany, Italy was not unified politically until the second half of the nineteenth century. Italy was ruled by diverse leading families including the Habsburgs (Lombardy, Tuscany, Parma, and Piacenza), the Savoy family (Piedmont and Sardinia), the Pope (the Papal Estates), the Bourbons (Naples and Sicily), and the Este family (Modena). In addition, there were smaller republics (Venice, Genoa, and Lucca).[55] Unlike Germany, however, Italy had natural geographical borders (the Alps, the Adriatic and Tyrrhenian Seas, and the Mediterranean Sea) and was considered to be a geographical entity from at least the third century B.C. By the late eighteenth century, however, Italy found itself essentially divided because of existing entrenched kingdoms and republics. Given this political situation, the unification of Italy was quite difficult.

The first efforts to unify Italy did not begin in earnest until 1831 with the political efforts of Guiseppe Mazzini.[56] Mazzini, like many other nineteenth-century European nationalists, was influenced by Johann von Herder's ideas regarding language as the basis for the creation of the nation-state.[57] Language-nationalism became a powerful movement in Europe in the nineteenth century, contributing to the momentum of the German, Polish, Hungarian, Czech, Romanian, Greek, and, of course, Italian national movements.

Mazzini faced a divided Italy with separate states and monarchies, with each city-state, province-state, or region adhering to distinct political identities and clan loyalties. In this context, the formation of a transregional Italian state was difficult. The Italians were clearly divided regionally, but the modern Italian language (based upon the Florentine dialect), despite the existence of other regional dialects, eventually provided the basis for successful linguistic nationalism. By wedding the glorification of the tradition of Italian culture and literature with forceful military action, Mazzini, Giuseppe Garibaldi, Camillo Cavour, and their collaborators helped found the modern state of Italy in 1861.

The Former Yugoslavia: Borders, the State, and Nationalism

The challenges of border consolidation, state formation, and nationalism in the Balkans (for example, the former Yugoslavia) and Africa (for example, the four countries in our study) are peculiar because they offer examples of how these processes became distorted as a consequence of colonialism. Whereas France, England, Germany, and Italy offer us examples of diverse paths to border consolidation, state formation, and nationalism, and while these examples reflected complex processes, none of these nations or states suffered from direct colonialism. In contrast, the Balkans and Africa both suffered this burden. Colonialism created borders while also creating and distorting power relations among emergent ethnic groups and political elites, seriously hindering national cohesion and state formation, especially when state building was attempted within the context of colonially imposed borders.

The political states within the Balkans and in our example of Yugoslavia provide good examples of the difficulties of establishing stable borders, stable states, and cohesive societies in postcolonial contexts. The former Yugoslavia was a complex multiethnic and multireligious society that tried to coalesce in the twentieth century into a nation-state. This experiment failed because, given the complexity of the society, the state did not have the ideological or institutional resources necessary either to entice or coerce multiethnic or multireligious cohesion. The predicament encountered in the former Yugoslavia, and elsewhere in the Balkans, is very similar to what has occurred in Africa. States in African and Balkan contexts have experienced serious political distortions because power relationships among ethnic groups and sometimes religious groups were often intentionally manipulated by colonial powers. An examination of these social and political distortions within the context of artificial borders reveals how the seeds for systemic instability have been sown and continue to be manifested in the postcolonial world.

The borders that became Yugoslavia were first defined by the Ottomans and the Habsburgs, both colonial powers. These borders were then redefined by the 1878 Congress of Berlin.[58] This congress arbitrarily demarcated the borders of many Balkan states as had been done for Africa. In this context of colonially imposed borders, separate religious or ethnic identities became important to the organization of many anticolonial movements. This combination of factors (artificially imposed borders, social heterogeneity, and colonization) distorted and destabilized consequent processes of political development. The existence of multiethnic and multireligious groups within these colonial borders has made state and nation formation in the Balkans remarkably similar to Africa. The states in the Balkans (using our particular example of the former Yugoslavia) and Africa (using our examples of Sudan, Ethiopia, DRC, and Sierra Leone) are multiethnic, multireligious, and polylinguistic. The social arrangements among these groups were then manipulated and distorted by colonial policy. The result of these similar processes has been social and political anomie. When these factors are viewed comparatively, the similarity between the Balkans and Africa is startling.

In addition to the language factor in the Balkans and in the former Yugoslavia, historical memory, especially the humiliation of wartime defeat, forms another complication. This second factor involves religious identifications with Eastern Orthodox Christianity, Roman Catholicism, or Islam. In this matrix of language, memory, and religion, Muslims and Christians vied for power and perquisites. Even within Christianity itself a deep social division was constructed between Serb Orthodox Christians and Croat Catholics. The linkage of historical memory to separate linguistic tendencies and religious identities created a highly distrustful and volatile sociopolitical environment. This distrust has inhibited the possibility of either transethnic or transreligious lines of cooperation.

Historical myths of origin and myths of military defeat have inhibited political unity. Croats and Serbs in particular have historical myths of origin that cause them to segregate themselves. The Croat historical myth is based upon the medieval kingdom of King Tomislav (tenth century) and King Kresîmir (eleventh century). The Serb historical myth begins with the royal house of Nemanjíc and the medieval state that flourished in the twelfth and thirteenth centuries in the geographic area of present-day Serbia, Herzegovina, and Macedonia. Another Serb myth focuses on the Battle of Kosovo in 1389 when Serb leader Prince Lazar Hrebljanovíc perished on the battlefield while fighting against the Ottoman Empire. This second myth serves as the origin of Orthodox Christian and Muslim animosity.[59] These myths were elaborated upon during the eighteenth and nineteenth century by literary movements seeking to create separate Serbian, Croatian, Macedonian, Montenegrin, Bosnian, Slovenian, Hungarian (Magyar), Bulgarian, Macedonian, and other identities.[60] Historical mythmaking and denial of cultural hybridity have long inhibited transethnic unity. When mythmaking, religious separatism, and distinctive linguistic traditions are thrown together within artificial borders created by colonialism, we then observe systemic sociopolitical distortions that are frequently encountered in Africa.[61]

Colonial intrusion in the Balkans and in most of Africa make the cases observed in those two regions quite unlike what we observed in France, England, Germany, and Italy. Colonialism has made all the difference. France and England developed without colonial intrusion. Consequently, when leaders in those states undertook the tasks of border consolidation, state building, and nationalism, they not only suffered no colonial interference, but they also had centuries to complete their objectives. In Germany and Italy, nationalism was articulated before the consolidation of borders and the stabilization of state institutions; but again in these cases colonialism did not interfere with these processes. In southeastern Europe the idea of separate national identities had been dormant and remained substantially unarticulated before the intrusion of colonialism. Ideas of ethnic separation developed in the context of resistance to Ottoman and Austro-Hungarian colonialism, which began during the fifteenth century. These trends continued into the twenty-first century. Colonialism assembled so-called different peoples into artificial spaces that were recognized as territorial states. Despite juridical recognition as territorial states, the peoples within remained internally disunited. In the southeastern European context, vibrant, powerful, and separatist ethnic identity movements did not mobilize substantially until the arrival of colonialism. The important fact, however, was that these movements toward ethnic separation became activated in the context of resistance to colonialism. By contrast, African anticolonial movements were first defined racially. They focused on themes of black Africans ousting white Europeans from their lands. Anticolonial resistance was first expressed racially while postponing ethnically based resistance movements. Now, however, Africa rivals southeastern Europe in terms of ethnic conflict. Because of similarity of processes in both postcolonial regions, ethnic conflict now reigns in southeastern Europe and Africa.

The colonial experience in the former Yugoslavia began in 1463 when the Ottomans seized Bosnia and colonized it directly. Ottoman authorities created effective state institutions, especially with regard to the creation of a state bureaucracy, a religious bureaucracy, a military, and centralized methods for tax collection and land adjudication.[62] All of these state institutions were colonial instruments, controlled directly by the Ottomans in Istanbul. Ottoman control in Bosnia reached its high point under Suleiman the Magnificent (1520–1566) after which the centralizing power of the Ottomans waned, opening up the opportunity for disparate development of Macedonian, Bosnian, Serbian, and Montenegrin peoples, especially in the nineteenth century.[63]

When Bosnia-Herzegovina was ceded to the Austro-Hungarian Empire at the Congress of Berlin in 1878, Serbian and Croatian subject peoples within Bosnia-Herzegovina and Serbia began improving their status vis-à-vis Bosnian Muslims, who had been previously privileged under the Ottoman regime. Under the new Austro-Hungarian regime, Muslims, Catholics, and Orthodox Christians were encouraged to establish separate schools (with financial support from the Austro-Hungarian Empire). The creation of these separate religious schools further encouraged the spread of ethnic subnational identities within Serbia, Croatia, and Bosnia-

Herzegovina during the nineteenth century.[64] Ironically, these subidentities grew under the Austro-Hungarian regime despite a fairly noticeable tradition of religious intermarriage within the region. Amidst these contradictory trends, perceptions of difference and division grew.

Whereas the primary tendency within political and social movements in the Balkans and the former Yugoslavia since the nineteenth century has been toward identification with separate ethnic and religious subnational identities, there have been countervailing intellectual and political efforts to create a transethnic or transreligious state and nation. This effort at crossreligious and cross-ethnic unity has been known as the "Yugoslav idea." The idea of a multiethnic, multireligious, and multilinguistic state had its origins in 1815 within a small student circle in Croatia led by Lyudevít Gaj.[65] Gaj's group started a newspaper (*Danicza, Horvatska, Slavonzska i Dalmatinzka*) that tried to foster Serb-Croat linguistic and political unity.[66] Gaj's efforts to use language as a basis for political unity was directly influenced by German and Italian linguistic-nationalist movements. Gaj, like Mazzini, was especially influenced by Johann von Herder.[67] His efforts were then extended in 1860 when Josip Strossmayer and Franjo Rački (both Croatians) set up the National Party, which focused upon Serbo-Croatian unity.[68] Again, using Italian and German unification efforts as their model, Strossmayer and Rački argued for South Slav unity.

Efforts to create a multiethnic Yugoslavia continued after World War II under the leadership of resistance leader Josip Broz, also known as Tito. After his successful leadership during the resistance, Tito in 1946 organized the Federal Republic of Yugoslavia. The republic's constitution officially provided for a form of decentralized socialism, with a purported federal relationship between the central government in Belgrade and the six federated republics (Slovenia, Croatia, Serbia, Bosnia and Herzegovina, Montenegro, and Macedonia). Power, however, was only formally devolved from the central authorities in Belgrade toward constituent republics. Realistically, until his death in 1980, Tito and his cohorts centralized power in their own hands. Despite political paeans to federalism and allegations that its constitution was different from the Soviet Union's in terms of the actual exercise of power, political authority was centralized.

As leader, Tito attempted to create a transreligious and transethnic Yugoslavia. The tendency within Yugoslavia and the Balkans, however, since the nineteenth century at least, has tended toward separateness rather than political union, toward independence of the constituent republics, or at most federation or confederation rather than political unification. Quite consistently, from the Corfu Declaration of 1917 to the first Provisional Government and Parliament of the Kingdom of Serbs, Croats, and Slovenes that was formed on 20 December 1918, to more recent times, the trend has been at most for a federal, multiethnic state.[69] More recently, especially since the 1990s, the trend has been toward ethnic separatism and the establishment of separate ethnic-exclusive republics.

While Tito tried to encourage multiethnic Yugoslavism versus separate ethnic identities, attachment to local (particularly Serbian and Croat) identities remained strong. To bridge this critical gap between the Serbs and Croats, Tito tried to propagate a merged language with a new alphabet during the 1950s and 1960s. He hoped this linguistic initiative would help unite the two largest ethnic groups within Yugoslavia, leading eventually to the unity of all Yugoslav peoples. Local linguistic activists, especially within Croatia (the third most important ethnic group), rejected this approach, preferring the preservation of local languages.[70] This Croatian-led linguistic countermovement proved deadly to the creation of a new cultural and linguistic base for national unity. Furthermore, despite Tito's attempt to encourage pan-ethnic Yugoslavism via multiethnic recruitment into the ranks of the civil service and the military, these quotas for ethnic recruitment into government actually enhanced ethnic and religious rivalries because rival groups felt that they were being discriminated against in employment. Ethnic quotas for employment backfired, contributing to the further disintegration of his hoped-for pan-ethnic Yugoslav identity.[71] Separate subnational identities began to flourish noticeably in the late 1960s. First, Muslim leader Alija Izetbegovíc published his Muslim Declaration in the late 1960s, emphasizing Muslim identity within a multiethnic Yugoslavia.[72] Soon afterward, Muslim Albanians in Kosovo placed claims for autonomy from Yugoslavia (in 1968), and Croatian leaders made their own claims for autonomy in 1970 and 1971.

Aleksandar Pavković has argued that the Yugoslavia that began disintegrating in 1991 had its institutional foundations in the 1974 Constitution. That constitution began the real process of devolving power and resources from Belgrade to local republics. Under this constitution, substantial decisionmaking power was transferred to constituent republics while Tito maintained control of the military and the foreign service.[73] Tito's control of the military enabled him to keep Yugoslavia together in the interim even though he had created the essential institutional basis for Yugoslavia's subsequent disintegration.

After Tito's death in 1980, local ethnic leaders, especially Serbia's Slobodan Milosěvić, encouraged ethnic separatism further. Beginning in 1981 in Kosovo and continuing through the beginning of the twenty-first century, the violent expression of ethnic nationalism in the former Yugoslavia has been the norm. Whether one examines Kosovo Albanian nationalism, Serb nationalism, Slovene nationalism, Croat nationalism, or Muslim (Bosnia-Herzegovina) nationalism during this period, the principal precept has provided for exclusive ethnic control of "ethnic" territories; power sharing or even dialogue with other ethnic groups has been precluded from political discussion. This is ethnic nationalism at its most extreme: the most uncompromising and most intolerant form of social and political discourse imaginable. Within this discourse, separatism is the primary political objective, and the economic and political benefits of confederation are rarely discussed. The historical memory of alleged grievances inflicted by competing ethnic groups has aggravated the sense of separation and has inhibited the possibility of interethnic dialogue or communication. The erstwhile benefits of Tito's militarily enforced federal systems were that they helped temporarily arrest historical memory and kept ethnic hatreds in check. With his death, Tito's artificial federation and republic lapsed and the dogs of ethnic hatred were set loose. The collapse of the state led to the eventual independence of Slovenia and Croatia, the partition of Bosnia-Herzegovina into a Muslim-Croat confederation and a Serb subrepublic, the incomplete movement toward independence in Kosovo, and the consistent application of policies of mass deportation of "nonnationals" from "national" lands.[74]

Back to Africa

Having examined border consolidation, state formation, and nationalism in western, central and southern, and southeastern Europe, we now turn our attention to these same issues in Africa. Like the states that we encountered in southeastern Europe, African states experienced colonialism and their territorial borders were demarcated by external European powers. Like the Balkans, states in Africa more often than not represent different ethnic groups who frequently speak different languages, and who have strong family and kinship networks that inhibit trans-kin or transethnic affiliations that ordinarily would lead to the consolidation of larger multiethnic and multilingual nations. Like conditions found in southeastern Europe, kinship relations, ethnic ties, myths of origin, and separate religious affiliations inhibit the construction of larger nation-states. When we add these factors to the rigidity of and reverence for artificial borders, we find a situation where the failure to consider the possible reformation of these borders inhibits the creation of alternate political formulas for peace and conflict resolution. The inherited territorial borders of many African states distort processes of political development and divide communities that otherwise would be organically constituted. The borders of African states have created "territorial states" that are legitimized in international law and that are relevant primarily to those who seek interim political power. These states and their borders are rarely meaningful, however, to the majority of the state's inhabitants, especially those who live in rural areas. When political elites capture the "territorial state," they often find governance difficult. The very artificiality of these states and their borders creates inhibiting conditions that stymie the realization of two key tasks for successful governance: the construction of effective governmental institutions and the encouragement of affective relationships that eventually lead to transethnic nationalism.

The first three concerns that need to be addressed regarding the future possible political effectiveness of African states are the following: borders and their possible reformation, enhancement of state capacity, and the encouragement of transethnic, transreligious, and translinguistic nationalism. To assess whether state effectiveness can be improved and whether nationalism can be reformulated, we will have to address the question of borders and their possible reformation. This challenge of border examination and border reformation is inevitable because state capacity and nationalism are eventually built within territorial spaces that we call "states." The question is whether these spaces contribute to or inhibit the growth of state capacity and nationalism. This question must be addressed squarely. In some cases we may find that borders should be left alone; in others they may have to be reformed.

However, we need not fear border reform. The politics of border reform can be ameliorative. In Europe, especially Central and Eastern Europe, borders have been redrawn constantly, primarily because of warfare. This has happened for centuries. At other times, borders have been reformed pacifically, via negotiation. As recently as 1992, the Czech and Slovak border was created via partition, and although President Vaclav Havel regretted the development, the change has led to beneficial relations for the two republics.

In Africa, however, since the establishment of the Organization of African Unity in 1963, there has been a clear policy, at least within the realm of international law as it has been applied to Africa, to respect the rigidity of colonially created borders.[75] (Exceptions are the partition of Ethiopia and Eritrea and the de facto separation of Somaliland from Somalia.) Reverence for these borders has led to their geographic stability. It also has created a clear logic that impels local political actors to seize power within what are artificial territorial spaces. The territorial "states" that have been seized most often are states on paper and maps only. These states are recognized internationally but often they do not function as states; they often do not govern effectively. When one scrutinizes the operation of the state within these internationally recognized borders, one finds weak states with weak governmental institutions that fail to serve the people. The state's capacity to rule effectively rarely extends beyond the capital and other large cities. The pressing concern seems to be, therefore, the building of effective state institutions. The corollary concern that needs to be addressed is whether these state institutions can be improved without concurrently assessing realistically whether the borders of these "paper" states are viable. As Charles Tilly has effectively argued, policing, war making, and taxation build states and enhance state capacity.[76] These processes often take place after borders have been stabilized. If we accept the present demarcation of the borders of African states and Tilly's axiom as political reality, elected leaders of internationally recognized "territorial" states must, therefore, pay attention to stabilizing and legitimizing their borders to build effective state institutions. Furthermore, they must extend governmental authority beyond the capital and large cities into rural and border areas. If they fail in these endeavors and if valuable economic and ideological resources can be found in the hinterlands, especially in rural and border areas, we will find a situation where local warlords will seize the opportunity to fill the political vacuum. They will contest for power in areas where the elected government has failed to extend its authority and they will seize opportunities to instigate and continue warfare, especially where there are either natural resources (in the form of diamonds, petroleum, and others) or ideological resources (in the form of fervent subnationalism) that will sustain them in their war-making efforts. These are essential questions that need analysis when we consider the question of borders and their possible reformation in Africa.

State capacity is a critical issue. State capacity can be built by the elected government or, if the elected government has failed to extend its authority into rural and border areas, state capacity will be built by local warlords, especially where significant economic or ideological resources are present. In this study, we will examine conditions in the Sudan, Ethiopia, the DRC, and Sierra Leone. We will see how these principles operate. Inevitably, in our examination of state capacity and nationalism in these four cases, we will have to address how the viability and legitimacy of borders affect these questions.

Besides addressing state capacity—whether expanded by warlords or the elected state—we examine the possibilities for building viable multiethnic nations. However elusive the goal of multiethnic nationalism and however difficult that objective may be to achieve, the pursuit of forms of multiethnic nationalism is inevitable in Africa and elsewhere because the global movement of peoples—both voluntary and involuntary—has created diverse and hybrid societies in many parts of the world. Heterogeneous rather than homogeneous societies are increasingly the norm despite insistence by racial and ethnic chauvinists for racial or ethnic purity and demands for "cleansing."

Given de facto heterogeneity, the new nationalisms ipso facto will move toward expressions that will embrace racial, ethnic, and religious heterogeneity. That will be the case in both the developed and the developing world. As we move forward toward multiethnic, multireligious nationalism there will of course be resistance; but given cognizance of global population movements, the need for talented yet racially and ethnically diverse labor pools, and the global transmission of culture that will improve eventual transcultural understanding, it is predictable that in the twenty-first century, given mass media's capabilities for the global transmission of culture, there will be a gradual but perceptible expansion of cultural knowledge that will lead to the diminution of fear of other peoples and societies and the enhancement of transnational understanding.

This shift toward multicultural nationalism, both globally and within Africa, is primarily a cultural project. Nationalism has always been a cultural project that has been closely linked to politics.[77] It involves that special combination of the efforts of politicians and artists that leads to a cultural product that transforms and mobilizes a society, motivating it to pursue political goals. The review of history reveals whether these nationalist movements have been inclusive or exclusive. It is almost always a question of choice. That choice has been exercised by political elites and their associates in the artistic community. Nationalism, whether inclusive or exclusive, whether multiethnic or uniethnic, whether religiously diverse or singular, is a question of choice and the expression of perceived interest by politicians and artists. In this book, interviews with political and artistic elites will reveal present tendencies to create either heterogeneous or homogeneous nationalism in the four countries in our study.

Beyond the primary questions of borders, state building, and nationalism, there are a series of secondary questions that also need consideration. These are the political formulas of federalism, confederation, partition, and independence. These alternatives can help enhance conflict resolution and the establishment and preservation of peace. Our view, however, is that they should be considered as secondary alternatives—not as a substitute for the examination of the primary questions of borders, state formation, and nationalism.

If we were to contemplate federalism as a means of reconciling social heterogeneity with the artificial geographical borders of African states, federalism would be desirable because it has often had salutary benefits that can eventually lead to both national unification and a more effective state. Federalism can only be undertaken seriously, however, when there is the political will among political elites and the masses to complete such a project. One critical advantage of the methodological approach employed in this project is that by using interviews with political elites and random surveys with mass audiences we will be able to discern whether there is real support for federalism as a viable political alternative in the countries being studied. Federalism may be a desirable solution for the resolution of ethnic, racial, and religious conflict in Africa, but as the tortured history of attempted federalism and partition in the former Yugoslavia reveals, we must have a real national commitment to federalism for it to succeed.

Federalism often is contemplated as a scheme for conflict resolution and hoped-for national unification in heterogeneous societies because the primarily considered alternative—a unitary nonfederal government—often exacerbates fissiparous tendencies among subnational ethnic and linguistic groups. Federalism (which does not provide the option for territorial secession) and even looser confederation (which does) have been used to defuse tensions in states where ethnic, linguistic, or religious subnationalisms are manifest. We have seen federalism employed in many regions of the world, from India to Mexico. Federalism has been tried with greater and lesser success in various regions in Africa, among the most notable being Ethiopia and Nigeria. There has been a modicum of success with federalism in Ethiopia while federalism in Nigeria is undergoing serious challenges. This work will explore the viability of federalism as a method of conflict resolution in these cases.

Beyond considerations of federalism and confederation, partition and secession are considered the most drastic alternatives. As Donald L. Horowitz has stated, partition is a form of "radical surgery" for the resolution of ethnic, racial, and religious conflict.[78] The argument for the "radical surgery" of partition is that it is better to keep differing groups apart—even if that involves large population transfers—rather than experiment with federalism or the building of new transethnic or transreligious nationalism that will either fail or take too long to implement. Partition is often a lamentable alternative; even when it has experienced a modicum of success it often remains unstable and does not engender fruitful political and economic relations between the entities that have decided to separate. (Two notable exceptions may be the partition of the Czech and Slovak republics in 1992 and the partition of Singapore and Malaysia in 1965). It is a solution that does not lead to complete resolution of the frictions that led to partition. It can provide for an absence of hostilities, but it does not lead to the promotion of positive peace. Nevertheless, partition and secession must be considered as final alternatives. It has somewhat stabilized relations between India and Pakistan, Northern Ireland and the Republic of Ireland, and the Greek and Turkish communities of Cyprus. Even in these cases, however, we must recognize that the relationships between the now-separated entities are not truly harmonious.

Finally, regardless of preferences expressed by academicians or public policy analysts, we must recognize that even if we prefer peace, stability, and tranquility, the borders of African states are being reformed on a de facto basis by warfare. This is evident. If we look at Sudan, Somalia, Eritrea/Ethiopia, Sierra Leone, and the DRC, the borders of African states are being redrawn before our eyes.

Notes

The author would like to acknowledge Edmond J. Keller for his comments on this chapter.

1. S. E. Finer, "State Building, State Boundaries, and Border Control," *Social Science Information* 13, no. 4/5 (1974): 79.

2. S. E. Finer, "State and Nation-Building in Europe: The Role of the Military," in *The Formation of National States in Western Europe*, ed. Charles Tilly (Princeton, NJ: Princeton University Press, 1975), 88.

3. Max Weber, "Politics as a Vocation," in *From Max Weber: Essays in Sociology*, ed. H. H. Gerth and C. Wright Mills (New York: Oxford University Press, 1958), 77–128; Perry Anderson, *Lineages of the Absolutist State* (London: NLB, 1974), 17; Ali A. Mazrui, *The African Condition* (Cambridge: Cambridge University Press, 1980); Crawford Young, *The African Colonial State in a Comparative Perspective* (New Haven, CT: Yale University Press, 1997).

4. Max Weber, "Politics as a Vocation," 78.

5. Charles Tilly, "Reflections on the History of European State-Making," in *The Formation of National States in Western Europe*, ed. Charles Tilly (Princeton, NJ: Princeton University Press, 1975), 70, 86.

6. Saadia Touval, "Partitioned Groups and Inter-State Relations," in *Partitioned Africans*, ed. A. I. Asiwaju (London: C. Hurst & Company, 1985), 223–224.

7. Rupert Emerson, *From Empire to Nation: The Rise to Self-Assertion of Asian and African Peoples* (Cambridge, MA: Harvard University Press, 1960), 95–96.

8. Eugen Weber, *Peasants into Frenchmen* (Stanford, CA: Stanford University Press, 1976).

9. Charles Tilly, *Coercion, Capital, and European States, A.D. 990–1990* (Oxford: Blackwell, 1992), 3.

10. Finer, "State-Building, State Boundaries and Border Control," 99.

11. Ibid., 108.

12. S. E. Finer, *The History of Government*, vol. 2 (Oxford: Oxford University Press, 1997 & 1999), 899–900.

13. Finer, "State and Nation-Building in Europe," 99.

14. John Bell Henneman Jr., "France in the Middle Ages," in *The Rise of the Fiscal State in Europe, c. 1200–1815*, ed. Richard Bonney (Oxford: Oxford University Press, 1999), 103–104.

15. Gabriel Ardant, *Histoire de l'impôt*, livre 1 (Paris: Fayard, 1971), 526; Pierre Chaunau, "L'État de Finance," in *Histoire Économique et Sociale de la France, Tome I: De 1450 á 1660,* ed. Fernand Braudel and Ernest Labrousse (Paris: Presses Universitaires de France), 132–135 (129–191); Henneman, "France in the Middle Ages," 106, 112.

16. Chaunau, "L'État de Finance," 138–139; Henneman, "France in the Middle Ages," 113.

17. Henneman, "France in the Middle Ages," 114.

18. Ibid.

19. Ibid., 115.

20. Perry Anderson, *Lineages of the Absolutist State* (London: Verso, 1979), 87; Ardant, *Histoire de l'impôt*, 530–531; Richard Bonney, *The King's Debts: Finance and Politics in France, 1589–1661* (Oxford: Clarendon Press, 1981), 13; G. R. R. Treasure, *Seventeenth Century France* (London: John Murray, 1966, 1981), 33.

21. Richard Bonney, *Political Change in France under Richelieu and Mazarin* (Oxford: Oxford University Press, 1978).

22. Ardant, *Histoire de l'impôt*, 454.

23. Chaunau, "L'État de Finance," 184–188; John C. Rule, "Louis XIV, Roi-Bureaucrate," in *Louis XIV and the Craft of Kingship*, ed. John C. Rule (Columbus: Ohio State University Press, 1969), 42.

24. Bonney, *The King's Debts*, 86; G. N. Clark, *The Seventeenth Century* (Oxford: Clarendon Press, 1953), 86; Treasure, *Seventeenth Century France*, 168.

25. Treasure, *Seventeenth Century France*, 168.

26. Emmanuel Joseph Sieyès, *What Is the Third Estate?* trans. by M. Blondel (New York: Frederick A. Praeger, 1964); Eugen Weber, *Peasants into Frenchmen.*

27. Hans Kohn, *Prelude to Nation States: The French and German Experience, 1789–1815* (Princeton, NJ: Van Nostrand, 1967), 89.

28. Ibid., 90.

29. Finer, *The History of Government*, vol. 2, 899–900.

30. Finer, "State Building, State Boundaries and Border Control," 115.

31. Edward Miller, "War, Taxation, and the English Economy in the Late Thirteenth and Fourteenth Centuries," in *Warfare and Economic Development*, ed. J. M. Winter (Cambridge: Cambridge University Press, 1975), 11; W. M. Ormond, "England in the Middle Ages," in *The Rise of the Fiscal State in Europe, c. 1200–1815*, ed. Richard Bonney (Oxford: Oxford University Press, 1999), 19–20.

32. Finer, *The History of Government*, vol. 2, 1039–1040.

33. W. M. Ormond, "England in the Middle Ages," 20.

34. Ibid., 36.

35. Patrick K. O'Brien and Phillip A. Hunt, "England, 1485–1815," in *The Rise of the Fiscal State in Europe, c. 1200–1815,* ed. Richard Bonney (Oxford: Oxford University Press, 1999), 54.

36. Ibid., 74.

37. C. D. Chandaman, *The English Public Revenue, 1660–1688* (Oxford: Clarendon Press, 1975), 38–39.

38. Ibid., 81.

39. Ibid., 63–65.

40. Ibid., 57.

41. Rudolf Braun, in *The Formation of National States in Western Europe,* ed. Charles Tilly (Princeton, NJ: Princeton University Press, 1975), 282.

42. Linda Colley, "Whose Nation? Class and National Consciousness in Britain, 1750–1830," *Past and Present* 113: 97–117.

43. Ibid., 110, 114.

44. Ibid., 112.

45. S. E. Finer, *The History of Government*, vol. 3 (Oxford: Oxford University Press, 1999), 1432.

46. Harry Hearder, *Italy in the Age of the Risorgimento, 1790–1870* (London: Longman, 1983), 156; Stuart J. Woolf, *A History of Italy, 1700–1860* (London: Methuen, 1979), 231.

47. Sieyès, *What Is the Third Estate?*

48. Friedrich Meinecke, *Cosmopolitanism and the National State*, trans. by Robert Kimber (Princeton, NJ: Princeton University Press, 1970), 10; Friedrich Meinecke, *The Age of German Liberation*, trans. Peter Paret and Helmut Fischer (Berkeley: University of California Press, 1977); Anthony D. Smith, *Nationalism and Modernism* (London: Routledge, 1998), 122–123; Eric Hobsbawm, *Nations and Nationalism Since 1780: Programme, Myth, and Reality* (Cambridge: Cambridge University Press, 1990), 102–133; see James J. Sheehan, "What Is German History?" *Journal of Modern History* 53, no. 1 (March 1981): 4–5.

49. F. M. Barnard, *Herder's Social and Political Thought* (Oxford: Clarendon Press, 1965), 29–30, 142; Isaiah Berlin, *Vico and Herder* (New York: Viking, 1976), 63; Hans Kohn, *Prelude to Nation-States: The French and German Experience, 1789–1815* (Princeton, NJ: Van Nostrand, 1967), 227.

50. Eugene N. Anderson, *Nationalism and Cultural Crisis in Prussia, 1806–1815* (New York: Octagon Books, 1939), 57–63; Barnard, *Herder's Social and Political Thought*, 161; Kohn, *Prelude to Nation-States*, 237–240.

51. Anderson, *Nationalism and Cultural Crisis in Prussia, 1806–1815*, 256; Kohn, *Prelude to Nation-States*, 252–257.

52. Kohn, *Prelude to Nation-States*, 183–184.

53. Peter F. Sugar, "Roots of Eastern European Nationalism," in *Nationalism in Eastern Europe*, eds. Peter F. Sugar and Ivo J. Lederer (Seattle: University of Washington Press, 1969), 11–15.

54. Ibid., 14.

55. Derek Beales, *The Risorgimento and the Unification of Italy* (London: Longman, 1971), 21–22; Hearder, *Italy in the Age of the Risorgimento*.

56. Beales, *The Risorgimento and the Unification of Italy*, 55.

57. Hearder, *Italy in the Age of the Risorgimento*, 184–185.

58. Misha Glenny, *The Balkans 1804–1999: Nationalism, War, and the Great Powers* (London: Granta Books, 1999), 135–151.

59. Aleksandar Pavković, *The Fragmentation of Yugoslavia: Nationalism and War in the Balkans*, 2d ed. (London: Macmillan, 2000), 7–8.

60. Ivo Banac, *The National Question in Yugoslavia: Origins, History, Politics* (Ithaca, NY: Cornell University Press, 1984), 70–155; Pavković, *The Fragmentation of Yugoslavia*, 9.

61. Sugar, "Roots of Eastern European Nationalism," 10.

62. John R. Lampe, *Yugoslavia as History*, 2d ed. (Cambridge: Cambridge University Press, 2000), 20.

63. Ibid., 21.

64. Noel Malcolm, *Bosnia: A Short History* (New York: New York University Press, 1994), 144–147.

65. Lampe, *Yugoslavia as History*, 59–60; Pavkovi'c, *The Fragmentation of Yugoslavia*, 11.

66. Ivo J. Lederer, "Nationalism and the Yugoslavs,'" in *Nationalism in Eastern Europe*, eds. Peter F. Sugar and Ivo J. Lederer (Seattle: University of Washington Press, 1969), 414.

67. Lampe, *Yugoslavia as History*, 43.

68. Ibid. 59–60; Ivo J. Lederer, "Nationalism and the Yugoslavs," 419; Pavkovi'c, *The Fragmentation of Yugoslavia*, 12.

69. Michael Boro Petrovich, *A History of Modern Serbia*, vol. 2 (New York: Harcourt Brace Jovanovich, 1976), 644–646.

70. Glenny, *The Balkans*, 585; Lampe, *Yugoslavia as History*, 305–306; Pavković, *The Fragmentation of Yugoslavia*, 62–63.

71. Pavković, *The Fragmentation of Yugoslavia*, 64–65.

72. Malcolm, *Bosnia: A Short History*, 219–221.

73. Pavković, *The Fragmentation of Yugoslavia*, 69–70.

74. For example, in 1995, Croatia expelled 200,000 Serbs from Croatia. In 1995, in Bosnia-Herzegovina, 1.4 to 2 million of 4.36 million Bosnians were "internally displaced."

75. The policy of inviolability of colonially inherited borders was adopted at the 1964 Cairo conference.

76. Tilly, *Coercion, Capital, and European States*.

77. Benedict Anderson, *Imagined Communities* (London: Verso, 1983).

78. Donald L. Horowitz, *Ethnic Groups in Conflict* (Berkeley: University of California Press, 1985), 588–589.

2

Sudan's Turbulent Road to Nationhood

Francis M. Deng

The war in Sudan is the result of immensely complicated internal factors, fraught with diversities, tensions, contradictions, and violent confrontations. The size and location of the country alone signal the monumental dimensions of the crisis. Sudan is geographically the largest country in Africa, covering a massive territory of nearly 1 million square miles and bordering nine countries—Egypt and Libya to the north; Eritrea and Ethiopia to the east; Kenya, Uganda, and the Democratic Republic of Congo (DRC) to the south; the Central African Republic and Chad to the west—and is separated from a tenth neighbor, Saudi Arabia, only by the Red Sea. As might be expected from its size and location, the Sudanese state was carved out of racial, ethnic, cultural, and religious diversities whose dynamic coexistence featured elements of conflict, coexistence, and cooperation well before colonial intervention and the formation of the modern state. Their current complex configuration can be aggregated into three principal categories: the Arabs and the non-Arab groups in the North, and the African peoples in the South.

Torn between aspirations for unity and pressures for partition, Sudan's painful process of self-reckoning as a modern nation has included a civil war that was initially separatist in its objectives, but was eventually recast into reconstructing the national framework to forge a new Sudan, turning the war into a contest for the soul of the nation. The combination of these trends has resulted in an ambivalent view of nationhood in which separatism is becoming intertwined with unity in a reconstructed Sudan. Whether unity or separation will prevail, however, is not a matter for the Sudanese alone to decide. Regional and international interests have become vested in the outcome and continue to influence the terms of negotiations and emerging visions of the contesting identity groups. A viable outcome may be the short-term accommodation of differences through a form of internal self-determination, and a longer-term process of evolution toward a more integrated nation that embraces the diversities of the country on the basis of mutual accommodation and respect. Nevertheless, the dynamics of the situation are such that no outcome is clearly in sight.

This chapter discusses the Sudanese case in four sections. The introduction provides an overview of the situation from the perspective of historical evolution, culminating in the challenges the country faces today. The second section elaborates on various themes and perspectives, with a focus on identity conflicts, the issues involved, and the incremental progress toward peace. The third section presents the results of surveys conducted among Sudanese within the country and living abroad on the issues of statehood and the evolution of national consciousness. The chapter ends with an assessment of the prospects for peace, unity, and national integration.

Precolonial Context

Diversities in the country's composition fall into two main divisions, North and South. The northern two-thirds of the country is inhabited by ethnic groups, the dominant among whom intermarried with incoming Arab migrants and traders and, over centuries, produced a mixed African-Arab racial group and corresponding "creolized" identities. The resulting racial characteristics resemble closely all of the African peoples cutting across the continent below the Sahara, from Ethiopia, Eritrea, and Somalia in the east, Chad, Niger, and Mali in the center, and Mauritania and Senegal to the west. Indeed, the Arabic phrase "Bilad al-Sudan," from which Sudan derives its name, means the Land of the Blacks and refers to all of these sub-Saharan territories. Arab immigration and settlement in the South, in contrast to the North, were discouraged by natural environmental barriers; difficulties of living conditions, including the harshness of the tropical climate for people accustomed to the desert; and resistance of the warrior Nilotic tribes. Those Arab adventurers who managed to travel in the South were primarily engaged in slave raids. They were not interested in Arabizing and Islamizing the southerners because that would have removed their prey from *dar al-harb* (land of war) and placed them in *dar al-Islam* (land of peace), thereby liberating them from slavery.

Sudan's conflict of identities therefore has deep historical roots. Sudanese contact and interaction with the Middle East via Egypt dates back thousands of years before Christ, taking the form of migration and trade in ivory, gold, and slaves. Throughout this time, Arab traders settled in Sudan and integrated themselves with the indigenous populations in the North, where Arab culture was valued and began to take root. This process intensified after the advent of Islam in the seventh century. The Arab Muslim empire invaded the Sudan, but met with ferocious and sustained resistance, which during the seventh to the ninth centuries eventually forced them to conclude treaties with the northern peoples of Nubia and Beja. That opened channels of communication and cultural exchange with the Arab world, but otherwise the Muslim Arabs left the Sudanese in relative peace and independence. Although the Arabs who settled were traders and not rulers, their privileged position, their more cosmopolitan and universalizing religious culture, and their superior material wealth, combined with the liberal assimilationist nature of the Arab-Islamic culture, opened the gates of assimilation and made them an appealing class for intermarriage with the leading Sudanese families. This process eventually resulted in the transformation of the pre-Islamic society.[1]

Islam was promoted by leading Sufi orders, which were introduced to the country during the fifteenth and sixteenth centuries. By the early 1800s, Sufi orders had become firmly established and had pervasive political and religious influence. One of the distinguishing factors of Sufi orders was the degree to which they accommodated pre-Islamic practices, allowing the syncretism of traditional African religious practices with Muslim rituals. There came a point in this process when Islamic values and institutions prevailed over preexisting practices, yet the latter continued to enhance the former. Such is the stage Jack Mendelsohn had in mind when he said that northern Sudanese "exercised their genius for assimilation by molding the religion of the Prophet to their tastes . . . They sang in it, danced in it, . . . paganized it a good deal, but always kept vivid the reality of its inherent unity under one God."[2] By recognizing and building on the traditional order, Islam became identified with the local community and adopted many uniquely Sudanese characteristics.

Rudiments of State Formation

Sudan as we know it today is an anomaly of a country with deep historical roots but, as a nation, it is at best a work in progress. Parts of modern-day Sudan can be traced back to ancient history and have been known by various names, such as Nubia and Kush. However, as a state and an evolving nation with definable borders, the country called Sudan is the creature of foreign intervention and domination. Prior to the Turko-Egyptian conquest of 1821, the territory below Egypt was viewed as a vast, uncharted land of opportunities, widely open for adventurers, exploration, and exploitation. During a period of some 135 years of foreign rule—since the Turko-Egyptian conquest—it became the task of the British-dominated Anglo-Egyptian Condominium Administration, which lasted only fifty-eight years, to define and consolidate the present borders of the country.

In 1820–1821, Turkish and Egyptian forces invaded and took over the northern regions of Sudan. Unlike the immigrant Arab traders, the Turko-Egyptians were an imperial power and came to Sudan with clear objectives; the most vehemently expressed was to recruit blacks as slave soldiers for the Egyptian army. While the Turkish-Egyptian administration maintained and used the tribal system, tribal chiefs became instruments of Turkish-Egyptian control and consequently lost respect and influence among the tribes. Further, the government's main source of wealth from Sudan, taxation, generated great discontent and resentment among the people. To the Sudanese, "the taxes were not only hateful by tradition but more than abominable when the revenues were not repaid in social services but sent to Egypt or pocketed by the Egyptian [colonial] officials who viewed their corruption as just compensation for their unpleasant exile in the Sudan."[3] The South, meanwhile, continued to be a hunting ground for slave raiders, adventurers, and traders in local commodities.

During most of the period of Ottoman-Egyptian rule, the slave trade flourished and slave traders used the North as the base of operations for their incursions into the South. However, under pressure from Europe, the government began to suppress slavery. General Charles Gordon, the British hero of the war with China, was sent to Sudan as governor-general with the objective of suppressing slavery. This obviously antagonized the slave traders, especially the Baggara Arab tribes of the west who were among the most deeply engaged in the slave raids and trade. General Gordon's efforts against slavery were largely imperceptible to the South, where no notable change was observed. Reaction to the Ottomans and the Egyptians came from both the North and the South, and had a unifying effect on the country as groups pulled together to resist foreign domination. Popular unrest culminated in a successful revolt that began in 1881 and brought Muhammad Ahmed al-Mahdi (the Mahdi) to power. General Gordon was killed in 1885 and the Ottoman-Egyptian rule collapsed. The Mahdi, seen by many as the awaited Islamic messiah, galvanized the various Sudanese peoples against the Ottomans. Though not converting to Islam, the South saw the Mahdists as a liberating force against the foreign rulers. The Dinka, the largest tribe within the South and also within the country, even conceived of the Mahdi as a holy man; they claimed the spirit of the Dinka divinity called Dengdit (The Great Deng) had descended to liberate the people.[4] Southern support of the Mahdi and his resistance movement was withdrawn after the Mahdiyya (the Mahdist movement) proved to be yet another source of oppression and slave raids from the North. The Mahdi had the opportunity to consolidate Sudan's nationhood, but foiled that opportunity by perpetuating the gross mistreatment of the people of Sudan. The Mahdists not only alienated the South, but they also generated divisions among the various tribes and regions of the North.[5]

These divisions worsened when the Mahdi suddenly died and was succeeded by Khalifa Abdullahi from the Taishi Baggara tribe of Darfur, under whose tenure the Mahdiyya abused their power and authority. This period was characterized by a complete breakdown of law and order, famine due to drought, and lack of state capacity to meet the drought emergency. The Mahdiyya thus paradoxically represented both progress toward the unification of the nation and an acute disruption that was extremely divisive, even among the Muslim communities of the North.

British Policies of Divisive Unification

The Anglo-Egyptian reconquest was reluctantly undertaken to avenge the death of General Gordon and to stop the French from encroaching into the country from the South. The outcome of the campaign was the collapse of the Mahdist state in 1898 and the establishment of the British-dominated Anglo-Egyptian Condominium Administration that was to rule the country for fifty-eight years. The Condominium, as the dual administration was known, established Sudan as a state with well-defined borders. It ended slavery and unified the country, but decided to administer North and South separately. This dual system reinforced Arabism and Islam in the North and encouraged southern development along indigenous African lines, while introducing Christian missionary education and rudiments of Western civilization in the South.

Paradoxically, while the reconquest imposed colonial domination on the country, it also brought relief to the peoples of Sudan, North and South. The Condominium was a unique colonial model in that its administration was accountable not to the colonial offices, but to the advisory jurisdiction of the foreign offices of the Condominium powers, Britain and Egypt. The administration tried to establish its legitimacy by demonstrating sensitivity to the local religious values and sentiments. The British were especially cognizant and respectful of the Arab-Islamic identity in the North, where the nationalist Islamic fervor of the Mahdiyya still prevailed. The resulting system was a compromise in which criminal and civil codes based on English law were adapted to fit the Sudanese condition, while such personal matters as marriage, divorce, and inheritance fell under the jurisdiction of *sharia* (Islamic) courts applying Islamic law.[6] The same policy was followed with regard to education, where Islam was taught in state schools as part of the curriculum, and the medium of instruction at the elementary and intermediate levels was Arabic.

In the South, given the persistent resistance to foreign rule, the Condominium Administration initially adopted a stringent policy of militaristic pacification and enforcement of law and order. This was gradually replaced by a policy of indirect rule, which meant building on the local cultures, values, and institutions. This implied recognizing, formalizing, and encouraging tribal identities as well as the North-South dichotomy. While the government invested considerably in the political, economic, social, and cultural development of the North, the South remained isolated, secluded, and undeveloped. Whereas the government felt that strict separation of religion and state was not acceptable to the North, it introduced state neutrality or impartiality on religious matters in the South.

From 1919, as Egyptian nationalism and anti-British political activism was on the rise in northern Sudan, the government became more stringent in its policy of separate development for the South. Following the 1924 rebellion led by Ali Abdel Latif, a young Dinka officer of slave background in the Egyptian army, the British cut off the South from the North and pursued their southern policy with greater vigor. This policy was developed in part to stem the tide of Egyptian nationalism that aspired to unify the entire Nile Valley.[7] However, it was also a means of containing the Africans in the

South, in particular the Nilotic tribes that had been the most resistant to British rule. It was feared that they constituted a potential nationalist threat if they were to become politically activated. Although the South resisted British rule into the late 1920s, long after the North had been pacified, British sensitivity to the cultures and concerns of the southerners—especially for peace, security, and autonomy—gradually won the confidence of the people.

When the structure of British colonialism began to weaken, northern Sudanese aspired to integrate the South into a unified state infrastructure and constitutional framework, but without southern participation in the process. When, in 1946, the governor-general set up an administrative conference to help determine the transfer of power to the Sudanese, southerners were not included in the discussions. When northerners, with the backing of Egypt, demanded the fusion of the North and the South, the British capitulated and decided upon a policy of ultimate unity of the country.[8] British policy until that point had recognized that

> the people of the Southern Sudan are distinctly African and Negroid, and that our obvious duty to them therefore is to push ahead as far as we can with their economic and educational development on African and Negroid lines, and not upon the Middle Eastern Arab lines suitable for northern Sudan. It is only by economic and educational development that these people can be equipped to stand up for themselves in the future, whether their lot is eventually cast with the northern Sudan or with East Africa (or partly with each).[9]

The new British policy, while recognizing the distinct identity of the South, nevertheless pushed for integration of the North and the South on the grounds that "economics and geography combine (so far as can be seen at the present time) to render them inextricably bound to the Middle-Eastern and Arabized northern Sudan."[10] British administrators in the South protested against this shift in policy and demanded that southerners be consulted. In response, in June 1947 the civil secretary convened the Juba conference to seek southerners' views on whether and how the South should be represented in the proposed legislative assembly, initially intended solely for the North. The conference revealed intense mutual suspicion and tension between the parties, with the North highly suspicious that the South wanted separation, and the South suspecting that the North wanted to dominate under the proposed unified framework. Representatives of the South, lacking the education, experience, and sophistication of northerners, found themselves at a disadvantage, and, rather than achieving a meeting of the minds during negotiations, were swayed to support national unity on the basis of a North-British agenda.

Although the South could not now be deprived of that distinct African cultural identity that had been safeguarded and fostered by earlier policies, emphasis was placed on conditioning southerners for increased contact with northerners, drawing the South into national political institutions, and making southern education compatible with the educational system established in the North. With less than seven years to go before the end of British administration, it was too late.[11] The parliament elected in 1953 decided on 16 August by a unanimous vote to carry out the requisite steps toward exercising the right of self-determination with a view to independence.

With unrelenting development toward a united Sudan under way at an accelerating pace, one incident after another intensified southern fear of the North: the disparaging attitude of northern officials toward southerners; the discrediting propaganda of northern political parties against one another in their scramble for southern votes; alienating strategies in which the government sought to intimidate southerners by transferring northern military forces to the South and attempting to move southern soldiers to the North; and above all, the announcement that eight hundred posts previously held by the British would now be Sudanized, in fact northernized, with only eight junior positions to go to southerners. This pattern of marginalization fanned southern opposition until a violent revolt erupted on 18 August 1955, in the southern town of Torit, less than four months before independence, triggering the first phase of a war that was to last for seventeen years.

The rapid march to independence was the achievement of an elite group of politicians, intellectuals, and sectarian leaders who were quite isolated from the rural masses and certainly isolated from the South. Even after the South had expressed fears of independence and the threat of northern domination, northern political leaders accelerated the pace toward independence with near total insensitivity to southern concerns. Only one day after the revolt of the South, Parliament passed a resolution to hold a direct plebiscite. The decision, however, was soon reversed: the vast, diversified country's population was largely illiterate, in the South the rebellion had caused the collapse of the security and administrative system, and more problems would be created and none solved. The people of Sudan were denied the right to participate in determining the future of their country.

At the critical point, the leaders of the nationalist movement "worked feverishly" for days to ensure the declaration of independence, effective 1 January 1956. With a tone that underscored the lack of sensitivity to southern concerns, Muhammad Ahmad Mahjoub, one of the main architects of the independence movement, recalled, "We encountered some difficulty in convincing the southerners, so we inserted a special resolution to appease them, pledging that the Constituent Assembly would give full consideration to the claims of southern Sudanese members of Parliament for a federal government for the three southern Provinces."[12] Whether Mahjoub and his colleagues intended to take this pledge seriously or not can only be judged from the cursory reference to it and the subsequent dismissal of the southern demand without anything near full consideration. The destiny of a people, indeed a nation, was thus determined by a ploy that was devoid of fundamental ethical and political principles other than the shortest-term objective of connived independence, and the South naively took it at face value as sincere. As Mansour Khalid noted, "Sudan's declaration of independence, in the words of one of its authors, was a take-in: a fraudulent document gained through false pretenses and subterfuge that does no honor to the northern political establishment."[13]

The crisis of legitimacy, however, went beyond southern Sudan and affected other parts of the country. As Tim Niblock observed, "To much of the population in the less developed fringe of the Sudan, then, the Sudanese state as it emerged at independence seemed a distant and alien entity, just as it did in the colonial era. The peoples of southern Sudan, and most of those in western and eastern Sudan, had little access to the benefits which the state bestowed (education, health services, remunerative government jobs, etc.) . . . the State personnel who faced them . . . appeared to share little of their cultural or ethnic background."[14]

The global perspective of the northern leaders in their interaction with the Condominium powers, Arab countries, and the world at large seemed more developed and refined than their comprehension of the internal situation, especially in the South. To the average southerner, the new government that took over on independence was northern, Arab, and foreign, and certainly did not signify southern independence. The commission of inquiry into the 1955 disturbances in the South reported, "The northern administration in southern Sudan is not colonial, but the great majority of southerners unhappily regard it as such."[15]

Evidence obtained by the author in interviews with former British administrators show that British postcolonial recollections and evaluations of their record of accomplishments in Sudan are generally glowing, but they remain ambivalent and even remorseful about their southern policy. They were also critical of the disparity in economic and social development that was allowed to develop over the period of colonial rule and then ignored in favor of a unity that was bound to be disadvantageous to the South.[16] Paul Howell, who had served in the South, observed that "one of the biggest [British] errors was to have a southern policy which not only led to a scandalous lack of investment in development and education in the South, but was really incompatible with the aims of a unitary state. This was, ultimately, a burden which had to be carried by the northern Sudanese no less than the southern."

Gawain Bell concluded with an acknowledgment of failure on the part of the British:

> The fact is that the government failed to solve the problem. And I think it
> failed to solve the problem because it did not appreciate early enough that

independence would come as soon as it did. What ought to have been done, I think, was that in the twenties there should have been much more cultural, educational, and administrative interchange between the North and the South. Not that . . . the South would have become a completely Islamic area. I think that the missions would have had their opportunity; but . . . . if the Sudan were going to become a really united country, then I think steps should have been taken to integrate the two parts of the country which, after all, geographically, were not a unit.

K. D. D. Henderson concluded, "The new Southern Policy . . . was conceived of at a time when men thought in terms of half centuries and centuries . . . It was designed to develop the South so that it could make its own choice in the fullness of time."[17] And according to the Commission of Enquiry into the 1955 disturbances, "very few people could visualize in 1947 what the political developments in the Sudan would be in 1955."[18]

The legacy of British rule is thus a mixture of ambivalences and contradictions. Although the British were the first to give meaning to the unity of Sudan, the northern Sudanese condemned their policies for deepening the North-South division and making it an obstacle to national unity. The southern Sudanese resented the policies aimed at keeping the South traditional, which, however well motivated, relegated them to a position inferior to the North, and then lumped them together in an unqualified unitary state. When the British belatedly realized that they were about to leave, they wanted to help the South catch up with the North and even accepted the principle of formulating programs of accelerated development for the South. But it was too late.

Challenges of Statehood and Nationhood

The crisis of statehood and national identity in Sudan is rooted in the British attempt to bring together diverse peoples with a history of hostility into a framework of one state, while also keeping them apart and entrenching inequities by giving certain regions more access to state power, resources, services, and development opportunities than other regions. This policy of divided unification took place both between the North and South and within the northern regions themselves. The inequities fostered by the system played out along regional, racial, ethnic, and cultural divisions, with the Muslim Arabs favored over the non-Arabs within the North, and with the South being by far the most neglected region. Disadvantaged in every respect, the South feared that independence threatened to return the country to the evils of the past, among which slavery was the most dreaded. That was the cause of the 1955 mutiny that triggered a seventeen-year war, perpetrated by the Southern Sudanese Liberation Movement (SSLM) and its military wing, the Anyanya, until it was ended by the dictatorship of Jaafer Nimeiri through the Addis Ababa Agreement of 1972, which he unilaterally abrogated in 1983, provoking the South into another war that raged until quite recently.

Since the resumption of the war in 1983 and the formation of the Sudan People's Liberation Movement (SPLM) and the Sudan People's Liberation Army (SPLA), the South's strategic shift toward unity and the reaction of the Arab-Islamists (who seized power by military coup in June 1989 and continue to assert their agenda with an ideological zeal), have created extreme polarization between the North and South, while also serving as a source of unification within and between regions. Racial, ethnic, and cultural marginalization has made possible cross-cutting alliances among non-Arab groups in the North and the South, as well as with liberal-minded Arabs who believe in an equality of citizenship that transverses the boundaries of racial, ethnic, or cultural identification. These alliances across the North-South divide have improved the prospects of unity in a restructured system, which, though not easily acceptable to those committed to an Arab Islamic model of the country, nonetheless make a powerful case for unity and integration within a secular and ethnically pluralistic framework. Other factors working in favor of unity include the strong bias in Africa and internationally against changing the colonial borders, notwithstanding the exception of Eritrea and the unfolding de facto partition in Somalia. While the commitment to unity is conditional to the equitable restructuring of the national framework, it would seem that the dynamics of the situation on the ground are creating a de facto reconciliation of unity and separatism among southerners. It is in that sense that the proposed formula of one country, two (or multiple) systems, becomes a creative way of reconciling contradictory aspirations and building a framework for evolutionary nation building.[19]

Perspectives on Borders, State, and Nationalism

Sudanese perspectives on borders, state, and nationhood are heavily weighted on the issue of national identity. While the country still has minor border problems with some of its neighbors (notably Egypt, Ethiopia, and Kenya), the only significant threat to the existing borders is the secessionist sentiment in the South. The territorial integrity of Sudan is recognized regionally and internationally within its established colonial borders, and the notion of the state in its varying political systems and forms of governance is also recognized and well established. The development of a sense of national unity, on the other hand, remains a precarious issue.

Identity, Power, and Economics

Identity is used here to describe the way individuals and groups define themselves and are defined by others on the basis of race, ethnicity, religion, language, and culture. In Africa, clan, lineage, and family are often vital elements of identity. Territory or region as an element of identification overlaps with one or more of these factors and is therefore a complementary or an affirmative consideration. Whatever the determining factors, identity is a concept that gives a deeply rooted psychological and social meaning to the individual in the context of group dynamics. As groups vie for power, material resources, and other values, these dynamics may involve cooperation, competition, or conflict. The source of conflict lies not so much in the mere fact of differences as in the degree to which the interacting identities and their overriding goals are mutually accommodating or incompatible. In the context of the nation-state, conflicts of identities often occur when groups—or more appropriately, their elites—rebel against what they see as intolerable oppression by the dominant group, expressed in denial of recognition, exclusion from the mainstream, marginalization, and perhaps the threat of cultural or even physical elimination.

Nationalism and identity are closely interconnected, in that the nationalist sentiment, in its essence, can be construed as an internalized sense of belonging that roots people in a common heritage and a shared destiny. This connection is profoundly internal, going much deeper than one's connection to the formal mechanisms of government, and touching on the very essence of an individual's or a group's perception of itself. National consciousness is often conceived of as a transcendental norm, wherein all citizens and groups within the state, having reconciled and synthesized ethnic, racial, and religious diversities, share a unified conception of themselves.[20] The path to nationhood can therefore be conceived of as an emergent process entailing reconciliation of diverse identities and the reconstruction of a unified vision of self and nation.

In the context of Sudan, identity has been rendered conflictual by the gross inequities that have characterized racial, ethnic, cultural, and religious differences. Ann Mosely Lesch has aptly described the implications of identity stratification in Sudan and its marginalization of the non-Arabs in these terms:

> Racial, linguistic and cultural categories have become the basis for crucially important power relationships that have resulted in the peoples who live in the northern and central Nile Valley wielding disproportionate political and economic power. Those citizens' Arabic-Islamic image of the Sudanese nation excludes citizens who reside in the geographic and/or ethnic margins: persons who define themselves as African rather than Arab, ethnically or linguistically. Those who reside in the South generally adhere to Christianity or traditional African beliefs, whereas the ethnic minorities in the North are largely Muslim. Their marginalization has intensified as political, economic and cultural power has remained concentrated in the hands of the Muslim Arab core and as the central government has intensified its drive to spread Islam and Arabic. In reaction, disaffection and revolts by the marginalized people have deepened and widened. Originally expressed by those in the South who are both African and non-Muslim, the revolt now includes many Muslim Africans who think that their ethnicity and particular forms of Islamic practices are denigrated and suppressed by the current ruling elite.[21]

Lesch concludes her account with a portrayal of more recent developments that are tentatively pointing to a demand for reform rather than secession: "Recently a process of rethinking the political alignments has begun that may, in time, cut across the divide and lead to the restructuring of power based on inclusive concepts of national identity. At present, that realignment is partial, tentative, and largely theoretical."[22]

From the perspectives of the dominant northern models of identification, these hard facts tend to be clouded with theoretical, often politically motivated discussion of the concept of identity to make northern self-identification with Arabism seem more benign and less racist. In his statement to the 1965 Round Table Conference on the problem of the South, Prime Minister Sirr al-Khatim al-Khalifa observed: "Gentlemen, Arabism, which is a basic attribute of the majority of the population of this country and of many African countries besides, is not a racial concept which unites members of a certain racial group. It is a religious, cultural and non-racial link that binds together numerous races, black, white and brown. Had Arabism been anything else but this, most modern Arabs, whether African or Asian, including the entire population of northern Sudan, would cease to be 'Arab' at all."[23]

Although the cultural notion of Arabism is widely used in the Arab world, it is particularly appealing to the Sudanese Arabs whose features look more black African than Arab. In reality, northern Sudanese "Arabs" conceive of their identity in both racial and cultural terms, even though they are quite flexible in their interpretation of those terms. As Professor Ali Mazrui, the renowned African scholar, noted, "Disputes as to whether such and such a family is really Arab by descent or not, and evaluations of family prestige partly in terms of lighter shades of color, have remained an important part of the texture of Sudanese life in the North."[24] One of those interviewed by the author on the issue of identity, Abd al-Rahman al-Bashir, while recognizing that Islam and the Arabic language are important factors in being considered an Arab, also emphasized genealogy:

> You must belong to something [a known genealogy] . . . say the Abassids [which means] that your great, great, great grandfather [original ancestor] is Al-Abbas, the Uncle of the Prophet, so that you are distinguished. Some of the Sudanese think of themselves as Ashraf [descendants of the Prophet's closest friends and associates]. This might be forced, but it gives them satisfaction. These are the things that are in the mind of the people: that you speak Arabic, the good language of the Koran, and you are from the Arab world which is the best nation God has created. Rightly or wrongly, this is the way people think. They find pride in this and in their origin, *asl*. The word *asl* is very important in the Sudan. If you want to marry, you should look for the *asl*. People think that way: How pure is this man? Is he contaminated or not? I am just explaining the way people think.[25]

Identification with the Arabs is often asserted as a dogma that defies the facts. As Al-Baqir al-Afif Mukhtar vividly explained, because the margin is conscious of its invisibility to the center, there is a need to advertise itself. Northerners' marginal identity therefore explains their overemphasis on Arab descent. "Statements such as 'I am an Arab. I have genealogy,' or 'I am an Arab, nationally and culturally, whether you like it or not,' are repeatedly issued by the political and cultural entrepreneurs. Unlike the elite of the Arab world, who do not need to state the obvious, northerners feel the need to complement their lack in features by words."[26] Here too, the Sudanese "Arabs" confront a serious dilemma and therefore a personal crisis of identity. Since the Arabs who have come to Sudan were mostly men who married into prominent Sudanese families, with their progeny inheriting positions of power, wealth, and influence through their maternal lines, then overturning the system in favor of their paternal Arab lineage, the psychosocial implications of this parental schism and implicit antagonism raise intriguing questions. Al-Baqir Mukhtar writes:

> Northerners live in a split world. While they believe that they are the descendants of an "Arab father" and an "African mother," they seem to identify with the father, albeit invisible, and despise the mother who is so visible in their features. There is an internal fissure in the Northern self between the looks and the outlook, the body and the mind, the skin color and the culture, and in one word, between the "mother" and the "father." Arabic culture standardizes [i.e., idealizes] the white color, and despises the black color. Northerners, in using the signification system of the Arabic language, and the value system and symbolic order of the Arabic culture, do not find themselves, but they find the embodiment of the center. The Northern self is absent as a subject in this order. It is only seen, as an object, through the eyes of the center, and hence the "misfits."[27]

Interestingly enough, northern "Arabs" do not recognize this complex within themselves; to the contrary, their outward appearance and discourse reflect a self-assurance that is strikingly in contrast with the marginality of their claimed Arabness, perhaps a successful case of overcompensation though exaggerated pride in Arabism. This exaggerated pride was so graphically articulated in an often-quoted statement by Ismail al-Azhari, one of the legendary figures of the nationalist struggle, who was to become the first prime minister and later president, expressed in unequivocal terms to the Round Table Conference on the problem of the South in 1965:

> I feel at this juncture obliged to declare that we are proud of our Arab origin, of our Arabism and of being Moslems. The Arabs came to this continent, as pioneers, to disseminate a genuine culture, and promote sound principles which have shed enlightenment and civilization throughout Africa at a time when Europe was plunged into the abyss of darkness, ignorance and doctrinal and scholarly backwardness. It is our ancestors

who held the torch high and led the caravan of liberation and advance-
ment; and it is they who provided a superior melting-pot for Greek,
Persian and Indian culture, giving them the chance to react with all that
was noble in Arab culture, and handing them back to the rest of the world
as a guide to those who wished to extend the frontiers of learning.[28]

The psychological roots of such an exaggerated attachment to Arabism
go deep into the history of the threatening and even humiliating relations
with the Christian West. Appreciating this psychological dimension is
important to understanding the threat of demotion to the supposedly inferi-
or African identity, which both the southerners and non-Arab northerners
pose to the northern Sudanese claims to Arabism by their demands for a
restructuring of the country's identity to include a more visible African element. This deeply entrenched inferiority complex has provoked an Arab
superiority complex that is so vigorously committed to the Islamic-Arab
identity and its agenda for nation building.

Edward Atiyah, a Syrian who arrived in Sudan in 1926, taught at the
Gordon Memorial College, and later joined the intelligence department of
the Anglo-Egyptian administration, observed this phenomenon closely:
"The educated Sudanese, as a class, were unhappy. Their minds were being
warped, their souls soured, and I knew the reasons . . . as no Englishman
could." For Atiyah, Sudanese nationalism and hatred of the British represented a reaction against humiliation and an attempt to retrieve a sense of
dignity that had been destroyed and supplanted by a feeling of inferiority.
His students displayed mixed emotions—excitement about the outside
world with its superior knowledge, power, and wealth, and a sense of self-
pity for being backward, poor, and ignorant. According to Atiyah, identification with the Arab East was as much a reaction against Western domination as it was an escape from the inferiority of the African background.
Sudanese emphasized their Arab descent, excluding from their consciousness any connection with Africa or the Negro elements, and they found
great consolation in the renaissance of the Arab East. Since that renaissance
had not much to offer in tangible terms, they sought comfort and encouragement in the past glory of the warlike Arabs who, inspired by their religion and the spirit of the Prophet, had swept victoriously through
Christendom.

Had not the Arabs been the masters and teachers of the world when the
now mighty Europeans were steeped in medieval night? Had they not
translated Aristotle into Arabic and transmitted to the European barbarians
the first gleams of the light of Greece? But the greatest consolation of all,
the one beyond doubt and dispute, the safe and sure anchorage of their
being was the knowledge that in their Book and Prophet they possessed
the Ultimate Truth. In this serene knowledge they felt superior to all out-
siders . . . Truly that knowledge was a rock of comfort.[29]

The northern Sudanese scholar, Muddathir 'Abd al-Rahim, confirms Atiyah's observation by explaining that a dominant theme in the writings and verbal utterances of the literate northern Sudanese at that time was the need for unity and solidarity based on principles of Islamism and Arabism rather than on Sudanese nationalism. Having been defeated and humiliated by the Anglo-Egyptian forces, the Sudanese, he explained, needed psychological reassurance, which they could not find in their past or in contemporary African identity. Instead of helping them to regain their lost self-confidence, Africa threatened to accentuate their feeling of inferiority in contrast to both the British and the Egyptians. "Almost involuntarily, therefore, the Sudanese . . . turned their backs on Africa and became passionately attached to the glorious past of Islam, which, together with the richness of classic Arabic culture and thought provided the necessary psychological prod."[30]

Since in reality most northern Sudanese families are mixed, the notion of race, *unsur* or *jins*, from which the word for nationality—*jinsiyya*—is derived, has to be flexible in terms of color. To be racially Arab then does not require being as light as the original Arabs. On the contrary, the Sudanese have developed their own color scheme, which favors the mixed mold as the ideal, relegating both black and white to a lesser order. Even within this color range, shades are critically important. Relating the notion of *asl* to color, Abd al-Rahman al-Bashir, a man of very dark complexion, noted, "Black is depicted in [Arabic] literature as something not good. That is why people are described as not black but brown or green. Green in Sudan means that their *asl* (origin) is not Negroid." Although Sudanese, northerners and southerners alike, range in skin color from exceedingly black to various shades of brown, Sudanese passports almost never describe the holder as "black." The description used for the overwhelming majority of the holders is "green," the standard of the nation in official eyes. Indeed, green is seen as the ideal Sudanese color of skin because it reflects a brown that is not too dark, giving associations with black Africa and possibly slavery, and it is not too light, hinting at gypsy (*halabi*) or European Christian forbears. Al-Baqir Mukhtar, however, provides an even more nuanced perspective on the complexities of northern color consciousness and stratification:

> The first color in rank is *asfar*. This literally means "yellow," but is used interchangeably with *ahmar* to denote "whiteness." The second in rank is *asmar*. This literally means reddish, but it is used interchangeably to describe a range of color shades from light to dark brown. This range usually includes subdivisions such as *dahabi* (golden), *gamhi* (the color of ripe wheat), and *khamri* (the color of red wine). The third in ranking is *akhdar*. This literally means green, but it is used as a polite alternative of the word "black" in describing the color of a dark northerner. Last and

least is *azrag*. This literally means "blue," but it is used interchangeably with *aswad* to mean "black," which is the color of the *abid* (slave).[31]

Mukhtar notes with refreshing candor: "The average Northerner views dark color as a problem that should be dealt with . . . Defense mechanisms must be put to work . . . In order to avoid describing the self as *aswad* (black), the collective Northern consciousness renamed the word *akhdar* (green) . . . Whereas a very dark Northerner is only *akhdar*, an equally dark Southerner is bluntly *aswad*."[32]

Increasingly, enlightened northern Sudanese are recognizing the paradoxes and dilemmas of the racial and cultural attitudes behind the crisis of national identity in the Sudan. Yet, there are those who still hold to the dogma of Sudan's being an Arab-Islamic country. In the interviews conducted by the author with Sudanese elites from both the North and the South, perhaps the most articulate voice among the northerners in defense of Sudan's Arabism was Khalid al-Mubarak. Personalizing the national question of identity, he said,

> Personally, I don't see any identity crisis as a northern Sudanese. I see myself as somebody within the Arab-Islamic culture. I am at peace with that. I do not deny the fact that I have African, Negroid, black blood in me. I know I am not an Arab in the same sense that a Syrian is an Arab. But that is not as problematic as some people try to present. I don't spend sleepless nights, for example, thinking whether I am an Arab or an African. I think there has been much fusion; all the characteristics have been fused in such a way that one is reconciled to the fact that one is a mixture of several strands.

Questioned on how he would explain the process that fostered in him the Arab-Islamic elements of identity, whether it did not entail looking down on the African elements that were regarded as the bottom of racial, cultural, and religious hierarchy, and how he felt about the fact that elements still visible in him are looked down upon, Khalid al-Mubarak responded:

> If part of me were looked down upon by others, I would not accept it. If it is being looked down upon by myself, then I would need psychiatric treatment. But I think many, even among the most enlightened Southern intellectuals, are unaware of the degree of awareness among the Northerners of the African strand of their character. I think there is a blind spot as far as this is concerned. We are also conscious of another dimension neglected by our Southern brothers; this is the consciousness of the black element within Arabic, Islamic countries about their [black] origin. The greatest writer in Arabic of all ages, Al-Jahiz, wrote a very long treatise about "Fakhr al-Sudan ala al-Bidan"—Why Blacks are superior to Whites. And he himself was, according to some sources, like the Northern Sudanese [in features].

Mukhtar explains that although Islam preached the unity and equality of humankind despite differences in tongues and colors and that "the most noble of you in the eyes of God is the most pious," and the Prophet taught that "no Arab shall enjoy superiority over the non-Arab, nor shall the white ever excel the black, nor the red the yellow, except in piety," the attitude of the Arabs toward the blacks never changed. Many blacks apparently internalized the contempt against them. Yet, often blacks took pride in their blackness. It is to this group that al-Jahiz, whom Khalid al-Mubarak exalts as a symbol of black pride in the Arab world, belonged. Al-Jahiz tried to remind the Arabs that the black people were creatures of God, and that God could not have intended to demean His own creation, as the Arabs tended to believe. He said: "God did not deform us by creating us black. Our black color came as a result of the country (environment)."

The second form of resistance usually accepted the negative view of blackness as ugly, apologized for it, but asserted positive moral and intellectual qualities in the blacks, along the lines of "yes, we are black, but we are virtuous." The poet Sahim Abd Bani al-Hassas, a Nubian, typifies that approach: "If I have been a slave my soul is free, and if my skin is black my virtues are white." There was, implicitly and sometimes explicitly, an element of self-deprecation even in this position: "Had I been rosy white, they (women) would have adored me, but my God has cursed me with a black skin." Khifaf Ibn Nadba, another black poet, accepted that his blackness was a negative mark, but took pride in his skills as a great warrior. Antra, the great warrior, is reported to have said that "during peacetime they call me son of Zabiba, and when it is war they say to me come, attack them, son of nobility."

Mukhtar concludes that the few works of resistance had little effect. "Prejudice [against] the black color intensified in Arabic culture as the empire grew and the Arabs set out to hunt slaves. Eventually, an association between slavery and al-Sudan, i.e., the blacks, became instilled."[33] Khalid al-Mubarak's assertion of blacks' being part of the exalted Arab identity and occupying a respectable place in Arab society was sheer myth or wishful thinking. The fact is that blacks were not accepted as Arabs and they suffered discrimination on account of their black color, which associated them with slave background, as it still does today in the Arab world.

Many northern Sudanese do not share Khalid al-Mubarak's strong defense of Sudanese Arabness and even see it as a form of inferiority complex. Magdi Amin, a northerner of Nubian-Arab descent, alludes to the psychological dimensions of northern ambivalences between Arabism and Africanism, which he describes as a "neurosis." "I do believe the problem of identity is of great importance because the South has been forced to endure the neurosis of the North trying to decide whether it is African or Arab . . . The reference points for the Northerners have always been in the Middle East, actually more Arab than even the Egyptians. Ultimately, it is a neurosis. . . . I think the North—just as they are looked upon as second class citizens . . . [in the Arab world] have to emulate that . . . and see whoever is South of them as second class." Mansour Khalid appears to support Magdi Amin's perspective on the northern psyche:

> The reason [for northern identification with Arabism] stems from an inferiority complex really. The Northern Sudanese is torn internally in his Arab-African personality. As a result of his Arabic Islamic cultural development, he views himself in a higher status from the other Sudanese not exposed to this process. Arabism gives him his sense of pride and distinction and that is why he exaggerates when he professes it. He becomes more royal than the king, so to speak.

Much of this change in northern attitude stems from exposure to the outside world. Many anecdotes abound about the experience of the northern Sudanese abroad. Although being identified as black in the West, and presumably experiencing discrimination on that account, what is particularly bewildering and hurtful to the northern Sudanese who have been to the Arab world is that they are considered black and discriminated against by other "fellow Arabs." As Mansour Khalid observed:

> The Arab whom this Northern Sudanese wants to be like looks down on him because the latter has specific images of his own culture. Today in Lebanon and in the East, the name given to blacks is slaves. Even peanuts are called "ful abid," "the nuts of slaves." In Africa, the Lebanese living there call Africans slaves. They do not mean this literally, but the word there is associated with color. This is the problem of the Sudanese northerner who when faced with this reality, overcompensates in order to alleviate his feelings of inferiority.[34]

The anthropologist Abd al-Ghaffar Muhammed Ahmed, who has had considerable professional experience inside Sudan and abroad, gave a personal illustration: "I went to Saudi Arabia and was outright rejected as an Arab. I was always told, 'You are an African. Even though you speak Arabic, profess Islam, and go to the Mosque, you are still . . . African.'" In comparison, he reports that in Africa he was often mistaken for an Ethiopian, a Nigerian, or other African, and never taken for an Arab. "I am in fact very proud of that," he remarked, referring to his identification as an African. Abbas Abdal-Karim Ahmed, an economist who served as lecturer at Juba University in southern Sudan and later worked in the Gulf and in Europe, offered an insightful analysis of the dynamics of the various considerations, both subjective and objective:

> Sudanese more and more realize that we are different from the Arabs, especially those of us who go to the Gulf. I went through the same experience. They come back understanding very much how different they are. Of course, they benefit and like to identify themselves as Arabs, because

otherwise they might not be permitted to stay there. But deep in them-selves they see that they are different. Many of the Sudanese migrants who went there had never met Arabs before. They find that in fact they are very different from them, not only racially but even culturally and social-ly. When they come back, I don't believe they look forward to being iden-tified with the Arabs. Of course, there are always the economic variables. If they see that this is going to enhance their position as individuals or groups they might continue to identify with the Arabs.

Despite the pride in Arab identity, the word "Arab" is sometimes used by the urban population of the North to connote an unsophisticated tribal nomad, with outmoded rural values and out-of-context manners. As Ahmed al-Shahi observed about the Nuri people of the Shaigiyya tribe in the Northern Province, "In one context the claim to descent from an 'arab' tribe is a matter of pride; in another context, to be an 'arab' indicates a nomadic way of life and an associated inferior social status. (Conversely nomads look down upon sedentary agriculturalists.)"[35] To complicate the picture even more, as al-Shahi implies, the association with rural life and values usually connoted by the word "tribe," *gabila*, is also positive. To say, even in urban circles, that one is *wad gabila*, "son of a tribe," or *wad gabail* (son of tribes), which has a more generic association with the concept of the tribe, or the even more pluralistic *awlad gabail*, "sons of tribes," carries a complimentary connotation that calls to mind generosity, courage, and integrity.

Such derogatory terms as *zunj*, "Negro," or *abid*, "slave," commonly applied to the southern Sudanese and black Africans in general, are now less rampant than they were even a few decades ago. But they are still pop-ular in casual conversations that sometimes have a serious and even racist edge. Nonetheless, there is no doubt that while the northern view of the southerner has improved considerably, the word *janubi*, "southerner," has its plural form, *janubiyeen*, and still carries a significant connotation of racial (and cultural) inferiority, backwardness, and socioeconomic distance from the northerner.[36] Mansour Khalid intimates that "in the closed circles of northern Sudan there is a series of unprintable slurs for Sudanese of non-Arab stock, all reflective of semi-concealed prejudice."[37]

The impression should not be given, however, that only the northerner has a condescending view of the southerner. Quite the contrary, the preju-dice is mutual. Southerners generally believe that the differences between them and the Arabs are genetic, cultural, and deeply embedded. They also acknowledge that their prejudices are mutual. But they realize that the Arabs have the upper hand, which gives their racial and cultural chauvin-ism the means to impose itself in the South. As a young Dinka put it, "The Arabs despise us, and we know it; we also despise them, but they do not know it."[38]

Southern scorn for the Arabs lies in the realm of moral values, which they believe to be inherent in the genetic and cultural composition of identity. In a set of interviews with Dinka chiefs and elders about the past, present, and prospects for the future of their people, this theme emerged recurrently. To give a few examples, in response to a question of whether, in light of the peace achievement of 1972, the peoples of Sudan would integrate or remain separate, one elder observed, "This question . . . whether people will mix or remain separate—why should we not remain separate? . . . God did not create at random. He created people with their own kind. He created some people brown and some people black. We cannot say we want to destroy what God has created. Even God would get angry if we spoiled his work."[39] Several others spoke in the same vein. One said he could not see how integration could take place. "It cannot happen, you will live together but there will always be South and North. Even living together is only possible if you handle the situation well. There are people who appear to be one, but inside them they remain two. I think that is how you will live. A man has only one head and one neck, but he has two legs to stand on." Another elder pleaded, "If you, our children, have survived, hold to the ways of our ancestors very firmly. Let us be friends with the Arabs, but each man should have his own way. We are one Sudan, but let each man be himself." Yet another elder, a man of renowned spiritual powers inherited from a long line of religious leaders, spoke in similar words: "Why don't we promote our own ways? Why do we take their [Arab] ways without our own plan? What have you people done to promote our own ways with the Arabs?" He proceeded to give a dramatic account of his resistance to Arab influence: "I don't speak Arabic, God has refused my speaking Arabic, and I asked God, 'Why don't I speak Arabic?' And he said, 'If you now speak Arabic, you will turn into a bad man.' And I said, 'There is something good in Arabic!' And he said, 'No, there is nothing good in it.'"

Southerners generally tend to accept the northerners' claim to be Arabs and react to them as such. According to Dunstan Wai, "Whether the North is both Arab and African, or exclusively one or the other, is not crucial. The significant point is that those who wield political power, generally the educated elites, think the North is Arab. Thus, even if biologically they are both Arab and African, they have opted in their choice of self-identification for Arabism."[40] For the southern Sudanese, the issue then is the struggle for power, in which identity, subjectively conceived, defines the contestants. In Ambrose Riny's words, "The ruling Arabs in Sudan think that it is important that they be of Arab nationality because it is a 'superior' race, and they are not prepared to share the country with the [non-Arab] people of Sudan regardless of race and religion." Riny continued his analysis of the situation:

> They want to use the racial and religious question in order to maintain dominance, in order to marginalize people they identify as not part of

what they are. Now, we know that any country can be shared by various nationalities across race. The United States is a great nation with a multiplicity of races, cultures, and religions. It has moved forward, ensuring that everyone has equal opportunity to develop and advance, and to aspire for a higher position in their state. This is not obviously the thinking of our compatriots in northern Sudan.

Riny recognized that not all northerners shared that attitude; some believed in pluralism and equality. But according to him, they are an ineffective minority: "Unfortunately, we wish their numbers were a little more than we are able to see. If they were able to become the majority, there would be the possibility for the people to develop a commonality in that position and establish a country. But in view of the fact that these are an extreme minority, while the majority insist on maintaining power on the grounds of race and religion, that to me is the crux of the Sudanese crisis."

Obviously, Mansour Khalid belongs to the northern elite minority that has begun to challenge the self-perception of northerners as Arabs. Khalid was one of the most important personalities behind the Addis Ababa Agreement and now is one of the prominent northern Sudanese members of the SPLM. He explains the complex interplay of the traditional and the transitional phases in the politics of sectarianism and the modern forces that are challenging them:

> For 30 years, and for reasons of myopia, ignorance, and unenlightened self-interest on the part of the Sudanese ruling elite, Sudan's national identity has been obscured and distorted. By "ruling elite" I refer to the politicized Arab/Islamic rulers coming from the urban and semiurban centers of the northern and central Sudan in Khartoum, White Nile, Gezira, and Kordofan provinces, which exert a political and economic hegemony over the marginalized social and cultural groups living in the rural and outlying regions of the country, including some parts of the geographic north. It is this ruling elite which alone has had the power to make and break governments, to mold public opinion, to tackle head-on the challenge of achieving unity in diversity, and to articulate a genuine vision of Sudan to the outside world.[41]

The issue for Sudan is whether what a person believes himself or herself to be racially or ethnically is what counts, even if it is not supported by genetic or physical evidence, or whether such perception, in order to be valid, must conform with features normally associated with racial or ethnic claims. This clear delineation of the issues tends to be blurred by the literature on ethnicity, which reflects some ambiguity between recognizing objective criteria for determining ethnic identity, and taking subjective claims to any identity as the determining factor. Logically, the latter position would extend to the scenario in which anyone who claims to be a member of any one race or ethnicity should be accepted as such, whatever the discrepancy between the claim and the appearance.[42] Where the discrepancies are minor and hardly noticeable, the issue poses no serious or difficult problems. Also, where such claims are personal and carry no consequences for others, no problem arises from a misplaced or distorted self-image. But where the gap is visible between what is claimed and what is accepted as standard, or where significant social consequences from the claims affect the interests of others, the matter cannot be considered purely personal.

On balance, recognizing identity (including its kinship and racial components) as subjective does not mean that it cannot be challenged, especially if the public interest justifies it. For policy purposes, if an exclusive identity comes into conflict with the requirements of national unity in a framework of diverse identities, then national identity must be redefined and broadened to include others, otherwise there is a justifiable case for the disadvantaged or excluded parties to go their separate ways.

Factors Shaping National Identity

Historically, a number of factors have played, and continue to play, a role in shaping the conflicting identities in the Sudan, both reinforcing divisiveness and pulling the various elements together. Power and economics were at the core of the initial involvement of the Arab traders and subsequent invasion of the Turko-Egyptian forces. They were motivated by a quest for gold, ivory, and slaves. The Nile and its waters have always been a vital factor in linking the South to the North and Sudan to Egypt. One of the reasons the British were reluctant to partition the country was that the South was too poor to be viable independently. Paradoxically, there were people who thought that the country's natural wealth was mostly in the South and that the North could not be viable alone. This prophecy has now been born out by the discovery of most of the country's petroleum reserves in the South, which in turn has been an aggravating factor in the conflict.

There is a general tendency to attribute conflicts in Africa to poverty and the competition for scarce resources. While this may be true, at least in part, it does not follow that the prospects for development dispose conflicting parties toward seeing the mutual interest in both moving toward peace and creating conditions for development. In Sudan, two major projects that could have brought relative prosperity to the country were deliberately blocked by the conflict. These were oil production and the construction of the mammoth Jonglei Canal that would retrieve water from the Sudd swamps and make it available for irrigation schemes in the North and Egypt. Economics has also pulled Sudan toward the Arab world because of its oil wealth. This played a significant role in the 1970s, following the Middle East War and the Arab mobilization of oil power in global politics.

As an Arab country with access to petrodollars, Sudan's vast potential in agriculture and animal wealth made it ideally suited for trilateral cooperation involving Western technology and Arab money. The country was projected as a potential breadbasket for the Middle East and North Africa.[43] Bilateral aid from Arab countries and the resources of several Arab funds became available to the country, and the Arab Authority for Agricultural Development was created with its headquarters in Khartoum. Sudan became its first recipient country. However, according to Bona Malwal, a southerner who was minister of culture and information at that time, the northern Sudanese projected themselves as having a special role to play in promoting Islam in Africa and saw this as a basis for receiving support from Muslim and Arab countries.

> We were always mindful of our Arab identity as a way of promoting ourselves . . . We always felt that if we, by which I mean the people who were making decisions in this process, identified ourselves as Muslims and Arabs, more capital would flow in. So, there is no denying that we became hostages of our own ideological tilt, and we linked it to our economic decisions, and our economic behavior.
> So many times when there was some little economic activity that we wanted to undertake, the first thing people thought of was that we could always go to Saudi Arabia and Kuwait to plead in the name of Arabism and Islam or in the name of the "breadbasket," and we would get the money.[44]

The discovery of oil in commercial quantities, mostly in the southern areas bordering the North, has added to the complexities of the situation. With sanctions still imposed on the regime for involvement in international terrorism, and Sudan still on the U.S. list of countries that promote terrorism, U.S. companies are barred from investing in Sudan. Pressure against investment by companies from other Western countries has also discouraged their involvement, leaving the field to the Chinese, the Malays, and the Indians. To ensure access to the southern oil fields and provide security for production, the government has forcefully displaced the indigenous populations in the respective areas. Oil revenues have also been used by the government to buy weapons and enhance its capacity for pursuing the war. Furthermore, northern interest in southern oil has made the South an even greater economic asset for the North, rendering it even more difficult for the North to go along with southern secession. Ironically, in the negotiations between the government and the SPLM/SPLA, specifically in the protocols relating to self-determination and wealth sharing, the parties agreed that the government will receive 50 percent of the revenues from the southern oil during the six-year interim period, after which the South will remain within a united Sudan or become fully independent, in which case the arrangement for sharing the oil revenue would end. In a sense then, oil has both added fuel to the conflict and strengthened the case for unity.

With respect to the influence of foreign relations on statehood and nation building in general, it is evident that the configuration of identities in Sudan has been the outcome of historical ties with the outside world. While most people accept historical explanations, there is controversy over the extent to which the causes of the present conflict in Sudan are internally or externally generated. Many would argue that the Sudanese conflict is essentially the result of internal causes and that external factors are marginally relevant. It is important to distinguish between foreign involvement in the conflict and external systems that act as models for the perceptions of Sudanese identity. While direct foreign involvement has had little lasting effect, externally based models of identity have been at the core of the racial, ethnic, and religious configuration of the Sudan. Even here though, a distinction should be drawn between popular self-perceptions and the elite's politicization of identity through domestic and foreign policies. While the first also affects the degree to which people are differentiated and perhaps stratified, the latter makes the identity question a public issue of nation building because it concerns the basis for participating in the shaping and sharing of power.

Mansour Khalid, who was foreign minister during the pivotal period of Nimeiri's rule, articulated the difference between foreign intervention and the relevance of external symbols to the Sudanese sense of identity: "The external factors, if anything, are a reflection of Sudan's crisis of national identity and the inability of northern Sudanese, particularly the ruling elite, to come to terms with themselves, face realities, and articulate a genuine vision of Sudanese national identity to the outside world."[45] Elaborating on the domestic roots of the problem, Khalid indicated the degree to which this elite perception has permeated the whole Sudanese political culture. "The Sudanese conflict is about national self-identification . . . There is still no consensus among Sudanese as to what kind of country Sudan is. Are we Arabs? Are we Africans? Are we Afro-Arabs? Are we Muslims? What is Sudan and what does it mean to be Sudanese?"[46]

Sudan's conflict of identities has thus evolved from a war for secession on the part of the South to a quest for a unified "New Sudan," in which non-Arabs of both the North and the South would have an equitable role with the Arabized Sudanese of the North. The visions for nationhood that have been advocated by the dominant parties have crystallized into two distinct options including, on the one hand, a theocratic, monolithic model with an Arab-Islamist orientation, and on the other hand, a secular, pluralistic model with strong African orientation, both vying for acceptance by the Sudanese people and, increasingly, for support from international stakeholders. The war is, therefore, being waged over the transcendent values of Sudanese nationhood, a process that challenges the people to identify and acknowledge their shared heritage and common destiny, and begin building consensus toward a reconstructed framework that values the enriching diversities encompassed within the nation and the state.

Documenting Injustice: The Black Book

It is significant that inequities of power sharing and the distributive system in the country are increasingly being seen in regional rather than racial terms, with the North and central regions being far more advantaged than all the other regions of the country. A book titled *Imbalance of Power and Wealth in the Sudan*, popularly known as *The Black Book*, prepared and published anonymously in Arabic by authors who refer to themselves simply as "The seekers of truth and justice," documents these inequities with remarkable statistical details covering the three principal organs of the state: the executive, the legislature, and the judiciary, with a fourth institution, the media, described as the consciousness of the nation, but portrayed as conforming to the stratifications of the system.[47] The study acknowledges that even within the favored northern region, three Arab tribes, making up just over 5 percent of the total population, dominate political and economic power in Sudan. It mentions specifically the Shaigiyya, the Jaalyeen (who consider themselves descendants of the Prophet's uncle, El Jaaly), and the Dongollawis, while also noting that even in the disadvantaged northern regions, Arabs fare better than the non-Arabs within them. The study points out that only in elections did disadvantaged northern regions fare well commensurate to their population percentages. But where representation in legislative bodies was decided by selection, the representatives chosen, though themselves residents of these marginalized regions, tended to have their origins in the favored regions of the North and the Center.

With respect to regional representation in the executive branch of national government from 1989 to 1999, *The Black Book* presents statistics revealing that the northern region, with a population of 5.4 percent of the total population of Sudan, provides 79.5 percent of national representation within governmental institutions, followed by southerners who, at roughly 24 percent (or 30 percent, according to the only reliable census, that of 1956) of the total population, provide 16 percent of national representation. The non-Arab northern regions (including the eastern, western, and central regions) meanwhile contain the remaining 70 percent of the population, but only provide 4 percent of representation within governmental institutions. The figures illustrate the inequitable distribution of regional representation and the political dominance of the minority northern Arab Sudanese who historically dominated the country economically as well. The authors then move on to examine the regional status of the ministers of national governments from 1964 to 1999: multiparty democracy (1964–1969), Nimeiri regime (1969–1985), Military Provisional Council (MPC) (1985–1986), second multiparty democracy (1986–1989), National Islamic Front (NIF)/National Salvation 1 (1989–1999), and the ongoing National Salvation 2. In these governments, the representation of the North ranged between 47 percent (under the second-multiparty democracy) to 70 percent (under the MPC), and averaged a grossly disproportionate 62 percent of national ministerial posts. During the same period, the representation of the South ranged from 7.8 percent under the Nimeiri regime (when most southern elites preferred to serve in the southern regional government) to 17.3 percent under the multiparty democracy (1964–1969). What would surprise most people is that, on average, the South has maintained 14 percent of national ministerial posts and therefore fared better than the other regions of the country.

The trends observed with respect to national executive and ministerial positions also hold true with regard to the judiciary, with the exception that here the South fares far worse; none of the attorneys general have come from the South, while eight (or 67 percent of the total) have come from the North and three (or 33 percent of the total) from the non-Arab northern regions. The authors conclude that "the leadership of the legal system at the level of the Minister for Justice and the Attorney General has been controlled by the executive powers which are characterized by nepotism and discrimination among the members of the nation."[48]

The authors reveal that wealth distribution has also been skewed in favor of the North, claiming that the Ministry of Finance has become an "estate" of the northern region, and in addition to favoritism in ministerial-level positions, even staff appointments such as drivers are recruited from among the advantaged groups of the North. This pattern of employment, the authors conclude, has affected government allocations for development projects. As an example, they cite the case of eight non-northern development schemes that "were not sold or privatized, but simply cancelled despite the fact that they were developmental in nature and had an impact on the ordinary citizens of these States."[49] The book further implies that the privatization of seventeen government enterprises was characterized by nepotism and favoritism toward the North that obviously went against national interests. Finally, with the exploration and production of oil, the National Council for Distribution of Resources was formed, whose composition is also severely skewed in favor of the North, which holds 76 percent of the seats on the council, followed by the South and non-Arab regions of the North, which received 12 percent each of the seats.

The Black Book goes on to say that this control has been exercised through the state security apparatus, which, ironically, maintains itself through black African manpower. The authors point out, as evidence of this phenomenon, that the only three successful coups in Sudan were led by members of the three tribes, the Shaigiyya, the Jaalyeen, and the Dongallawis, combined with the fact that there has never been a head of the state security apparatus who was not a member of the three Arab tribes. Those unsuccessful coup attempts by forces not associated with the tribes, *The Black Book* asserts, were discredited as racist. The book notes, however, that "[the central government's] loss of . . . credibility has been one of the prime consequences of [the] injustice."[50] Northern non-Arab groups are beginning to question the current state's legitimacy, and are looking to other models of nation building, including the secular pluralist model of the SPLM/SPLA. Interestingly, the authors, using the statistics, point out that the South has been able to obtain more representation within the central government than the marginalized non-Arab northern regions, and credits southern resistance as being the main factor in this southern success. "The marginal cost of rebellion in the South," explained the SPLM/SPLA leader, John Garang, many years before *The Black Book* was published, "became very small, zero, or negative; that is, in the South, it pays to rebel."[51]

This regional contextualization of the problem provides opportunities for cross-cutting alliances that challenge the status quo and postulate a more equitable basis for building an inclusive and cohesive nation. It would be a valid question to ask if this makes for an opportunistic alliance aimed at overthrowing the government to bring into power interest groups that would perpetuate the system to their own advantage. There is, however, potential for a fundamental restructuring of the nation to bring the South closer strategically to the marginalized regions of the North as part of a program of ethnic pluralism.

Although *The Black Book* does not discuss the cultural dimension, Arab dominance has been very much associated with the language policy in the country, which heavily favors the Arabic language, despite the fact that in both the North and the South many indigenous languages are still spoken. During the period of British rule, both English and Arabic were used as official languages, with English favored as a language of instruction from the secondary school level upward and also favored as the working language at the national level. With independence, the policy of Arabization discouraged the use of English and replaced it with Arabic. The Addis Ababa Agreement of 1972 recognized Arabic as the national language, with English as the working language in the South. Any peace agreement between the government and the SPLM/SPLA is bound to recognize indigenous language, especially in the South, as national languages, but favor Arabic and English as the working languages, with the latter particularly relevant to the South. The North will probably continue to be unified by the Arabic language, while the marginalized non-Arab groups will continue to forge closer alliances with the South.

Whatever the outcome of these regional dynamics, it is worth noting that, surprisingly, not only the non-Arabs, but also Arab groups from these regions, have reportedly been in contact with the leadership of the SPLM/SPLA, complaining about the way they have been exploited by various governments in the war against the South, how their region has suffered from neglect by the central government, and how they share the vision of the SPLM/SPLA for a just Sudan.[52] It is also significant that

Daoud Yahya Bolad from Darfur, who, as a university student had been a
Muslim brother and a leader of the Islamist movement in the country, was
one of the first northern Sudanese to join the SPLM/SPLA and led a rebellion in Darfur, where he was killed by the government forces. Ironically,
The Black Book exalts his name as a martyr and praises him for his fore-
sight in having observed and rebelled against the inequities that his region
suffered. A man who died a rebel and was labeled a traitor is now being
hailed as a hero. In fairness to his people, however, his rebellion and tragic
death have already been documented by scholars from the region who concluded that racism between the Arab and non-Arab peoples of Sudan differentiated the Muslims, marginalizing even the non-Arab leaders of the
Islamic movement, such as Bolad.[53] All this shows that Sudan has reached
a critical juncture and that the need for reform is gaining broad support that
may make it unnecessary for the South to secede.

Prospects for Peace

The civil war in Sudan is now widely acknowledged as the longest-lasting
and most destructive conflict in the world today. The Sudanese people,
under pressure from concerned neighbors and an international community
that is outraged by the suffering of the innocent masses, are charting an
admittedly difficult path to peace. For years, the conflict has drawn attention from individuals and groups who have sought to mediate for peace but
with no visible successes. Longer running has been the mediation of the
Horn of Africa's Inter-Governmental Authority on Development (IGAD),
which in September 1993 mandated Kenya, Uganda, Ethiopia, and Eritrea
to undertake that task of peace negotiations, under the chairmanship of
President Daniel Arap Moi of Kenya. After a series of meetings, mediators
produced the Declaration of Principles (DOP), which, briefly stated, pro-
poses that:

- The right to self-determination of the people of the South to determine their future status through a referendum must be recognized.
- The unity of Sudan, however, should be given priority.
- Religion and the state shall be separate.
- The government of Sudan should recognize and respect fundamental human rights in a framework of a multiracial, multiethnic, multireligious, and multicultural society; separation of religion from the
  state, the equitable distribution of national wealth between the various parts of the country; and a constitution that guarantees the independence of the judiciary, and such other basic rights as are internationally recognized.
- In the event of failure to guarantee such rights, the southerners have
  a right to self-determination.

While the government initially rejected the DOP, it was eventually persuaded to accept the principles as a basis for negotiations, and talks resumed. Though a series of meetings were held, resulting in short-lived cease-fires and agreements to facilitate the delivery of international humanitarian assistance, the process—which was much supported financially and politically by a group of Western "Friends" who became "Partners" to the IGAD forum—did not seem to make any notable progress toward peace. The IGAD process, after being stalled and on the verge of being pronounced dead, has recently been reinvigorated by the active involvement of the United States and other Western countries, including the United Kingdom, Norway, and Italy. The role of the United States has so far proved pivotal and indeed indispensable. Those interested in peace in the Sudan, including the IGAD countries, the Western countries who have been supporting the peace process as friends of IGAD, Egypt and Libya (who have offered their own peace initiative), and the Sudanese parties to the conflict, all have welcomed the involvement of the United States in the search for peace.

Whatever the factors behind U.S. involvement, the role of the United States Institute of Peace–funded Center for Strategic and International Studies Task Force on U.S. Sudan Policy (for which this author served as cochair) is often mentioned as having been instrumental. Initially, the task force saw Sudan as marginal to U.S. interests, with the exception of the negative impact of the regime's alleged involvement with international terrorism, destabilization of U.S. friends in the region, and concern over humanitarian tragedy inside the country. It was assumed that whichever party was to win the elections, the United States would probably only support the efforts of European allies in the peace process. However, those who believed in the strategic importance of Sudan, particularly as a potential point of linkage and cooperation or confrontation and conflict between sub-Saharan Africa and North Africa, extending into the Middle East, argued for the United States to play a leadership role in favor of ending the war. The gist of the analysis was that the war was between two contrasting visions that were not reconcilable in the short run and that the formula that stood a chance of success was that of coexistence through a framework of one country/two systems. The Nuba and other marginalized areas of the North later objected to the division of the country into two systems, as it leaves them out of the equation, which is why, instead of two systems, it might be more appropriate to conceive of multiple systems.[54]

President George W. Bush surprised most observers with the concern he showed over the tragic situation in the Sudan, which led to his appointment of former Senator John Danforth of Missouri as his special envoy for peace in Sudan and the appointment of Andrew Natsios, administrator of USAID, as special humanitarian coordinator. The hope that the United

States would build on the Danforth report to reinvigorate the peace process in collaboration with other parties was borne out. Danforth's central recommendation was that efforts for peace continue on two tracks: One was a pragmatic, catalytic, and incremental approach toward alleviating humanitarian crisis through cease-fire arrangements in areas most affected, the first achievement in this regard being the internationally monitored agreement in the Nuba Mountains, with less ambitious steps in the South. The other was a more vigorous search for a comprehensive peace, which eventually led to the negotiations at the Kenyan town of Machakos. These negotiations have generated optimism about ending the war in the Sudan. The first positive outcome was the Machakos Protocol, signed by the government and the SPLM/SPLA on the 20 July 2002, which, in addition to affirming the right to self-determination of the southern people, postulates a six-year interim period aimed at encouraging the government to build an environment conducive to unity. This would provide a period for self-reckoning for the Sudanese people to address the issue of nationhood through a widely participatory process carried out in an environment of peace, security, and relative harmony.

Since the Machakos Protocol, the parties have thus far (July 2004) negotiated and concluded a series of agreements and protocols on a wide range of issues: the 25 September 2003 agreement on security arrangements during the interim period, which provides for integrated units as well as the retention of the respective armed forces; the 7 January 2004 agreement on wealth sharing during the interim period, which recognizes the interests and needs of the various states, the South, and Sudan as a whole; the 26 May 2004 power-sharing protocol, which provides for self-government in the South and an equitable role in the national government during the interim period; the 26 May 2004 understanding on the administration of the conflict areas of the Nuba Mountains and Southern Blue Nile, with provisions for popular consultation of the people about their future, short of the self-determination granted the South; and the 26 May 2004 protocol on the resolution of the conflict in the Abya area, which grants the people of Abya the right to decide by a referendum to be carried out with the self-determination in the South whether to join the South or remain under the administration of the North. The two issues that remain to be negotiated are permanent cease-fire arrangements, on which talks are under way (July 2004) and modalities of implementation to follow an agreement on cease-fire.

While the country appears to be irreversibly headed toward peace between the North and the South, the region of Darfur exploded in 2003 in a conflict pitting two rebel movements, Sudan Liberation Movement and the Justice and Equality Movement, in a brutal confrontation against the Sudanese government, using a local Arab militia known as Janjaweed, which has terrorized the non-Arab tribes of the region. This has resulted in what is widely recognized as one of the worst disasters of the new century, and its first certified case of genocide. Some thirty thousand civilians have been brutally murdered, over a million displaced internally, while nearly two hundred thousand have fled across the borders to Chad. Villages have been razed to the ground, crops destroyed, livestock killed or looted, and women raped. The activities of the Sudanese army, including bombings, appear to be coordinated with the raids by the Janjaweed. The crisis has generated an intense debate on whether what is happening in Darfur is ethnic cleansing or genocide, with the consensus that war crimes are certainly being committed. Even as the world appears more responsive in the wake of the Rwandan genocide, millions remain at risk from murder, starvation, and disease, with humanitarian pledges from the international community tragically falling short of the needs.

The parties and the mediators have wisely kept the situation in Darfur separate from the peace talks between the government and the SPLM/SPLA. Nevertheless, the two situations are connected in a number of ways. First, the people of Darfur are reacting against the marginalization of the non-Arabs, which though not identical with the cause of the South, has elements in common. Second, the experiences of the South, the Nuba, and Southern Blue Nile indicate that armed struggle pays. Third, although there is no formal alliance between the SPLM/SPLA and the rebel movements in Darfur, it should be recalled that the initial rebellion led by Daoud Yahya Bolad was in partnership with the SPLM/SPLA. It is inconceivable that the SPLM/SPLA will agree with the government and together continue the war in Darfur. John Garang, the leader of the SPLM/SPLA, has pledged to facilitate a peace agreement with the Darfur rebel movements.

What the situation in Darfur calls for is action on several parallel lines: address the humanitarian crisis with a sense of urgency; restore security and stability so that people can return to their areas of normal residence; and initiate serious peace talks to bring the region into a comprehensive peace for the country, perhaps building on the arrangements for the Nuba and the Southern Blue Nile as models to be adapted to the conditions of the region.

It now appears that the vision of a "New Sudan" postulated by the SPLM/SPLA is unfolding. With the Nuba and the Southern Blue Nile closely allied with the South, the Beja asserting their own non-Arab identity, the people of Darfur now up in arms, and even the Nubians neighboring Egypt reviving their proud ancient identity, the dominating vision of Sudan as an Arab country is being severely contested and is unlikely to survive in the long run. Although there are southerners, perhaps the overwhelming majority, who still see the future of the South as an independent state, these developments and alliances across the North-South divide clearly favor a trend toward unity in a reconstructed Sudan.

Sudan's internal dynamics should also be seen within the broader context of relations with its neighbors in both black Africa and the Arab regions of North Africa and the Middle East. Egypt, of course, has strong ties with Sudan, largely centered around the Nile River that runs the length of Sudan from south to north. The Nile has for thousands of years been the source of life and civilization in Egypt.[55] For Egypt, there is also the perception that Sudan is an Arab-Muslim country whose territorial integrity should be protected by the Arab-Muslim world. This, combined with Egypt's historical connections to Sudan, makes the Egyptian position uncompromisingly committed to the preservation of Sudan within its present borders.[56]

While the orientation of the North has been toward the Arab world, the southern liberation movements, in particular the SPLM/SPLA, have gained support and legitimacy from their non-Arab African neighbors. Initially, the major source of outside support for the SPLM/SPLA was the Ethiopian government under Mengistu Haile Mariam, which until 1991 provided bases for training and operations, as well as military equipment and logistical support.[57] Ethiopia's interest in supporting the SPLM stemmed primarily from its differences with the Islamist NIF government that it not only suspected was sponsoring insurgent Islamist groups in Ethiopia and Eritrea, but was also in genuine support for the cause of the South. With the coming to power of President Musevini in Uganda in 1986, the SPLM found another ally, both in support for the cause and because of its fight with the Khartoum-backed Lord's Resistance Army, a rebel group along the Uganda-Sudan border, whose ruthless violence against their own people, the Acholi, has been well documented.[58] Uganda's identification with the cause of the South is also historically rooted, as the two were closely connected under British rule.

The general position of regional African countries on Sudan has been ambivalent. On the one hand, they feel strongly about the plight of their black brethren in the South. On the other hand, there is an overriding concern over the possible secession of the South and the regional implications for the stability of the colonial borders on the continent. Most of these states are marked by acute ethnic and regional diversities, with competing nationalistic sentiments that strive either to capture the state or break away from it. It was to forestall the threat of disunity and disintegration of the new nations that the Organization of African Unity adopted, in 1963, the principle of preserving colonial borders, thereby implicitly legitimizing the governments and regimes within those borders. The result has been that these nations, while sympathetic to the cause of the South, have been hesitant to support self-determination that might lead to secession.[59]

The tendency in favor of unity and against secession is found not only in Africa but also globally. Despite notable exceptions, such as the consensual breakup of Czechoslovakia and the disintegration of Yugoslavia and the Soviet Union, the international community has been generally antagonistic to partitioning countries. The attitude toward the de facto division of Somalia, the anomalous position of Kosovo, and the brutal suppression of the Chechnyan separatist movement in the Russian Federation are outstanding examples.

In the Sudanese context, the outcome has been that the processes of statehood and nation building have been evolving in an ambivalent, but on balance, progressive manner. Colonial power in Sudan left in its wake a divided state in which the successor northern governments inherited control over the country, only to face direct challenges to their legitimacy by the South in the form of resistance against Arab-Islamic hegemony. The North-South divide, while forming the most distinct line of demarcation in the conflict, is being bridged by a variety of other contending interests in the North which are also challenging state legitimacy. Trends among the marginalized non-Arab northern groups and their increasing alignment with southerners on a shared vision for a secular, pluralist Sudan, as well as the maturation of southern Sudanese national consciousness (including, most ironically, the effect of the war itself and the resulting internal displacement), and not least, the fragmentation within the South, are all working toward a new emphasis on reform rather than secession. The first stage was that the North-South divide tended to mute intraregional differences, thereby reinforcing a duality of national identity rather than ethnic or tribal fragmentation. The notion of unity in diversity continues to characterize the state of Sudan today and binds the country in an increasingly contested, yet closely shared framework of national identity.

Statistical Evidence:
Views on the State, Citizenship, and Nationhood

Relevant Elite Interviews

While a major source on views about the state and rights of citizenship discussed in this chapter come from statistical analysis of surveys conducted specifically for this study, this chapter also makes reference to materials obtained from several sets of interviews by the author, as well as an important statistical analysis of power and wealth sharing published by an anonymous source. The author conducted the first set of interviews between 1973 and 1981; they formed part of a study aimed at a closer examination of the colonial experience and its interracial and intercultural dimensions. The interviews were conducted among three groups of respondents: former British colonial administrators in Sudan, northern Sudanese who had worked with the British, and their southern Sudanese counterparts. In collaboration with historian Martin Daly, who had written extensively on the history of British rule in Sudan, the author then published the results in a book.[60] Since colonial intervention constitutes the foundation of the Sudanese state, the views contained in these interviews, though not representing an objective historical perspective, nonetheless aid significantly in understanding the Sudanese situation.

The second source consists of materials from the author's interviews with Dinka chiefs and elders about the past, present, and projected future. The author carried out these interviews immediately after the 1972 Addis Ababa Agreement and the return of peace. The views expressed by the interviewees, therefore, reflected a degree of cautious optimism about the future of the country.[61] Much of the Dinka historical myths and oral history revealed deep-rooted connections with the North—even with respect to religion—as reflected in the myths of creation, original leadership, and earliest migration, even while the Dinka still saw themselves as very distinct and different from the Arabs of the North. The investigation and understanding of these differences, perceived by the interviewees in spiritual and moral terms, also significantly contribute to the long-term prospects for peace and unity in a pluralistic framework.

The author conducted the final set of elite interviews among northern and southern Sudanese (both within Sudan and around the world), focusing the inquiry primarily on the issue of the national identity crisis. These interviews, conducted in the late 1980s and early 1990s, provide information most directly relevant to the main themes of this study.[62] The examination of Sudanese views indicates that although the crisis of national identity has achieved wide recognition, and although the agenda for dialogue and negotiation consistently addresses the issue, considerable controversy still exists over the identity crisis among the Sudanese themselves, northerners and southerners alike.

As noted at the outset, the main body of the chapter contains excerpts from these earlier interviews, and this section summarizes the results of surveys conducted specifically for this study. The respondents' views summarized herein, on issues of diversity, self-perceptions, and the perceptions of others with respect to nationhood, the role of the state as provider of basic protections and services, as well as national unity versus group and individual rights and interests, form the culmination of an analysis of the evolutionary process toward national consciousness, unity, and the challenges they present to the nation.

The analysis supports the themes discussed in the previous sections, particularly the ambivalence among Sudanese people concerning issues of national identity. First in this regard, the analysis attempts to scrutinize perceptions that seem incongruous with objective facts, and thus tend to distort the reality of shared structures and a national framework that truly involves all identities. Second, and related to the first theme, the analysis reveals changing perceptions of Sudanese identity from an Arab-centered view to one that bolsters the authenticity of other groups, and demands an equitable voice for them within an evolving pluralistic framework. The third theme explores the extent to which non-Arab northerners are allied with either the

Arabs or the southerners around critical issues of state legitimacy and nationhood. A final, cross-cutting theme emerged, not from previous sections, but from an analysis of the survey data, namely, how group responses differed by interview location (i.e., Sudan, Cairo, and the United States). Where significant differences among the locations emerged, an inferential analysis follows.

Survey Sources and Methods

Surveys, conducted randomly in Khartoum (803 respondents), Cairo (100 respondents), and Washington, D.C. (180 respondents), form the base data set. The responses from each country sample were then aggregated into one data set, which in turn forms the basis for most of the analytical discussion contained in this section. The analysis provides a further segmentation by ethnic group/region to comport with the overall focus of this chapter (see Table 2.1). The three focus groups include Arabs, non-Arab northerners, and southerners. The Arab group was derived by combining responses from respondents who identified themselves as Arabs of the northern states; non-Arab northerners were obtained by combining responses of those who identified themselves as being from non-Arab ethnic groups in the North;

Table 2.1   Location, Ethnic Group, and Gender[a]

Location	Sample Size		Arabs		Non-Arab Northerners		Southerners	
Sudan	Male	515	Male	78	Male	271	Male	170
	Female	285	Female	73	Female	127	Female	72
	Missing[b]	3	Missing	0	Missing	0	Missing	1
	Total	803	Total	151	Total	398	Total	243
Cairo	Male	54	Male	13	Male	24	Male	16
	Female	46	Female	12	Female	18	Female	16
	Missing	0	Missing	0	Missing	0	Missing	0
	Total	100	Total	25	Total	42	Total	32
U.S.	Male	124	Male	43	Male	44	Male	36
	Female	54	Female	17	Female	16	Female	21
	Missing	2	Missing	2	Missing	0	Missing	0
	Total	180	Total	62	Total	60	Total	57
Total	Male	693						
	Female	385						
	Missing	5						
	Total	1,083						

Notes: a. Those noted as "missing" in the three columns entitled "Arabs," "Non-Arab Northerners," and "Southerners" identified themselves by ethnic origin but failed to indicate gender.

b. Those noted as missing in this column are among those who failed to identify a gender, and include the two respondents who did not provide an ethnic identity.

southerners were derived by combining responses from those who identified themselves as being from the southern ethnic groups. Of the total sample analyzed, non-Arab northerners comprise roughly 46 percent, followed
by southerners at 31 percent, and Arabs at 22 percent. The individuals who
conducted the surveys made an effort to balance factors such as gender,
age, income, and education level among the respondents.

The subject matter of the surveys can be roughly divided into the following general categories:

- State capacity, including perceptions about the role and adequacy of
  state apparatus in the provision of basic services and protections
- Selected objective characteristics of the sample population (i.e.,
  gender, age, education level, income, and employment status)
- National identity in the context of national unity vs. the protection
  of individual and group rights and interests
- Perceptions of one's group and other groups with regard to being
  truly Sudanese
- Impact of regional and transcontinental actors, including states and
  nongovernmental organizations on peace and conflict in Sudan

The observations listed below highlight the major qualifying characteristics of the research data:

- The sample size (N = 1,083), permits statistical analysis and discussions of obvious correlations.
- Of the 1,083 people surveyed, 11 chose "other" when asked to identify their group. The analysis, in keeping with an ethnic/regional
  group focus, therefore omits their responses. Additionally, two
  respondents failed to check any ethnic category, and thus the analysis omits their responses as well. This leaves a total of 1,070
  respondents upon whom the analysis is based.
- The survey sample taken in Sudan, though it includes a fair percentage of people who identified as southerners (30 percent), was
  nonetheless carried out mainly in the North, and thus may limit the
  prescriptive value of some of the survey responses (i.e., to the questions seeking to determine who in Sudan provides basic protections
  and services).
- The sample, while gender-biased (unintentionally) in favor of males,
  nonetheless includes a significant portion of female responses (385
  respondents comprising roughly 36 percent) and thus adequately
  incorporates the perceptions of Sudanese women. Special attention
  will be paid to women's perspectives in the following analysis.
- The randomness of the sample notwithstanding, the survey coordinators made an effort to ensure that the major cultural and geo-

graphic groups received adequate representation, thus enhancing generalizations drawn from the analysis.

Since the views reflected in this survey may reveal the prevailing sentiments at a given moment of time, the period within which the interviews were conducted, which ranged from August (Washington), October (Cairo), and November (Sudan) of 2001 (with additional surveys taken on women in Sudan in June 2003), has significant bearing on the outcomes discussed. The coordinators commissioned in Sudan and Cairo conducted the surveys through a number of other interviewers. Two project consultants conducted the Washington survey.

The Role of Government:
Who in Sudan Provides Basic Protections and Services

Government, as a provider of basic protections and services, figures prominently across all groups, accounting for the majority in all instances (see Table 2.2). On average, however, southerners (51 percent) indicated that government played a less important role in providing basic protections and

Table 2.2 Perceptions of Who Provides Basic Services and Protections

Group	Sample Size	Crime Protection %		Foreign Violence Protection %		Health Care%		Children's[a] Education %		Average %
Arabs	238	Govt.	76	Govt.	79	Govt.	69	Govt.	70	74
		No One	10	No One	9	No One	9	No One	6	9
		Self[b]	10	Self	6	Self	9	Self	18	11
		Other[c]	3	Other	5	Other	5	Other	3	4
		Missing	<1	Missing	1	Missing	8	Missing	3	3
Non-Arab Northerners	500	Govt.	86	Govt.	90	Govt.	75	Govt.	66	79
		No One	5	No One	7	No One	11	No One	14	9
		Self	6	Self	2	Self	10	Self	13	8
		Other	2	Other	1	Other	4	Other	4	3
		Missing	1	Missing	0	Missing	<1	Missing	7	2
Southerners	332	Govt.	65	Govt.	68	Govt.	51	Govt.	35	55
		No One	20	No One	18	No One	20	No One	25	21
		Self	6	Self	4	Self	12	Self	12	9
		Other	7	Other	8	Other	10	Other	24	12
		Missing	2	Missing	2	Missing	2	Missing	4	3
Total	1,070[d]									

Notes: a. Calculation excludes respondents who identified as having no children.

b. The variable "Self" includes self, family, tribe, group, and community.

c. The variable "Other" includes a range of nonroutine responses including such examples as "God," "Conscience," and "Good Behavior," among many others.

d. Total reflects total respondents (1,083) less those who identified as "Other" (11) and those who failed to identify with any ethnic group (2).

services than either Arabs (67 percent), or non-Arab northerners (74 percent).

The less-central role of government among southerners when compared to the other groups is congruent with the overall trend in the data in which southerners feel less benefit from the government, and correspondingly placed less importance on national unity than individual rights. Still, the majority of southerners cited government as the provider of basic services and protections, suggesting that, at least to some extent, all Sudanese people share the benefits provided by major governmental and social institutions. On the other hand, because none of the actual surveys were carried out in the South, it may be difficult to gauge the actual role of government as perceived by southerners who are currently living there. One suspects, however, that given the relatively smaller role of government among southerners in the North when compared with Arabs and non-Arab northerners, those in the South, where governmental services and protections do not extend, would place even lesser importance on the role of the central government in Khartoum. Non-Arab northerners, on the whole, appear more closely aligned with Arabs on the role of government as a provider of basic protections and services, as might be suggested by the fact that many of those groups, like the Arabs, live under the administration of the central government in Khartoum, and have, over time, attempted to work within the system to obtain a share of government resources.

Gender roles, as they are inextricably intertwined with the issue of national identity in Sudan, deserve close attention in conducting any serious consideration of the issues. Sudanese people remain largely rooted in traditional familial structures, whether in the northern, largely Muslim context, or in the South, where indigenous cultures still survive. In both instances women play a primary role as caregivers and protectors of families. With the intensity of war and its humanitarian consequences in terms of internal displacement or refuge abroad, women become particularly vulnerable, but also resilient, resourceful, and self-reliant in seeking sources of support for their families, as men either go to war or feel helpless with the loss of their traditional position of dominance. It may be instructive, therefore, to observe that while female respondents to the surveys closely matched the overall sample in terms of their perception of the government's role in providing basic protections, they tended, in the aggregate, and among each ethnic group, to be less likely to view the government as the provider of basic services. Only 51 percent of the women surveyed perceived government as the major provider of health care, compared to 65 percent in the overall sample, and only 35 percent saw the government as a provider of children's education as compared to 57 percent of the overall sample. Strikingly, the marginalization of women in this respect almost mirrors that of the southerners, and consistently recurs across all ethnic categories. These differences highlight the impact that a lack of government responsibility for provision of basic services has on families, groups, and ultimately on the state of the nation itself.

The Adequacy of Government in Providing Basic Services

"Part of the role of a central government is to provide services and protection to its citizens. We would like to ask you some questions that relate to the adequacy of services and protection that the central government in the Sudan provides its citizens. In the Sudan how satisfied or dissatisfied are you with the following?"

While all groups expressed general dissatisfaction with the government's provision of basic protections and services, non-Arab northerners and southerners on average (and in each category) expressed more dissatisfaction than did Arabs. On the whole, all groups expressed less satisfaction with the provision of basic services than of basic protections, though Arabs expressed much more satisfaction with protections than services. This would support the overall trend of Arabs' feeling some form of political affinity to the government even if the quality of services is poor. In some sense, they may enjoy the protections of the state while hoping for more in the way of civil administration and social services.

Southerners' views on the inadequacy of government services may, when compared to the above responses to the question of who provides services, reveal some ambivalence. On the one hand, southerners largely agree that the central government provides basic services and protections; on the other hand they seem overwhelmingly dissatisfied with the adequacy of such provision. The same applies for non-Arab northerners. This trend may reflect ambivalence in that southerners acknowledge, in a sense, the role of the central government, while at the same time feeling extremely marginalized. It

Table 2.3 Perceptions of the Adequacy of Government Provision of Protections and Services

Group	Sample Size		Crime Protection	Foreign Violence Protection	Basic Health Care	Education	Roads	Average
Arabs	238	Sat.	45	45	24	22	24	32
		Dissat.	55	55	76	78	76	68
Non-Arab Northerners	500	Sat.	36	34	13	9	14	21
		Dissat.	64	66	87	91	86	79
Southerners	332	Sat.	24	23	14	11	12	17
		Dissat.	76	77	86	89	88	83

Note: Sat. = percentage Satisfied; Dissat. = percentage Dissatisfied.

may also reflect normative ambiguity between who should provide, and who does in fact provide, these protections and social services. Clearly the government should provide, but from the evidence does not do so adequately.

Unity Versus Self-Determination

Question set

> One thing that a central government can do is to help the people of a country work toward a feeling of national unity, to bring the people together for common cause and purpose. So that we can understand better how you feel about this, I want to ask you to listen to a few statements and tell me how strongly you agree or disagree with each.

- The unity of Sudan is more important than the interests of any particular group or people in the country.
- The central government of Sudan represents the interests of most of the people of Sudan.
- It is more important that individual groups or people have the right to determine their own future than it is for the country to have a sense of unity and common purpose.
- In Sudan, the central government represents the interest of all the people in the country.
- Sudan should remain united even if it requires armed force to do so
- Military force should be used to keep Sudan united.
- The central government has been effective in trying to seek solutions to the problems among the peoples of the country.

Table 2.4 Perceptions of National Unity vs. Individual Rights and Interests

Group	Sample Size		National Unity More Impt. than Group Interests	Govt. Represents Most People	Individual or Group rights More Impt. Than National Unity	Govt. Represents All People	Armed Force to Achieve Unity if Necessary	Military Force Should Be Used	Govt. Is Effective in Seeking Solutions
Arabs	238	A	87	15	48	13	48	47	29
		D	10	80	44	82	46	48	64
		M	3	5	8	5	6	5	7
Non-Arab Northerners	500	A	81	11	65	10	36	37	19
		D	17	86	32	89	61	59	78
		M	2	3	3	1	3	4	3
Southerners	332	A	47	12	78	5	15	18	8
		D	52	84	20	92	79	79	90
		M	1	4	2	3	6	3	2

Note: A = percentage Agree; D = percentage Disagree; M = percentage No Opinion or Missing.

A large majority of Arabs (87 percent) placed national unity above group interests, while only a minority of southerners (47 percent) agreed that national unity is more important. Conversely, a sizeable majority of southerners (78 percent) placed individual or group rights above national unity, while only a minority (48 percent) of Arabs placed more importance on individual rights. Majorities of non-Arab northerners placed national unity above group interests (81 percent), and also placed individual and group rights above national unity (65 percent). While the non-Arab northerner's responses may seem contradictory at first glance, it is important to note that the first question juxtaposed national unity with group interests while the second juxtaposed national unity with individual or group rights. The difference between rights and interests in the context of national unity may account for the seeming discrepancy. Respondents may have perceived interests as self-serving, and therefore not more important than national unity, whereas they may have viewed rights as more fundamental, and thus superseding the need for national unity.

Among all groups, one finds more or less uniform agreement that the government was not widely representative of all or even most people in Sudan. Related to this, all groups seemed to acknowledge the ineffectiveness of government in addressing the needs of all or even most Sudanese. Thus, it appears significant that a large minority of Arabs (29 percent) perceived the central government as effective in trying to seek solutions to the problems among the people of Sudan, even though they also agree that the government does not widely represent the interests of all the people. In contrast, only 19 percent of the non-Arab northerners and 8 percent of the southerners agreed that the government was effective. This could point to a view held by Arabs that the government can effectively seek solutions to problems without being representative of groups (which, though not defined in the survey, can be interpreted to imply ethnic, religious. and regional groups) within Sudan.

Such a view, if consciously held by Arabs, seems incongruous with Arabs' general dissatisfaction with government provision of basic services. The incongruity about a perception that government, in the context of national unity, effectively seeks solutions, but that, in the context of state capacity, has proven grossly inadequate, may reveal symptoms of a reflexive defense of the central government's legitimacy against ethnic self-determination. Viewed in isolation, this dynamic among Arabs could be explained away by a view that the problems with government services have little to do with its lack of representativeness, or its effectiveness in seeking solutions in the context of national versus group identities. However, when one juxtaposes the responses of non-Arab northerners, a trend comes more clearly into view. The non-Arab northerners, whose rate of dissatisfaction with government protections and services closely matches that of southerners (79 percent and 83 percent, respectively), seem more unlikely than

Arabs to agree that the government is effective in finding solutions in the context of national unity and group rights. Their views on the subject rested almost directly between that of southerners and Arabs. Further, non-Arab responses to these juxtaposed questions appear more congruent with each other than those of the Arabs, further suggesting a reflexive defensiveness of the Arabs.

Ambivalence about the issue of national unity and (ethnic) group self-determination has begun to provide the creative tension needed to advance the development of Sudanese nationhood. The relative advantage of the South over the non-Arab areas of the North, according to the statistics of *The Black Book*, indicates that the conflict itself has forced the Arab North to make compromises in power and wealth sharing.

Correspondingly, responses by female respondents tended to fall in line with the overall themes with women on average agreeing that national unity is more important than group interests (74 percent of women agreed as compared with 72 percent of the overall sample). Women also perceived the government as ineffective in seeking solutions to the problems of national unity and self-determination (69 percent), though in slightly lower proportion than did the overall sample (77 percent). On the questions involving armed force, however, women appeared more willing (50 percent) than the overall sample (33 percent) that armed force should be used if necessary to achieve national unity. Surprisingly, this increase is reflected across all ethnic groups, with southern women (38 percent), Arab women (43 percent), and non-Arab women of the North (56 percent) all appearing more willing than the overall sample to achieve unity through armed force.

Interestingly, Sudanese women, especially southern women, have been presumed to be very much against going to war to achieve political objectives either for unity or ethnic self-determination. Anecdotal evidence indicates that southern women have tended to view marginalization by Arabs as ignorable, preferring to maintain their households and cultural traditions even in the face of Arab prejudice. However, in the face of civil war and greater negative penetration of the government into the affairs of all groups at all levels, Arab discrimination can no longer be viewed as distant and inconsequential. The finding that Sudanese women appear, in larger percentages than the overall sample, to be willing to use armed force to achieve unity is therefore contradictory and demands a closer inspection and will be the subject of ongoing research and analysis.

Identity and Self-Perception

"Of the following people, which do you consider to be truly Sudanese?"

"Do any of the following peoples see your people as being truly Sudanese?"

Table 2.5   Perceptions of Claims to Sudanese Identity of Other Groups

Group	Sample Size		Arabs of Central Sudan	Arabs of Western Sudan	Beja and other Easterners	Fur and other Westerners	Nilotics and other Southerners	Nubians and other Northerners	Nuba and other Border Groups
Arabs	238	Y	65	65	61	61	82	73	90
		N	3	4	2	5	7	4	1
		M	32	31	37	34	11	23	9
Non-Arab Northerners	500	Y	21	25	34	48	92	58	99
		N	8	6	3	3	1	1	1
		M	71	69	63	49	7	41	1
Southerners	332	Y	27	25	37	35	94	57	92
		N	37	23	14	7	1	29	2
		M	36	52	49	58	5	14	6

Note: Y = percentage Yes; N = percentage No; M = percentage Missing.

Table 2.6   Perceptions of Others' "Perceptions of One"

Group	Sample Size		Arabs of Central Sudan	Arabs of Western Sudan	Beja and other Easterners	Fur and other Westerners	Nilotics and other Southerners	Nubians and other Northerners	Nuba and other Border Groups
Arabs	238	Y	73	78	68	67	63	71	71
		N	5	4	5	4	9	4	5
		M	22	18	27	29	28	25	24
Non-Arab Northerners	500	Y	52	53	60	68	83	77	91
		N	6	6	2	3	14	2	2
		M	42	41	38	29	3	21	7
Southerners	332	Y	32	34	49	65	89	64	88
		N	36	35	22	13	2	6	5
		M	32	31	29	22	9	30	7

Note: Y = percentage Yes; N = percentage No; M = percentage Missing.

A large majority of Arabs indicated that southerners viewed them as being truly Sudanese, while only a minority of southerners indicated that Arabs viewed them as being truly Sudanese. Contrastingly, Arabs almost unanimously agreed that southerners are truly Sudanese, while few southerners agreed that Arabs are truly Sudanese. Majorities of non-Arab northerners indicated that both Arabs (53 percent) and southerners (83 percent) viewed them as being truly Sudanese. This view roughly reflects the answers given by Arabs and southerners to the question of whether they view non-Arab northerners as being truly Sudanese. Southerners, in the majority, indicated that non-Arab northerners considered them to be truly Sudanese.

The striking factor about this data set is the degree to which peoples' perceptions of other people's views on who is truly Sudanese seem to be widely dissonant with how the others actually view them. What, one wonders, is the overall effect on national unity of Arabs feeling that southerners see them as being truly Sudanese when in fact they are not? Conversely, what is the effect on ethnic self-determination among southerners who feel that Arabs do not view them as being truly Sudanese, when in fact they do? Are Arabs merely being deferential when acknowledging the Sudaneseness (for lack of a better term) of southerners? Are southerners being inordinately exclusive when refusing to acknowledge the authenticity of Sudanese Arabs? And are they being unduly suspicious or out of touch with northern attitudes when they think the Arabs do not consider them to be truly Sudanese? Further, are the Arabs too self-assured or out of touch with the South as not to know that the majority of southerners do not consider them to be truly Sudanese? What accounts for the fact that they do not realize their marginalization by the southerners on the question of their being Sudanese? A theme that might cut across answers to these questions may be that things are changing and perceptions have not caught up with the changes. The Arabs formerly saw themselves as the true inheritors of the land and the non-Arabs as marginal. Their perspective has changed, according to the answers of the surveys, but the non-Arabs have not caught up with northern Arab perspectives.

When one isolates Arab responses by the three survey areas, a potentially explanatory trend reveals itself. Arabs in Sudan were much less likely (50 percent) than Arabs in the United States (87 percent) and Cairo (76 percent) to believe that southerners viewed them as being truly Sudanese. Correspondingly, southerners in Cairo (60 percent) were much more likely than southerners in Sudan (40 percent) to believe that Arabs viewed them as being truly Sudanese. Southerners residing in the United States, however, were less likely (28 percent) to believe that Arabs viewed them as truly Sudanese than southerners in the other two locations.

Racial and socioeconomic conditions in the United States, where even so-called Arab Sudanese would be considered black or of African origin, might lead Arabs to perceive the differences between themselves and southerners as less salient than in Sudan. The congruent position on the part of southerners would indicate that in the United States a majority would believe that Arabs perceived them as being truly Sudanese, but this does not appear to be the case. The anomalous result, however, could be a factor of the limited sample size (there were only 57 southerners in the U.S. sample), or might reflect a heightened sensibility by southerners in the United States (especially in the Washington, D.C., area where the surveys were taken) about issues of identity and authenticity. Whatever the case, however, it appears that southerners in the United States and Sudan share the sentiment that Arabs do not view them as being truly Sudanese, when, in fact, those identifying as Arabs, across all three sample locations, overwhelmingly do.

This incongruity in perspectives also reflects the controversy over the issue of national consciousness or nationality that this chapter has tried to portray. While northerners have tended to identify themselves as Arabs, considerable rethinking is under way, as the elite interviews so vividly demonstrated. Southerners also reflect two competing trends. One permits northerners to be acknowledged on their own terms as Arabs, the implication being that there is no basis for a national unity that accommodates the identities of both northerners and southerners. The other trend, found among a minority but increasing numbers of southerners, particularly the leadership, challenges northern self-perceptions as Arabs, while presenting a vision of a "New Sudan" as a unified nation guided by race-neutral, secular, and pluralistic principles.

The fact that perceptions differ sharply from objective facts may point to the existence of shared identities that are not acknowledged or reflected in intergroup dynamics. That the authenticity of southerners is unquestioned by the Arabs and non-Arab northerners, while the Sudanese identity of the Arabs is deeply questioned by southerners, may provide a glimpse of the challenge facing both to explore their common identity.

Sudan's Relations with Other Countries/International Civil Society Networks

"Have any of the following nations contributed to creating and sustaining peace and order in the Sudan?"

Majorities of Arabs cited Egypt (64 percent) and Libya (63 percent) as having contributed to sustaining peace and order in Sudan. Among southerners,

Table 2.7 Perceptions of Other Countries Creating and Sustaining Peace in Sudan

Group	Sample Size	Egypt	Ethiopia	Eritrea	Kenya	Libya	Saudi Arabia	Uganda	DRC	United States
Arabs	238	64	22	16	20	63	25	15	7	21
Non-Arab Northerners	500	55	13	12	18	53	15	12	5	43
Southerners	332	39	38	27	46	37	6	39	7	72

Note: Numbers = percentage Yes.

a large majority (72 percent) cited the United States as contributing to sustaining peace and order, with significant minorities citing Kenya (46 percent), and Uganda (39 percent) as contributors to peace and order. Significant minorities of southerners also pointed to Egypt (39 percent), Ethiopia (38 percent), and Libya (26 percent) as contributing to peace and order. Among non-Arab northerners, majorities cited Egypt (55 percent) and Libya (53 percent), while significant minorities cited the United States (43 percent) as contributing to peace and order. In general, Arabs cited regional Arab countries as contributing to peace and order, whereas southerners cited transcontinental interests such as the United States as being the biggest contributors. Non-Arab northerners tended to see neighboring Arab nations as well as neighboring non-Arab nations and Western interests as contributing to peace and order in Sudan.

These figures also tend to reflect the dynamics of the peace process, especially the role of the IGAD mediators and their Western partners, particularly the troika of Norway, the United Kingdom, and the United States, which have recently reinvigorated the search for a just peace in which the South stands to gain. Parallel to the IGAD process has been the Egyptian-Libyan initiative that is more tilted in favor of the North, especially as it is premised on an opposition to self-determination for the South. Given the progress that has been made in the peace process, with the increased role of the United States, Norway, and the United Kingdom in support of the IGAD-sponsored talks in Machakos, Kenya, if the surveys in this section were taken today, their rating as peace promoters, among all the groups surveyed, would likely be even higher.

"Have any of the following countries contributed to war and violence in the Sudan?"

Majorities of Arabs cited Eritrea (59 percent), Ethiopia (57 percent), and Uganda (58 percent) as being contributors to war and violence in Sudan, while significant minorities cited the United States (46 percent). Southerners saw Egypt (63 percent) as the major contributor to war and

Table 2.8   Perceptions of Other Countries' Roles in Contributing to War and Violence in Sudan

Group	Sample Size		Egypt	Ethiopia	Eritrea	Kenya	Libya	Saudi Arabia	Uganda	DRC	United States
Arabs	238	Y	24	57	59	17	22	7	58	4	46
Non-Arab Northerners	500	Y	36	49	51	13	25	4	50	4	29
Southerners	332	Y	63	20	20	5	39	25	12	6	15

Note: Y = percentage Yes.

violence in Sudan, with significant minorities pointing to Libya (39 percent) and Saudi Arabia (25 percent). Non-Arab northerners cited Eritrea (51 percent), Uganda (50 percent), and Ethiopia (49 percent) as being major contributors to war and violence, followed most closely by Egypt (36 percent) and the United States (29 percent). In sum, Arabs viewed their non-Arab neighbors as well as Western interests as contributing to war and violence, while southerners saw their Arab neighbors as being the major contributors. Non-Arab northerners were more likely than southerners to view non-Arab neighboring nations and Westerners as contributing to war and violence, and more likely than Arabs to point to Arab nations.

These results more or less mirror the results of the previous question in which southerners particularly saw a more positive role being played by the neighboring African countries and Western partners in the search for peace than the Arab neighbors to the north. Here, the role of these countries for peace is reversed in favor of contributing to violence.

"Has the United Nations or any other international agency contributed to creating and sustaining peace/order or war/violence in the Sudan?"

Large majorities of southerners (78 percent) and non-Arab northerners (79 percent) cited the UN and international agencies as contributing to peace, whereas a much smaller majority (55 percent) of Arabs cited the UN as a contributor. The three groups also varied in terms of the percentage of respondents who answered positively to the question of whether the UN and other international agencies have contributed to war and violence, with more Arabs answering affirmatively to the question (38 percent), while southerners (9 percent) and non-Arab northerners (27 percent) were more likely to answer negatively.

The influence of international interests (i.e., the United States, the UN, and international agencies) is evident in the southerners' responses. The question was what influence those powers have had on the issue of national unity versus self-determination in Sudan. Historical analysis reveals a complex situation, in which international influence, while undermining tradi-

Table 2.9 Perceptions of UN and Other International Agency Roles as Contributing to Peace and War in Sudan

Group	Sample Size	UN Peace		UN War	
Arabs	238	Y	55	Y	38
Non-Arab Northerners	500	Y	79	Y	27
Southerners	332	Y	78	Y	9

Note: Y = percentage Yes.

tional culture, inculcated a respect for diversity and separation between religion and state.[63]

Arabs, being more oriented toward the Arab-Islamic world, were more antagonistic toward Western ideas and attempts to counter the Arab-Islamic orientation of the country. Related to this was the northern assumption that southerners do not have an independent voice, but are considered subject to the influence and control of the Western Christian–Zionist world. Even the humanitarian aid that goes to the South sometimes tends to be interpreted as undue interference in the affairs of the country and a threat to its national sovereignty.

The competing influence of outside actors indicates that Sudanese perspectives on national vision are not entirely dependent on the Sudanese themselves. Southerners see the North as supported by the Arab-Islamic world, while the Arabs feel that without the support of the West and black Africa, the South would not have been able to resist northern assimilation into the Arab-Islamic orientation of the country.

Conclusion

"[Sudan's] major problem," in the words of SPLM leader John Garang, "is that it has been looking, and is still looking for its Soul; for its true identity."[64] The trends illustrated by this survey, while broadly reflective of significant differences among the three groups, nonetheless reveal creative tensions that have helped develop and strengthen integrative forces of identity and unity. Non-Arab northerners' responses to the survey indicate that there are at least some in the country that can agree with both sides to a significant degree. To the extent that they act as a buffer between Arabs and southerners, they also bolster and support both sides. Non-Arab northerners were for national unity and for individual and group rights. On questions of national identity, non-Arab northerners seemed to agree more with southerners about authentic Sudanese identity belonging to African groups, rather than Arabs. On questions of war and peace, they tended to be more aligned with the Arab population with regard to the option for achieving national unity through armed force. In sum, non-Arab northerners tend to embody within themselves both sides of the ambivalence created by the tension between North and South, Arab and African. This raises the distinct possibility that the key to resolving the crisis of national identity may be not in finding one soul, but in helping individuals to recognize, reconcile, and ultimately celebrate the multiple souls within themselves. In this way, what may now appear to be irreconcilable strivings among the groups might be mediated as individuals begin to come together on the basis of shared interests and, over time, become groups who can be identified more by their substantive positions on issues of common concern rather than by the currently entrenched identities of tribal affiliation, race, or religion.

The dynamic of creative ambivalence is not restricted merely to the buffer group of non-Arab northerners, but also contained within the responses of the Arabs and southerners themselves. Arabs were much more satisfied with government protections than with government services. Protection in this sense may be more associated with military defenses against internal and external threats than respect for the human rights and civil liberties of individuals. In this sense, the survey may be indicating dissatisfaction with a regime that, while purporting to provide military protection against the threat of non-Arab groups, offers little in the way of basic social services. Arabs also seemed to exhibit ambivalence in their response to questions of self-perception. While only half of the Arabs indicated that they believed themselves to be truly Sudanese, overwhelming majorities expressed the opinion that southerners viewed them as being truly Sudanese. These two beliefs might seem to be completely incongruous with each other—but when viewed in the context of a contest of identities, they begin to make sense. Arab claims on religious, racial, and cultural inheritance logically extend beyond Sudan to the Middle East, and make them less likely to identify themselves as being of Sudanese origin. On the other hand, the Arabs' notion of cultural dominance within Sudan might, in their view, imply that other groups view them as being truly Sudanese.

Ambivalence among southerners mirrored that of the Arabs in that they overwhelmingly believe themselves to be truly Sudanese, but perceive that the Arabs do not believe them to be truly Sudanese. This difference in perception might appear to be less conflicted than that of the Arabs, especially in light of the obvious marginalization of the South within the framework of political power and wealth distribution. But if asserting their claim to true Sudanese identity rests in opposition to the Arab identity, unwittingly both groups agree on their common Sudanese identity. Southerners are also ambivalent about the role of central government. While overwhelming majorities felt that government was ineffective, most also pointed to the government as the provider of basic services and protections. This may, however, indicate a dichotomy between what is and what ought to be.

The survey data can be compared to a snapshot, a captured moment in time, rather than a movie containing a beginning, middle, and end. However, the picture reveals clearly the dynamic tensions at work within and among the groups defined in this survey. These nodes of interactivity, when viewed in historical perspective where positions existed in almost "splendid isolation," reflect a turbulent search in which groups are now called upon to come together and define the common ground.

The survey data used for this analysis has also provided fertile ground for further study along the lines of issues discussed in this chapter. Even within the focus of national and ethnic identity discussed, there are many additional questions raised by the survey data. Differences of perceptions across gender, particularly as they relate to the questions dealing with national unity and individual rights, are especially demanding of further inspection. Moreover, the differences in replies by survey location may shed more light on an emerging Sudanese national identity that is not as easily perceived by Sudanese in the national context, but that comes into view when the Sudanese interact with each other abroad.

Notes

The author would like to acknowledge with gratitude the research assistance of Robert L. Ostergard, Omari West, and Daniel Deng. Their help in the analysis of the survey data discussed in this chapter was invaluable.

1. Yusuf Fadl Hasan, *The Arabs and The Sudan* (Edinburgh: Edinburgh University Press, 1967), 90.

2. Jack Mendelsohn, *God, Allah and JuJu: Religion in Africa Today* (New York: Thomas Mendelsohn & Sons, 1962), 102.

3. Ibid., 11.

4. See Godfrey Lienhardt, *Divinity and Experience, Religion Among the Dinka* (Oxford: Clarendon Press, 1961), 164–165. See also Francis Mading Deng, *Tradition and Modernization: A Challenge for Law Among the Dinka of The Sudan* (New Haven and London: Yale University Press, 1971), 48–49.

5. Mansour Khalid, *The Government They Deserve: The Role of the Elite in Sudan's Political Economy* (London and New York: Kegan Paul International, 1990), 4.

6. E. Guttman, "The Reception of Common Law in the Sudan," *Common Law Quarterly* 61 (1957): 401–417, somewhat overstated the success of the adaptation when he said that the Sudan Penal Code was "neither British, Indian, French, or indeed wholly marked with the system in force in any other country. It was a scheme which may be correctly called Sudanese, insofar as it was truly framed with a special view to meet the requirements of the country" (p. 402). See also W. Twinning, "Some Aspects of Reception," *Sudan Law Journal and Report* (1957): 229–252. For a comprehensive treatment of the subject and in particular the creative application of the qualifying clause "justice, equity, and good conscience," as both justification for and a limitation on the application of English law, see Zaki Mustafa, *The Common Law in the Sudan: An Account of the Justice, Equity and Good Conscience Provision* (Oxford: Clarendon Press, 1971).

7. Gabrial R. Warburg, "The Nile Waters, Border Issues and Radical Islam in Egyptian Sudanese Relations: 1956–1995," in *White Nile Black Blood: War, Leadership, and Ethnicity from Khartoum to Kampala,* eds. Jay Spalding and Stephanie Beswick (Lawrenceville, NJ: Red Sea Press, 2000), 74. The author contends that "Unity of the Nile Valley" was a direct outcome of the reality of Egypt's dependence on Nile waters, whose importance was recognized by the rulers of Egypt long before it became the slogan of Egyptian nationalists at the end of the nineteenth century.

8. See Civil Secretary's Memorandum on Revision of Southern Policy, 1946, CS/SCR/ICI, 16 December 1946; Muddathir 'Abd Al-Rahim, *Imperialism and Nationalism in the Sudan: A Study in Constitutional and Political Development 1899–1956* (Oxford: Clarendon Press, 1969), appendix 8.

9. Dispatch no. 89 (1945) to the British Colonial Government in Sudan by Killearn. Quoted in Dunstan M. Wai, *The African-Arab Conflict in The Sudan* (New York and London: Africana Publishing Company, 1981), 38.

10. 'Abd Al-Rahim, *Imperialism and Nationalism in the Sudan,* 254.

11. Tim Niblock, *Class and Power in the Sudan: The Dynamics of Sudanese*

Politics, 1898–1985 (Albany: State University of New York Press, 1987), 156.

12. Muhammad Ahmed Majoub, *Democracy on Trial: Reflections on Arab and African Politics* (London: Andre Deutsch, 1974), 57.

13. Khalid, *The Government They Deserve*, 231. And as Niblock noted, "Southerners remained peripheral to the debate over independence arrangements during 1955, except when their votes were needed in parliament. Such attention as the major northern parties did give to the Southern Sudan, moreover, was motivated by short-term political interest and often had destructive consequences. Promises were made by northern politicians in the course of the 1953 elections which bore little relation to what these politicians intended, or were able to do." *Class and Power in the Sudan*, 215.

14. Niblock, *Class and Power in the Sudan*, 146.

15. Republic of Sudan, *Report of the Commission of Inquiry into the Disturbances in the Southern Sudan During August 1955* (Khartoum: McCorquedale & Co. Ltd., 1955), 7.

16. For the views quoted below, see Francis M. Deng and M. W. Daly, *Bonds of Silk: The Human Factor in the British Administration of The Sudan* (East Lansing: Michigan State University Press, 1989), 96–97.

17. In a private letter to the author, cited in Francis M. Deng, *Dynamics of Identification* (Washington, DC: Brookings Institution, 1995), 36; and Francis M. Deng, *War of Visions* (Washington, DC: Brookings Institution, 1995), 97.

18. Republic of Sudan, *Report of the Commission of Enquiry*, 31.

19. For background to the proposed one country, two systems, see Francis M. Deng and J. Stephen Morrison, *U.S. Policy to End Sudan's War, Report of the CSIS Task Force on U.S. Sudan Policy* (Washington, DC: CSIS, February 2001).

20. Abdullahi A. An-Na'im, "Islam and National Integration in Sudan," in *Regional and National Integration in Africa: Islam, Christianity and Politics in The Sudan and Nigeria,* ed. John O. Hunwick (Chicago, IL: Northwestern University Press, 1992), 11.

21. Ann Mosely Lesch, *Sudan: Contested National Identities* (Indianapolis: Indiana University Press, 1998), 3.

22. Ibid.

23. See text in appendix 15 in Muhammad Omar Beshir, *The Southern Sudan: Background to Conflict* (London: C. Hurst and Company, 1969, and reproduced by Khartoum: Khartoum University Press, 1979), 168.

24. Ali Mazrui, "The Black Arabs in Comparative Perspective: The Political Sociology of Race Mixture," in *The Southern Sudan: The Problem of National Integration,* ed. Dunstan M. Wai (London: Frank Cass, 1973), 69. Michael Wolfers argues, "So much of the debate on race relations is conducted on the interaction of black and white groups and peoples that we do not have a ready terminology for what is occurring in a country like Sudan" ("Race and Class in Sudan," in *Race and Class* 23, no. 1 [Summer 1981]: 65–79).

25. This and other views quoted in the following pages, unless otherwise noted, come from elite interviews conducted by the author on the issue of identity in Sudan in the late 1980s and early 1990s. The material was used in my *War of Visions.*

26. Al-Baqir al-Afif Muktar, "The Crisis of Identity in the Northern Sudan: A Dilemma of a Black People with a White Culture," a paper presented at the CODESRIA African Humanities Institute tenured by the Program of African Studies at Northwestern University, undated and unpublished, p. 20.

27. Ibid., 13.

28. Deng, *War of Visions*, 421.

29. Edward Atiyah, *An Arab Tells His Story: A Study in Loyalties* (London: John Murray, 1946), 158.

30. Abd Al-Rahim, "Arabism, Africanism, and Self-Identification in the Sudan," in *The Southern Sudan: The Problem of National Integration,* ed. Dunstan M. Wai (London: Frank Cass, 1973), 39.

31. Al-Baqir al-Afif Mukhtar, "The Crisis of Identity in the Northern Sudan," 14–15.

32. Ibid., 15. In a conversation with a prominent dark-skinned northern Sudanese, whose daughter was a fellow student in Khartoum University, this author, in response to the father's question as to whether he knew her, recalled similarities with the father, and said "Yes, I think I know. She is dark (*azrag*), isn't she?" The response was, "No, she turned out to be like her mother."

33. Al-Baqir al-Afif Mukhtar, "The Crisis of Identity in the Northern Sudan," 36.

34. From an interview with the author in Addis Ababa, September 1989, as quoted in Deng, *War of Visions,* 431.

35. Ahmed S. al-Shahi, "Proverbs and Social Values in a Northern Sudanese Village," in *Essays in Sudan Ethnography,* eds. Ian Cunnison and Wendy James (London: Hurst, 1972), 92.

36. Mansour Khalid told the author of a conversation he had with a northern Sudanese graduate of Khartoum University with advanced degrees, indeed a university lecturer, who questioned his membership in the southern-dominated SPLM: "Even we, the descendants of the Arabs, you hold a low opinion about our lack of culture and sophistication. What could possibly have brought you together with the Janubiyeen?"

37. Khalid, *The Government They Deserve*, 135.

38. Evidence of a leading southern politician given to the author.

39. Francis M. Deng, *Africans of Two Worlds* (New Haven, CT: Yale University Press, 1978).

40. Dunstan M. Wai, "Revolution, Rhetoric and Reality in the Sudan," *Journal of Modern African Studies* 17, no. 1 (March 1979): 74.

41. Mansour Khalid, "External Factors in Sudanese Conflict," in *The Search for Peace and Unity in the Sudan,* eds. Francis M. Deng and Prosser Gifford (Washington, DC: Wilson Center Press, 1987), 110.

42. See Crawford Young, *The Politics of Cultural Pluralism* (Madison: University of Wisconsin Press, 1976), 23–24; Nelson Kasfir, "Peace Making and Social Cleavages in Sudan," in *Conflict and Peace Making in Multiethnic Societies,* ed. Joseph V. Montville (Lexington, MA: DC Heath, 1990), 365–366; and Peter Woodward, *Sudan (1898–1889): The Unstable State* (Boulder, CO: Lynne Rienner, 1990), 7.

43. Niblock, *Class and Power in the Sudan*, 279–280.

44. Interview with Bona Malwal, quoted in Deng, *War of Visions*, 379.

45. Mansour Khalid, "External Factors in the Sudanese Conflict," in *The Search for Peace and Unity in the Sudan,* eds. Francis Deng and Prosser Gifford (Washington, DC: Wilson Center Press, 1987), 109.

46. Ibid., 109–110.

47. Since its mysterious appearance in Sudan in 2000, which seems to have been a well-planned and coordinated campaign, the distribution of the book took a life of its own through spontaneous photocopying. The book has no copyright: indeed its free duplication constituted the greatest bulk of the distribution, as most readers have never seen the original copy of the book.

48. *The Black Book*, 28.

49. Ibid., 43–44.

50. Ibid., 58–59.

51. Lesch, *Sudan: Contested National Identities*, 88.

52. From conversations with the leadership of the SPLM/SPLA.

53. Sharif Harir, "Racism in Islamic Disguise? Retreating Nationalism and Upsurging Ethnicity in Darfur, Sudan," Center for Development Studies, University of Bergen, p. 9, cited in G. Warburg, *Historical Discord in the Nile Valley* (London: C. Hurst, 1992), 188; See also Deng, *War of Visions*, 460–463.

54. For the report of the task force, see Francis M. Deng and J. Stephen Morrison, eds., *U.S. Policy to End Sudan's War: Report of the CSIS Task Force on U.S.-Sudan Policy* (Washington, DC: CSIS Africa Program, February 2001).

55. The historian Robert Collins wrote: "Without the Nile there would be only sand and rock and wind in Egypt and much of the Sudan. . . . For thousands of years, man's greatest fear in Egypt and the Sudan was that the Nile would cease to flow." Robert O. Collins, *The Waters of the Nile* (Oxford: Clarendon Press, 1990), 2–3.

56. "War and Peace: Egypt's Stakes in the Future of Sudan," editorial page, *The Daily Star Online*, 18 November 2002, www.dailystar.com.

57. Lesch, *Sudan: Contested National Identities*, 90.

58. Thomas P. Ofscansky, "Warfare and Instability Along the Sudan-Uganda Border: A Look at the Twentieth Century," in *White Nile, Black Blood: War, Leadership, and Ethnicity from Khartoum to Kampala,* eds. Jay Spalding and Stephanie Beswick (Asmara: Red Sea Press, 1999), xxiii.

59. Lesch, *Sudan: Contested National Identities*, 172.

60. Deng and Daly, *Bonds of Silk*.

61. The results of these interviews were presented in two publications by Francis Mading Deng: *Dinka Cosmology* (London: Ithaca Press, 1980), comprising the verbatim translations with an analytical introduction; *Africans of Two Worlds: The Dinka in the Afro-Arab Sudan* (New Haven and London: Yale University Press, 1978) comprises an analysis of the materials in *Dinka Cosmology*.

62. The results of these interviews are summarized in chapter 11 of Deng, *War of Visions*, 436–483. The themes represented here are from the concluding section of the chapter entitled "Perceptions in Perspective," 478–483.

63. Deng, *War of Visions*, 18–19.

64. Quoted in Khalid, "External Factors in the Sudanese Conflict," 110.

3

Making and Remaking State and Nation in Ethiopia

Edmond J. Keller

Although the Ethiopian state can trace its history back more than two thousand years, what is known as the modern state did not begin to come into view until the mid-1800s. The formation of the modern state contemporaneously coincided with the European "Scramble for Africa." Four successive emperors—Tewodros, Yohannes, Menelik II, and Haile Selassie I—in one way or another contributed to the consolidation of the territorial boundaries of the modern state, the creation of a national professional army, and development of a national system of bureaucratic administration.[1] At first the process of state building involved no more than conquest and subjugation of the conquered peoples, accomplished under the auspices of a monarchy that broadcasted its power from the central highlands to disparate areas of the periphery. Rather than submitting to alien authority based upon some sense of its legitimacy, subjugated peoples were brought to heel more by its raw coercive power than anything else.

Significantly, the modern state of Ethiopia began to emerge at a time when the Westphalian model of state organization was spreading throughout the world. In the process, state boundaries became fixed and accepted legally in international law. At the same time state leaders made an effort to instill in their subjects a sense of belonging collectively to a single nation based on a shared history, culture, and often language. In many places, belonging to a particular state came to be seen as simultaneously belonging to a particular *nation*. In some cases, such as modern France, this sense of identity emerged partly as a result of force and partly organically. In others, the development of a sense of common national heritage among a multiplicity of ethnic groups, such as in Italy, had to be cultivated by cultural and political leaders over a period of time.[2]

The history of the modern state of Ethiopia has been punctuated by failed attempts to develop a multiethnic unitary state in which all citizens feel a primary allegiance to the state itself rather than to their particular ethnic group. Initially, there was no clear sense of an ethnically based national identity on the part of Ethiopia's constituent groups. However, with the onset of modernization in the late eighteenth and early nineteenth centuries, and the rise of nationalism throughout the colonized world, Ethiopia proved not to be immune from the centripetal forces of ethnic nationalism. In fact, such forces contributed greatly to the demise of the imperial state system and to the introduction of a new system of Marxist-Leninist governance. Like the imperial regimes before it, the Marxist-Leninist regime that ruled between 1975 and 1991 failed to resolve the issue of national political integration, and efforts to deal with this problem since 1991 have consumed the new regime headed by the Ethiopian Peoples' Revolutionary Democratic Front. Rather than attempt to ignore or suppress ethnic nationalism, the new regime has committed itself to the celebration and promotion of Ethiopia's diverse cultures, and to equal citizenship rights for all groups and individuals. These principles are enshrined in the Constitution of 1994, which created the Federal Democratic Republic of Ethiopia.[3] The primary vehicle being used toward this end has been a form of federalism, styled as "ethnic federalism."[4]

The purpose of this chapter is to evaluate critically the attempts by successive Ethiopian regimes during the modern era to consolidate the multiethnic state, while at the same time attempting to create a democratic culture in which all citizens, regardless of their ethnic affinities, feel that they willingly belong to and are citizens of the larger political entity, Ethiopia. The remainder of the chapter is divided into two major sections. The first section, employing the methodology of historical sociology, is concerned with the origins of the modern state and the attempts by the imperial regime and the Marxist-Leninist regime to construct a multiethnic, unitary state in which all ethnic groups share a common "Ethiopian" identity. The second section homes in on the effort of the current regime to use ethnic federalism as a strategy for consolidating democracy and social justice throughout the country.

The Origins of the Modern State and the Issue of National Political Integration in Ethiopia

The core of the traditional state originally centered on the ancient city-state of Axum in what is the present-day regional state of Tigray. The Axumite kingdom, based on trade and conquest, came into focus during the sixth century B.C., flourished between the first and eighth centuries A.D., and was finally decimated in 970 A.D. by hostile neighboring groups.[5] At this time we could not speak of a centralized bureaucratic empire, but a patrimonial conquest empire, held together by force, particularistic loyalties, and trade.[6] Nevertheless, it was during the Axumite era that the inhabitants of the state began to refer to themselves as Abyssinians, and began to refer to their preeminent leader as "the King of Kings" or "Emperor."

Abyssinia maintained relatively close trading links with the Roman Empire, and this may have contributed to the adoption of Christianity as the official religion during the middle of the fourth century.[7] From this point on the Christian religion and the Geez language—the language of the

Church—became the vehicles through which Abyssinian culture was spread to conquered peoples.

From the time of the collapse of Axum in 970 until 1135, the Christian empire fell on hard times. Muslim Arabs threatened it from the north, Muslim Somalis threatened it from the southeast, and it was otherwise surrounded by hostile, largely animist neighbors who entered the region from the south. By 1135 what remained of the original state had been pushed to the south and west, but it was able to reconstitute itself, although in a seriously weakened form.

Between the early fourteenth and fifteenth centuries, the state was able to become strong enough to venture expansion again. During this period the core was significantly reconsolidated, and the Abyssinian-Christian culture was diffused to all regions of the state. Kings from the Amhara ethnic group dominated this phase of expansion, and there was a conscious effort to bring conquered peoples firmly under the sway of the Amhara- and Christian-dominated culture. They were often forced to abandon their animist beliefs, adopt Coptic Christianity, and speak the Amharic language outside the home.

By the beginning of the sixteenth century, the Abyssinians were again severely challenged by hostile peoples who were also expanding their domains: the Ottoman Turks, the Somalis, and the Oromo. In 1557 the Ottomans captured the Red Sea port of Massawa, and also succeeded in penetrating the fringes of the Tigray highlands. For the most part, however, they confined themselves to the coast. The Ottomans provided arms to the Afar and Somali people in the region, enabling these groups to pressure Abyssinia from the east.

Even as the Christian Abyssinians and the Muslim Somalis were engaged in protracted struggle for hegemony in the Horn of Africa, the Oromos were making inroads into the territories of both protagonists. At the height of their expansion, the Oromo occupied as much as one-third of the Abyssinian heartland. The Oromo culture mingled with the Abyssinian culture to the extent that the Oromos had a presence and influence in the royal court of the Abyssinians.[8]

Between 1769 and 1855 the Abyssinian Empire became moribund, and eventually ceased to exist in all but its name. This was a period that came to be known as the "Era of the Princes" (Zemene Mesafint), and parochialism among regional nobles reached crisis proportions.[9] Abyssinia was then only nominally a state, being ruled by fifteen different figurehead emperors during the period.

Building the Modern Imperial State

After almost ninety years of political instability and lack of state cohesion, the end of the Zemene Mesafint began with the rise of a regional warlord, Ras (Duke) Kasa, around 1853. For the next two years, Kasa won battle after battle, and forced the nobility that he defeated to submit to his authority. Before long it was clear that Kasa saw himself as having been ordained to reconstruct the Abyssinian state. Upon subduing the region of Tigray in 1855, Kasa had himself crowned "King of Kings" in the traditional manner, thus ending the fratricidal Zemene Mesafint in the Abyssinian core. He took the title of Emperor Tewodros II, claiming that according to one of the religious documents that forms the basis of Ethiopian myth and custom, Fikkare Iyesus (the Interpretation of Jesus), he was the righteous, just, and popular king who would come to the throne after a period of divine punishment that had been meted to the Abyssinian people for their evil deeds. It was allegedly prophesied that the king would be called Tewodros and that he would rule for forty years, restoring Abyssinia to its former unity and greatness.[10] This marked the beginning of the modern Ethiopian Empire. Tewodros was the first in a succession of four Ethiopian emperors responsible for consolidating the Ethiopian state.

The Reign of Tewodros II

Tewodros instituted two primary measures designed to strengthen his imperial authority. First, he fragmented traditional administrative divisions and thus deprived many local princes and kings of their bases of power. Administrators for the reconstructed administrative units were chosen—except in rare circumstances—by the emperor himself. Most were trusted officers in his military or members of the royal family. They were responsible for collecting tithes and taxes on behalf of the sovereign and were instrumental in Tewodros's efforts to break the power of patrimonial, feudal lords. He also jailed most of his potential enemies. This facilitated the maintenance of law and order in the countryside, and buttressed the emperor's centralizing efforts.

Second, Tewodros began to create a disciplined, professional state army for the first time. He often employed Europeans and Turks who had military expertise to train his forces, and he also provided his soldiers with regular salaries, clothes, and equipment. This did much to strengthen both his empire's military and the administrative capacity of the government. Tewodros's centralization policies were continued, but not significantly improved, by Yohannes IV who succeeded him in 1872.[11]

The Reign of Yohannes IV

During the reign of Yohannes, centralization in fact began to break down and some powerful provincial aristocrats began to regain their strength and semiautonomy. Most of the emperor's efforts were directed toward territorial expansion. He pushed the periphery of his domain to the west from his capital in the region of Tigray, leaving hegemony over the south to his most powerful vassal, Menelik.

Yohannes's most outstanding accomplishments were in the field of foreign policy.[12] Before him, Tewodros had been unsuccessful in securing diplomatic recognition from European powers that were already beginning to show interest in the Horn of Africa. Yohannes followed the course of patient diplomacy, buttressing his authority and legitimacy with a relatively strong, modernizing army that deterred reckless incursions into Abyssinia by any real or potential enemies. He entered into a peace treaty with Egypt and trade agreements with Britain. He also purchased arms from both public and private European agents.

Yohannes's diplomatic and military moves provided him with a measure of security, but he was still threatened on his western border by Sudanese Mahdists (Muslims). In 1889, Yohannes was killed in a western campaign against these antagonists. Before his death he had decreed that the throne would pass to Menelik I of Shoa.

The Reign of Menelik I

As King of Shoa, Menelik had already begun to expand and consolidate the territory under his control. Between 1890 and 1906, through conquest or diplomacy, he succeeded in stretching the boundaries of Ethiopia to its present configuration. This did not include Eritrea, which at the time was a colony of Italy.

Historically, the territory now constituting the independent state of Eritrea had passed from one imperialist power to the next. In 1885 Britain controlled the Eritrean port city of Massawa, and Italy, Britain's ally, expressed interest in establishing a colony on the Red Sea. Britain decided to allow the Italians to have Eritrea as its own colony. Italy proceeded to solidify its control over the Eritrean lowlands and it became clear that Italy was not satisfied to stop with Eritrea; it also wanted to control Abyssinia itself. Previous to the death of Yohannes, Italy had concluded several treaties between 1883 and 1887 with Menelik, then king of Shoa, designed to facilitate Italy's dealing with Yohannes.

Between 1887 and 1889 the relationship between Menelik and the Italians continued to strengthen, and just seven weeks after he became emperor, Menelik concluded the Treaty of Wichale with Italy.[13] The treaty was officially described as a treaty of "perpetual peace and friendship." According to the agreement, Italy officially recognized Menelik as emperor of Abyssinia. For its part, Abyssinia ceded part of the Tigray highlands to be used as a buffer to Italy's interests in Massawa, and granted certain commercial, industrial, and judicial privileges to the Italians. The sphere of the Italian occupation and influence, however, was to be confined to a small, well-circumscribed area at the coast, which was already occupied by Italy at the time the treaty was signed. This was the nascent Italian colony of Eritrea.

Initially, the treaty seemed to have value for both signatories. Before long, however, it became apparent to Abyssinia that the Treaty of Wichale was not in its own interests. Menelik discovered that the treaty, which had both Amharic and Italian versions, contained different language in the two versions with regard to the relationship between the signatories. The Amharic version suggested that Abyssinia had the authority to designate Italy as its political agent in international affairs. By contrast, the Italian version asserted that Abyssinia was *obliged* to go through Italy in the conduct of its foreign policy. Through duplicity, Italy had declared Abyssinia its protectorate.

This controversy resulted in a war between Italy and Abyssinia that is now widely known as the Battle of Adowa. The first skirmish in the war occurred in December 1895, and by early March of the following year, the war was over. Menelik's well-armed and numerically superior forces handed the Italians a resounding defeat. The Abyssinian victory sent shock waves throughout Europe, and caused the reigning Italian government to fall.

In October 1896, at Addis Ababa, a peace treaty was signed between the two antagonists. The Treaty of Wichale was abrogated and Italy was allowed to maintain possession of Eritrea as long as it did not penetrate the Abyssinian hinterland. Between 1896 and 1897, Menelik quickly entered into other agreements with France, Britain, and the Mahdists in an effort to ensure the sovereignty of his empire. In securing recognition from the European powers, Menelik had succeeded in accomplishing what his predecessors—and indeed many other African leaders of his time—could not. This success contributed immensely to the almost mythical image of Ethiopia as the epitome of African independence. What is generally ignored, however, is that the modern Ethiopian bureaucratic empire consolidated itself as a state at the same time that the European powers were engaged in the so-called Scramble for Africa. In the process Ethiopia's sovereignty and territorial integrity became a matter of historical record among other states in the international community. Until this time, the geographic as well as ethnic boundaries of the state were fluid and had never been rigidly defined.

In newly conquered territories the contrast between agents of the empire and local inhabitants was extremely sharp. Under Menelik, no effort was made to integrate subject peoples effectively into the expanded political system except to impose by force the culture and institutions of the dominant highlanders, the Amharas and Tigreans. For many, particularly outside of the highlands, this was an obstacle to the development of a clearly defined sense of national, Ethiopian identity among many subjects. A feudal economic system was developed in the south, with the northern representatives of the empire taking on the role of lords, and the southerners being relegated to the status of vassals or serfs.[14] The inequalities, exploitation, and discrimination visited on southerners by the empire and its representatives sowed the seeds of ethno-regional conflict that continue to plague Ethiopia today.

Menelik began the process of consolidating and modernizing imperial dominance in Abyssinia, but was unable to complete the modernization project due to his death in 1913. The task of completing the wedding between modernity and tradition was left to Emperor Haile Selassie I, who assumed the throne in 1930.

The Reign of Haile Selassie I

As emperor, Haile Selassie was dedicated to continuing the centralization and modernization policies begun by Menelik. This meant the further development of a secularized, professional bureaucracy, a professional army, and an indigenous middle class, all of which were committed to modernization. Moreover, he cultivated foreign alliances that provided his regime with capital for economic development and arms for his police and military. The latter not only aided in the consolidation of national borders but also in maintaining domestic order.

Haile Selassie's plans were interrupted in 1936 when he was driven from the throne into exile by Mussolini's invading Italian army. The occupation of Ethiopia lasted for five years. Allied forces led by Great Britain eventually forced the Italians out, enabling Haile Selassie to return and to continue consolidating his power. From this moment, it was clear that the emperor was bent on establishing linkages with foreign powers, while at the same time laying the basis for Ethiopia's endorsement of a capitalist development strategy.

As early as the 1930s, Haile Selassie had begun to secularize his rule and to lessen the influence of the traditional nobility. Among his early achievements were the expansion of a modern educational system, the abolition of slavery, the construction of all-weather roads and other public works, the organization of local police forces and local administration, and the publication of newspapers in Amharinya. Perhaps the most significant early reform, and one that clearly was aimed at strengthening the position of the sovereign relative to religio-traditional classes, was the proclamation of a constitutional monarchy in 1931.[15] The constitution was the first document of its kind in Ethiopia. It lessened the role of the Church in legitimating the emperor and centralized more power in the hands of the absolute monarch. Partly as a control mechanism and partly in an effort to create a semblance of political modernization, national quasi-representative institutions were created: the Chamber of Deputies and the Senate. Despite these reforms, the emperor continued to face considerable opposition to his innovations from provincial aristocrats. However, war with Italy intervened and the emperor was removed from the throne for five years. During this time, the Italians succeeded in significantly weakening the authority of traditional Ethiopian leaders. Ironically, this created a more favorable climate for Haile Selassie's modernization efforts once he was restored to the throne in 1941.

On reassuming power, Haile Selassie introduced three major structural reforms in imperial administration. First, he established a standing national army that was completely under the control of the emperor, making regional armies and their commanders obsolete. The British provided the training for this new army. However, Haile Selassie was acutely aware that if he did not take effective countermeasures to British initiatives, Ethiopia could well become a de facto protectorate of Great Britain. This led Ethiopia to sign lend-lease agreements with the United States in the early 1950s. In 1953, a mutual defense pact was signed, guaranteeing U.S. military assistance, resulting in Ethiopia's receiving more than $200 million in military aid over a twenty-two-year period. This military aid and other such aid from Sweden, Israel, India, the Soviet Union, and other countries enabled Haile Selassie to use the national army not only to protect Ethiopia's sovereignty and territorial integrity from outside forces, but also to suppress domestic rebellions.[16] This development significantly enhanced Ethiopia's bureaucratic capacity well into the modern era.

The second major postoccupation reform involved the establishment of a new fiscal system under the Ministry of Finance. For the first time, taxes paid in a new currency were collected by salaried civil servants and forwarded directly to the national treasury. The significance of this measure was that it professionalized the national bureaucracy and, at least in theory, deprived district administrators of the right to appropriate for their own personal use certain amounts of taxes they collected. For income, bureaucrats could now rely on their monthly salaries, on rents they collected from tenants on land they held privately, and on what they could produce from land they cultivated.

Third, the provincial administration was reorganized under the control of the Ministry of the Interior. Provincial boundaries were redrawn to reduce the power of aristocrats in certain areas that had been traditionally semiautonomous administrative regions. Administrators at all levels were simply made employees of the Ministry of the Interior and were provided with support staff such as clerks and secretaries who were also paid salaries directly by the national government. To go along with these changes, many discretionary powers of local administrators were curtailed.

On the diplomatic front, Haile Selassie sought to present the image of being the ruler of a viable and cohesive multiethnic nation-state. After World War II, Ethiopia was among the first states to join the United Nations. Subsequently, it was designated the headquarters of the Organization of African Unity, and several other international and regional organizations also established offices in Addis Ababa.[17]

In addition to Haile Selassie's diplomatic moves and administrative reforms, he attempted to use domestic policies to construct a modernizing political economy. Historically, agriculture has been the backbone of Ethiopia's economy, and initially the emperor felt that his regime was compelled to strengthen the extractive ability of the state in this area. The emperor was more concerned with increasing the tax base of the national government than with improving agricultural production techniques. Later, he decided to encourage the commercialization of agriculture and to develop a nascent industrial base.[18]

Haile Selassie's idea of modernization revolved around an educated elite—predominately from the Amhara and Tigray ethnic groups—and during his reign he emphasized education for these groups and more or less ignored the poor and culturally subordinate ethnic groups. As often as he could, Haile Selassie recruited young, educated individuals who had been exposed to Western values to fill positions of responsibility in his government. Instead of choosing members of the nobility, as had traditionally been the case, these persons were usually commoners or exceedingly loyal individuals from the nobility.

Perhaps the most significant aspect of Haile Selassie's social policy was that it almost completely ignored the need to build a sense of genuine Ethiopian national identity among the majority of that country's non-Amhara or non-Tigray ethnic groups. Some individuals from non-Amhara/Tigray groups were incorporated into the ruling class, and in the process they acquired a sense of loyalty to the Crown and a sense of "Ethiopian" identity. This, however, was far from universal. Although there was an endless stream of rhetoric from the emperor and his representatives devoted to the idea of the actual existence of a united Ethiopia, there were no actual policies designed to facilitate national political integration. For the most part, the state provided the majority of the country's population with only meager social services and even fewer opportunities to improve their opportunities in life. Instead, emphasis was placed on the control and exploitation of subordinate populations.

Social Inequalities as an Underlying Cause of Revolution

Throughout his reign, Haile Selassie demonstrated a strong commitment to royal absolutism, while at the same time publicly espousing modernization and economic development. Contradictions and conflict necessarily emerged from these seemingly incompatible goals. Capitalist development in Ethiopia following World War II fueled the process of modernization. This highlighted contradictions relating to the remnants of a quasi-feudalistic agricultural sector and grinding poverty throughout most of the country. Most importantly these processes and social conditions also contributed to crystallizing the sense of ethnic consciousness among many of Ethiopia's subordinate groups.

By the mid-1960s it was apparent that the progressivism of some elements of the new classes the emperor worked hard to create had come to exceed his own. Instead of buttressing him during the period of modernization, newly educated and cosmopolitan elites—many of them non-Amhara or non-Tigray—increasingly spoke out about the contradictions between the values they had and those values held by the old, feudalistic classes, between conspicuous wealth and abject poverty and inequality, between democratic rhetoric and authoritarian practice. Thus, the seeds for the 1974 revolution were sown.

Among Haile Selassie's political reforms directed at easing the modernization of autocracy, perhaps the most significant were reforms relating to the constitutional monarchy and the quasi-representative institutions that legitimized it. In 1955, in an effort to enhance his domestic authority and his international prestige, the emperor encouraged the revision of the 1931 Constitution. That constitution provided for a popularly elected representative Chamber of Deputies for the first time.[19] However, the 1955 Constitution did not provide for political parties, and the emperor reserved the right to appoint and dismiss the prime minister. As in 1931, the established nobility opposed these changes, but the emperor's will was allowed to prevail as long as the aristocracy was allowed to maintain most of its traditional privileges.

The Chamber of Deputies had the power to amend and even veto proposals made by the government, but it was several years before deputies felt confident enough to do so. However, by 1966 it was apparent that the Chamber had become more than a rubber stamp for the government. In that year, after a bitter struggle between the Ministry of Finance and the lower house, a revised tax bill was finally forwarded to the emperor for his signature.

Ironically, it was the constitutional reforms of 1955 that appeared to have contributed most to a sharpening of the contradictions between the feudalistic values held by the traditional elites and the bourgeois-democratic values held by the new classes. Between 1965 and 1974, young intellectuals and students began to question the legitimacy of feudalism and royal absolutism. What came to be characterized as the "student movement" emerged in February 1965, crystallizing in a demonstration before Parliament. While Parliament was discussing a land reform bill, the rallying cry of the students was, "Land to the Tiller."[20] Such demonstrations became common from this moment on and, in 1969, students openly distributed pamphlets attacking the emperor directly. They called for radical social, economic, and political reforms. Nevertheless, there appeared not to have been an overwhelmingly leftist orientation among them. In these demonstrations, the contradictions inherent in the remnants of the old order were clearly identifiable; all that was left was for precipitating ingredients to be added to this inherently explosive situation.

Other contradictions emerged from the emperor's socioeconomic policies. As indicated above, throughout the postwar period, Haile Selassie's socioeconomic policies were aimed at economic extraction, control, and macroeconomic development rather than at social justice and national integration. In no case was this more evident than in the policies pursued by the imperial regime outside the highland core of the country.

In all aspects of social and economic policy, Amharas, Tigrays, and elites from other ethnic groups that had been assimilated into the dominant culture were favored over the rest of society. The emperor would occasionally pay visits to dissident areas in order to give symbolic assurances to subordinate groups that he was concerned with their plight, but seldom were such visits followed by significant policy changes. The result, in most of the periphery, was deep-seated resentment of the ruling class.

The situation of Eritrea under imperial rule was illustrative. Despite widespread opposition among several segments of the Eritrean population, Ethiopia annexed Eritrea in 1962, thus incorporating the last segment of the bureaucratic empire. For a decade, Eritrea, the former Italian colony, had existed in a federation with Ethiopia, but the act of annexation meant that it was now relegated to being a mere province of the Ethiopian state.

The union between Ethiopia and Eritrea had initially been accomplished under the auspices of the United Nations, but it was seen by many Eritreans, particularly those who did not adhere to the Ethiopian Orthodox religion, as a confirmation of Ethiopia's imperialist designs on their territory. Opposition groups generally preferred their own nation-state, and resistance movements were formed even before the union was consummated. Once Eritrea was annexed in 1962, such groups stepped up their activities. Significantly, at the time Eritrea was federated with Ethiopia, it possessed more political freedoms and democratic, participatory institutions than Ethiopia. Following annexation, political parties were banned and other institutions had to be changed to conform to the Ethiopian pattern.[21]

In the Ogaden region to the southeast of the country, Somalis who had briefly been united with the other parts of the Somali nation during World War II engaged in sporadic resistance against Ethiopia after the British returned the area to Ethiopia in 1948. Effective occupation of the Ogaden by the Ethiopian government did not begin to take shape until 1954–1955.

Between 1954 and 1960, Haile Selassie made sporadic attempts to "integrate" subject Somalis into the empire. Urban administrative centers, schools, and hospitals were established to present the trappings of an effective administration and allegedly to avail Ogaden Somalis of the same opportunities available to other Ethiopians. An effort was also made to absorb Somali elites gradually into the provincial administration. Despite these efforts, resistance continued.

In 1960 former British Somaliland and Italian Somaliland each achieved independence and quickly merged, forming the Somali Republic. From this time on, Somali nationalists, particularly through the many branches of the Somali Youth League, began to press more seriously for the creation of an independent "Greater Somalia." This movement contributed to the intensification of a Somali irredentist movement in the Ogaden.

The main impetus for militaristic irredentism in the Ogaden, however, involved the founding of the Western Somali Liberation Front (WSLF) in 1960. The aim of the WSLF was to separate the territories Somalis occupied in Ethiopia and to join these areas to the Republic of Somalia.[22]

The WSLF relied heavily on Somalia for military and logistical support until the October 1969 coup that brought Mohamed Siad Barre to power. At first, Siad Barre attempted to reverse his government's policies toward the WSLF, withdrawing military support and jailing several of its leaders. He preferred to modernize his own regular army with assistance from the Soviet Union, always keeping the goal of "Greater Somalia" clearly in sight. WSLF leaders retreated to Aden, where they maintained an office in exile and attempted to continue guerrilla struggle with support from abroad. When Aden and Addis Ababa concluded a treaty in 1976, however, the WSLF was forced to turn to Somalia once again. By this time Siad Barre was more receptive to a relationship between the WSLF and his government.

By the early 1970s, during the last days of the imperial regime in Ethiopia, Somali resistance in the Ogaden had again intensified. In 1976, the Ethiopian Revolution that overthrew the imperial system entered a "reign of terror," creating widespread political instability throughout the country as competing political groups struggled to have their voices heard at the center of government. Siad Barre decided to take advantage of Ethiopia's unrest, and in 1977 made a bold and decisive bid to wrest the Ogaden from its control.

Oromo Claims

Another major issue confronted the imperial regime in Ethiopia as it attempted to modernize autocracy. The Oromo people claimed social injustice and some of their leaders asserted that their nation had a right to self-determination. The Oromo people are the largest ethnic or nationality group in Ethiopia. They account for approximately 26 million of a total population of 65 million. Oromos are disproportionately represented in the southern parts of Ethiopia and were militarily incorporated into the empire during the late nineteenth and early twentieth centuries, resulting in the configuration of the present boundaries of the state.[23]

Under Haile Selassie's rule, the Ethiopian state attempted to secure Oromo fealty through developing alliances with certain Oromo leaders. The most favored among the Oromo were those who chose to become totally assimilated into the dominant culture of the Amhara, often adopting Christian names. Historically, the Wollega and Shoan Oromos were the

most receptive to this approach, but as Haile Selassie became more concerned with firming up the boundaries of the modern state and its bureaucratic authority in the periphery, other Oromo were assimilated.

The state was represented by bureaucrats in the field, including some
officials indigenous to the particular area (*balabats*) and some highlanders
in service of the Crown (*neftegnyas*). These administrators viewed the
majority of the Oromo as mere subjects. They were regularly the victims of
corrupt bureaucrats and judges, all of whom invariably tended to be
Christian northerners. In the distribution of scarce resources, Oromo needs
were considered to be secondary to those of the dominant highlanders.
When attempting to understand current ethnic tensions in Oromo regions,
the inferior status accorded the Oromos and their culture must be considered, along with the fact that Oromo areas constituted the backbone of the
Ethiopian economy. These areas were and are the main source of the country's chief export crops (coffee, oil, seeds, hides, and skins).[24]

Despite the fact that most Oromos had not enjoyed full rights as citizens of Ethiopia during the imperial era, a sense of Oromo national consciousness did not begin to surface until the mid-1960s when the Oromo
self-help association, Macha-Tulama, was founded.[25] The organization,
named after two of the major Oromo clans, was established in 1963 as a
self-help club dedicated to promoting Oromo self-identity and improving
the lot of the Oromo. Since political parties were not allowed, associations
such as Macha-Tulama often took on political roles.

The organization attempted to involve Oromo in both the cities and the
countryside. It was most successful in the south, Bale and Arussi in particular, where Oromos had been relegated to the status of tenants on land that
was once theirs. At the height of its development, Macha-Tulama claimed
as many as three hundred thousand members.[26] The leadership comprised
educated Oromos who had initially accepted assimilation into the dominant
culture, but rediscovering their own Oromo culture, decided to fight for a
fair share of the spoils of modernization for their people.

The most prominent leader of the Macha-Tulama movement was
Tadesse Biru, a former general in the Ethiopian police force and the territorial army. By late 1966 the Haile Selassie regime had become sufficiently
alarmed at the growth in Macha-Tulama's popularity that it decided to
arrest Tadesse Biru and other top officials of the organization. The pretext
for this arrest was a bomb explosion in an Addis Ababa movie house that
was attributed to Macha-Tulama. The organization was banned shortly
thereafter. Tadesse Biru was brought to trial in 1968 and condemned to
death, a sentence later commuted to life in prison.

Although Macha-Tulama was suppressed, Oromo nationalism did not
disappear. In fact, more serious Oromo nationalist militancy emerged less
than a decade later, with the founding of the Oromo Liberation Front (OLF)
in 1973. The OLF was dedicated to the "liberation of the entire Oromo

nation from Ethiopian Colonialism."[27] The OLF began an offensive against the Ethiopian government in Hararge Province in 1974, but sustained activities did not occur until 1976, after the collapse of the imperial regime.

The Demise of the Imperial State

By the early 1970s, Ethiopian society was rife with contradictions, and the imperial regime appeared less and less capable of resolving these accumulating contradictions through its policies. The emperor until then had been able to rely on the support of significant flexible resources at his disposal (e.g., the military, the police, the Church, the bureaucracy, the educated classes, and diplomatic and military alliances) to help him survive. But this was no longer the case. The cumulative effect of the failure of Haile Selassie's polices to resolve multiple inconsistencies, which were themselves by-products of the process of modernization, could be considered the underlying cause of the 1974 revolution. Other debilitating factors, however, did not begin to come together until about 1973. During this period, two main precipitating causes manifested themselves. First, a catastrophic drought gripped large segments of Ethiopia, beginning in 1973. As a consequence, more than a hundred thousand people died of malnutrition, disease, and starvation, while the regime appeared to ignore the tragedy. By 1974, students and intellectuals had brought this problem to the attention not only of other Ethiopians but also of the world community. Second, in urban centers people suffered from unemployment, inflation, gasoline shortages, and food shortages of basic commodities; and groups such as teachers, students, taxi drivers, and industrial workers pressured the government to address their economically based grievances. The government either ignored these demands or responded meekly.

In this climate, critical contradictions evolved into open conflict. For example, the interests of old and new classes clashed in Parliament over land policy, government corruption, and democratic reform. Traditionalists attempted to block or moderate land reform proposals, and progressives pushed for more decisive policies to overcome Ethiopia's chronic underdevelopment and increasing dependence on foreign capital.

When a series of military mutinies in various regions rocked the country in February 1974, the government found itself in an untenable position. If it were to survive, a loyal military would be essential. Junior officers and enlisted men revolted not for revolutionary purposes but because of corporate grievances relating to salary and terms of service. Not only did these mutinies succeed in forcing the authorities to succumb to the soldiers' demands within a month, but these revolts also brought down the imperial regime. Ethiopia's bureaucratic empire had failed to modernize itself.

In an effort to stem growing discontent in several sectors of society, the regime made a last-ditch effort to reform national political institutions. In August 1974, yet another national constitution was proposed. This version called for the abolition of royal absolutism, the introduction of parliamentary democracy, and the relegation of the emperor to only figurehead status. It was also proposed that there would be a separation of powers among the branches of government, universal suffrage, guaranteed civil rights, and a complete separation of church and state.

Even as the terms of the new constitution were being debated in Parliament, various groups throughout the country were becoming more and more politically emboldened. In many areas of the rural south even tenants and peasants had begun to express their concerns publicly. In some areas they began to appropriate land and other property claimed by *neftenyas* and *balabats*. They attacked the symbols of authority and the landed classes.

The military officers and enlisted men who mutinied in February 1974 also became more and more politicized as the year wore on, so much so that they were moved to preempt the enactment of the new constitution in September, only one month after its provisions were made public. Moreover, the military committee, beginning in April 1974, injected itself into matters of national public policy, albeit from behind the scenes. In September, however, the committee decided to go public and staged the coup that led to a resounding finale to the imperial regime of Haile Selassie.

Rather than being guided by an elaborate ideology, the coup makers claimed that they were motivated by a sense of patriotism. They adopted as their motto "Ethiopia Tikdem" (Ethiopia First), and they began referring to themselves as, the "Derg"—an Amharic term meaning "committee." Over the next three years, the Derg began to define its revolutionary objectives through its policy edicts. Its intention was to move away from feudalism and nascent capitalism to socialism under the leadership of the Derg itself. By 1976, the new regime declared its intentions to follow the Program for the National Democratic Revolution (PNDR) and its commitment to creating a political system and government based upon the principles of "scientific socialism."[28]

The Rise and Fall of the Marxist-Leninist Regime
Upon assuming power, the first order of business for the Derg was to solve the Eritrean "problem." Some in its ranks pressed for a decisive military solution to what most Ethiopians perceived to be Eritrea's attempted secession. The PNDR was a first attempt to articulate the regime's position on this issue. This document asserted the right to self-determination of all nationalities within Ethiopia, including Eritreans.

In general, despite serious efforts at the beginning of its rule to create conditions for its widespread acceptance, the Derg was not able to convince significant segments of the population that it was legitimate or that its vision of the new society was the correct one. Its opponents included ideologically (e.g., Ethiopian Peoples' Revolutionary Democratic Front) and ethnically based movements (Tigray People's Liberation Front [TPLF], WSLF, OLF). However, with the assistance of the Soviet Union, Cuba, and Yemen, the Derg was able to stabilize the country somewhat by late 1978 and to push the Eritrean liberation movement to the west. It was in this context that the construction of socialist institutions was begun, and by 1984 the Workers' Party of Ethiopia (WPE) was inaugurated. Ironically, amidst these significant political transformations, Ethiopia was in the midst of yet another catastrophic drought and famine. The government practiced a scorched-earth policy in areas of intense rebel activity, instituting a villagization program in some parts of the country, and relocating whole communities to uninhabited or sparsely inhabited and difficult areas of the southern periphery. During this period, the regime diverted resources that would have been used for famine relief to military purposes, and relied upon the largess of the international community for humanitarian assistance.[29]

In early 1987, the new constitution, a hybrid that resembled the Soviet and Romanian Marxist-Leninist constitutions, was submitted to the populace for their consideration. There was a referendum on the document, which was officially said to have received 82 percent approval from 96 percent of those eligible to vote. The constitution established the People's Democratic Republic of Ethiopia (PDRE), with an 835-member national assembly that gave strong powers to the president. Once the assembly was elected and held its first session in September 1987, one of the main pieces of enabling legislation had to do with the administrative reorganization of the country. In an effort to defuse nationalist discontent, the assembly created twenty-four administrative regions and five so-called autonomous regions.

Despite this gesture of regional reorganization, the response of most nationalist movements fighting the Mengistu regime was threefold and swift. They rejected the PDRE initiative, increased their military activities, and began to cooperate among themselves. Between 1987 and 1990 both the Eritrean People's Liberation Front (EPLF) and the TPLF scored major victories over the Ethiopian National Army and came to control vast amounts of contested terrain in their respective regions. On its part, the TPLF organized a coalition of forces opposed to the regime. This coalition came to be known as the Ethiopian Peoples' Revolutionary Democratic Front (EPRDF), comprised of a TPLF core and other ethnically based groups.

The late 1980s also coincided with a decision by the Soviet Union to reform itself and to withdraw its economic and military support for the Mengistu regime. Having become desperate, Mengistu in 1989 declared a state of emergency and engaged in a rapid buildup of the national army. The beginning of the end for the Marxist regime—and also a sign of the state's collapse—was an abortive coup in May 1989, while Mengistu was on a state visit to East Germany in search of military aid. The army—which had expanded to more than six hundred thousand—began to implode. Whole military units defected, taking their arms and equipment with them to join opposition forces. Over the next two years, the TPLF and its umbrella organization, the EPRDF, came to control all of Tigray and large segments of Wollo, Gondar, and Shoa provinces. In Eritrea, the EPLF took over all but the major towns of Asmara, Massawa, and Assab. By 1990 the rapidly declining military position of the Ethiopian forces on both the Eritrean and home fronts and the loss of political will on the part of Mengistu himself had overtaken U.S. attempts to broker a peace between Ethiopia and the EPLF and Italian efforts to do the same with the TPLF.[30]

Even as plans were being made for an all-parties peace conference in London, the EPRDF tightened its encirclement of Addis Ababa, and the EPLF overran Ethiopian garrisons at Massawa and closed in on the Eritrean capital, Asmara. Finally, on 21 May 1991, the Mengistu regime finally fell and he went into exile. Over the next week, law and order throughout the country broke down and soldiers of the Ethiopian army defected in droves. One garrison after another on the road to the capital fell as the rebels advanced. By the end of the month, the EPRDF had assumed power and was in the process of filling the vacuum left by the fallen Marxist regime.

Ethnic Federalism, Development, and Democracy

A primary challenge facing any new regime is to restore state effectiveness while being guided by competent, politically committed leaders, working systematically to establish legitimacy and develop trust among society's disparate groups. The EPRDF at first tried to present the public image that it had the political will to address many of Ethiopia's past problems, including ethnically based discontent. Within a few weeks it had established a transitional government. A national conference was convened in July 1991 in an attempt by the EPRDF to secure widespread acceptance. It resulted in the signing of a transitional charter by representatives of some thirty-one political movements, the creation of a Council of Representatives with eighty-seven members, and the establishment of the Transitional Government of Ethiopia. The EPRDF had the largest single bloc in the council with thirty-two seats, and the OLF, until its withdrawal from the government in late June 1992, was the second largest, with twelve seats.

The charter declared that the transitional period was to last no more than two and a half years. The council was charged with organizing a commission to draw up a draft constitution. The draft constitution was first submitted for public discussion 1994 and then voted into effect by a constituent assembly.

Ethnic Politics in the Context of Administrative Reform

In 1992, the EPRDF government organized the first multiparty elections in Ethiopian history. These elections were for local and regional offices during the period of transition to a multiparty democracy. In the days leading up to these elections in June, ethnic tensions ran high. Although ethnic parties had been included in the broad-based governing coalition, there were fears among groups such as the Oromo, Amhara, and Somali, that these elections would not be free and fair, and that the elections would simply provide a cover for the rule of the Tigray minority through the EPRDF. Days before the elections, major parties including the OLF, the Ethiopian Democratic Action Group, the Gideo People's Democratic Organization, the Islamic Front for the Liberation of Oromia, and the All Amhara People's Organization announced that they would not participate in the process. At the same time, the armed wing of the OLF left camps to which they had been confined in the lead-up to the elections, and engaged in low-intensity warfare against the forces of the EPRDF. Because they refused to lay down their arms, the OLF was barred from participating in electoral politics.

In 1993, the EPRDF issued a proclamation relating to the registration of political parties. In order to operate freely and to engage in activities normally associated with political parties (e.g., organizing, campaigning, holding rallies, etc.), political organizations had to be registered. The only groups that were barred were those who attempted to pursue their objectives through the use of arms, and those that behaved irresponsibly and fomented conflict, hatred, racism, religious intolerance, etc.[31] In addition, the former Marxist ruling party, the WPE, was specifically excluded.

By the end of 1993, the governing coalition had narrowed considerably. In April of that year, the transitional government ousted five political groups (who called themselves the Southern Coalition) from the Council of Representatives for the endorsement of a resolution sponsored by opposition groups meeting in Paris, calling for dissolution of the council. Consequently, the membership of the council was reduced to the representatives of the EPRDF and the ethnic-based parties it had created. Organized opposition inside the country by this time was generally repressed. Major ethnically based parties were completely shut out of the pact that now formed the transitional government or were forced out over the first two years of the transition.[32]

In December 1993, the government allowed a "peace and reconciliation conference," organized by internal as well as exiled opposition groups, to take place. But some who returned from abroad to participate were arrested and government agents harassed participants. Moreover, the transitional government itself boycotted the conference, demonstrating that there was still a wide chasm between the EPRDF and opposition leadership. What was also made clear by this conference was that the opposition was badly fragmented along ethnic lines. Only the urban-based Ethiopian National Democratic Party and the Joint Political Forum were not organized along ethnic lines.

Elections for a constituent assembly to approve a new democratic constitution took place in 1994. All registered political parties were entitled to participate, and indeed, thirty-nine did. However, the outcome could have been predicted. Member organizations of the EPRDF won 484 of 547 seats. The EPRDF had the advantage of incumbency and a wealth of resources at its disposal, including patronage with which it could co-opt opposition leaders. Currently, the EPRDF and affiliated parties hold 518 seats in the 547-seat federal assembly. EPRDF and affiliated parties also hold all regional parliaments by large majorities, except in the capital, Addis Ababa, where opposition parties hold about 30 percent of the regional council.

Clearly what has emerged in Ethiopia is a type of what Alfred Stepan has termed a "putting together" federation[33] that is based upon the ruling EPRDF working through ethnically based elites and parties that are beholden to it.[34] Although authority is constitutionally devolved to subnational governments, this devolution is only apparent at the regional, zonal, and, in some cases, *woreda* (district) levels. Under most circumstances, subregional authorities have power and authority to make autonomous policy decisions only when this involves using non-federal resources. Given the heavy emphasis on following central directions, one could even argue that what Ethiopian federalism resembles is more a case of the deconcentration of authority rather than devolution of authority.

Foundations of Ethnic Federalism in Ethiopia

Even before the passage of the federal constitution, the EPRDF utilized selected proclamations and the transitional charter to create a new system of governance that was federal in form and based on a commitment to ethnically based self-determination. Perhaps the two most important provisions of the transitional charter in this regard were Articles II and XIII. Article II asserted the right of all Ethiopian nationalities to self-determination, the preservation of the national identities of each group, and the right of each nationality to govern its own affairs within the context of a federated Ethiopia. Article XIII stated that "there shall be a law establishing local and regional councils defined on the basis of nationality." These provisions represented a dramatic departure from the policies of previous regimes regarding the right of various ethnic groups to self-determination. The new policy quickly prompted protests among Ethiopian nationalists both at home and abroad who violently opposed what they saw as the balkanization of Ethiopia. Despite this, the EPRDF regime showed its determination to follow through on the administrative reorganization of the country along ethno-regional lines. This policy commitment was formalized with the enactment of the Federal Constitution of 1994.

Even as the constitution was in the final stages of being drafted, the EPRDF issued a major policy statement outlining its political views and policy objectives in regional reforms.[35] It declared its intention to imple-

ment a plan to devolve power from the center to states and local governments. This was billed as a form of "devolved federalism" without extensive subnational control over technical policies, laws, regulations, and
taxes. This contrasts with the "coming together" type of federalism resulting from bargaining and negotiating among states that seek to voluntarily
join in some type of federal arrangement. In such cases, each state surren-
ders a certain amount of its sovereignty, power, and authority to the center
for the good of the collective. However, when it finally took shape,
Ethiopia's federal system was clearly of the "holding together" variety,
having been imposed from the top, and it quickly transformed into a "putting together" federal exercise, where there are federal features, but little or
no liberal democracy.

Further evidence of this can be seen in the fact that although the constitution states that regional states may prepare their own constitutions, decide
their own official language, develop their own administrative systems,
establish separate police forces, and collect certain taxes, again the initiative for these arrangements came more from the center than from the constituent states.

Article 39 of the constitution, "The Rights of Nations, Nationalities
and Peoples," declares that "every nation, nationality and people shall have
the unrestricted right to self-determination up to secession." This action can
be taken when at least two-thirds of the legislature of the nation, nationality, or people concerned vote to do so, and when the action is ratified in a
statewide referendum three years later. Before secession can in fact occur,
however, there are constitutional provisions for review by the
Constitutional Court and the Council of the Federation, a national political
and deliberative body with 108 elected representatives from all states.
Article 39 also gives nations, nationalities, or peoples the right to speak,
write, promote, and develop their own languages.

The constitution further proclaims the establishment of the Federal
Democratic Republic of Ethiopia, consisting of nine states. Five of these
states (Afar, Amhara, Harari, Oromia, Somalia, and Tigray) are dominated
by a single ethnic group, and four—Benishangul-Gumuz, Gambella, and
the Southern Nations, Nationalities and Peoples (SNNP)—are multiethnic
states, without one dominant ethnic group. In the multiethnic regional
states, although each group uses its own language on a day-to-day basis,
Amharic is the working language. In the others, the working language is the
language of the predominant group in the state.

The objectives of the EPRDF seemed noble. They claimed to want to
reduce the ethnic tensions and conflicts that had dominated the modern history of Ethiopia; to forthrightly tackle social and economic problems in
such a way that all ethnic groups were treated as equals; to build a democratic society; and to construct effective, efficient, and incorrupt systems of
governance.[36] To do this, a new social compact for the polity was needed.

However, rather than such a compact being negotiated among elites representing the major groups in society, or emerging in an organic manner, it was imposed from above. What has evolved is an asymmetrical form of federalism that is "hypercentralized."

The Practice of Ethnic
Federalism and Revenue Sharing in Ethiopia

Some outside observers see the Ethiopian experiment with "ethnic federalism" as "bold and thoughtful."[37] By the standards of public administration, this would seem to be the case. However, there is a political dimension that most outside observers such as the World Bank and other international development agencies seem to ignore or simply downplay. Ethnic federalism has *not* resulted in a widespread consensus in the general population of Ethiopia. There are some in the public at large—particularly among the Amhara and some others—who see themselves as Ethiopians first and members of an ethnic group second, and who contend that by definition a development strategy involving ethnic federalism is fatally flawed. This is the predominant view of citizens who feel that such a strategy will ultimately result in the demise of a unitary Ethiopian state.[38] Some scholars question this approach because they claim it is likely to lead to more rather than less ethnic-based conflict.[39] This sentiment was clearly evidenced among some participants in a national conference called by the government that involved academics from institutions of higher learning throughout the country. The *Ethiopian Herald* reported that "some conference participants . . . said that as . . . Article 39 does not encourage unity or tolerance among the people it should be *rubbed out*. They vehemently condemned the existence of the Article in the constitution saying that it can be the major cause of some opposition parties to raise the issue of secession."[40]

Despite such concerns, the EPRDF government forged ahead with its plans, justifying this approach based on the fact that its first priority was the removal of social inequalities founded upon ethnicity. In 1995, one of the government's chief ideologues, citing the historic failure of previous Ethiopian governments to address the problem of ethnic disharmony, stated, "We must find a solution which is beneficial to the Ethiopian people today, therefore, history will not provide the answer."[41] Prime Minister Meles Zinawe recently reinforced this point when he asserted that the EPRDF government was "resolved to empower and promote democratic principles by giving affirmative actions [*sic*] to historically disadvantaged groups and relatively backward states."[42]

Hybrid federalism. The experiment currently under way is indeed hybrid federalism with many features that are characteristically Ethiopian. In structural terms, the Federal Democratic Republic of Ethiopia resembles federal states in most parts of the world. As mentioned above, it consists of nine regional states, and two special cities, Addis Ababa and Dire Dawa. In addition, Ethiopia is made up of 66 administrative zones (provinces), 550 *woredas* (districts), and six special districts. Each of the four levels of government has more or less the same structures, with executive, legislative, and judicial branches. The regional state bureaucracy carries out the day-to-day operations of government.

State versus federal powers. Regional state powers include the implementation of state constitutions as well as social (e.g., language policy, education policy) and economic development policies and plans; the policing function; the administration of land and natural resources according to federal law; taxation in such areas as personal income (except for federal, state, and international employees); certain producer and manufacture taxes; and certain joint taxes with the federal government.

Although most taxing powers rest with the federal government, most of the expenditure obligations of government in this federal system are the responsibility of regional states, zones, and *woredas*. The central government has rather narrow responsibilities. It is responsible for collecting most taxes, including import and export taxes; setting national economic and social policies; and establishing national standards in areas such as commerce and trade, finance, and transportation. Also, like central governments in all federal states, it is responsible for the conduct of foreign policy, ensuring national defense, monetary policy, and setting policy relating to interregional state transportation and commerce.

Despite the fact that the constitution gives a great deal of power and administrative authority to regional states, the overwhelming amount of political power in this system rests with the central government. As a result, Ethiopia in practice operates more like a unitary state, with regional states closely following the policy lead of the center, mainly as represented in the EPRDF's Five Year Program, rather than asserting their policy independence. This system has been described as a form of "cooperative federalism," characterized by a policy consensus between the federal and state governments in most sectors. What is revealed here is the manner in which the EPRDF government has systematically neutralized political opposition; political elites and party cadres who support it have been placed in positions of power and authority at the regional level. At the same time, the central government has set up a devolved system of administration, ostensibly in an effort to bring government closer to the people and to create an environment conducive to peoples' empowerment.

In poor and deeply divided countries such as Ethiopia, administrative devolution under the best of circumstances would be risky business. Poverty and weak, uncoordinated administrative institutions have generally proven to be anathema to the successful implementation of devolved federalism. Such an approach has the tendency to limit population movement between and among regional states; it could lead to demands for secession from the federal state; it could limit the ability of the central government to take an effective lead in the development of the country; and it is likely to inhibit the development of an open and free market that integrates all parts of the country.

For devolved ethnic federalism to work, there should at the very least be a widespread sense in the general population of national unity, and a sense that ethnically based federalism, rooted in the principles of administrative devolution, is appropriate to the development of the country. Moreover, there should be the administrative and financial capacity to implement such a strategy effectively. However, at the time the strategy of devolved ethnic federalism was embarked upon, there was a consensus only among a narrow circle of elites within or close to the EPRDF that this strategy was desirable.

In structural terms, what is the driving mechanism of ethnic federalism in Ethiopia? Does this policy achieve what it is meant to achieve in structural terms? In terms of their effectiveness and appropriateness, how are various levels of government perceived by the agents who are supposed to implement federalist policies as well as by the general population these policies are meant to affect? We turn our attention to these questions in the next two subsections.

Federalism and Revenue Sharing: The Engine of Devolved Governance

The engine of Ethiopia's devolved federalism is a hybrid system of revenue sharing that includes block grants through which the central government shares with regional states tax and other revenues it is able to generate.[43]

The Causes and Consequences of Fiscal Imbalance

The dominance of the Ethiopian federal government in revenue generation has resulted in state governments' relying extensively on transfers from the central government to meet their obligations. Ideally, a federal arrangement would be characterized by a fiscal balance whereby regional governments would have taxing powers sufficient for them to meet their service delivery and governance obligations. However, in Ethiopia this has not been the case. In fact, present-day Ethiopia has been characterized by vertical imbalances, with mismatches between their expenditure responsibilities and their revenue-generating capacities. For example, in the 1993–1994 fiscal year, out of a total expenditure of Birr 3,145 million[44] by the regions, only Birr 807 million (26 percent) was generated by the states; the rest was in the form of grants and subsidies from the central government. These numbers highlight the fact that between 80 percent and 90 percent of all revenue is controlled by the federal government. Moreover, the expenditure patterns of the states are centrally monitored, and thus controlled.

The World Bank has estimated that in 1994–1996 the regional states collected only 15 percent of the total national revenues. By 1996–1997 that figure had risen by 2 percent.[45] This change does not represent a significant erosion of the dominance of the federal government in revenue generation, and only serves to highlight the relative weaknesses of regional states in such matters.

Revenue Sharing and the Reduction of Regional State Inequalities

Acknowledging the significant disparity in terms of levels of economic development, the widespread poverty and inequality throughout the country, and differences in the revenue-generating capacities of the states, the federal government of Ethiopia has turned to a form of revenue sharing as a way of implementing an equity-based development strategy. Taxes are collected at the center and then devolved to the regions according to a formula that has a significant equity component.

Ethiopia's approach to revenue sharing involves the provision of "budgetary subsidies" or block grants from the center to the states. Grants are determined according to a formula. The share of the budget subsidy that is accorded each region is based on such objective factors as the region's population share, its relative level of development, and its relative projected revenue-generation capacity.

Conditionalities and Block Grants to Regional States

In principle, block grants to states come with no strings attached. In developed countries revenue sharing generally involves tax sharing. But in developing countries it often takes the form of block grants to regions, based on needs, and intended to compensate for the differences in regional resource endowments and levels of economic development. Regions under such circumstances theoretically have the power and authority to identify the policy preferences of their constituents, to formulate their own development plans, and to make decisions about the allocation of their own budgets between sectors as well as between capital and recurrent expenditures. However, as mentioned above, state spending decisions most often are heavily influenced by priorities set nationally in the EPRDF Five Year Program. In other words, officials at the regional state and zone levels, who are generally party loyalists, structure the choices at the *woreda* and sub-*woreda* levels so that they conform to centrally determined priorities.

Making Spending Decisions at the Regional State Level

While there generally has been a policy consensus between states and the federal government, there have been occasions when intraregional conflicts have emerged over how to allocate the revenues received from the center. For instance, the World Bank reported that in the Amhara region there was an incident recently where zonal preferences did not match regional preferences. One zone wanted to allocate its entire budget to roads, at the expense of such important activities as improving educational infrastructure and instruction, health care, and agricultural programs. Another wanted to use its entire budget to construct a sports stadium. However, each zone was persuaded to change its plans and to follow guidelines set at the federal and regional levels "for a more balanced approach to development."[46] Such incidents show that there are limits to autonomous decisionmaking on the part of lower levels of administration, especially when they stray too far outside nationally and regionally determined priorities. This is especially true at the *woreda* level. Rather than popular participation being enhanced at that level, it is constrained by the heavy hand of the center and its representatives at the state and zonal levels.

Interregional Imbalances

In addition to the fiscal imbalance that exists between the center and the regional states, there are also imbalances between and among regions themselves. For instance, the city of Addis Ababa finances almost all its public spending from revenues that it generates independently. In fact, Addis Ababa accounts for an average of 34 percent of the revenues raised by all states. The state that collects the next largest percentage of revenues is Oromia (28 percent), followed by the Amhara Regional State (12 percent), and the SNNPR State (11 percent). The lowest collections tend to be in Gambella, Benishangul-Gumuz, Harari, and Afar. (See Table 3.1.)

It is interesting to note that of all the tax revenues individual states are able to generate on their own, in Gambella, one of the poorest states, most of the state's revenues collected come from personal income tax paid primarily by government employees. Another interesting statistic is in the category of sales tax on goods—Tigray and Afar (another extremely poor state) far outpace other states in terms of the percentage of their revenues collected in this category. This is in large measure due to taxes levied by state governments against public and private enterprises doing business in those regions. The regions of Benishangul-Gumuz and Gambella are barely able to finance 10 percent of their public expenditures on their own.

The Limits of Revenue Sharing as a
Strategy for Democracy and Development

The heavy reliance of regional states on the federal government for fiscal resources is only part of the story. Despite an admirable development strategy centered on the principle of revenue sharing, regional states tend not to be able to exercise independent authority. There are a number of reasons for this including the following:

The reality of an underdeveloped private sector, and a lack of access to credit for this sector. In most regions except for Amhara, Addis Ababa, Tigray, and

Table 3.1   Regional Revenue Indicators, 1994/95–1997/98

	Total	Tigray	Afar	Amhara	Oromia	Somali	Benesh.-Gamuz	SNNP	Gambel.	Harari	Addis Ababa	Dire Dawa
Share of Total State Revenues	100.00	6.98	0.91	12.12	27.51	4.07	0.48	11.02	0.48	0.60	34.16	1.67
Per Capita Revenue/GDP	0.05	0.05	0.02	0.02	0.04	0.06	0.03	0.03	0.08	0.12	0.36	0.21
1994 Population (millions)	52.64	3.14	1.11	13.83	18.73	2.32	0.46	10.38	0.18	0.13	2.11	0.25
Share of 1996/97 State Totals	100	100	100	100	100	100	100	100	100	100	100	100
Personal Income Tax	15	15	26	19	12	11	31	17	47	19	13	12
Business Profit Tax	13	13	14	8	28	78	2	19	2	44	16	41
Agricultural Income & Land Fees	10	10	0	33	25	0	12	25	2	1	0	0
Ag. Income Tax	4	4	0	16	13	0	6	14	1	0	0	0
Rural Land Use Fee	6	6	0	16	12	0	6	11	1	0	0	0
Sales Tax on Goods	32	32	39	4	14	2	2	15	6	0	5	15
Service Sales Tax	2	2	0	1	0	1	0	1	0	1	2	3
Urban Land Lease Fee	0	0	0	0	0	0	0	0	0	0	14	0
Gov't Sale of Goods & Services	5	5	8	13	7	1	15	7	21	0	5	9
Stamp Sales & Duty	6	6	0	1	1	1	0	1	0	2	11	5
Charges & Fees	10	10	3	7	4	0	3	3	1	4	3	9
All Others	9	9	8	14	9	6	34	13	20	10	33	6

Source: World Bank, *Ethiopia: Review of Public Finances*, vol. 2. Report No. 18369-ET, 30 December 1999, 45.

Note: The share of state revenue is the average for the period 1993/94 through 1996/97.

Oromia, this sector is either at a very low level of development or no development.[47] Moreover, given the heavy reliance of regional states on revenues emanating from the center, there is a disincentive for private capital to invest locally.

The shortage of administrative capacity, particularly in the poorest regions.[48] There is a significant regional difference in the availability of skilled administrative and technical staff, and this is a major constraint on their autonomous development. This is a natural consequence of attempting to implement a federalist system under conditions of abject poverty and underdevelopment. Decentralization comes at a high price. It involves the duplication of institutions and functions in a hierarchical pattern from top to bottom. In order to meet staff needs, regional bureaucracies must either employ individuals who may not be qualified for the positions they hold, or force skilled bureaucrats to underutilize their talents. This problem is particularly acute in the poorest regions.

The practice of "pooling" is used in an effort to address shortages in qualified administrative manpower at the regional state and particularly the *woreda* level. That is, the sharing of individuals with needed administrative skills among various offices in different branches of government or in different policy sectors. This works in some cases, but in areas of the judiciary and legislative branches of government it is problematic.[49]

The record shows that while popular participation at the regional level has improved, including citizens' ability to determine how public funds are spent and what services are given priority, there has not been an equivalent improvement in the efficiency of administration. In most regions basic public services such as drinking water, sanitation, education, public health, and public works are generally unavailable or available only on a limited basis.

A second approach to dealing with the problem of low levels of administrative capacity at the regional level has involved the federal government's providing state governments with training and technical assistance for capacity building. This support, however, has been quite modest in relation to the amount of public fiscal resources the states have been asked to distribute. The absorptive capacity of shared revenues by such regions as Afar, Somali, Gambella, and Benishangul-Gumuz is quite low, and this serves as a drag on regional development. States are required to give their recurrent needs the highest priority, followed by ongoing noncapital projects. New investment projects are given the lowest priority. The poorest regions most often are only able to address their recurrent needs.

Problems with breaking in the system of ethnic federalism. Besides the limited availability of sufficient numbers of trained and skilled civil servants at the regional level and below, a problem also exists with the fact that devolved federalism is new, and regional and local administrators and politicians do have a great deal of discretion to set their own rules in dealing with constituents. In some cases this has led to serious excesses in administration. For example, although the constitution guarantees citizen freedom of assembly, this right is not always adhered to by local administration. The U.S. State Department's 1999 Human Rights Report cited a January 1999 case in which the Coalition of Ethiopian Opposition Political Organizations held a rally in Addis Ababa to announce its political agenda, but its organizers claimed that they were hindered in carrying out their plans because local authorities did not approve a permit for the rally until a day before.[50]

Pitfalls of donor dependence. Regional states, in addition to being heavily reliant on grants from the federal government, tend also to be dependent on donor assistance. Neither situation has proved anywhere to be conducive to the achievement of autonomous development on the part of states. In the case of Ethiopia, the practice has been for states to attempt to cut their dependence on donor assistance even before they can reduce their reliance on block grants from the center. In part this is due to a sense of nationalism that is encouraged by the EPRDF, and in part due to the fact that state administrators know that there is no value added with donor assistance. Assistance provided by donors is distributed and tightly controlled by the federal government. It is subtracted from the amount that would otherwise be allocated through the revenue-sharing scheme. Moreover, the strings attached and stringent reporting requirements of many donor-driven projects make them less desirable to state administrators.

Official corruption. A final negative aspect of devolved federalism in Ethiopia, particularly given the nascent stage of its regional and subregional bureaucracy, is official corruption.[51] As in the past, the EPRDF regime promotes the use of *gim gama* (self-criticism) sessions for bureaucrats as a way of addressing charges of corruption. However, in recent years this method has proven to be grossly inadequate in addressing the problem of official corruption.

In May 2001 the EPRDF government established the Federal Anti-Corruption Commission, and within six weeks twenty-four businessmen, bankers, and government officials had been arrested on charges of corruption. They included two former TPLF ministers who were accused of anti-democratic sentiments. Most of the corruption charges had to do with the sale of government-owned businesses and the provision of loans by the national bank without adequate security.

Significantly, this anticorruption campaign was launched at the same time that the TPLF and other EPRDF-affiliated parties engaged in purges of their leadership as well as all levels of government. Differences had begun to emerge in the TPLF leadership as early as 1996 over governance and ideological issues, but these differences did not become evident publicly until during the border war with Eritrea (1998–2000). In March 2001, twelve members of the TPLF Central Committee walked out of one of its meetings. Hard-line Tigray nationalists had felt that the war with Eritrea should have been prosecuted further and that the TPLF should not abandon its Marxist orientations in favor of liberal democracy and capitalism. The so-called "splinter group" was arrested, and a six-month debate within the TPLF and EPRDF leadership ensued, finally resulting in the neutralization of the splinter group and the affirmation of EPRDF's leadership under Meles Zinawe. At its Fourth Party Congress, the EPRDF called for "renewal," and reaffirmed the democratic values in the constitution.[52] Subsequently, there were significant changes at all levels of government. Many who lost their positions after the onset of the renewal were alleged to be supporters of the splinter group or their allies within EPRDF-affiliated parties (e.g., the Amhara National Democratic Movement, the Oromo Peoples' Democratic Organization, Southern Ethiopian Peoples Democratic Front), or implicated in electoral irregularities in 2000 and 2001. The Final Report of the EPRDF Congress proclaimed that capacity building at all levels of governance and in party activities would be fundamental to the tasks of renewal and rehabilitation.

What is clear is that despite pledges by the EPRDF to build and improve administrative capacity and policy effectiveness, the continuing lack of good governance at various levels of Ethiopia's government could well continue to undercut any efforts to tackle serious problems such as poverty, inequality, and discrimination. At the same time, if the majority of people have favorable opinions of the efforts being made by those who govern only have responsibility for implementing policy, this might be an indication of support for the regime and its development strategy. How satisfied is the population at large that various levels of government are meeting their security needs? How satisfied are members of various ethnic communities that the government's policies uphold their equal rights as citizens?

Public Perceptions of the Adequacy of Service Delivery, Identity, and Citizenship

The data and methods. In addition to various primary and secondary sources, the data in this study come from (1) public documents; (2) personal, open-ended, and nonstructured interviews with government officials at the national and regional levels, and with private citizens throughout the country; and (3) a purposively selected survey sample of 277 respondents in the regional states of Oromia, SNNPR (Southern Nations, Nationalities, and People's Regional State), Tigray, Amhara, Benishangul-Gumuz, and Ethiopia's capital city, Addis Ababa. The data were gathered over a two-year period between 2001 and 2003. The statistical data are analyzed via cross-tabulation and regression analysis.

The voice of the people: cross-regional comparisons. Among the main objectives of the survey sampling exercise was to gauge public opinion regarding citizens' evaluation of the adequacy of government service provision involving the central government as well as the *woreda*. It was assumed that the information we received would allow some insight as to the effectiveness of the policy of administrative devolution. The devolution of administrative authority down to the *woreda* level is very recent, and it could be that the populace do not quite understand implications of this change, or they might not perceive that level of authority to have clearly established its role in the provision of social services. The social services that were inquired about were policing, health care, education, road maintenance and development, the courts, the provision of safe water, and food security. Let us now turn our attention to the data as it relates to the provision of services by these seven categories.

Central Government Service Delivery

In terms of the opinion of citizens of the adequacy of the delivery of social services by the central government, while controlling for the region in which they reside, the data clearly indicate that the citizens of the Tigray state are consistently more satisfied than citizens of other regional states with the performance of the government in delivering the social services about which we inquired. (See Table 3.2.)

However, like the citizens of other regions, those from Tigray were least satisfied with the performance of the court system and with the provision of food security. Fifty-six percent of the Tigray respondents were either somewhat dissatisfied or dissatisfied with the performance of the central government in the delivery of services in these categories. These same respondents seemed particularly satisfied with progress being made by the central government in the areas of formal education, police services, and the provision of safe water. Table 3.2 further indicates that respondents from Oromia state were the least satisfied across the board with central government service provision, followed by respondents from Amhara state. In no category was the Oromo level of satisfaction more than 11 percent. The highest levels of dissatisfaction among the Oromo were in the areas of health care delivery (98 percent) and road development and maintenance (100 percent). It is interesting to note that in the multiethnic states of Benishangul-Gumuz and SNNPR, the safe water and food security categories revealed the highest level of dissatisfaction. Furthermore, among the respondents from SNNPR state only one in four was satisfied with the court services available to them.

In addition to controlling for the region of residence, the study also controlled for the nationality of the respondents. (See Table 3.3.)

Tigrayan respondents again tended to be the most satisfied with services being provided by the central government, particularly regarding police

Table 3.2 Satisfaction with Central Government Services by Region

Region	Degree of Satisfaction/ Dissatisfaction	Police %	Health Care %	Education %	Roads %	Court %	Water %	Food %
	Most Satisfied	14	0	4	4	0	4	0
	More Satisfied	29	10	19	22	5	16	2
Addis Ababa	Satisfied	10	18	19	8	7	24	4
	Less Satisfied	35	27	21	22	27	24	15
	Dissatisfied	12	45	38	43	61	31	79
	Most Satisfied	9	4	37	8	0	4	2
	More Satisfied	23	19	22	30	11	21	11
Tigray	Satisfied	51	44	28	25	32	52	30
	Less Satisfied	6	17	6	21	21	12	25
	Dissatisfied	11	17	7	17	36	12	32
	Most Satisfied	2	2	33	11	0	21	6
	More Satisfied	19	54	40	41	23	53	6
Amhara	Satisfied	14	9	5	16	4	6	0
	Less Satisfied	14	2	2	5	4	2	2
	Dissatisfied	51	33	19	27	69	17	85
	Most Satisfied	2	0	2	0	2	0	0
	More Satisfied	0	0	0	0	0	2	0
Oromia	Satisfied	6	2	9	0	2	6	5
	Less Satisfied	17	23	28	4	13	23	7
	Dissatisfied	75	75	62	96	83	69	88
	Most Satisfied	3	0	3	6	0	15	0
	More Satisfied	18	14	20	11	10	12	9
SNNPR	Satisfied	32	20	29	31	14	21	9
	Less Satisfied	26	31	26	37	38	32	9
	Dissatisfied	21	34	23	14	38	21	74
	Most Satisfied	29	7	22	4	9	4	8
	More Satisfied	17	30	7	22	22	7	12
Beneshengul- Gamuz	Satisfied	33	30	30	37	26	19	12
	Less Satisfied	0	7	15	4	13	22	8
	Dissatisfied	21	26	26	33	30	48	60
Total Satisfied/ Dissatisfied Numbers (percents)	Most Satisfied	22(9%)	5(2%)	44(17%)	14(5%)	3(1%)	20(8%)	6(2%)
	More Satisfied	44(18%)	53(20%)	47(19%)	55(21%)	22(10%)	51(20%)	16(6%)
	Satisfied	60(24%)	53(20%)	48(19%)	45(18%)	32(14%)	57(22%)	26(10%)
	Less Satisfied	43(17%)	47(18%)	40(16%)	40(16%)	44(20%)	47(18%)	29(12%)
	Dissatisfied	82(33%)	101(39%)	74(29%)	102(40%)	122(55%)	82(32%)	173(69%)
Total number of respondents		251	259	253	256	223	257	250

services, health care, education, the provision of safe water, and road maintenance and development. However, more than half of the Tigrayan respondents were somewhat dissatisfied or dissatisfied with the courts as well as with the provision of food security. On the one hand the favorable ratings could well be related to the fact that the central government, which is domi-

Table 3.3   Satisfaction with Central Government Services by Nationality

Region	Degree of Satisfaction/ Dissatisfaction	Police %	Health Care %	Education %	Roads %	Court %	Water %	Food %
Amhara	Most Satisfied	5	0	23	9	0	12	4
	More Satisfied	22	33	23	31	16	35	5
	Satisfied	18	20	14	12	5	16	1
	Less Satisfied	24	9	12	15	21	12	4
	Dissatisfied	32	39	28	33	58	25	87
Tigrayan	Most Satisfied	13	5	31	5	0	7	1
	More Satisfied	25	24	29	34	10	20	11
	Satisfied	43	37	26	23	29	48	30
	Less Satisfied	10	18	5	20	24	12	23
	Dissatisfied	10	16	10	18	36	13	34
Oromo	Most Satisfied	9	1	7	1	1	1	0
	More Satisfied	9	9	3	6	6	6	5
	Satisfied	10	10	12	11	9	11	7
	Less Satisfied	16	23	28	7	13	24	8
	Dissatisfied	56	57	51	74	70	57	80
Sidama	Most Satisfied	8	0	8	15	0	17	0
	More Satisfied	8	15	15	0	0	0	8
	Satisfied	42	15	46	38	27	25	15
	Less Satisfied	17	46	23	46	27	33	15
	Dissatisfied	25	23	8	0	45	25	62
Berta	Most Satisfied	33	17	17	17	17	17	17
	More Satisfied	0	0	17	0	0	0	0
	Satisfied	33	33	50	50	33	17	17
	Less Satisfied	0	0	0	0	17	17	17
	Dissatisfied	33	50	17	33	33	50	50
Other Southern Nationalities	Most Satisfied	6	0	0	0	7	13	7
	More Satisfied	25	13	20	27	13	20	7
	Satisfied	38	19	20	20	7	20	0
	Less Satisfied	19	38	40	33	33	40	27
	Dissatisfied	13	31	20	20	40	7	60
Other	Most Satisfied	0	0	0	0	0	0	0
	More Satisfied	17	14	17	14	14	14	0
	Satisfied	0	0	17	14	0	0	0
	Less Satisfied	33	14	0	0	0	29	0
	Dissatisfied	50	71	68	71	86	57	100
Total Satisfied/ Dissatisfied Numbers (percents)	Most Satisfied	22(9%)	5(2%)	44(18%)	14(6%)	3(1%)	20(8%)	6(2%)
	More Satisfied	44(18%)	53(21%)	45(18%)	55(22%)	22(10%)	49(19%)	16(7%)
	Satisfied	60(24%)	53(21%)	48(19%)	44(17%)	32(14%)	57(23%)	26(11%)
	Less Satisfied	43(17%)	47(18%)	40(16%)	40(16%)	44(20%)	47(19%)	29(12%)
	Dissatisfied	79(32%)	97(38%)	72(29%)	100(40%)	120(54%)	80(32%)	169(69%)
Total number of respondents		248	255	249	253	221	253	246

nated by the TPLF, has made a special effort to make up for the historically woefully inadequate provision of social services in Tigray. At the same time, as mentioned above, the court system, especially at the local levels, is characterized by many undereducated judges, limited operational resources, and overloaded court dockets. The findings regarding food security are not surprising given Ethiopia's frequent problem with drought and famine in Tigray and other parts of the country.

Significantly, the Amhara and Oromo respondents generally tended to be critical of the central government's service delivery efforts. The highest levels of satisfaction with central government service delivery among the Amhara respondents were in the education and safe water categories. However, 91 percent of these respondents were unhappy about the central government's ability to provide for food security, and only 21 percent were somewhat satisfied or satisfied with the court services. By contrast, the Oromo respondents tended to across the board be dissatisfied with the central government's provision of services. The range of Oromo dissatisfaction was from a low of 72 percent in the area of police services to highs of between 78 percent and 89 percent in the areas of health care, education, roads, courts, water, and food security. Moreover, only 12 percent of the Oromo were either somewhat satisfied or satisfied with their food security plight; none were very satisfied. How are we to understand the attitudes of respondents from Ethiopia's two largest ethnic groups? The Amhara tend to feel that the EPRDF government's ethnic federalism policy undermines the unity of the Ethiopian nation, and that their group is the object of particular marginalization by the regime. Many Oromos are torn between wanting to exercise their right to self-determination and separating Oromia from the Ethiopian state, or sticking with it, but demanding their equal-citizenship rights. In either case, the level of popular disaffection comes through in these data. The Sidama are the largest nationality group in the SNNPR state, where there are more than forty distinct nationalities, and the Berta hold a similar position in Benishangul-Gumuz. Local conditions seem to have influenced the responses we got from respondents in those states. Sidama respondents were most concerned with health care, the court system, and food security issues. The Berta respondents of Benishangul-Gumuz were generally supportive of the central government's service delivery effort, particularly in the education sector (84 percent), but they registered some dissatisfaction with the government's delivery of services in the court system (50 percent), the provision of safe water (67 percent), and food security (67 percent).

Government Service Delivery

The pattern of respondent's satisfaction/dissatisfaction levels with service delivery by the central government carried over to the *woreda* level (see Table 3.4).

Table 3.4 Satisfaction with Woreda Services by Region

Region	Degree of Satisfaction/ Dissatisfaction	Police %	Health Care %	Education %	Roads %	Court %	Water %	Food %
	Most Satisfied	18	0	2	2	0	19	3
	More Satisfied	16	7	18	9	3	19	8
Addis Ababa	Satisfied	27	14	18	13	3	21	12
	Less Satisfied	22	27	18	22	28	19	5
	Dissatisfied	18	52	44	54	67	23	72
	Most Satisfied	4	6	19	2	2	6	2
	More Satisfied	26	29	19	20	13	15	8
Tigray	Satisfied	49	31	38	34	21	48	27
	Less Satisfied	11	19	17	26	28	17	33
	Dissatisfied	9	15	8	18	36	13	31
	Most Satisfied	2	0	21	17	0	20	2
	More Satisfied	15	58	51	52	17	56	13
Amhara	Satisfied	22	7	8	10	9	4	0
	Less Satisfied	7	2	3	2	9	2	9
	Dissatisfied	54	33	18	19	65	18	76
	Most Satisfied	2	0	0	0	0	0	0
	More Satisfied	0	0	0	2	0	4	0
Oromia	Satisfied	8	2	8	0	2	2	7
	Less Satisfied	10	17	23	0	9	23	12
	Dissatisfied	80	81	69	98	89	71	81
	Most Satisfied	14	3	9	9	3	18	3
	More Satisfied	14	9	9	3	3	0	9
SNNPR	Satisfied	24	26	38	38	23	30	6
	Less Satisfied	24	35	24	35	20	30	13
	Dissatisfied	24	26	21	15	50	21	69
	Most Satisfied	32	8	19	12	14	4	8
	More Satisfied	16	20	15	15	18	8	0
Beneshengul-Gamuz	Satisfied	24	20	38	27	23	8	24
	Less Satisfied	4	20	0	0	9	4	4
	Dissatisfied	24	32	27	46	36	75	64
Total Satisfied/ Dissatisfied Numbers (percents)	Most Satisfied	24(10%)	6(12%)	27(11%)	15(6%)	5(2%)	27(11%)	6(3%)
	More Satisfied	35(15%)	51(21%)	45(18%)	42(17%)	16(8%)	45(18%)	16(7%)
	Satisfied	64(27%)	40(16%)	58(24%)	47(19%)	26(13%)	49(20%)	29(12%)
	Less Satisfied	32(13%)	48(20%)	37(15%)	36(15%)	37(18%)	40(16%)	32(14%)
	Dissatisfied	86(36%)	101(41%)	78(32%)	106(43%)	121(59%)	84(34%)	150(64%)
Total number of respondents		241	246	245	246	205	245	233

Again the strongest endorsements of the service provision efforts of their *woredas* came from respondents in Tigray state, followed by relatively moderate endorsements from the two multiethnic states in the study, SNNPR and Benishangul-Gumuz. Among these two sets of respondents, those from SNNPR seemed more prone to express dissatisfaction than their counterparts from Benishangul-Gumuz. Again, the most disaffected region seems to be Oromia. In no category of service provided by the *woreda* did respondents in Oromia express any level of satisfaction above 8 percent; on the other hand, in five of the seven categories of service (police services, health care, road development and maintenance, the court system, and food security) the dissatisfaction score was between 90 percent and 98 percent. Significantly, respondents from Amhara state were generally satisfied with the provision of social services by their *woreda*. In that state, the areas of most dissatisfaction were the *woreda's* role in the provision of police services (61 percent), the courts (74 percent), and food security (85 percent).

What is most striking about regional differences in respondents' perception of the adequacy of service delivery by their respective *woredas* is the high levels of dissatisfaction among the residents of the capital, Addis Ababa, particularly in the areas of health care (79 percent), education (62 percent), roads (76 percent), the courts (95 percent), and food security (77 percent). One would have expected that because Addis Ababa is the most well-endowed state in terms of its administrative personnel, technical expertise, and independent sources of revenue, its administration would be in a better position to secure the approval of its citizens. However, this seems not necessarily the case. Even if most services in the city are better than in most other regions, generally residents feel they could be much better.

When we consider the nationality of the respondents along with their satisfaction/dissatisfaction with *woreda* government service delivery, the patterns reported above continue to hold (see Table 3.5).

The support Tigrayan respondents give their *woredas* in the area of the provision of social services is generally high, except in the areas of food security and the court system, where the level of dissatisfaction is 62 percent and 66 percent respectively. Among the Amhara, respondents expressed limited satisfaction only with the provision of police services, formal education, and the provision of safe water. But these respondents were most dissatisfied with the court services (78 percent) and food security (82 percent) provided by their *woredas*.

Again, the highest level of dissatisfaction occurred among our Oromo respondents, who across the board tended to be dissatisfied with the effort of their *woredas* to deliver social services. Consistently, more than 70 percent in each category were either somewhat dissatisfied or dissatisfied. The highest levels of Oromo dissatisfaction with *woreda* service delivery were in the health care (88 percent), road development and maintenance (85 percent), court services (90 percent), safe water (88 percent), and food security (88 percent) categories.

Among the Sidama and Berta respondents, the results were mixed. The Sidama were most satisfied with police services (72 percent), and education (77 percent), and least satisfied by far with food security (88 percent). The

Edmond J. Keller

Table 3.5 Satisfaction with Woreda Services by Nationality

Region	Degree of Satisfaction/ Dissatisfaction	Police %	Health Care %	Education %	Roads %	Court %	Water %	Food %
Amhara	Most Satisfied	12	1	18	12	2	17	3
	More Satisfied	13	35	29	27	8	36	9
	Satisfied	24	13	15	14	13	10	6
	Less Satisfied	13	9	8	9	15	9	9
	Dissatisfied	38	42	30	38	63	27	73
Tigrayan	Most Satisfied	7	5	15	0	2	7	2
	More Satisfied	30	29	24	23	13	20	10
	Satisfied	42	29	32	30	19	46	27
	Less Satisfied	12	24	17	28	29	14	31
	Dissatisfied	10	14	12	19	37	14	31
Oromo	Most Satisfied	9	0	1	3	0	2	0
	More Satisfied	6	6	9	8	6	5	2
	Satisfied	14	6	13	5	3	6	11
	Less Satisfied	11	22	21	2	8	22	9
	Dissatisfied	61	66	55	83	82	66	79
Sidama	Most Satisfied	18	0	6	6	0	6	0
	More Satisfied	18	6	6	6	0	0	6
	Satisfied	36	38	65	53	44	44	6
	Less Satisfied	18	38	18	29	13	25	13
	Dissatisfied	9	19	6	6	44	25	75
Berta	Most Satisfied	20	20	20	20	20	20	20
	More Satisfied	0	0	0	0	0	0	0
	Satisfied	20	0	20	20	20	0	20
	Less Satisfied	20	20	0	0	20	0	0
	Dissatisfied	40	60	60	60	40	80	60
Other Southern Nationalities	Most Satisfied	7	0	7	7	7	40	7
	More Satisfied	7	13	7	0	7	0	14
	Satisfied	40	20	33	40	0	13	7
	Less Satisfied	20	33	27	33	50	40	14
	Dissatisfied	27	33	27	20	36	7	57
Other	Most Satisfied	20	20	20	20	20	25	20
	More Satisfied	0	0	0	0	0	0	0
	Satisfied	20	0	40	0	0	25	20
	Less Satisfied	40	20	0	40	0	25	0
	Dissatisfied	20	60	40	40	80	25	60
Total Satisfied/ Dissatisfied Numbers (percents)	Most Satisfied	24(10%)	6(2%)	27(11%)	15(6%)	5(2%)	27(11%)	6(3%)
	More Satisfied	35(15%)	51(21%)	43(18%)	40(17%)	16(8%)	43(18%)	16(7%)
	Satisfied	64(27%)	40(16%)	58(24%)	47(19%)	26(13%)	49(20%)	29(13%)
	Less Satisfied	32(13%)	48(20%)	37(15%)	36(15%)	37(18%)	40(16%)	32(14%)
	Dissatisfied	83(35%)	101(41%)	76(32%)	104(43%)	118(58%)	82(34%)	143(63%)
Total number of respondents		238	242	241	242	202	241	226

Berta respondents were too few in number to permit a reasonable assessment of their opinions.

Identity and Citizenship

The central government in deeply divided societies such as Ethiopia has a special role to play in engendering a sense of national identity and commitment on the part of the country's disparate nationality groups. Frances Deng et al. suggest that this would require the following:

> Defining national identity to be equitably accommodating to all the contending groups; developing principles of constitutionalism or constitutive management of power that creatively and flexibly balance the dynamics of diversity in unity to promote national consensus and collective purpose; designing a system of distribution or allocation of economic opportunities and resources that is particularly sensitive to the needs of minorities and disadvantaged groups and induces them to see unity as a source of security and enrichment and not of subjugation and deprivation; and through all these measures to challenge every group to recognize that it has a distinctive contribution to make to the process of nation building.[53]

To what extent do the respondents in this study have a sense of their identification with their particular group that is stronger than their sense of Ethiopian identity? To what extent do the respondents, based upon their nationality group identity, assess the efforts of the central government to address this issue?

In order to get at respondents' sense of the performance of the central government in promoting a widespread sense of a common Ethiopian identity, and their relative affinity to their particular nationality group as opposed to the Ethiopian nation as a whole, they were asked four questions:

- Do you feel that the interests of the Ethiopian people as a whole are more important than the interests of particular nationality groups? (Table 3.6A)
- Is it more important that a certain nationality group have the right to determine its own future rather than the country as a whole to have a sense of common purpose and unity? (Table 3.6B)
- In your opinion, does the central government of Ethiopia represent the interests of most of the people of Ethiopia? (Table 3.6C)
- How effective has the central government been in trying to solve problems among the different people of the country? (Table 3.6D)

As is indicated by Table 3.6A, among the four largest sets of respondents by their nationality the Oromo respondents were the most likely to feel that the interests of particular nationality groups were more important than that

Table 3.6A   Opinions About National Identity, Group Relations, and National Unity

Do you agree/disagree that the interests of the Ethiopian people as a whole are more important than the interests of particular nationality groups?

Nationality	% Strongly Agree	% Agree	% Disagree	% Strongly Disagree	Total number of respondents
Amhara	53	27	9	11	81
Tigrayan	28	47	20	5	60
Oromo	26	18	33	23	61
Sidama	74	4	4	17	23
Berta	0	20	60	20	5
Other Southern Nationalities	89	6	6	0	18
Other	50	0	17	33	6
Total Number of respondents	112	64	45	33	254

Table 3.6B   Opinions About National Identity, Group Relations, and National Unity

Is it more important that a certain nationality has the right to determine its future rather than the nation to have a sense of common purpose and unity?

Nationality	% Strongly Agree	% Agree	% Disagree	% Strongly Disagree	Total number of respondents
Amhara	12	13	39	36	69
Tigrayan	22	38	29	10	58
Oromo	54	22	14	11	65
Sidama	29	8	8	54	24
Berta	40	60	0	0	5
Other Southern Nationalities	22	6	6	67	18
Other	17	0	50	33	6
Total Number of respondents	70	51	59	65	245

of the Ethiopian community as a whole, but only by a slight margin (56 percent). Three in every four Tigrayans place the interest of Ethiopia as a whole ahead of that of any nationality group. Among the Amharas and Sidamas the percentage that apparently had a strong affinity toward the Ethiopian nation was much higher, 80 percent and 78 percent respectively. This finding seems to confirm the observation made above that there is no national consensus in the general population of Ethiopia that ethnic federalism is a desirable strategy for the country. However, this does not mean that

Table 3.6C   Opinions About National Identity, Group Relations, and National Unity

Do you agree that the central government of Ethiopia represents the interests of most of the people of Ethiopia?

Nationality	% Strongly Agree	% Agree	% Disagree	% Strongly Disagree	Total number of respondents
Amhara	8	20	14	58	71
Tigrayan	16	46	30	9	57
Oromo	9	6	21	64	66
Sidama	22	26	4	48	23
Berta	40	60	0	0	5
Other Southern Nationalities	0	19	6	75	16
Other	20	0	40	40	5
Total Number of respondents	29	56	45	113	243

Table 3.6D   Opinions About National Identity, Group Relations, and National Unity

How effective has the central government been in trying to solve problems among the different people of the country?

Nationality	% Very Effective	% Somewhat Effective	% Somewhat Ineffective	% Very Ineffective	Total number of respondents
Amhara	4	24	30	42	74
Tigrayan	25	47	19	8	59
Oromo	10	10	16	64	69
Sidama	36	9	18	36	22
Berta	25	25	25	25	4
Other Southern Nationalities	31	13	13	44	16
Other	0	14	43	29	7
Total Number of respondents	39	59	54	98	251

the national identity of individual groups is unimportant to them. Further credence to this observation can be seen in the responses to the question about whether it is most important for nationality groups to have the right to self-determination or more important for Ethiopia to remain a unified multinational community. Among the Amhara respondents, 75 percent put Ethiopian unity first, and 62 percent of the Sidama felt the same. Interestingly, however, 60 percent of the Tigrayan respondents, and 76 percent of the Oromos, put the rights of nationality groups to determine their own futures ahead of maintaining Ethiopian national unity. This seems to suggest that nationality groups for the most part will give ethnic federalism a chance for now, but they will continue to hold out their preference for ethnic self-determination.

How do respondents from various ethnic groups feel about the central government's efforts to build an Ethiopian national community? More than half of all respondents (65 percent) were of the opinion that the central government was not doing an adequate job in representing the interests of all Ethiopian people. As might be expected, the highest level of disapproval was among the Oromo (85 percent), followed by the Amhara (72 percent) and Sidama respondents (52 percent). Also as might be expected, Tigrayan respondents (62 percent) were most satisfied with the central government's efforts to promote national unity.

Tigrayan respondents were most likely to agree that the central government has been very effective or somewhat effective in trying to solve problems among different people in the country (72 percent). However, only 45 percent of the Sidama, 28 percent of the Amhara, and 20 percent of the Oromo respondents held similar opinions. This is a clear indication that the Tigray-dominated central government still has a ways to go before its building a multiethnic federal state meets with widespread acceptance.

These findings notwithstanding, how do the respondents from the different nationality groups feel about their own self-identity, the importance of passing on this identity to their children, and their relationship with other nationality groups? This is another way of getting at the issue of citizenship and citizenship rights within the context of Ethiopian federalism.

Most respondents felt a strong affinity to their particular national group, but this sentiment was strongest by far among Tigrayan respondents (see Table 3.7A). Ninety-three percent of respondents from this group said they felt proud to be Tigrayan, and 92 percent of the Oromo respondents felt the same about their group identity. This compares to 80 percent of the Amhara respondents, who said they were proud to be Amhara. However, only 46 percent among Sidama respondents expressed great pride in belonging to their nationality group.

When asked whether they would want their children to have a strong sense of identification with their nationality group, 83 percent of all respondents said yes, but the strongest views in this regard came from the Tigrayan respondents (92 percent) and the Oromo respondents (86 percent). Seventy-seven percent of the Amhara respondents and 82 percent of the Sidama respondents said that they would like their children to have a sense of identity with their nationality group. (See Table 3.7B.) This trend is not surprising—the Amhara culture forms the basis of Ethiopian identity, and the Sidama were historically the object of intense policies of acculturation. The Oromo and Tigrayans, on the other hand, generally resisted wholesale adoption of an Ethiopian national identity.

Table 3.7A   Nationality, Identity, Citizenship, and Group Relations

Do you agree/disagree with the statement that you are proud to be a member of your nationality group?

Nationality	% Strongly Agree	% Agree	% Disagree	% Strongly Disagree	Total number of respondents
Amhara	70	10	8	11	71
Tigrayan	60	33	7	0	58
Oromo	72	19	4	4	67
Sidama	32	14	5	50	22
Berta	100	0	0	0	6
Other Southern Nationalities	62	15	8	15	13
Other	60	20	20	0	5
Total number of respondents	157	45	16	24	242

Table 3.7B   Nationality, Identity, Citizenship, and Group Relations

Do you agree/disagree that you would want your children to think of themselves as having a close affinity to your nationality group?

Nationality	% Strongly Agree	% Agree	% Disagree	% Strongly Disagree	Total number of respondents
Amhara	67	10	10	13	69
Tigrayan	59	33	7	2	58
Oromo	65	21	6	8	63
Sidama	29	53	6	12	17
Berta	83	0	17	0	6
Other Southern Nationalities	25	42	8	25	12
Other	60	40	0	0	5
Total number of respondents	137	55	18	20	230

Despite Sidama response to the foregoing question, surprisingly, three out of every four Sidama respondents said that they felt a stronger affinity to their nationality group than to other Ethiopians. This compares to 65 percent among Amhara, 87 percent among Tigrayan, and 70 percent among Oromo respondents. (See Table 3.7C.) In response to the question, "Do you agree/disagree that all people born in this country, regardless of nationality, should be treated equally?" 98 percent of all respondents agreed. In fact, 98 percent of the Amhara, 98 percent of the Tigrayan, 95 percent of the Sidama, and 99 percent of the Oromo respondents agreed with this state-

Table 3.7C Nationality, Identity, Citizenship, and Group Relations

Do you agree/disagree that you feel stronger ties to your nationality group than to other Ethiopians?

Nationality	% Strongly Agree	% Agree	% Disagree	% Strongly Disagree	Total number of respondents
Amhara	59	6	16	19	68
Tigrayan	47	40	7	7	45
Oromo	55	15	25	5	65
Sidama	74	4	4	17	23
Berta	33	0	17	50	6
Other Southern Nationalities	31	8	23	38	13
Other	0	40	60	0	5
Total number of respondents	120	36	38	31	225

Table 3.7D Nationality, Identity, Citizenship, and Group Relations

Do you agree/disagree that all people born in this country, regardless of nationality, should be treated equally?

Nationality	% Strongly Agree	% Agree	% Disagree	% Strongly Disagree	Total number of respondents
Amhara	96	2	0	1	82
Tigrayan	87	11	1	0	61
Oromo	97	2	0	1	58
Sidama	91	4	0	1	23
Berta	100	0	0	0	6
Other Southern Nationalities	100	0	0	0	17
Other	60	40	0	0	5
Total number of respondents	235	13	1	3	252

ment. (See Table 3.7D.) What is most remarkable about these findings taken as a whole is that even though nationality groups have a clear sense of their ethnic identity, they also have a clear sense that they are Ethiopians. They feel strongly that any person born in Ethiopia has citizenship rights that are equal to those of any other person from any other nationality group. If one takes a long-term view of the implications of these findings, it would be reasonable to expect that with political stability and economic growth, the sense of having a common Ethiopian identity along with one's own ethnic identity will become institutionalized. Paul Collier and associates have presented empirical evidence that there is a close relationship between economic development, political stability, development, and democracy. Social conflicts such as civil wars and various forms of cultural conflict retard development; at the same time, development retards war.[54]

Conclusion: A Balance Sheet

Ethiopia is presently involved in attempting to implement what is officially billed as a form of ethnic federalism. Typically, federal systems emerge organically as political entities that must coexist, and they decide to organize themselves into a system of self-rule and shared rule. In Ethiopia, however, this approach has been dictated from above. This experiment initially started off looking like what Alfred Stepan has termed a "holding together" federation: decisions were taken by ethnic elites to create subnational states from a unitary state. But it has now evolved into a form of "putting together" federation, as the federal government and ruling party have created new states but staffed them with party cadre and personalities loyal to the ruling group. This practice is in contrast with the method for choosing regional state representatives, which involves local elections.[55]

The government claims that this approach is best for achieving democratic consolidation in this multiethnic polity. A central element in the process of consolidation is a system of devolved administration giving state, *woreda*, and zonal authorities the major roles in making decisions relating to socioeconomic development and the building of democratic institutions. This study has found, however, that decisionmaking at subnational levels of governance is constrained by the EPRDF Five Year Development Program, which does not permit much deviation from the dictates of the center.

Revenues collected at the center are shared with regional states, but most of these resources are used to cover the salaries of state, zonal, *woreda*, and local officials, and other recurrent expenses. Most states, because of the lack of resources, are not able to engage in new capital projects. Moreover, there is in most cases a severe lack of skilled administrative capacity below the national and state levels, and this too serves as a drag on democracy and development.

In reality, what is billed as a unique form of ethnic federalism in Ethiopia operates very much like a centralized, unitary state, with most power residing at the center. While official rhetoric proclaims that ethnic communities are now empowered and free to exercise their right to self-determination, Ethiopia is characterized by limited autonomous decision-making below the regional state level, and a great deal of central control and orchestration. As a consequence, while some institutional forms associated with consolidated democracies such as political parties and periodic multiparty elections with universal suffrage may exist, this is more of a "pseudodemocracy" than anything else.[56]

Ethiopia possesses a highly centralized form of federalism, with the "power of the purse" giving the federal government enormous power and control over policymaking at the subnational levels. The choice of a federal system as well as the policies and programs that undergird such a system were political decisions, primarily to enhance the controlling hand of the central government. What is unique about Ethiopia in contrast to other federal systems in the world today is the emphasis it places on organizing most states along ethnic lines.

Despite the efforts of the EPRDF government to exercise central control over politics while at the same time presenting the public image of being committed to power sharing with Ethiopia's various ethnic communities, by the summer of 2002 it was clear that some adjustments in the form of the federal system would have to be made. National discussions led to a second round of administrative devolution, this time down to the *woreda* level. Also, the EPRDF government announced that it would address its shortcomings in governance with a program of "renewal." This would demand the empowerment of the people and further popular participation according to democratic principles. It remains to be seen, however, whether the EPRDF will in the future be able to continue to pursue what it terms "ethnic federalism" as an approach to addressing the claims of various ethnic groups. Resource constraints would present formidable obstacles to the effective and realistic implementation of such an approach. The heavy coercive hand of the central government will continue for the foreseeable future to be a fact of everyday life in Ethiopia.

The results of the survey research make it clear that the EPRDF government is making some headway in engendering a sense of Ethiopian identity that either transcends or coexists with a clear sense of ethnic identity among the country's various nationality groups. Respondents identified some of the shortcomings in the efforts of both the central government and *woreda* governments in the delivery of vital social services. Their views sometimes were shaped by the regional state they resided in, but in other cases, their nationality affiliation was the most determinative. The most satisfaction with the delivery of social services tended to be found among the Tigrayan respondents, and the least among the Amhara and Oromo respondents. However, these views varied according to the type of social services being discussed. For example, respondents, no matter what their ethnic affiliation, tended to identify the court system and food security as the most unsatisfactory aspects of both central and *woreda* government service delivery.

Interestingly, although virtually all respondents, regardless of their nationality group, had pride in their national identity, they generally did not see a contradiction between their group identity and their identity as Ethiopian citizens. Moreover, most felt that any individuals born in Ethiopia, no matter what their nationality group, had equal rights as Ethiopian citizens. What all this seems to indicate is that continued progress toward the structural transformation of Ethiopian society and administrative reform will be necessary for the EPRDF regime to ultimately achieve its objectives through its policy of ethnic federalism. This, no doubt, will be a lengthy, halting, and arduous journey.

Notes

On a personal note, I am grateful for the research assistance on this project provided by Lahra Smith, Dawit Zegaye, Debela Goshu, Habtamu Alabachew, Yemane Zeray Mesfin, and Mismak Ta'ame Hagos. I am also indebted to James Polhemus for his keen insights on the dynamics of Ethiopian development and change.

1. Edmond J. Keller, *Revolutionary Ethiopia: From Empire to People's Republic* (Bloomington: Indiana University Press, 1988).

2. See Chapter 1 of this volume, "Borders, States, and Nationalism," by Ricardo René Larémont.

3. See *Constitution of the Democratic Republic of Ethiopia.* Addis Ababa, Ethiopia (8 December 1994).

4. In some ways the public commitment of the regime of the EPRDF could be considered nothing more than a fiction, since in practice not all states are ethnically homogenous. Four of the nine regional states (Gambella, Benishangul-Gumuz, Harar, and the Southern Nations, Nationalities, and Peoples' Region states) are comprised of several different ethnic groups.

5. See Donald Levine, *Greater Ethiopia: The Evolution of a Multiethnic Society* (Chicago: University of Chicago Press, 1974), 70–71.

6. S. N. Eisenstadt notes that, historically and analytically, empires are states that belong somewhere between what we might classify, for lack of better terms, "premodern" and "modern" political systems. Historically, a monarch whose claims to authority and legitimacy were established by sacred traditions governed most empires. However, there was also a conscious attempt on the part of emperors of bureaucratic empires to secularize certain aspects of their authority (e.g., Ottoman, Roman, Persian, Ethiopian Empires). Those bureaucratic empires that survived into the mid to late twentieth century faced similar challenges of modernization: They each attempted to cope in similar ways—centralizing and modernizing their bureaucracies and militaries, developing stable and reliable military alliances, reducing the power of traditional elements, and strengthening the hand of secular authorities vis-à-vis religious actors and institutions. See S. N. Eisenstadt, *The Political System of Empires* (London: Free Press of Glencoe, 1963), and Samuel P. Huntington, *Political Order in Changing Societies* (New Haven, CT: Yale University Press, 1968), especially 140–191.

7. See Tadesse Tamrat, *Church and State in Ethiopia, 1270–1527* (London: Oxford University Press, 1972), 21–68.

8. See A. H. M. Jones and E. Monroe, *A History of Abyssinia* (New York: Negro University Press, 1969), 118–119.

9. See M. Abir, *Ethiopia: The Era of the Princes* (London: Longman, 1968).

10. See Levine, *Greater Ethiopia,* 157.

11. Tewodros, who had taken some representatives of Queen Victoria of England as hostages for two years, committed suicide rather than surrender to an invading military force intended to liberate the hostages.

12. See Zewde Gabre-Selassie, *Yohannes IV of Ethiopia* (London: Oxford University Press, 1975).

13. Sven Rubenson, *Wichale XVII* (Addis Ababa, Ethiopia: Haile Selassie University Press, 1964).

14. See Keller, *Revolutionary Ethiopia*, 50–64.

15. See Christopher Clapham, *Haile Selassie's Government* (New York: Praeger, 1969), 34–35.

16. See John H. Spencer, *Ethiopia, the Horn of Africa, and U.S. Policy* (Cambridge, MA: Institute of Foreign Policy Analysis, 1977).

17. See Haile Selassie I, *The Autobiography of Emperor Haile Selassie I: My Life and Ethiopia's Progress, 1892–1937* (London: Oxford University Press, 1976).

18. See John Markakis and Nega Ayele, *Class and Revolution in Ethiopia* (London: Spokesman, 1978), 55.

19. Peter Schwab, *Decision-Making in Ethiopia: A Study of the Political Process* (Rutherford, NJ: Fairleigh Dickinson University Press, 1972), 89–140.

20. See Richard Greenfield, *Ethiopia: A New Political History* (London: Pall Mall Press, 1965), 456; Randi R. Balsvik, *Haile Selassie's Students: The Intellectual and Social Background to Revolution, 1952–1977* (East Lansing: African Studies Center, Michigan State University Press, 1985).

21. See Ruth Iyob, *The Eritrean Struggle for Independence: Domination, Resistance, Nationalism, 1941–1993* (Cambridge: Cambridge University Press, 1995).

22. See Patrick Gilkes, *The Dying Lion: Feudalism and Modernization in Ethiopia* (London: Julian Friedmann, 1975), 215–216.

23. See Asmarom Legesse, *Gada: Three Approaches to the Study of African Society* (New York: Free Press, 1973); Asafa Jalata, "The Cultural Roots of Oromo Nationalism," in *Oromo Nationalism and the Ethiopian Discourse,* ed. A. Jalata (Lawrenceville, NJ: Red Sea Press, 1998); Mohammed Hassen, *The Oromo of Ethiopia: A History 1570–1860* (Cambridge: Cambridge University Press, 1990).

24. Keller, *Revolutionary Ethiopia*, 161.

25. See Mohammed Hassen, "The Macha-Tulama Association and the Development of Oromo Nationalism," in *Oromo Nationalism and the Ethiopian Discourse*, ed. A. Jalata (Lawrenceville, NJ: Red Sea Press, 1998), 183–221.

26. Patrick Gilkes, *The Dying Lion: Feudalism and Modernization in Ethiopia* (London: Julian Friedmann, 1975), 225–226.

27. "Oromia Speaks: An Interview with a Member of the Central Committee of the Oromo Liberation Front," *Horn of Africa* 3 (1980): 24.

28. A noncapitalist approach to development was supposed to be dictated by the fact that African states had not matured as capitalist systems but instead were characterized by "medieval survivals." This was said to make conditions in countries such as Ethiopia different from the conditions that gave rise to the Russian Revolution of 1917. Logistically, then, it was assumed that the general theory and practice of socialist transformation had to be adapted to the specific conditions of Ethiopia. This was justified on the basis that Lenin himself had come out categorically against overemphasis on technical-economic prerequisites as well as against rigid, deterministic political preconditions for socialist revolution. The fact that Ethiopia's leaders exhibited a "socialist orientation" was deemed enough reason for the Soviets to consider embracing them as clients. See Keller, *Revolutionary Ethiopia*, 197–198, and A. S. Shin, *National Democratic Revolutions: Some Questions of Theory and Practice* (Moscow: Nauka, 1982).

29. See Edmond J. Keller, "Drought, War, and the Politics of Famine in Ethiopia and Eritrea," *Journal of Modern African Studies* 30, no. 4 (1992): 609–624.

30. See Edmond J. Keller, "Remaking the Ethiopian State," in *Collapsed States: The Disintegration and Restoration of Legitimate Authority,* ed. I. W. Zartman (Boulder, CO: Lynne Rienner Publishers, 1995).

31. See The Political Parties Registration Proclamation, No. 46 of 1993, *Negarit Gazeta* (Addis Ababa, 15 April 1993); and Sandra Fullerton Joireman, "Opposition Politics and Ethnicity in Ethiopia: We Will All Go Down Together," *Journal of Modern African Studies* 35, no. 3 (1997): 397–398.

32. Keller, "Remaking the Ethiopian State," 136–137.

33. A "putting together federation" is orchestrated from above by a ruling group and is characterized by some form of coercion. This contrasts with what Stepan calls "coming together" and "holding together" federations. Coming together federations emerge when sovereign states agree to join together in a federal arrangement. Holding together federations are the outgrowth of a consensual parliamentary decision to preserve a unitary state by creating a multiethnic federal system. This involves compromises among ethnic elites and is most often done to avoid or manage divisive ethnic, regional, or other types of group conflict within a polity.

34. See Alfred Stepan, *Arguing Comparative Politics* (New York: Oxford University Press, 2001), 320–323.

35. Prime Minister of the Federal Democratic Republic of Ethiopia, *The System of Regional Administration in Ethiopia* (Addis Ababa, Ethiopia, 1994).

36. Ethiopian Peoples' Revolutionary Democratic Front, "EPRDF's Five-Year Program of Development, Peace and Democracy" (Addis Ababa, Ethiopia, August 2000).

37. See World Bank, *Ethiopia: Regionalization Study*, Report No. 18898-ET (February 1999), 1.

38. See Worku Aberra, "Tribalism Rules in Ethiopia," *New African* (September 1993); Paul Brietzke, "Ethiopia's 'Leap into the Dark': Federalism and Self-Determination in the New Constitution," *Journal of African Law* 40 (1995); and Merere Gudina, "The New Directions of Ethiopian Politics," in *New Trends in Ethiopian Studies: Ethiopia 94*, eds. Harold G. Marcus and Grover Hudson (Lawrenceville, NJ: Red Sea Press, 1994).

39. See Walle Engedayehu, "Ethiopia: Democracy and the Politics of Ethnicity," *Africa Today* 40, no. 2 (1993): 29–30.

40. *Ethiopian Herald*, "Sound Discussion for National Consensus," 4 August 2002.

41. Quoted in Kjetil Tronvoll and Oyvind Aadland, "The Process of Democratization in Ethiopia: An Expression of Popular Participation or Political Resistance," *Human Rights Report No. 5* (Oslo, Norway: Norwegian Institute of Human Rights, 1995), 47.

42. See "Forum Discusses Decentralization Affirmative Actions," *Ethiopian Herald*, 6 August 2002.

43. *Negaret Gazeta of the Transitional Government of Ethiopia, Proclamation No. 33/1992: A Proclamation to Define the Sharing of Revenue Between the Central Government and the National/Regional Self-governments*, no. 7 (20 October 1992), 25.

44. One (1) $US is equivalent to Birr 8.2.

45. World Bank, *Ethiopia: Review of Public Finances Volume One*, Report No. 18369-ET (30 December 1998), 42.

46. World Bank, *Ethiopia: Regionalization Study*, 7.

47. See John Young, "Development and Change in Post-Revolutionary Tigray," *Journal of Modern African Studies* 35, no. 1 (1997): 83.

48. See Tegegne Gebre Egziabher, "The Influences of Decentralization on Some Aspects of Local and Regional Development Planning in Ethiopia," *Eastern Africa Social Science Research Review* 14, no. 1 (January 1998): 41; and John M.

Cohen and Stephen B. Peterson, *Administrative Decentralization: Strategies for Developing Countries* (West Hartford, CT: Kumarian Press, 1999), 136–137.

49. Personal interviews conducted with government administrators by James Polhemnus and Lissane Yohannes, October 2002, in Tigray and the Southern Nations, Nationalities, and People's Regional State.

50. U.S. State Department, Bureau of Democracy, Human Rights, and Labor, *1999 Country Reports on Human Rights Practices: Ethiopia* (25 February 2000), 18.

51. See John Young, "Along Ethiopia's Western Frontier: Gambella and Beneshengul in Transition," *Journal of Modern African Studies* 37, no. 2 (1999).

52. *EPRDF Fourth Congress Report* [Non-official Translation by USAID/Ethiopia] Addis Ababa (August 2001).

53. Francis M. Deng et al., *Sovereignty as Responsibility: Conflict Management in Africa* (Washington, DC: Brookings Institution, 1966), 214.

54. See Paul Collier, V. L. Elliott, Harvard Hegre, Anke Hoeffler, Marta Reynal-Querol, and Nicholas Sambanis, *Breaking the Conflict Trap: Civil War and Development Policy* (Washington, DC: World Bank, 2003).

55. Stepan, *Arguing Comparative Politics.*

56. See Larry Diamond, "Prospects for Democratic Development in Africa," *Hoover Institution Essays in Public Policy, No. 7* (Stanford, CA: Stanford University Press, Hoover Institution, 1997).

4

The Enduring Idea of the Congo

Herbert F. Weiss & Tatiana Carayannis

This chapter examines public attitudes toward the Kinshasa government and rebel authorities in the Democratic Republic of Congo (DRC). Analysis of public attitudes provides a basis for understanding the construction of Congolese national and state identities. Our conclusions are based on a series of public opinion surveys conducted in five cities throughout the DRC in January and June 2002.

Based on these data, the central thesis of this chapter is twofold. First, we postulate that the identification of the Congolese with the Congolese nation over the last forty years has become stronger, despite predatory leaders, years of war and political fragmentation, devastating poverty, ethnic and linguistic diversity, and the virtual collapse of state services. We also suggest that while Congolese identity has become stronger, it has also become exclusionary with regard to one particular ethnic group, the Rwandaphone peoples.

The Legacy of the Belgian Colonial Experience

The geographic frontiers of the DRC have largely remained unchanged since a company under the leadership of King Leopold II of the Belgians, the Association Internationale du Congo, established a private colonial, commercial empire in Central Africa in 1875. The boundaries of this empire were largely arbitrary and separated many large precolonial African nations and tribal groups such as the Bakongo, who resided, and still reside, in northern Angola, Belgian Congo, French Congo, and in Cabinda; the Lunda, who lived in Angola, northern Rhodesia (now Zambia), and the Belgian Congo; the Zande, who are found both in southern Sudan and northern Belgian Congo; and the Tutsi and Hutu, who resided mainly in Rwanda and Burundi but also across the frontier in Congo.

In the late nineteenth century, Belgium's security was threatened both by external conflict and internal divisions. The war between its neighbors, France and Germany, and the divisions within Belgium itself—between Flemings and Walloons, Free Thinkers and Catholics—threatened its very survival. For Leopold II, a colony would not only ensure Belgium's survival, but also bring it into the ranks of the great powers:

What my country needs is a safety valve for her surplus energies. Now the late King [Leopold I] believed no better answer would be found than by establishing a Belgian colony—not only to develop our commercial interests, but to raise the morale of the army and create the merchant navy which we lack . . . It's time that she [Belgium] takes her part in the great work of civilization, following in the footsteps, however modestly, of England.[1]

With the acquisition of the Congo, Belgium—a small state of 30,520 square kilometers—increased its territorial control almost a hundredfold, thus greatly enhancing its political influence and prestige. However, the Belgian government, unlike Leopold II, was opposed to the idea of establishing a colony, considering it too risky a business venture. Therefore, the Association Internationale du Congo was created and financed privately.

Desperate to receive international recognition for a hoped-for colony, Leopold became one of the founders of the 1884 Berlin Conference, which carved up the African continent among the European colonial powers. The Berlin Conference not only established rules to govern this partition and the almost total colonization of Africa by European states, but also resulted in the international recognition of the boundaries of Leopold's colony, renamed the "Congo Free State."

The Congo Free State lacked the capital and military resources of a state-sponsored colonial takeover, and thus rapidly faced severe financial constraints. This resulted in particularly harsh conditions of rule and economic exploitation in the territory that focused primarily on the forced collection of rubber and ivory, and which produced "atrocities on a large scale."[2] The growing international scandal surrounding the treatment of the Congolese under Leopold's brutal "one-man rule" pressured a reluctant Belgian parliament into accepting responsibility for the territory. In 1908, the Congo Free State became a colony of the Belgian state and was renamed the "Belgian Congo."

The Belgian colonial system employed three instruments of penetration: a virtually unsupervised state colonial administration, private concessionary companies dating back to the period of the Congo Free State, and the widely present Catholic Church and its missionaries.[3] One of the most important aspects of colonial policy was the creation of an adequate work force both for the mining industry and for agricultural concessions.

The Catholic Church was highly influential in the determination of a Belgian colonial philosophy. The Church was primarily concerned with the conversion of the Congolese people to the Catholic faith. With this goal in mind, it achieved not only a great deal of influence over the administration and the concessionary companies, but also over the Belgian government, which it often indirectly controlled through the Christian Democratic Party. With this influence, the Church achieved virtual control over colonial policy in education, relations with traditional elites, policies toward modern elites, and employment strategies for the Congolese. The Church also had great influence over who became colonial administrators.

The most important effect of this influence was in the area of education policy. The Belgian Congo followed neither the French-Portuguese pattern of elite assimilation and promotion, nor the British policy of indirect rule and support for traditional elites. Instead, Belgian colonial policy sought to undermine traditional elites because they represented resistance to religious conversion. It also prevented the development of a modern assimilationist elite because the creation of a university-level educated elite was believed to encourage African competitors for leadership and possible protest movements.

There was one important and significant exception to this approach—the formation of a Congolese clergy. Significantly, the first Congolese Catholic priest was ordained in 1917, while the first lay university student was graduated in 1956.[4] Thus, while there were very few university graduates at the time of independence, many Congolese had, in fact, achieved university-level training in Catholic seminaries. Basic primary-level literacy was widely achieved in a relatively short time, and the Church was resoundingly successful in its goal of conversion to Catholicism. Although Church policy was profoundly paternalistic, unlike the conscious separation of the races in other aspects of life under Belgian colonial rule, the Church aimed at some measure of racial equality within its own institutions. However, this was limited to the confines of Church activity:

> The Church was, in effect, the only modern structure in the Congo that was progressively Africanized. It . . . probably explains why the Church was the only national structure to survive the collapse of 1960. But, it is also important to note that not only did the Church-controlled education system not produce secular equivalents to the Congolese clergy, but the clergy was never allowed to exercise leadership functions outside the narrow confines of Church activities. On the contrary, the Congolese priest was instructed to cooperate with the colonial administration, sometimes even in a humiliating fashion.[5]

The triad of Belgian colonial rule operated quite independently of the Belgian government and presented a hassle-free picture of the Congo to the Belgian people: "au Congo, pas de problème," was a common saying in Brussels, suggesting that there was little discontent about Belgian rule among the Congolese. Indeed, when an anti-Belgian riot erupted in Leopoldville [6] in January 1959, it took the Belgian public and the Belgians living in the Congo completely by surprise, as they somehow thought that all the political changes that had taken place in Africa, and even across the river in Brazzaville, since the end of Word War II, would not touch "their" colony.

Nationalism and the Road to Independence

After World War II, the Belgian Congo experienced an economic boom. The Congo was transformed by Belgian investment policies and by the creation of a broader social-service delivery program. By 1956, the Belgian government began to change its policy and encouraged or allowed some Congolese *evolués*—relatively well-educated Congolese but without university training—to express protopolitical ideas. The Congolese, until then, had been insulated from the growing pan-Africanist and anticolonial movements taking hold throughout the continent, largely because they had been denied travel outside of the Congo. Indeed, the earliest protests began with specific demands for greater Congolese participation in colonial administration. The grievances were often formulated by urban ethnic associations, but also by vaguely ideological "debating" societies inspired by Belgian political parties and nongovernmental organizations (NGOs). Later, some of these groups transformed themselves into political parties.

In these early years of quasi-political mobilization, the most radical group was created by the Bakongo, who supported what was at the beginning a cultural organization and later a political party, the Association des Bakongo (ABAKO). The ABAKO was the first Congolese organization to demand independence. Its leaders were held responsible for the January 1959 riots in Leopoldville and were jailed. The Bakongo felt betrayed by the rest of the Congolese who neither followed their lead at that time, nor undertook any protests at the jailing of their leaders. This was one factor, coupled with the deep cultural and historical pride that the Bakongo manifested in the past glory of the Kongo empire, which led to their considering the possibility of separating from other groups and creating a homogeneous Kongo state with the Kongo in Congo-Brazzaville and Angola.

Another region in which such centrifugal forces manifested themselves was in South Katanga, where a political party dominated by the Lunda developed. The Confédération des Associations Tribales de Katanga (CONAKAT) exhibited strong federalist tendencies, encouraged by conservative Belgian circles, and argued that most of the wealth in the Congo was produced by the copper mines in Katanga while all of the revenue went to the capital. At that time CONAKAT also had links to the white settler–dominated Federation of Rhodesia and Nyasaland.

Therefore, in the period just before independence, not all Congolese people embraced the notion of a united Congo. Bakongo separatism evaporated when the Belgians accepted rapid decolonization and when their leader, Joseph Kasavubu, was elected president of the country. On the other hand, CONAKAT separatism resulted in a real secession movement supported by Belgian military and white mercenaries. It ended only after UN military action two years after independence.

The final phase of anticolonial nationalism in the Congo began with the aforementioned Leopoldville riots in January 1959. The importance of the riots lay not only in the fact that the colonial forces lost control over the African neighborhoods of Leopoldville for several days, but far more importantly, also because for the first time in memory the Congolese saw their white rulers express fear. The subsequent policy of the colonial administration to expel unemployed Congolese men from Leopoldville and forcibly return them to their villages simply had the effect of breaking the broom of the sorcerer's apprentice. These events opened the door for the mobilization of the rural masses by the elite-dominated nascent political parties. In some instances, entire regions allowed themselves to be mobilized and paid party membership dues within a matter of a few weeks. Some key regions, such as the Bakongo-dominated Lower Congo Province, became totally ungovernable as people refused to pay taxes, attend courts, or even avail themselves of medical services. In this atmosphere, Belgium had the choice of reasserting control militarily or bending with the wind and accepting independence. Expediting military forces would have involved a vote in the Belgian parliament where sufficient support did not exist for such an intervention. Belgian policy at that point fell back on the only path available—agreeing to immediate negotiations in the hope that this would isolate the more radical leaders and their supporters, and bring what they thought would be the pro-Belgian majority to power. This policy decision was based on the knowledge that the Congolese nationalist movement at the time of the independence struggle was much more fragmented than its counterparts elsewhere in Africa. The meeting to decide the Congo's future, however, resulted in the first negative surprise for Belgian leaders—all of the Congolese delegates united and demanded the participation of Patrice Lumumba, who at that time was in prison. Lumumba was recognized as the most radical nationalist leader. He was released from his Katanga jail cell and flown directly to the conference in Brussels. A second major disappointment came when all the Congolese participants at the conference demanded immediate independence. With its back against the wall, hoping for the emergence of moderate Congolese leadership after the projected national elections, the Belgian cabinet modified its plans and accepted 30 June 1960 as the date for the transfer of power to a Congolese government. The third major disappointment to Belgian policy occurred in May 1960 when the more radical of the political parties—Patrice Lumumba's Mouvement National Congolais (MNC), Joseph Kasavubu's ABAKO, and Antoine Gizenga and Cleophas Kamitatu's Parti Solidaire Africain (PSA)—won the election.

After very difficult negotiations, Congolese political leaders agreed to elect Kasavubu president and Lumumba prime minister, with a cabinet of national union that included both friends and enemies of the new prime minister.[7] But this uneasy compromise was shattered a few days after independence was declared when the Force Publique, the colonial army, mutinied. Until Lumumba's emergence as prime minister, the policy of the

Belgian government had been to oppose any division of the Congo after independence, anticipating that the government of an independent Congo would bring moderate pro-Belgian political forces to power and thus preserve Belgian influence, as had been the case with France in French West and Equatorial Africa. When radical nationalist forces and leaders—perceived to be pro-communist and anti-Belgian—emerged from the elections, some powerful Belgian circles supported the attempted secessions of Katanga and South Kasai provinces. In both cases, the motivation for those Belgian circles was antagonism toward Lumumba, whom they and other Western powers demonized as a communist puppet. Furthermore, they were also motivated by their desire to retain Belgian mining rights in South Kasai and Katanga, the main loci of diamond and copper mining at that time. In sum, the beginning of Congo's independence was a particularly difficult one; the anticolonial nationalist movement had not achieved anything resembling unity, the colonial army mutinied a few days after independence was declared, the richest provinces attempted to secede, and almost as soon as independence was won, it was to a considerable extent lost.

The Independent State
In the hectic months following the mutiny of the Force Publique and the expedition of a UN force to the Congo, Joseph Mobutu was appointed by Lumumba to be the chief of staff of the new Congo army, the Armée Nationale Congolaise (ANC).[8] Mobutu was instrumental in halting the decomposition of the ANC and reestablishing discipline, but in the process he betrayed Lumumba. One of the key tools that Mobutu employed in maintaining army discipline was payments to the mutinous soldiers—payments he was able to make through support from Western powers. This suggests that he had an established relationship with the West, particularly the United States and Belgium.

In September 1960, a little more than two months after independence, differences between President Kasavubu and Prime Minister Lumumba reached the point where Kasavubu dismissed Lumumba and Lumumba declared the act to be unconstitutional. This gave Mobutu the opportunity to engage in a Western-supported military coup, arguing that in the interest of "order" he had neutralized both Kasavubu and Lumumba. He received substantial help from the West and the United Nations to accomplish this. However, at this point, Mobutu did not take over the reins of government but handed them over to a "College of Commissioners" made up of young Congolese university graduates who were supposed to act as technical caretakers of government services. In effect, the Congo was virtually under a UN protectorate and the amount of power that the college possessed was quite limited. However, Mobutu, the College of Commissioners, and politicians who had sided with either Kasavubu or Mobutu, all feared

Lumumba's capacity to mobilize the Congolese masses and thus tried to imprison him. International pressures were such, however, that the UN presence in the Congo found it expedient to "protect" Lumumba's residence. For weeks, Lumumba was under effective house arrest surrounded by a cordon of UN troops, who were in turn surrounded by Mobutu-loyal ANC forces.

To remain politically active, Lumumba had to escape from his paralyzing position in Kinshasa, and an escape was organized with the objective of reuniting him with supporters in his home base, Kisangani. While initially successful, Lumumba was captured by forces loyal to Mobutu and ultimately shipped off to Katanga, led by secessionist leader, Moise Tshombe, where he was assassinated almost immediately upon arrival.

The Congo Rebellions

Lumumba's assassination was not the end of the alliance of radical political leaders that had formed around him. First, some of them had come together in Kisangani and formed a government claiming to be the legitimate central authority for the country. This regime, competing with Kinshasa, was able to gain the support of some army units and thus continued to exist for some time. Those of Lumumba's collaborators who stayed in the Kinshasa-controlled areas either compromised or were driven from positions of power, and often went into exile.

During these early years, the standard of living of the Congolese people dropped precipitously and the high hopes that they had held for the results of independence were bitterly disappointed. In the summer of 1963, one of Lumumba's closest associates, Pierre Mulele, returned from exile and began to organize a revolutionary movement in the Kwilu District, his home region east of Kinshasa. This movement held a vaguely Marxist ideology and gained some support from sympathetic states. Within a matter of weeks, a full-scale rebellion was under way against the Western-supported government in Kinshasa. A few months later, a second arena of revolt started in the northeast of the Congo. With the exception of the ABAKO-controlled area, most of the areas that rose up had voted for the more radical parties in the May 1960 elections and had supported the pro-Lumumba alliance.

There is little doubt that left to its own resources the Kinshasa government would have fallen to the forces of rebellion. When this revolutionary movement began, UN forces had virtually withdrawn from the Congo, and the Kinshasa authorities were saved by massive Western aid. External assistance for the government consisted of arms supplies from the United States; a small, relatively secret air force piloted by Miami-recruited Cuban pilots organized by the U.S. Central Intelligence Agency; the recruitment of battalion-sized white mercenary units largely made up of French, Belgian, and South African soldiers and adventurers; and the organization of an airlifted commando attack against the capital of the movement, Kisangani, by Belgium and the United States.[9]

When the revolutionary movement was defeated, there was an attempt to return to party politics in the Congo, but the governments that ensued were weak and divided. In 1965, Mobutu openly asserted a power he, in fact, held since 1960 but had never formalized. He outlawed political parties and appointed himself state president. This move was initially quite popular, as there was general disillusionment with political leaders and a sense that the great pain and loss of life the country had experienced during the period of revolutionary uprising and its suppression should not be repeated.[10]

Mobutu's Thirty-Year Rule and the Decline of the State

In the years that followed, Mobutu transformed a military coup into a single-party system of government and an authoritarian state.[11] He created what he claimed was a popular movement rather than a political party, the Mouvement Populaire de la Republique (MPR), and financed a mass mobilization effort that made every Congolese, from childhood to death, a member of the MPR. By the late 1960s and early 1970s, the MPR rivaled the power of the state, and a competitive balance developed between the state structure and the party structure. Both government administrators and the party presidents had the power to report to their highest authorities where the two structures intersected. This system produced an extraordinary degree of grievance articulation that could have been developed into an instrument of governance responsive to the interests of common people. The eternal quarrels that it also produced, however, were anathema to Mobutu's vision of authoritarian governance. Institutional changes were made that resulted in the synchronization of the two structures at all levels of the party and the government so that administrators became ex officio party presidents, pay scales were synchronized, and grievance articulation by and large died.

Under the Mobutist system, higher levels of governance systematically followed an endless process of group favoritism, division, payoff, and neutralization. Due not only to revenue from the export of resources, but also to massive loans from international financial institutions and private banks, the state's wealth and relative stability during this period resulted in one of the most corrupt systems of governance in the world. The state became completely nonresponsive to the interests of common citizens whose standard of living continued to decline while the regime's favored went from one ostentatious excess to another.

During Mobutu's thirty-year rule, the state abandoned virtually all social-service delivery functions and the country's socioeconomic infrastructure completely deteriorated. The informal economy thrived. Inflation was so high that only the lowest level of the economy employed the national currency; any substantial transaction was conducted with U.S. dollars.

By the late 1980s, the Mobutu regime had ceased to have any legitimacy with the Congolese people.

The political aristocracy that formed around Mobutu preyed on a Congolese economy based upon exports of primary products—mainly copper, cobalt, industrial diamonds, and other minerals. Revenues collected from mining concessions to foreign firms and from the largest state mining consortium, Gécamines, rarely went directly into the state treasury. This theft by the highest echelons of the state was replicated among the lower echelons that needed to secure some income, since civil servants and soldiers often went months without a paycheck. The *matabiche*, or "gift," became a standard operating fee for any official business transaction.

Economic decline was further evidenced by the total neglect of agriculture. In the rural areas the Mobutu regime was unable to control productivity that declined with each passing year. Unlike the situation that prevailed in the mining sector, which the state could tap with relative ease for revenue even when productivity declined sharply, revenue from agriculture virtually collapsed.[12] Some large-scale agriculture did survive under Mobutu, but it was mostly in the hands of large private capital—former colonial companies, multinational enterprises, and foreign-managed industrial enterprises—and it produced little income for the state coffers. The rural population was increasingly reduced to subsistence farming or small-scale food production that fed the growing urban population.[13]

In 1973, the Mobutu regime announced a policy of the "Zairianization" of all foreign-owned business. These businesses were appropriated by the state and handed over to friends and family of President Mobutu, who, in turn, used the money to buy new cars, homes, and clothes. Inventories were liquidated and not replenished, and by mid-1974, shortages and long lines for foodstuffs and other consumer goods were commonplace in all cities, including Kinshasa. These new business owners not only pillaged their businesses, but fired workers and either replaced them with family members or did not replace them at all since there was often no business left to run. By 1980, in a country with total population of over 24 million, many of those of working age were unemployed. In Kinshasa, with half of the country's wage earners, the rate was over 40 percent for males over eighteen years of age; Kananga and Mbuji-Mayi had an unemployment rate of 80 percent.[14]

The economy, already vulnerable due to the long-standing predatory practices of the state, was deeply affected by external shocks suffered by many African states during the late 1970s after the tripling of petroleum prices. In addition, the closing of the Benguela railroad as a result of the Angolan civil war; the two Shaba (Katanga) invasions (by the so-called Katanga Tigers, former supporters of Moise Tshombe who had fled to Angola after the defeat of Katanga secession); and the severe drop in world copper prices further impacted the state. By the early 1990s, the national currency, the Zaire, valued at US$0.50 in the early 1970s, was valued at US$1 for 7,500 Zaires.

It is, however, interesting that these conditions did not result in an internal upheaval. Some would argue that this was due to the coercive system in place, and although that was one factor, in fact stiff coercion was rarely used. In our view, the reason for this absence of violent protest has to be seen in the history of the Congo after 1960. The price paid by the Congolese during the 1963–1968 revolutionary period was so heavy and the number of deaths so great that subsequently up to 1990 there was no organized nationwide mobilization of a movement willing to employ political violence against Mobutu's rule. Some protests did occur, such as the 1977–1978 invasions by the Katanga Tigers, who had been in exile in Angola since the 1960s. In the face of this violent challenge, the Mobutu regime proved very weak, but was immediately given military support by Morocco, France, Belgium, and the United States. Of course there were a number of nonviolent protests, such as anti-Mobutu demonstrations by students. The foreign support given to Mobutu was seen by opponents as proving that the Congolese would not succeed in overthrowing him. But this situation changed, slowly but radically, with the end of the Cold War and the gradual withdrawal of U.S. support for Mobutu.

Liberalization, Political Opposition, and the Sovereign National Conference

The process of democratization in the Congo began at least as early as January 1990, when President Mobutu, facing growing internal pressures for reform and democratization during a sustained economic crisis and a significant drop in international support, took steps toward reform.

There had already been defections from the MPR. What ultimately became the largest opposition party, the Union pour la Démocratie et le Progrès Social (UDPS) had its beginnings in 1980 when a few members of the ostensibly Mobutu-controlled parliament called for multiparty democracy. They were met immediately with repression. Nonetheless, they persisted and in 1982 formed the UDPS.

The UDPS maintained a consistent policy of demanding democratic reforms and rejecting all forms of armed opposition. Indeed, there were moments in the declining days of the Mobutu dictatorship when elements of the military as well as foreign actors appealed to the UDPS leader, Etienne Tshisekedi, to lead a coup d'état backed by force. These proposals were always rejected.

Under pressure from the UDPS and others in the opposition, Mobutu invited individuals to submit written lists of grievances—an opportunity that thousands enthusiastically adopted—and in April 1990 he announced the end of single-party rule. This led to the convening, on 7 August 1991, of the National Sovereign Conference (CNS—Conference Nationale Souveraine), a body of 2,842 delegates taken from political parties and civic and religious organizations across the country that produced a widely accepted plan for a peaceful transition to democracy. The CNS terminated its work on 6 December 1992. This national constitutional conference opted for a power-sharing plan (with Mobutu), and elected Etienne Tshisekedi, the leader of the political opposition, as interim prime minister. In full public view with live television coverage, it reviewed Mobutu's performance and the country's history of corruption, political assassinations, and theft from public coffers. Although constantly undermined and manipulated by the Mobutu regime, the conference had a lasting legacy and legitimacy, because it provided a framework within which the nonviolent opposition to the Mobutu regime could formulate its demands for change. Later, the Kabila regime was challenged to uphold the decisions of the CNS—which it refused to do.

All this, however, failed to dislodge Mobutu. Tshisekedi lasted no more than three months as prime minister. Mobutu forcibly evicted all newly appointed ministers from their offices and brazenly reasserted his dominance. While the CNS was ultimately unsuccessful in establishing a new order, it laid the foundation—should it be adopted—for a democratic Congo, a transition from dictatorship toward elections, and a federalist constitutional order.

Mobutu fell from power in May 1997, after a coalition of neighboring states invaded the country in September 1996 and forcibly removed his government.

The Three Congo Wars Since 1996

Since 1996, the Congo has been the battleground for wars and wars within wars, involving, at various times, at least nine African countries as direct combatants and many more as military, financial, and political supporters of those fighting. To this, one must add a number of internal rebellions that are often involved in complex and shifting military and diplomatic networks. These wars have resulted in one of the most devastating humanitarian disasters of our day, resulting in what some have estimated as 3.5 million deaths from war, famine, and disease, and an internal displacement rate of nearly 10 percent of the population.[15]

A series of tragic events transformed an impoverished, yet relatively nonviolent, Congolese society into an arena of conflict and war. The first was the genocide of the Rwandan Tutsi in 1994.[16] The failure of international interventions in Rwanda[17] had a profound impact on the Congo. When the deteriorating security situation on the ground led the UN to withdraw most of its Assistance Mission for Rwanda (UNAMIR I) forces two weeks into the genocide, France offered to lead a humanitarian mission to the region until the United Nations could mobilize support for a new operation. On 22 June 1994, UN Security Council Resolution 929 authorized, with Organization for African Unity (OAU) support, a temporary French mission—Opération Turquoise—"for humanitarian purposes in Rwanda until UNAMIR is brought up to the necessary strength."[18] Its mandate was to use "all necessary means" to ensure the humanitarian objectives spelled out in the Security Council's earlier Resolution 925 on UNAMIR[19] to protect internally displaced persons, refugees, and civilians by establishing "secure humanitarian areas," and "provide security and support for the distribution of relief supplies and humanitarian relief operations." Moreover, the resolution authorizing the French intervention stressed "the strictly humanitarian character of this operation which shall be conducted in an impartial and neutral fashion."[20]

Opération Turquoise, however, did something quite contrary to its mandate of neutrality: it allowed the Hutu militias, known as the Interahamwe, the defeated Forces Armées Rwandaises (FAR) units,[21] and their political leaders, along with masses of Rwandan Hutu civilians, to escape across the border into the Congo virtually under French protection while the Rwandan Tutsi population received little protection from the ongoing killings. The influx of about 1 million Rwandan Hutu, in turn, resulted in the profound destabilization of eastern Congo.

By August 1994, after the RPF had defeated the Hutu government in Rwanda, several UN High Commissioner for Refugees (UNHCR) camps were established in eastern Congo near the Rwandan border to shelter the Rwandan Hutu refugees, *génocidaires, army* units, and leaders. For the next two years, while the international community fed the inmates of the camps, the camps were used as staging grounds from which these Interahamwe/ex-FAR regrouped and launched offensives against the new Tutsi-dominated government in Rwanda. The presence of this large, new, armed population of Hutu changed the ethnic balance in the Kivus, especially in the southern portion of North Kivu where indigenous Hutu joined forces with the Rwandan Hutu.

Despite the local conditions engendered by the influx of Hutu from Rwanda, the Mobutu government, some Kivu politicians and administrators, and some Congolese military officers in particular, made common cause with the Hutu. A campaign was launched against the Banyamulenge, a Congolese Tutsi community of a particular migration, who live on the High Plateau in South Kivu Province. By the summer of 1996, this campaign had reached crisis proportions, with some Kivu politicians and administrators threatening to expel all Banyamulenge from the country. This threat against the Congolese Tutsi population was deftly used by the Rwandans to legitimate their invasion of the Congo. This invasion was coordinated with the Banyamulenge who also attacked the Hutu in their UNHCR camps in September 1966. The Rwandan government had repeatedly asked the international community to disarm the Hutu in the UNHCR camps, but nothing concrete was done, despite repeated Rwandan warnings that if the international community did not act, Rwanda would take the matter into its own hands.

In September 1996, Rwanda attacked the camps with the goal of eliminating the Interahamwe/ex-FAR threat and to strike a blow against the Hutu-sympathizing Mobutu regime. This joint assault on the camps resulted in dismantling the Interahamwe/ex-FAR's base of operations and allowing the vast majority of Hutu refugees in the camps to flee back over the border into Rwanda. It also marked the beginning of the First Congo War.

The First Congo War

The Rwandans were soon joined by Uganda for similar, although less pressing security reasons. Anti-Museveni insurrection movements, some of which were supported by the Sudanese government, for years operated out of bases in the Congo with support from the Mobutu government, or at least some of Mobutu's generals.[22] Several months later, Angola joined the alliance against the Mobutu government, also for similar reasons. Its principal adversary, the National Union for the Total Independence of Angola (UNITA), continued to have bases in the Congo and had received substantial support from the United States via Mobutu during the Cold War. Therefore, Angola, Uganda, and Rwanda coalesced around a common goal—to cripple the insurgency movements challenging their governments from bases in the Congo.

To avoid being seen as aggressors and invaders, the Rwandan and Ugandan governments immediately sponsored the creation of an alliance of small and obscure exiled anti-Mobutu Congolese revolutionary groups. Laurent Kabila emerged as the principal spokesperson of the Alliance des forces Démocratiques pour la Libération du Congo (AFDL) and became the protégé of the coalition's foreign sponsors. Kabila was the only one of the Congolese recruited into this alliance who was even remotely known outside the Congo. He had been a zone commander in the Congo rebellions of the mid-1960s, a Lumumbist, and for over twenty years the leader of a small revolutionary redoubt in South Kivu where Che Guevara and a few hundred Cubans joined the Congo rebellion in 1964. The attempt to give a Congolese revolutionary character to this conflict was largely successful because of the worldwide rejection of Mobutu, but there is little doubt that the overwhelming military force employed against Mobutu was foreign.

By the end of 1996, Mobutu's army was in full retreat, looting, raping, and killing Congolese civilians along the way. Mobutu desperately sought help from his friends and allies abroad, but with the end of the Cold War and the new emphasis on democratic principles and transparent governance, his corrupt rule had become an embarrassment to most Western governments. His appeals fell on deaf ears. The patent fact that his country was undergoing an invasion did not even elicit a Security Council condemnation. Mobutu's African friends acted in much the same fashion; no African leader sent help. The only support he received was from UNITA in Angola. France gave him some help with which he was able to hire some Serbian mercenaries, but they were largely ineffective. Dying from prostate cancer, Mobutu was ultimately packed off into exile, where he died shortly after. The anti-Mobutu alliance marched across the Congo and into Kinshasa in a matter of eight months.

The conduct of Mobutu's army, after years of scarcity and neglect under his dictatorship, helps explain why the Congolese people, by and large, welcomed and gave aid to the anti-Mobutu alliance. The AFDL recruited thousands of young men and boys as the alliance advanced toward Kinshasa. Entire units of Mobutu's army defected to it. Some of Kabila's actions on the path to Kinshasa, such as instituting local elections for town administrators—crudely organized but by all accounts free[23]— gave the appearance of a commitment to democratic rule. Reports claiming that alliance forces were systematically rounding up and executing retreating Hutu, however, followed the advancing alliance. The international press began referring to it as a "clean-up" operation aimed at eliminating the remaining perpetrators of the Rwandan genocide.[24] There is no doubt that massacres of Rwandan Hutu occurred, but there is considerable controversy over who conducted them and the extent to which Kabila had the power to stop them even if he had wanted to do so. On 26 April 1997 Aldo Ajello, the European Union's special representative, met Kabila and received his authorization to visit Hutu camps south of Kisangani where massacres were alleged to have occurred. What follows is Ajello's account of what he saw and experienced:

> We reached the main camp [about 30 km from Kisangani] and we could see a few terrorized people who had been pushed back by the soldiers to the camp that same day. The largest part of the camp was empty and devastated. The signs of the aggression were evident everywhere. The holes of the bullets were visible in the tents. The poor belongings of the refugees were spread over the camp. Six dead bodies were lying in the bush a few meters from the camp. We were able to approach some of the refugees and the stories they told us were always the same. They had been attacked during the night by a few civilians supported by a large number of soldiers who started shooting blindly at the tents. Some of them had been able to run away but many had been killed.
>
> What we had seen was sufficient to sustain the allegations that a huge massacre had taken place there, but we decided to proceed in the direction of Ubundo. Unfortunately, we were stopped a few hundred meters from the camp, at a Rwandan checkpoint . . . We informed the officer in charge that we had Kabila's authorization to go up to Ubundo, but we were refused permission to proceed. . . . It was evident that the area was under direct Rwandan control and that Kabila's authority was neither recognized nor respected.[25]

Before Kinshasa was captured, South African president Mandela attempted to mediate between Mobutu and Kabila in an effort to ensure a smooth transition and to avoid unnecessary bloodshed. However, Kabila thwarted this effort by humiliating Mobutu. A more serious side effect of the mediation was the complete exclusion of all Congolese political forces from these and other negotiations. International actors were focused on two goals: getting rid of Mobutu and avoiding military confrontation. One particular worry was the fear that the final assault on Kinshasa would result in a bloodbath. This did not happen, as the last troops loyal to Mobutu retreated and allowed the alliance to march into Kinshasa on 17 May 1997. Kabila assumed the presidency and was beholden to no Congolese forces other than the young *kadogos* who had been recruited during the previous months.[26]

It is important to note that at no time since the early 1960s was the Congolese state structure weaker than at this juncture. The Congolese army was so weakened that foreign armies were able to march across the country and change the regime with little resistance. Local Congolese opposition leaders enjoyed great popular support and were under no control or restraint from the capital. Secession would have been possible had anyone chosen to lead one. Indeed, the governments of the invading armies might well have welcomed the partition of the Congo. Rwanda did have ambitions to annex a part of the Kivus in eastern Congo. Yet, not a single significant Congolese leader or group mobilized in favor of splitting up the country. All aimed, instead, to capture the whole prize. Moreover, they knew there would be no public support for partition.

Although Kabila had a relatively short postwar honeymoon, he did make some initial domestic changes that were welcomed by the Congolese people. The rate of inflation was reduced, but foremost among these was the real improvement in personal and property security that resulted from the elimination of arbitrary and capricious roadblocks and arrests by unpaid soldiers and police officers, a daily phenomenon during the latter years of Mobutu's rule. This change was less appreciated by the elites, however, as many not only experienced a direct loss of access and influence, but also experienced property seizures with the changing of the guard.[27] In a symbolic gesture aimed to eliminate all traces of the Mobutu regime, Kabila renamed the country the Democratic Republic of Congo, changed the flag, national anthem, and national currency, and renamed streets, towns, and the national football team, mostly reverting to the names used at independence.

However open the nonviolent opposition was initially to giving a new Kabila government a chance, relations between them deteriorated very quickly. Kabila went on to reject all power-sharing arrangements with the numerous political parties that had been established during the last few years of the Mobutu regime; he prohibited all party activity and refused to cooperate with NGOs, which became increasingly critical of his authoritarian rule. Kabila not only refused to give some recognition to the long struggle that groups such the UDPS had conducted against Mobutu, but imposed a new dictatorship inspired by his long association with Marxist revolutionaries. He attempted to initiate a "cultural revolution" in which ordinary citizens were to be watched by street committees, and only the AFDL was allowed to function; civil society was to synchronize its activities with the AFDL, and most trials were to be held before military courts. The behavior of Rwandan soldiers in Kinshasa added to the alienation of the population from the AFDL. Many began to see the Rwandan troops in the capital as an army of occupation rather than an army of liberation. None of this corresponded to the desires of the Congolese public, and Kabila's popularity dropped rapidly.

In the short fifteen months between the end of the First Congo War and the start of the second, Kabila managed to antagonize the UN, Western donors, his domestic opposition, and his foreign sponsors. By early 1998 it became increasingly clear that the leaders who had been most responsible for putting Kabila into power were dissatisfied with his performance. His presidency had not produced the results they wanted. Kabila had not succeeded in ending the problem of border insecurity by neutralizing the insurgency groups threatening Uganda, Rwanda, and Angola from the Congo—the principal reason that motivated their intervention in the first place. It was, however, somewhat unrealistic to expect Kabila to deal with the foreign insurgency groups still operating in the Congo: He had barely begun to create a new army; the Rwandans and Ugandans had de facto military control of the east where the main insurgency concentrations were located; and the Rwandans held top leadership in the organization of the new Congo army, the Force Armée Congolaise (FAC).

Kabila had a further problem in getting himself accepted by the Congolese public. His claim to leadership was largely based on having led a "revolution" against Mobutu. But as time passed it became increasingly obvious that the "revolution" was more a foreign invasion than an uprising of the Congolese against a hated dictator. In addition, two groups of Congolese who had fought in the war, the *kadogos* and the Banyamulenge, both became increasingly unpopular—the *kadogos* because of their ruthless, arbitrary, and violent behavior toward the civilian population, and the Banyamulenge because they were increasingly confounded with all other Tutsi and thus seen as Rwandan foreigners (on this issue see the survey results presented later in this chapter). The Banyamulenge were also seen as suspect because they held high positions in Kabila's new government and army.

The split between Kabila and his foreign sponsors may have been inevitable because any Congolese leader would have tried to seek popular legitimacy, which would have required an effort to distance himself from foreign, militarily present sponsors. Indeed, public opinion surveys conducted by the Bureau d'Études, de Recherches et de Consulting International (BERCI) in Kinshasa during 1997 and 1998 clearly show that the Rwandan presence was profoundly unpopular, and that when Kabila ousted the Rwandans, his popularity skyrocketed.[28]

The Second Congo War

There were numerous indications in June and July 1998 that relations between Kabila and the Rwandans had deteriorated to a point of mutual distrust. Kabila increasingly fell back on his supporters from Katanga, his home province. The chief of staff of the FAC, the Rwandan officer James Kabarebe, was fired and replaced by Kabila's brother-in-law. On 27 July, the Rwandan military was asked to leave the Congo immediately and they did so in an atmosphere of biting antagonism and mutual suspicion.

On 2 August 1998, the Second Congo War broke out when two of the best and largest units in the new Congolese army mutinied. They were stationed in the east and were in close contact with the Rwandan military, and Rwandan army troops crossed the border to support them. In Kinshasa, Congolese Tutsi soldiers in the FAC refused orders to disarm and were attacked by FAC soldiers of other ethnic backgrounds. Most of them were killed and a pogrom against all Tutsi, civilian or military, men, women, and children included, took hold. In subsequent weeks, the pogrom was extended to all the areas of the country under Kabila's control. On 4 August, in a spectacular cross-continental airlift, a hijacked plane full of Rwandan and Ugandan soldiers landed at Kitona army base in western Congo where some ten to fifteen thousand former Mobutu soldiers were being "reeducated." These soldiers joined the Rwandan and Ugandan forces and began a march on Kinshasa. Within two weeks, and with the Kabila regime facing almost certain military defeat, a group of Congolese politicians, ranging from former anti-Mobutu alliance leaders to former Mobutists, united in Goma to form the political wing of the anti-Kabila movement, the Rassemblement Congolais pour la Démocratie (RCD).

On 23 August 1998, in striking contrast to its actions in the First Congo War, Angola intervened militarily on behalf of Kabila. It attacked the Rwanda-Uganda forces in the western Congo from its bases in Cabinda and defeated them.[29] Although this cross-continental maneuver aimed at overthrowing Kabila failed as a result of Angola's intervention, the "rebellion" was able to achieve military control over eastern Congo. This second war would no doubt have ended very quickly if it had not been for the Angolan intervention. President Mugabe of Zimbabwe also supported Kabila militarily, but Zimbabwe was too far from the Congo to have saved the regime on its own. Kinshasa would have fallen before sufficient Zimbabwean aid would have arrived. Angola's decision to change its policy had a profound impact on the war and on politics in the region. The Angolan intervention was probably due to its concern that the anti-Kabila alliance had struck a deal with Angola's standing enemy, UNITA.

Zimbabwe, Angola, and Namibia invoked Kinshasa's recent Southern African Development Community (SADC) membership as a reason to launch an SADC military intervention to defend the Kabila government from foreign aggression.[30] Zimbabwe's president Mugabe held the chairmanship of SADC's Political, Defense, and Security Organ during that time, and used his position to secure an SADC umbrella for Zimbabwe's, Angola's, and Namibia's military intervention. This deeply divided the subregional organization, as there were members, most notably South Africa, who strongly opposed an SADC commitment to Kabila and instead argued that the organization should take a more neutral stand and support negotiations between the parties in conflict.

For the next year, the Congo became the arena of a regional war. Kinshasa received direct military support from Angola, Zimbabwe, Namibia, and Chad, while the "rebels" were supported by Uganda, Rwanda, and later, and to a lesser extent, Burundi. Significantly, Kabila mobilized the Interahamwe/ex-FAR and other Rwandan Hutu from the Congo and the region, and incorporated them in ethnically homogeneous battalions in his army. Seeking support wherever he could find it, Kabila also made an alliance with many Mai Mai guerrillas in eastern Congo, particularly in the RCD-controlled area. The Mai Mai are Congolese guerrilla fighters, often in ethnically homogeneous groups, who had a very checkered past in their relations with Kabila.[31] These groups have never managed to come together under a central leadership structure but share one common goal: opposition to any nonlocal rulers over eastern Congo. For Kabila, the Mai Mai constituted one of the best weapons at his disposal against the RCD and the Rwandan occupation of eastern Congo. He helped the Mai Mai with weapons shipments and gave them moral support by naming some of their leaders to high positions in the FAC. Kinshasa even declared that the Mai Mai were a part of the FAC, and that Mai Mai–controlled areas of eastern Congo were FAC-controlled areas.[32]

Kinshasa's support of the Mai Mai and mobilization of the Rwandan Hutu had another effect in eastern Congo—it created an alliance of opportunity between Interahamwe/ex-FAR (later renamed Armée pour la Libération du Rwanda and still later, Forces Démocratiques de Libération du Rwanda) guerrilla units still operating against Rwandan interests and the Mai Mai. As time passed, this alliance between Kinshasa, the Mai Mai, and the Interahamwe/ex-FAR, to which one can also add the Burundian Hutu insurgency movement, the Forces de défense de la démocratie (FDD), became Kinshasa's strongest card in a war in which its army and its allies were never able to gain important military victories against the RCD-Rwanda-Uganda alliance.

The RCD alliance was weakened by internal division and by armed challenges to its legitimacy in much of eastern Congo, specifically in North and South Kivu. The relationship between Rwanda and Uganda deteriorated, and each laid claim to its own sphere of influence. The RCD split into two factions with separate military establishments, one supported by Rwanda, the other by Uganda. RCD-Goma, the seat of the original rebel movement, was under Rwandan influence. RCD/ML (Mouvement de libération) was under Ugandan influence. Uganda also helped to create a completely new anti-Kinshasa movement, the Mouvement de libération du Congo (MLC) which soon became dominant in northern Congo.

As in 1996–1997, this moment in the Congo's history could have given rise to a leader or movement seeking the division of the Congo into separate states. A de facto division had taken place with political and military establishments having created what became recognized borders between the Kinshasa and the rebel-controlled zones. At a later stage, these borders were even monitored by MONUC, the UN observer mission in the Congo. Yet, despite the deep antagonisms that existed between the leaders of the different movements, not a single one postulated a breakup of the Congo.

There were at least twenty failed efforts by the UN, OAU, SADC, and individual mediators to stop the war, but most active military engagements during the Second Congo War only ended when a stalemate emerged and each side realized that military victory was not possible. In addition, considerable Western pressure was exerted, especially on the rebel forces and their foreign patrons, to stop advancing. The result of the stalemate was the Lusaka Cease-Fire Agreement in the DRC, ultimately signed by all belligerents in August 1999.[33] The genius of the Lusaka Agreement was that it recognized the overlapping layers of interstate and intrastate actors involved in the war, and recognized the serious concerns of Rwanda and Uganda regarding insurgency movements based in the Congo. The agreement specifically called for disarming foreign militia groups in the Congo—the so-called negative forces—and the withdrawal of all foreign forces from the country. The agreement also provided for an all-inclusive Congolese process, the "Inter-Congolese Dialogue," whose charge was to produce a new transitional political order for the Congo. To achieve this, the Lusaka Agreement mandated a "neutral facilitator" to organize this process, and the former president of Botswana, Sir Ketumile Masire, was appointed as facilitator in December 1999. An important provision was that all parties to the internal dispute, whether armed or not, including the government in Kinshasa, were required to participate in this dialogue as equals.

Congolese armed groups in eastern Congo such as the Mai Mai, were neither represented at the peace negotiations in Lusaka, nor were they asked to sign the agreement. They were also not mentioned as participants in the internal dialogue. The omission of the Mai Mai from the agreement has been particularly serious, since they continued to fight and were under no formal obligation to respect a cease-fire; this resistance continued

Map 4.1 Military Groups in the Democratic Republic of Congo, 2000

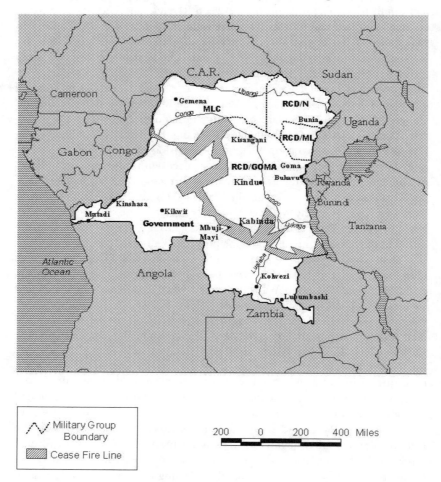

Source: Binghamton University GIS Core Facility.

despite their close relationship with, and indeed incorporation into, the FAC.

The agreement also called for a UN Chapter VII force to enforce the cease-fire and disarm the foreign militias. After first deploying a small technical assessment team, the Security Council adopted Resolution 1279 on 30 November 1999, which authorized the United Nations Observer Mission in the Democratic Republic of Congo (MONUC or Mission de l'Organization des Nations Unies en République Démocratique du Congo). That force was expanded to 5,537 military personnel in 2002 and to 10,800 in 2003, numbers that have been widely criticized as far too small to monitor a peace agreement effectively.[34] The mission has the authority, under Chapter VII, "to take the necessary action . . . to protect United Nations personnel . . . ensure the security of and freedom of movement of its personnel, and protect civilians under imminent threat of physical violence." However, as MONUC's failure to intervene to stop the 14 May 2002 massacres in Kisangani as well as the May 2004 clashes in Bukavu indicate, even this limited mandate has not been followed—a failure due as much to earlier internal management problems within MONUC and the ultra-prudent interpretation its leaders have given to the terms of reference under which it operates. Moreover, while MONUC is mandated with coordinating the disarmament, demobilization, reintegration, repatriation, and resettlement (DDRRR) of foreign militia, it is not authorized to disarm them by force. The problem with voluntary compliance, of course, is that many do not wish to be disarmed.

The Lusaka Agreement envisioned a six-week-long national dialogue between armed and unarmed Congolese groups about the future institutions and the interim government of the Congo. This dialogue was to concur with the disarming of armed groups and the departure of foreign armies. Until his assassination in January 2001, Laurent Kabila repeatedly refused to cooperate not only with the United Nations, but also with the dialogue's neutral facilitator, former president Masire. Kabila never did accept the agreement's provision that all parties, including the government, would enjoy the same status in the inter-Congolese dialogue. After Kabila's assassination, his son Joseph Kabila, who took power in January 2001, took steps to revive the national dialogue, which finally took place in Sun City, South Africa, in February 2001. Despite numerous efforts by South Africa, the dialogue failed to achieve even a general agreement among the key actors—the government, RDC-Goma, and the MLC. A separate agreement, outside the Sun City framework, for a transitional power-sharing arrangement in which Joseph Kabila would remain president and MLC leader Jean-Pierre Bemba would be named prime minister was signed by the government and the MLC. This was rejected, however, by the Rwanda-backed RCD-Goma, and by the nonmilitarized political opposition.

The Sun City dialogue failed because the balance achieved by the Lusaka Agreement (the interests of the foreign states and the disarming of foreign militia) was ignored, as was the emerging Third Congo War in the east and its devastating consequences. Once it became clear that national unification under its domination was not forthcoming, the Kinshasa-MLC pact ceased to have any interest for Kinshasa. The government walked away, choosing instead, to enter into bilateral agreements with Rwanda and Uganda, and to marginalize other rebel movements opposing it. A bilateral agreement signed between Kinshasa and Kigali in Pretoria on 30 July 2002 resulted in the withdrawal of most—though probably not all—Rwandan forces in return for Kinshasa's promise to dismantle the Rwandan Hutu militias, purge Hutu leaders from government and military positions, and hand over *génocidaire* leaders to the International Court or Rwanda. This was, in fact, a return to the Lusaka Agreement in which the "exchange" is implicit. A similar agreement was concluded with Kampala in Luanda on 6 September 2002, resulting in the withdrawal of most, but not all, Ugandan troops. The withdrawal of foreign troops, however, created a power vacuum in the east, and a significant increase in violence, partly because the departing occupation forces left behind proxy movements. But it also paved the way to a continuation of the dialogue under South African auspices, and the eventual establishment, in July 2003, of a new transitional government of national unity composed of representatives from all armed and unarmed parties. Modeled loosely after South Africa's transitional government, the new Congolese government is a power-sharing arrangement between President Kabila and four vice-presidents drawn from the two major rebel movements, the former Kinshasa authorities, and civil society. In addition, the cabinet is made up of over sixty ministers and deputy ministers drawn from an even broader group of movements, including representatives of political parties, smaller rebel movements, and the Mai Mai.

The Third Congo War

Since the signing of the Lusaka Agreement, violence and the accompanying humanitarian disaster has been largely limited to two eastern provinces—South and North Kivu. In South Kivu, the violent struggles have been between Mai Mai, Interahamwe/ex-FAR, FDD forces on the one side and the Rwandan, RCD-Goma forces on the other. None of the Mai Mai leaders accepted the Lusaka Agreement cease-fire and argued that as long as there were Rwandan troops in their area they would go on fighting them and their proxy, the RCD. Consistent with the notion that the "enemy of my enemy is my friend," they frequently forged alliances with the Interahamwe/ex-FAR and with the FDD, even though for the Mai Mai these groups are also foreigners they would want out of their region. And, as indicated earlier, they have been materially and morally supported by Kinshasa.

In 2002, the Banyamulenge community on the High Plateau of South Kivu mobilized against the RCD/Rwandan forces, as increasing numbers of Banyamulenge came to the conclusion that being allied to Rwanda was counterproductive for them, especially regarding their goal of being accepted as Congolese citizens (see survey data on this issue). They also felt that the RCD and the Rwandans were not doing enough to protect them from attacks by Congolese neighbors who viewed all Tutsi as Rwandan nationals. A Banyamulenge officer who defected from the RCD found substantial support on the High Plateau in 2001. In opposing the RCD, he was able to forge an alliance between the High Plateau Banyamulenge and the ethnic

Bembe and surrounding Mai Mai groups. This, however, was viewed as a dangerous provocation by the Rwandans and the RCD, and they launched a massive military campaign against the High Plateau in mid-2002.

North Kivu and the district of Ituri have witnessed a different but equally unresolved and deadly series of more localized conflicts over land and resources that have been largely ignored until 2003 by the UN and foreign states involved in the broader conflict in the region. Here, a series of divisions in the RCD/ML has resulted in small, ethnically based Mai Mai groups, often allied with or against Ugandan military officers who profited handsomely—and in some cases continue to do so—from their presence in the Congo. In late 2002, the Kinshasa government struck an alliance with the latest leader of the RCD/ML, Mbusa Nyamwisi, with the aim of gaining a Kinshasa-linked base in the area, which up to that point had been a rebel-controlled (RCD/ML) area. Not only was this not declared a violation of the cease-fire agreement that requires all signatories to hold their positions at the time of its signing, it resulted in an MLC campaign against Mbusa with disastrous consequences for the civilian population in that area. An older interethnic conflict between Hema herders and Lendu farmers has exploded again in recent years because of the absence of effective state power in the area and because such conflicts were often nurtured and encouraged by different Ugandan officers. In yet another division of forces, a new party emerged to control yet another militia, the Uganda People's Congress (UPC).

The Third Congo War is fundamentally different from the first and second. It is far less structured and involves many more, though smaller, military actors. In the First and Second Congo Wars, elements of the international community sought to contain conflict and achieve, at the minimum, cease-fire agreements. This pressure contributed to the Lusaka Agreement. The Third Congo War has not benefited substantially from such initiatives and the result has been endless violence while the rest of the country, though divided, in fact survives without the plague of daily, bloody confrontations. The deepening of hostilities in northeastern Congo and daily reports of gross civilian massacres by rival militia in that region led to a Security Council authorization on 30 May 2003 (Resolution 1484) for a French-led Interim Emergency Multinational Force deployed in Bunia for three months to stabilize Ituri until MONUC could mobilize additional resources to replace the Interim Force. Security Council Resolution 1493 of July 2003 gave MONUC a more robust enforcement mandate in addition to authorizing an increase in its personnel. MONUC has since redeployed most of its peacekeepers to conflict zones in the east, rather than along the old cease-fire lines.

Regarding the main focus of this study, it should be noted that even though the Mai Mai and rebel groups in these arenas of conflict are smaller and weaker than the three "partners" who have dominated the negotiations on the national scene (Kinshasa government, the MLC, and the RCD-Goma), they all are focused on participating in or controlling the central government in Kinshasa. None have articulated, in any way, programs aiming at secession, integration with surrounding states, or independence.

The State of the Nation

Mobutu—"Father" of a Nation
In the core period of the independence struggle, Congolese nationalism was framed in terms of ending Belgian colonial rule. How the Congolese people were to relate to each other, whether they were to remain in the same state, what ideology and form of government to adopt, were all questions to which there were no single answers. During the period of the independence struggle, some Congolese leaders flirted with the idea of splitting up the Belgian Congo at independence and creating separate states. The regions where such sentiments were strongest were Katanga, South Kasai, and also Lower Congo. Belgian policy was initially strongly opposed to such proposals. Two events, however, changed that. First, Lumumba was elected prime minister and that was viewed in many Belgian circles, especially the more conservative ones, as a disaster. Second, immediately after independence, the Force Publique (the colonial army) mutinied. A republic that was independent for four days was thrown into a state of anarchy. One of the consequences of the resulting power vacuum was the secession of Katanga and what was called, appropriately, the "Mining State of South Kasai." Both of these attempts were given considerable support by Belgian forces. In the case of Katanga, units of the Belgian army "protected" the secessionist regime. However, international opposition to these secessionist movements and the deployment of a UN force resulted in their ultimate failure, although in the case of Katanga it did take two military operations by the UN to put an end to this attempt to divide the frontiers inherited from the colonial period.

Shortly after independence and the Katanga secession, a split in leadership occurred along ideological lines. Kinshasa excluded Lumumbists, and Lumumbist ministers and supporters created a "second" national government in Kisangani. However, neither of these movements significantly challenged the unity of the state or the notion of a united Congolese nationality.

The next important chapter in developments along the trajectory of nation formation occurred when the so-called Congo rebellions began. Here again, the issue was ideological with strong Cold War influences and interferences—Kinshasa was supported by the West, especially the United States; and revolutionary forces were supported by the communist world and the radical third world (including Cuba). Neither side contemplated dividing the country or challenging the notion of a single nationality for all

Congolese, although this struggle involved profound ethnic antagonisms, some of which have had long-lasting impact. With some exceptions, mobilization tended to occur along ethnic lines, with ethnic groups either supporting the revolutionary movement or opposing it.

With the defeat of the revolutionary forces and the beginnings of the formal Mobutu dictatorship, a concerted effort was made by the national government to strengthen the national identity and instill values and pride in a common nationality.[35] Mobutu did this by instituting a single political party that went to great lengths to mobilize the public around a personality cult for the leader; he would be the embodiment of the nation. Other instruments used were the organization of successful sports teams, the invitation of the Muhummad Ali–George Foreman world boxing championship and of Apollo astronauts to Kinshasa, and various other exorbitant attempts to inculcate national pride.

These policies did not stop ethnic and regional identities or indeed antagonisms. However, Mobutu was a master in balancing them against each other, and he was, in the end, credited by many observers with having contributed significantly to the acceptance of a single, national identity for most Congolese people. This undoubted achievement was marred by some of his policies toward the end of his tenure of power when, at the close of the Cold War, he could no longer count on the unqualified support of his foreign allies. At that moment he began to use ethnic violence as a means of retaining power. This resulted in the massive ethnic cleansing of Kasai Luba in Katanga in 1993. It also heightened enormously the antagonism toward Congolese Tutsi. While Mobutu cannot be held responsible for all anti-Tutsi sentiment, he did nurture an alliance with the Habyarimana regime in Rwanda and did, at a minimum, permit anti-Tutsi politicians in Kinshasa and in the Kivus to generate a campaign that resulted in the expulsion of the Tutsi from North Kivu and in threats for the mass expulsion of the Banyamulenge from South Kivu. These actions were strongly supported by Kivu politicians expecting to run in elections scheduled to take place—but never held—in the waning years of the Mobutu regime.

National identity was reframed again in the context of the First Congo War. The AFDL, under Laurent Kabila's leadership, adopted a radical, leftist, anti-Western ideology that harkened back to the 1960s. Two things were significant during this period. First, it provided a golden opportunity for a secessionist movement, yet there was no leadership or following in favor of such a move in any region of the Congo. Second, as the Kabila regime took hold, it became apparent that resentment against foreign sponsors of the regime and their troops was its greatest weakness vis-à-vis the public. Although almost unique in contemporary African history, the country's double name change from Congo to Zaire, and then from Zaire back to Congo, seems not to have influenced the Congolese citizenry's identification with the state and nation.

With the development of the Second Congo War, the country was in fact divided into several politicomilitary zones controlled by elites supported in each zone by foreign allies. Once again, if there was any inclination to break up the Congo, these divisions easily could have served the purpose of a claim for an independent state. In fact, none of the leaders sought any solution other than joining and participating in a national government in Kinshasa. The aversion to any form of breakup or separatism is so great that in the Kivus, the notion of federalism, indeed even the word—surely a reasonable, possible institutional structure for a country as vast as the Congo—has become anathema as people fear that support for a federal solution implies separation from the whole.

As shown by the public opinion evidence below, there is pervasive acceptance among all Congolese of their common Congolese nationality. There is one glaring exception, and that concerns the Rwandaphone populations, i.e., the Tutsi, the Hutu, and the separately identified Banyamulenge Tutsi, who are not accepted as Congolese. One can postulate that the three wars that the Congolese have endured and the humiliation they have experienced at the hands of foreign armies has had a powerful strengthening effect on their sense of national identity. It may also explain the rejection of the Tutsi, all of whom have been linked with the Rwandan invaders. However, this does not explain why the Hutu are also rejected. This is particularly interesting in view of the campaign initiated among Congolese and, indeed, African elites claiming that a profound division and antagonism exists among Africans of Bantu as against Hamitic or Nilotic backgrounds. This ideological claim, which has dubious scientific basis, placed the Hutu among the Bantu and the Tutsi among the Hamitic/Nilotic peoples. Its political purpose was to mobilize antagonism against the Tutsi and the Tutsi-led Rwandan government and to legitimate the Kinshasa government's alliance with the Rwandan Hutu insurgents in the Congo. This ideological formulation could be observed not only all over the Congo, but also in Zimbabwe and Gabon. The survey data give almost no support to this ideology. The data suggest that the Hutu are rejected almost as much as the Tutsi and are part of the only group that is excluded from the national community. In sum, at the same time that the identity of the nation over the last forty years has become stronger, it has also become more exclusionary with respect to one particular ethnic group—the Rwandaphone peoples.

Public Opinion Surveys: Data Collection and Analysis

The sheer size of the Congo (roughly the size of Western Europe), warfare, and the Congo's ethnic, linguistic, and geographic diversity complicate survey research.[36] Such a geographically large and complex case mandates surveys in major cities in each region to ensure that ethnic as well as regional dimensions are reflected in it. This would also require surveying samples of the rural populations. Unfortunately, physical and financial restraints did not permit achieving this goal.

These public opinion surveys were first administered in Gemena, in the Congo's northern Equateur Province, in January 2002, and then in the cities of Kinshasa, Mbuji-Mayi, Lumumbashi, and Kikwit in June 2002, thus including the nation's capital and major cities in the south, north, and central Congo. These were conducted with a local polling firm, the Bureau d'Études, de Recherches et de Consulting International (BERCI). While we were able to administer the survey in MLC rebel-controlled territory in the northern town of Gemena, we were prevented by the RCD rebel authorities from administering the survey in the east, despite several efforts to do so.[37]

Most respondents had at least a secondary education, and were evenly split between males and females, except in Gemena where 99 percent were male. The majority of respondents in the BERCI surveys were between the ages of eighteen and thirty-four years. In the Gemena survey, they were between the ages of twenty-five and forty-four. The differences between the BERCI and Gemena samples indicate more arbitrary sampling methods in the Gemena survey.

In terms of the ethnic composition of each city surveyed, at least as reflected in the survey samples, Kinshasa was the least homogeneous. This diversity is not surprising given that it is the capital and a large urban center. It stands to reason that the larger the city, the more diverse the population, which might explain why Kikwit, Mbuji-Mayi, and Gemena were more ethnically homogenous.

The earlier Gemena survey allowed us to fine-tune the questionnaire and clarify, eliminate, or add questions, and amend politically sensitive language.

Training of pollsters focused on three major issues: (1) accurate translation—the survey would have to be administered either in French, Lingala, or Kiswahili[38]; (2) interpretation—how each pollster interpreted the meaning of a question; and (3) ensuring the neutrality of the pollster for questions that were politically or ethnically charged.

Interviews were conducted face-to-face in respondents' homes and responses were kept anonymous. Quality control checks were also built in.

The sample size used for these surveys was 250 for each city regardless of population size. Samples were based on the most recent demographic data available, the 1984 national census. There have been significant demographic changes since the 1984 census, including greater urbanization, but since our samples were taken from urban centers, the assumed change in demography since 1984 can only have resulted in samples that are more representative of the whole population.

Because the interviews were usually conducted in respondents' homes, the high rate of nonresponses to some questions may have been due to fear of reprisals or government persecution.

The Gemena survey was administered somewhat differently and under the auspices of the MLC, the rebel movement that controlled Equateur Province. Because we were not present on the ground during the polling, there was no way for us to verify that the surveys were administered in an unbiased manner.

The analysis of the surveys addresses the following four variables: public commitment to national unity, satisfaction with government and rebel authorities and their services, attitudes toward minority groups, and attitudes toward external state and nonstate actors.

Commitment to National Unity

It is commonly thought that the Congo, given its size, heterogeneity, and history, as well as the current state of conflict, is a divided country. However, in one of the most important questions for this study, the vast majority of respondents—both in the BERCI and Gemena polls—identified themselves as Congolese, suggesting that there may in fact be a strong national identity among the Congolese people.[39]

In order to better understand whether there is a common perception of "national unity," respondents in the BERCI polls were asked what they thought when one spoke of unity of the Congo (see Table 4.1). Gemena was not polled on this question because it was added later. Respondents in Kinshasa and Kikwit responded similarly. Nearly one-third thought of it as the Christian value of brotherly love (29 percent and 33 percent respectively); and nearly half of respondents in both cities showed some nostalgia for the days of Mobutu and colonialism by thinking of it as Mobutu's Zaire (23 percent and 21 percent respectively) or the Belgian Congo (23 percent and 20 percent respectively). In contrast, only 11 percent of respondents in Lumumbashi thought to equate unity with Mobutu's Zaire, and only 14 percent with the Belgian Congo. Reflecting the secessionist past of Katanga Province, 35 percent of its residents in Lumumbashi equated unity with the territorial integrity of the state, the highest such response rate.

Table 4.1   "What Do You Think of When One Speaks of Unity of the Congo?"

	Brotherly Love	Territorial Integrity	Peace and Democracy	Mobutu's Zaire	Belgian Congo
Kinshasa	29	22	4	23	23
Kikwit	33	10	16	21	20
Lumumbashi	25	35	15	11	14
Mbuji-Mayi	32	20	7	27	14

Note: Numbers represent percentages explained in the text for this and following tables.

Only 4 percent of respondents in Kinshasa, 7 percent in Mbuji-Mayi, 15 percent in Lumumbashi, and 16 percent in Kikwit equated unity with peace and democracy, which suggests that they do not consider peace a determinant of unity—a logical conclusion given that they were at war under a nondemocratic government, yet felt united under a common national identity.

When asked whether the Congo must remain unified, the vast majority of respondents in all five cities said yes and advocated the use of force, if necessary, to do so (see Table 4.2). Earlier BERCI polls conducted in Kinshasa[40] show respondents from all regions (residing in Kinshasa) categorically rejecting the idea of partitioning the country. For example, in an October 1996 survey in Kinshasa, less than one month into the first war, respondents overwhelmingly rejected carving up the country into independent states, with less than 5 percent in favor. In a November 1998 poll in Kinshasa, an overwhelming 89 percent were against partitioning the country. The response rates against any threat to the unity of the state have been consistently high every time this type of question has been asked.

In some cases, responses indicate that the disintegration of the country was not even seen as a possibility. In surveys conducted prior to Mobutu's ouster, respondents did not fear that his death would result in the division of the country.[41] This qualifies the once-popular "Mobutu or chaos" theory in the West, and seems to indicate that for the Congolese people, national unity is not tied to one leader or one regime.

When asked if the unity of the Congo is more important than the interests of any particular group or ethnicity, respondents in all five cities answered overwhelmingly that unity superseded any one group's interests (Table 4.3). Although this has potentially grim consequences for minority rights in the country, it appears to suggest that ethnic identity is not the primary identification of the Congolese people, whereas a unitary Congolese nation is.

The responses about the importance of ethnic ties in earlier BERCI surveys is consistent with this observation. The majority of respondents surveyed in a September–October 2000 BERCI poll[42] in Kinshasa, Matadi,

Table 4.2 **"The Congo Must Remain Unified, Even If the Use of Force Is Necessary to Achieve This"**

	Agree	Disagree
Kinshasa	90	8
Kikwit	85	9
Lumumbashi	69	22
Mbuji-Mayi	84	9
Gemena	62	33

Table 4.3 **"Unity of the Congo Is More Important than the Interests of Any Particular Group or Ethnicity"**

	Agree	Disagree
Kinshasa	96	2
Kikwit	76	18
Lumumbashi	83	9
Mbuji-Mayi	88	8
Gemena	99	1

Lumumbashi, and Mbuji-Mayi, indicated that ethnicity was not an important factor in their lives, and that it should not be a factor in political leadership. Most respondents in each city indicated that they did not consider ethnicity an important factor in either their public or private lives. The one exception is Matadi, where respondents made the distinction between the importance of ethnicity in their public versus their private lives. Nearly half of those respondents thought that ethnicity was an important factor in one's public life.

There has been a gradual shift in Congolese preferences in systems of government since the start of the war. In BERCI surveys through 1998, among the three choices given—federal state (authority decentralized and constitutionally given), unitary state (authority highly centralized), and decentralized unitary state (authority decentralized and conferred by the state)—a federal system of government was preferred by most respondents.[43] However, there was a marked difference in opinion between the capital and cities in the interior. Interior cities indicated a strong preference for federalism, while respondents in Kinshasa indicated a slight preference for a unitary, yet decentralized, system. Although this shows a national preference for some kind of decentralized system, it also shows a concern in the capital of devolving too much power to provincial authorities. Since then, support for federalism has dropped drastically, with only 29 percent of all respondents in this survey favoring that system of govern-

Table 4.4 **"What Type of State Would You Prefer in the Future of the Congo?"**

City	Federal State	Unitary State	Decentralized Unitary State	No Opinion
Kinshasa	23	36	34	8
Kikwit	29	49	15	8
Lumumbashi	23	17	22	39
Mbuji-Mayi	39	14	32	16
Gemena	15	40	42	3

ment. Federalism, in a country divided into four politico-military zones by six years of war, has come to be seen as code for partition. The tendency in recent years, therefore, has been to move away from decentralized government because of fears that that decision possibly would lead to the permanent partition of the state.

In this survey (see Table 4.4), 70 percent of respondents in Kinshasa favored some form of unitary state system. Only 23 percent of Kinshasa respondents favored federalism, compared to 41 percent in 1998. Sixty-four percent of respondents in Kikwit and 82 percent in Gemena favored some form of unitary state system. In Mbuji-Mayi, 46 percent of respondents favored some form of unitary state system, and 39 percent favored federalism. Although this is the highest response rate in favor of federalism of the five cities, when compared to earlier polls it is a dramatic drop; in a 1998 poll, for example, 73 percent of respondents in Mbuji-Mayi, the stronghold of Etienne Tshisekedi, the national leader of the nonviolent opposition, favored federalism. In Lumumbashi, 39 percent favored some form of unitary state, and only 23 percent favored federalism—a change from four years earlier when 53 percent favored federalism.

It is worth noting that the two cities with secessionist pasts had the highest rate of nonresponses: Lumumbashi (39 percent) and Mbuji-Mayi (16 percent), due perhaps to a fear of being perceived as secessionist.

We asked respondents in Kinshasa, Kikwit, Lumumbashi, and Mbuji-Mayi whether they thought the war was over.[44] The great majority in all four cities (76 percent total) said that they thought the war was *ongoing*. In Kinshasa, a greater percentage of respondents (18 percent) thought the war was over, compared to 11 percent of respondents in Mbuji-Mayi, 7 percent in Kikwit, and 4 percent in Lumumbashi. Of the total, 76 percent in all four cities who responded said that the war was *not* over. When asked what solution they would support to end it, 44 percent favored the resumption of a national dialogue and reconciliation; 7 percent favored reorganizing the national army to launch an offensive against enemy forces with or without foreign allies; 2 percent saw God and 2 percent saw elections as the solution; and only 1 percent considered the implementation of UN decisions as the best solution for ending the war. Although the use of force was strongly rejected,[45] one-quarter of all respondents registered that they did not know what would end the war.

Satisfaction with State and Rebel Authorities' Services

The surveys sought to capture the degree of satisfaction with the public services provided by the state or, in rebel-held territories, by the rebel administration. They polled respondents' attitudes toward the following five public services: road maintenance (Table 4.5), the provision of personal security and that of property (Table 4.6), access and quality of education (Table 4.7), primary health care (Table 4.8), and access to education (Table 4.9).

An overwhelming 80 percent of respondents in the BERCI polls and 72 percent in the Gemena poll indicated that they were dissatisfied with the roads in their city. There was a similarly high rate of dissatisfaction in all five cities with the way roads are maintained, except in Gemena. There, 69 percent of respondents indicated that the roads were being maintained, and 42 percent gave credit to the rebel authorities for that maintenance. Of those who thought the roads were being maintained in the other cities, over half in Kinshasa credited NGOs, missions, and private companies; and half of those in Kikwit, 86 percent of those in Lumumbashi, and 73 percent of those in Mbuji-Mayi credited the state.

In earlier BERCI surveys, respondents consistently pointed to the improved security situation over person and property as Laurent Kabila's greatest success. A survey conducted in Kisangani, Mbuji-Mayi, and Lumumbashi three months before the outbreak of the second war had 62

Table 4.5   "Are Roads in Your City Maintained?"

	No	Yes
Kinshasa	75	23
Kikwit	79	21
Lumumbashi	84	13
Mbuji-Mayi	81	17
Gemena	31	69

Table 4.6   "Are You Satisfied with Your Personal Security and the Security of Your Property?"

	Satisfied	Dissatisfied	Neither Sat./Dissat.
Kinshasa	58	29	12
Kikwit	47	47	6
Lumumbashi	35	41	23
Mbuji-Mayi	11	62	25
Gemena	45	42	13

Table 4.7   "Do You Feel Protected Against Crime?"

	Satisfied	Dissatisfied	Neither Sat./Dissat.
Kinshasa	53	29	18
Kikwit	53	42	6
Lumumbashi	41	40	18
Mbuji-Mayi	33	67	18
Gemena	67	26	7

Table 4.8 "Are You Satisfied with Your Primary Health Care?"

	Satisfied	Dissatisfied	Neither Sat./Dissat.
Kinshasa	51	28	20
Kikwit	45	51	5
Lumumbashi	23	45	30
Mbuji-Mayi	33	46	21
Gemena	28	60	11

Table 4.9 "Are You Satisfied with Your Access to Education?"

	Satisfied	Dissatisfied	Neither Sat./Dissat.
Kinshasa	35	47	17
Kikwit	18	75	7
Lumumbashi	27	49	23
Mbuji-Mayi	11	68	19
Gemena	33	56	10

percent of respondents approving Kabila's policies to ensure the security of people and property.[46] However, these surveys indicate that the security situation seems to have improved only in Kinshasa, where 58 percent of respondents feel secure. Overall, only 38 percent of respondents in the BERCI polls and 45 percent in the Gemena poll were satisfied with their security. When asked if they felt adequately protected against crime, 67 percent of respondents in Gemena indicated that they were, compared to 53 percent in Kinshasa and Kikwit, 41 percent in Lumumbashi, and the least satisfied, only 33 percent in Mbuji-Mayi. This question, of course, relates to who is in control of the local police.

Most respondents, with the exception of Kinshasa, were dissatisfied with their access to and quality of primary health care. Gemena had the highest rate of dissatisfaction, with 60 percent of respondents claiming to be dissatisfied with their health care. The high rates of "neither satisfied or dissatisfied" may indicate that respondents were dissatisfied with the situation but used to it.

Respondents in all five cities indicated an even higher level of dissatisfaction with the educational system than with the health care system. Only one-quarter of respondents in the BERCI polls, and one-third of those in Gemena said they were satisfied.

Attitudes Toward Minority Groups

When asked about the absolute right of different groups to determine their future, half of the BERCI poll respondents and 79 percent of those in

Gemena said that minority groups should not have the right to determine their own future. The question itself, however, was fairly ambiguous and could, therefore, be interpreted in various ways, including options from the right to self-determination and secession to the right to pursue an education.[47]

The Rwandaphone populations are a dramatic exception. Their citizenship rights have been challenged on several occasions, as their qualifications for citizenship have been, during long periods of time, legally different from other ethnic groups residing in the Congo since independence. While there is no currently available polling data that indicates what the popular attitude toward Rwandaphone populations was prior to the outbreak of the war in 1996,[48] the Congo wars have no doubt had a dramatic impact on the degree of acceptance the public is willing to accord them. We would assume that the impact has been to reduce their acceptance sharply.

In order to determine attitudes toward these groups, a series of questions in the questionnaire were tailored for each city. Respondents were given a list of ethnic groups and were asked which of the ethnic groups on the list living in the Congo are Congolese (see Table 4.10). The list included ethnic groups prevalent in their particular city, as well as Hutu, Tutsi, and Banyamulenge. All the ethnic groups other than Rwandaphone groups were overwhelmingly considered Congolese, except in instances when the respondent was unfamiliar with a particular ethnic group. In those cases, the unfamiliarity was demonstrated by a high rate of nonresponse for that ethnic group rather than a high rate of objection to that group's nationality status. Of the respondents in the BERCI polls, an aggregate average 26 percent considered the Banyamulenge Congolese, and another 20 percent were unsure. This indicates a much greater willingness to consider the Banyamulenge to be Congolese than the Hutu and Tutsi. The two latter groups were categorically rejected as Congolese: 83 percent said the Tutsi were not Congolese and 82 percent said that the Hutu were not. This is consistent with earlier BERCI polls. For example, in a poll taken in Kinshasa four months into the second war, when respondents were asked about the nationality question of the Tutsi, an overwhelming majority of respondents said that they were not Congolese—only 4 percent said they should be granted citizenship, even as a solution to the war.[49] The exception to this trend is Gemena, where the Tutsi and especially the Hutu, fared slightly better than the Banyamulenge. Eighty percent of respondents in Gemena said that the Banyamulenge are not Congolese, 74 percent said that of the Tutsi, and 66 percent said that of the Hutu.

From an internal Congolese point of view, one of the more interesting results of these polls is the sharp difference in the acceptance of Tutsi as a general category in contrast to the Banyamulenge. The Banyamulenge, unlike other Tutsi, live in a homogeneous community in the High Plateau in South Kivu and are cattle herders. Although there is no consensus on exact

Table 4.10   "Are the Tutsi/Hutu/Banyamulenge Congolese?"

	Yes	No	No Opinion
		Kinshasa	
Tutsi	6	86	8
Hutu	15	77	8
Banyamulenge	16	67	17
		Kikwit	
Tutsi	15	74	11
Hutu	13	75	12
Banyamulenge	39	42	20
		Mbuji-Mayi	
Tutsi	9	81	10
Hutu	7	83	10
Banyamulenge	38	36	26
		Lumumbashi	
Tutsi	4	94	2
Hutu	5	93	2
Banyamulenge	12	73	15
		Gemena	
Tutsi	13	74	13
Hutu	22	66	12
Banyamulenge	9	80	11

dates, the age of this community is estimated at two hundred years, and thus probably it is the longest-residing Rwandaphone community in the Congo. It is possible that their greater acceptance as Congolese by the Congolese people is due to their longevity in the country. However, it is more likely that recent events explain the difference in attitudes between the Banyamulenge and the Tutsi and Hutu. In January 2002, Rwanda and the RCD undertook a military campaign against the largely Tutsi/

Banyamulenge community in the High Plateau because a mutinous Banyamulenge officer had organized a rebellion against their authority. He was suspected of having ties to Kinshasa, the Mai Mai, and the Armée pour la Libération du Rwanda, and Banyamulenge viewed as sympathetic to him were persecuted.

This inter-Tutsi war resulted in some modification in the attitudes of some members of the Congolese political class vis-à-vis the Tutsi. These leaders tended to view all Tutsi as one united bloc and some advocated their expulsion from the Congo. Since the struggle has been quite violent, it may be that the Banyamulenge are beginning to gain some modest acceptance as genuine Congolese who have paid with blood for their divorce from their fellow Rwandan Tutsi. However, the more recent escalation of tensions between Congo's transitional government and Rwanda may negatively affect any such change.

These polls show that the Congolese believe that certain minority groups deserve and require special protection. In this regard, the survey focused not only on ethnic minorities, but also on such groups as "internally displaced persons," "child soldiers," "invalids," etc. It is interesting to note that in a country in which interethnic conflicts have fairly frequently resulted in great hardships, it is the nonethnic minority groups that are seen as deserving special protection by the largest number of respondents. It is also interesting to point out that the Rwandaphone minorities are seen as deserving of special protection by a substantial number of respondents even though this could be interpreted as being inconsistent with other responses regarding these groups.

Specifically, the BERCI poll produced the following positive responses for special protection: refugees (89 percent), international displaced persons (77 percent), child soldiers (70 percent), the infirm (70 percent), invalids (64 percent), Pygmies (52 percent), Hema (ethnic group in Ituri) (36 percent), Lendu (ethnic group in Ituri) (36 percent), Banyamulenge (33 percent), Hutu (28 percent), and Tutsi (26 percent). It should be noted that the ethnic minorities not only received a lower percentage of approval for special protection than the other minority categories, but also a higher nonresponse rate. In the Gemena survey, Pygmies received a much lower degree of support for special protection. This can of course be linked to the fact that a relatively large number of Pygmies live in Equateur Province.

The results in the Gemena poll were largely consistent with the BERCI ones except that the level of support for special protection was across-the-board lower for all groups.

Respondents were also asked what type of special protection they supported. In the BERCI and in the Gemena polls, the protection favored was legal rather than through the use of force or such methods as civic education.

The majority of respondents everywhere thought the government had been ineffective in resolving intergroup, interethnic, and interregional conflicts. Mbuji-Mayi, the home of political opposition leader Etienne Tshisekedi, and Gemena, a rebel stronghold, were the most critical of the government's effectiveness. Again, it is interesting to note that Lumumbashi, located in Kabila's province of origin, had the highest rate of nonresponses. Gemena respondents were also given the opportunity to judge the effectiveness of the MLC rebel administration in their area. Respondents were split down the middle: 47 percent found the MLC effective, while 48 percent found it ineffective—higher marks, however, than they gave the Kinshasa government (see Table 4.11).

When asked whether the Kinshasa government represented the interests of all Congolese, the majority said it did not. Of the five cities polled, Kinshasa respondents indicated the most favorable assessment of the government's representation of the interests of all Congolese interests. Respondents in the Gemena survey were also asked to assess the rebel authorities' performance in this area. They indicated that the MLC defended the interests of all Congolese more effectively than the Kinshasa government.

Attitudes Toward External Actors
Public attitudes in the Congo vis-à-vis external actors is an important variable in state and nation formation, not only because of the international legitimacy, through the recognition of state sovereignty, that they confer. External intervention in the Congo has been a familiar phenomenon since well before independence; and since the start of this recent conflict, foreign armies have created spheres of influence, with Congolese allies, within the Congo.

When asked what states most contributed to peace efforts in the Congo, respondents in the BERCI polls pointed primarily to members of SADC, (not surprising, since SADC has supported the Kinshasa government and Kinshasa, Kikwit, Lumumbashi, and Mbuji-Mayi are in government-held territories): South Africa (70 percent), Angola (61 percent), Zambia (58 percent), Namibia (43 percent). Of the Western powers,

Table 4.11   "How Effective Is the Kinshasa Government/the MLC Rebel Administration?"

	Effective	Ineffective	No Opinion
Kinshasa	41	52	6
Kikwit	35	59	7
Lumumbashi	27	57	16
Mbuji-Mayi	9	83	9
Gemena	13	79	8

Belgium (45 percent) was seen as having contributed to the peace process more than either France (32 percent) or the United States (31 percent); and of the intergovernmental organizations, about half of respondents viewed the UN, the OAU, SADC, MONUC, and the OAU-appointed facilitator of the national dialogue, ex-President Masire of Botswana, as having made roughly an equal contribution to peace. Those who were viewed as having contributed the least to peace were, predictably, Rwanda (7 percent), Burundi (10 percent), Uganda (11 percent), and the Central African Republic (CAR) (19 percent). These have been invaders or backers of the rebellions.

When one looks at the disaggregated results, Lumumbashi stands out from the other three cities in the BERCI poll. It consistently has the highest nonresponse rate (between 30 percent and 40 percent), shows a marked mistrust of Western peace efforts—Belgium (27 percent), France (16 percent), United States (9 percent); and thought that of all the intergovernmental organizations listed only SADC (40 percent) and the facilitator (34 percent), had made a contribution to peace.

The results from the Gemena survey, not surprisingly, are different, being in rebel-held territory. When asked what states most contributed to peace efforts in the Congo, respondents pointed to Zambia, which hosted the Lusaka Cease-Fire Agreement (81 percent), Belgium (73 percent), France (57 percent), and the United States (56 percent). Of the intergovernmental organizations, they pointed to the facilitator (90 percent); the UN (88 percent); MONUC (85 percent); the EU (79 percent); the OAU (67 percent); and the United Nations Development Program (50 percent). SADC was not viewed as a contributor peace. It is surprising that two of the MLC's allies, the CAR and Congo-Brazzaville, were not viewed by more respondents as having contributed to peace: only 15 percent said the CAR had, and only 26 percent credited Congo-Brazzaville. Moreover, the latter received one of the highest nonresponse rates in this question, 31 percent.

Conclusion

Put very simply, the survey data presented here clearly shows that a national consciousness and identity has been emerging in the Congo. This comes as no surprise to social scientists and other observers of Congolese society who have had direct contact with the people of this country during recent years.

The particular value of this study and its data lies in the fact that they probe "public" rather than "elite" opinion. A second conclusion is also no surprise to "Congo watchers"—it is that all administrations during the three wars, i.e., Kinshasa and the rebel authorities, have failed to perform most services that are usually considered to be normal, or even minimal, responsibilities of governments vis-à-vis their citizenry. Given the economic decline of the country over the last forty years, it is surprising how much "satisfaction" with these services is reported by the data. What this may mean is that years of hardship and declining state support have so reduced expectations that some respondents consider what they are receiving as adequate or what past experience has suggested is the norm.[50] But the essential, abstract, lesson to be drawn from a coupling of the "national identity variable" and the "services rendered variable" is that a national consciousness can develop, even to a strong degree, without any obvious material benefit to the citizenry emanating from the governing structures of the state in question.

In this sense, the data must be viewed as challenging an entire school of political science, notably that led by Karl Deutsch. One thing is clear: Social communication among all Congolese cannot, under present circumstances, be said to be intense, nor are the levels of transactions among them high.[51] And although we would agree with Benedict Anderson[52] that the Congolese nation is "imagined" and not a primordial given, the social construction of nationhood in the Congo suggests that national identity formation is a continual process and not a onetime event.[53] Congolese identity is a moving force that has been, and continues to be, reframed by the nationalization of political space.

While the majority of the respondents clearly affirm the importance of their identity as Congolese and their commitment to Congo unity, this issue would be meaningless if it involved the exclusion of major groups in the society. In other words, one could well imagine Ivorians who view Muslim northerners as foreigners giving answers similar to those of the Congolese respondents in this survey. It is therefore vital to join the questions dealing with identity to the question, "Who is Congolese?" In this regard, the responses clearly show that the overwhelming majority of the people living in the geographic confines of the DRC are considered by all to be Congolese. This is of some interest when one recalls that a mere decade ago an ethnic cleansing campaign in Katanga Province expelled approximately one million Kasai Luba. Today, as the data show, the respondents in Lubumbashi accept the Luba to be Congolese. The issue there was, and possibly will be in the future, whether people from different provinces should be accorded equal rights with the "natives" of the province in question. There is, in fact, much historical data that suggest a divide between the concept of a common nationality and emotional attachment to the Congo nation, on the one hand, and perceived regional or local "rights" to exclude Congolese from other regions from commercial advantages or administrative posts. In this regard, it should be recalled that Mobutu attempted to fight the latter concept by preventing government administrators from exercising their function in their home territories. But, when it came to high posts or the armed forces, Mobutu unashamedly favored people from his own family, clan, ethnic group, and region.

The one—dramatic—exception to the general acceptance of all residents as Congolese is the Rwandaphone population, whose claim to Congolese nationality is widely rejected. But even here a nuance has to be emphasized. Some, perhaps most, of the current rejection of the Rwandaphone population is linked to the effects of the Rwandan genocide on the Congolese people—the sudden immigration of about one million Rwandan Hutu in 1994, and the subsequent invasions of the First and Second Congo Wars by Tutsi-dominated Rwanda, bringing war and disaster to the Congo. Nonetheless, when an intra-Tutsi violent conflict erupted in South Kivu pitching the RCD and the Rwandan forces against Banyamulenge militia, respondents everywhere in the Congo immediately made a distinction between "Tutsi" and "Banyamulenge." Although the acceptance of the Banyamulenge is still extremely low, it is substantially higher than that of the generically identified "Tutsi." It is noteworthy that many respondents, even while rejecting the Rwandaphones as Congolese nationals, nonetheless believe that they need special protection, along with a number of other groups.

This study measures the positive elements of unification and identification with the state and nation, and thus may be more optimistic about the Congo's prospects than realities on the ground warrant. While it is evident that the Congolese people will resist any effort—external or internal—to undermine the national unity and territorial integrity of the state, they will fight equally hard for the spoils contained within it. A strong national consciousness does not, therefore, preclude crippling internal divisions over power and resources. That relationship we leave for future research.

It is little recognized that for the last thirty years—since the end of the so-called Congo Rebellions—the Congolese people have manifested little tolerance for those who would mobilize them for violent protest. Only the extreme conditions that have developed in eastern Congo have broken with this nonetheless long-lasting tradition. The attitudes and values reflected in this study suggest that the Congolese are a people who are determined to maintain and support their national identity and unity. With few exceptions, and despite horrific social conditions, they are consistent, tolerant, and aware of the realities that surround them. The same cannot always be said of those who wish to lead them.

Notes

1. Leopold to Lambermont, 22 August 1875, AMAE Lambermont V, 9. Roeykens, *Débuts*, 95–96, cited in Thomas Pakenham, *The Scramble for Africa* (New York: Random House, 1991).

2. Roger Anstey, *King Leopold's Possessive Legacy* (London: Oxford University Press, 1966), 2. See also Adam Hochschild, *King Leopold's Ghost: A Story of Greed, Terror, and Heroism in Central Africa* (New York: Houghton Mifflin Company, 1998).

3. Georges Balandier, *Sociologie des Brazzavilles noires* (Paris: Librairie Armand Colin, 1955), 123. Cited in Crawford Young, *Politics in the Congo:*

Decolonization and Independence (Princeton, NJ: Princeton University Press, 1965), 197.

4. Herbert F. Weiss, "Comparisons in the Evolution of Pre-Independence Elites in French-Speaking West Africa and the Congo," in *French-Speaking Africa: The Search for Identity,* ed. William H. Lewis (New York: Walker and Company, 1965), 130–142.

5. Ibid., 136.

6. Now the state capital, Kinshasa.

7. Left out of these negotiations were the Congolese members of the colonial army, the Force Publique. Four days after independence, they mutinied, seeking the ouster of their white officers just as their social equivalents, the teachers and clerks, had taken power away from Belgian colonial administrators.

8. Mobutu was initially a close ally of Lumumba's. He had been a member of the Force Publique, and later a journalist.

9. Catherine Coquery-Vidrovitch, Alain Forest, and Herbert Weiss, *Rebellions-Revolution au Zaire: 1963–1965* (Paris: Editions L'Harmattan, 1987); Benoit Verhaegen, *Rebellions au Congo* (Brussels: Les Études du CRISP, 1969).

10. Some estimates put the death toll of these clashes at 1 million lives.

11. For an analysis of Zairian state formation under the Mobutu regime, see Thomas M. Callaghy, *The State-Society Struggle: Zaire in Comparative Perspective* (New York: Columbia University Press, 1984); and Crawford Young and Thomas Turner, *The Rise and Decline of the Zairian State* (Madison: University of Wisconsin Press, 1985).

12. Jean-Philippe Peemans, "Accumulation and Underdevelopment in Zaire: General Aspects in Relation to the Evolution of the Agrarian Crisis," in *The Crisis in Zaire: Myths and Realities,* ed. Georges Nzongola-Ntalaja (Trenton, NJ: Africa World Press, 1986).

13. Ibid.

14. Janet MacGaffey, "Fending for Yourself: The Organization of the Second Economy in Zaire," in *The Crisis in Zaire,* 144.

15. See the mortality study on the DRC released by the International Rescue Committee in 2001 and 2003. Recent UNHCR estimates suggest that there are currently nearly 3 million internally displaced persons in the country, one of the highest rates of displacement in Africa.

16. For a more detailed account of the Congo wars on which this summary is based, see Tatiana Carayannis and Herbert F. Weiss, "The Democratic Republic of Congo: 1996–2002," in *Dealing with Conflict in Africa: The Role of the United Nations and Regional Organizations,* ed. Jane Boulden (London: Palgrave Macmillan, 2003), 253–303.

17. See Gérard Prunier, *The Rwanda Crisis: History of a Genocide* (New York: Columbia University Press, 1995); Linda Melvern, *A People Betrayed: The Role of the West in Rwanda's Genocide* (New York: Zed Books, 2000); J. Matthew Vaccaro, "The Politics of Genocide: Peacekeeping and Disaster Relief in Rwanda," in *UN Peacekeeping, American Policy, and the Uncivil Wars of the 1990s,* ed. William J. Durch (New York: St. Martin's Press, 1996), 367–407; Philip Gourevitch, *We Wish to Inform You That Tomorrow We Will Be Killed with Our Families: Stories from Rwanda* (New York: Farrar, Straus, and Giroux, 1998); Scott Peterson, *Me Against My Brother: At War in Somalia, Sudan, and Rwanda* (New York: Routledge, 2000); Bruce D. Jones, *Peacemaking in Rwanda: The Dynamics of Failure* (Boulder, CO: Lynne Rienner Publishers, 2001); United Nations, "UN Report of the Independent Inquiry into the Actions of the United Nations During the

1994 Genocide in Rwanda," 15 December 1999.

18. Although the Security Council authorized a *multinational* force under French command and control, it was de facto an exclusively French military intervention authorized under Chapter VII of the UN Charter—a problem, since the Rwandan Hutu-dominated government had been supported by the French since 1990. Thus, the operation appeared to be biased in favor of the government.

19. Resolution 925 was adopted on 8 June 1994 to extend UNAMIR's mandate for another six months, until 9 December 1994.

20. UN Security Council Resolution 929 was adopted on 22 June 1994.

21. Once out of power, known as "the ex-FAR"; later, Armée pour la Libération du Rwanda when they recruited others, not connected to the 1994 genocide, into their ranks; and more recently, Forces Démocratiques de Libération du Rwanda.

22. Some of these insurrection movements included the Lord's Resistance Army, the West Nile Bank Front, and the Allied Democratic Forces.

23. See Alphonse Maindo Monga Ngonga, *Voter en temps de guerre: Kisangani (RD-Congo) 1997* (Paris: L'Harmattan, 2001).

24. Howard W. French, "Zaire Rebels Blocking Aid, UN Says," *New York Times,* 23 April 1997.

25. Interview with Aldo Ajello by the authors, 16 April 2002.

26. Kabila's armed youth, often children, who lorded over the population, sometimes killing people arbitrarily.

27. Herbert F. Weiss, *War and Peace in the Democratic Republic of the Congo* (Uppsala, Sweden: Nordiska Afrikaninstitutet, 2000), 6–7.

28. BERCI surveys conducted between 1997 and 1998 show a gradual decline in Kabila's popularity in his first year in power, and then a sharp increase when he broke with his Rwandan and Ugandan allies. He was most popular in the weeks following the outbreak of the second war in August 1998. However, his popularity gradually declined after that, as the toll of war began to register. It is worth noting that at the height of Kabila's popularity, respondents overwhelmingly characterized his government as a dictatorship, while at the same time advocating for a transition to democratic elections. This may indicate that the population initially made a distinction between Kabila the person and leader, and government policy.

29. Henceforth referred to as *the* "anti-Kabila alliance" or the "rebellion."

30. The DRC became a member of SADC on 28 February 1998.

31. When Kabila was in alliance with the Rwandans the Mai Mai fought against the alliance.

32. Subsequently, Kinshasa transformed this claim by indicating that the Mai Mai are Forces d'Auto-défense Populaires (FAP or Self-Defense Forces).

33. The text of the agreement is available from http://www.monuc.org/english/geninfo/documents/documents.asp (24 May 2002) or http://www.usip.org/library/pa/index/pa_drc.html (1 February 2003).

34. As of 30 September 2002, 4,309 out of the authorized 5,537 uniformed personnel had been deployed.

35. See Kevin C. Dunn, *Imagining the Congo: The International Relations of Identity* (New York: Palgrave Macmillan, 2003).

36. See Emanuel Uwalaka, "Conducting Survey Research in an African Country: Suggestions for Other Researchers," in Abdul Karim Bangura, ed. *Research Methodology and African Studies,* vol.1, (Lanham, MD: University Press of America, 1994), 165–176.

37. It is widely speculated, and supported by anecdotal evidence, that the population in the east views the RCD as the pawns of the occupying Rwandan forces,

and supports the armed efforts of the Mai Mai and their allies aimed against the rebels.

38. Lumumbashi is Kiswahili-speaking. Also, at that time, we were still planning to administer the survey in the eastern city of Goma, where Kiswahili would also have been necessary.

39. The following percent of respondents in each city identified themselves as Congolese: Kinshasa, 96 percent; Kikwit, 99 percent; Lumumbashi, 98 percent; Mbuji-Mayi, 99 percent; Gemena, 100 percent. The vast majority of respondents in all five cities also felt that other ethnic groups identified them as Congolese: Kinshasa, 88 percent; Kikwit, 64 percent; Lumumbashi, 85 percent; Mbuji-Mayi, 93 percent; Gemena, 95 percent.

40. See, for example, October 1996, November 1998.

41. In an October 1996 survey conducted in Kinshasa by BERCI, respondents were more concerned about a military coup (40 percent) than of the country being carved up (31 percent) in the event of Mobutu's death. In fact, more respondents indicated that the death of Mobutu would not likely result in the division of the country (43 percent) than those who thought it likely to divide the country (31 percent).

42. BERCI, "Une pauvreté insupportable," September-October 2000. Moreover, in this survey, fewer than 3 percent of respondents in all four cities (3 percent in Lumumbashi only) said that they were best represented by ethnic associations.

43. In the April 1998 BERCI survey conducted in Kinshasa and the May 1998 survey conducted in Kinsangani, Lumumbashi, and Mbuji-Mayi, most respondents noted a preference for federalism (60 percent nationally), although that sentiment was much stronger outside of the capital. In Kinshasa, there was an even split between federalism and some form of unitary state (centralized or decentralized). Support for federalism dropped in Kinshasa in the first year of the Kabila regime; however, it was still the most popular system of government throughout the country then.

44. Gemena was not polled on this; the question was added later.

45. Although less so by respondents from Lumumbashi, 14 percent of whom suggested that alternative, compared to 4 percent or less in other cities.

46. BERCI, May 1998.

47. A common sentiment among Congolese people is that they all are ethnic minorities.

48. BERCI surveys did not distinguish between Tutsi and Banyamulenge until very recently. Survey questions asked about the Tutsi only.

49. BERCI survey, November 1998.

50. In this regard, it may be possible to employ the data along with additional research to qualify differences—and their causes—between the different regions and urban centers surveyed.

51. Karl Deutsch, *Nationalism and Social Communication* (Cambridge, MA: MIT Press, 1953).

52. Benedict Anderson, *Imagined Communities: Reflections on the Origin and Spread of Nationalism* (New York: New Left Books, 1991).

53. See Rogers Brubaker, *Nationalism Reframed: Nationhood and the National Question in the New Europe* (Cambridge: Cambridge University Press, 1996).

5

Ethnicity and National Identity
in Sierra Leone

Jimmy D. Kandeh, Ricardo René Larémont & Rachel Cremona

One of the intriguing peculiarities of Sierra Leone's descent into war and criminal terror in the 1990s was the relative absence of a grievance narrative rooted in ethnicity among armed combatants and their victims. This is not to suggest the irrelevance of ethnicity in the mobilization of grievance, nor is it to discount earlier portraits of the insurgency as a Mende war, instigated by the Mende people. Indeed, the Revolutionary United Front (RUF) was sustained in its first few years of operations not only by mercenaries from Liberia and Burkina Faso but also by a steady stream of Mende recruits from Pujehun district, a disaffected area of the country that had experienced intense repression under the one-party dictatorship of the All People's Congress (APC). Some ethnic politicians bandwagoned the RUF rebellion, with notable opposition elements (mainly southern Mende) supporting the RUF when the APC was in power and APC politicians (mainly northern Temne and Limba) forging common cause with the RUF after losing power in 1992. Rank opportunism, however, rather than ethnic disadvantage or tensions, explained the shifting relationships between unscrupulous politicians and criminal insurgents. The best example of this degeneracy was former President Joseph Momoh (1985–1992), against whom the RUF insurgency was first launched but who later supported the rebels in a desperate attempt to make a political comeback.

To the degree that the composition of the RUF was predominantly Mende, it is implausible to argue that the RUF fought against Mende-dominated governments (NPRC—National Provisional Ruling Council; SLPP—Sierra Leone People's Party) because of, rather than in spite of, ethnicity. The Kamajors who fought the rebels were also Mende and in some instances had seen prior fighting as RUF combatants. Disadvantaged rural Mende youth were just as alienated from the state, irrespective of who ran it, as were youth elements throughout the country. The RUF leader, Foday Sankoh, was Temne as was his replacement, Issa Sesay. The vast majority of RUF recruits were abducted children whose murderous agenda spared or favored no ethnic group, family member, or prior acquaintance. In the aftermath of the brutal 1997–1998 military interregnum, many renegade soldiers (mostly northerners) joined the RUF, a development that made the conflict even more intractable and irreducible to ethnicity. Although the RUF later fractured into northern and southern factions before the 2002 elections, with northern and southern former RUF combatants respectively supporting the APC and the incumbent SLPP, the RUF insurrection was never based on an ethnic script. This is in sharp contrast to Liberia, where ethnicity textured the grievance narrative of combatants.

Two types of grievances, those felt by out-of-power elites and those experienced by impoverished masses, were critical to the initiation and prolongation of armed conflict in Sierra Leone. Elite grievances stemmed mostly from greed, political exclusion, and lack of access to state offices and resources, while the grievances of the masses were rooted in social deprivation and political disenfranchisement. The war in Sierra Leone, wrote David Keen, "cannot be understood without comprehending the deep sense of anger at the lack of good government and educational opportunities."[1] It was government performance that devoured the state and alienated popular sectors. The imposition of a one-party constitution in 1978 criminalized political opposition and disenfranchised the majority of citizens. This power grab was clearly designed to protect the interests of "a kleptocracy whose main objective was to loot the land."[2] Contrary to John Hirsch, who argues that "geographically based ethnic tensions, manipulated by politicians, were at the root of the state's progressive collapse," ethnic tensions were at best epiphenomenal, masking an underlying unanimity of purpose among competing factions of the political class. Predatory accumulation, rather than ethnic tensions manipulated by opportunistic politicians, was the underlying cause of armed rebellion and state collapse in Sierra Leone.

Porous borders, especially Sierra Leone's border with Liberia, and the diminished capacity of the state to secure its borders and regulate the movement of people into the country, paved the way for the RUF insurgency, which started as an incursion launched from Liberia. The territorial borders of Sierra Leone were delimited by agreements in 1895 (Sierra Leone–Guinea border) and 1911 (Sierra Leone–Liberia border) but this has not prevented Guinea and Liberia from making claims to parts of Sierra Leone territory. Guinea is presently occupying Yenga in northeastern Sierra Leone and has produced maps to support its contention that the area falls within its jurisdiction. However, there was no Guinean presence in Yenga prior to the late 1990s when its troops moved into the area in hot pursuit of RUF commandos accused of raiding Guinean towns and villages. The inability of the state to police its borders not only eased the commencement of the RUF rebellion; it has historically deprived successive governments of the revenue needed to build state capacity. Compounding the problem of unconsolidated borders was the presence of Charles Taylor in Liberia, a brutal warlord determined to destabilize Sierra Leone and lay hands on its diamonds.

This chapter explores the historical linkages between state formation, nation building, and the mobilization of ethnic identities in Sierra Leone. As a failed state, Sierra Leone has fared just as poorly in constructing a coherent national imaginary as it has in establishing legitimate and durable political institutions. Sierra Leone's configuration as a state and its post-colonial reinvention as a nation continue to be works in progress. Anticolonial nationalism did not give birth to a new nation, nor has state performance brought disparate ethnic communities any closer. Competition for state power and perquisites prompted the mobilization of ethnic loyalties, which in turn subverted progress toward the elaboration of a new national identity and consciousness. That the state failed to create a nation in Sierra Leone is largely due to its own lack of effectiveness. Effective states control their borders, protect citizens, regulate societies, and routinely extract and allocate resources. State failures have far-reaching implications not only for security and development, but also for the very idea of a nation as cultural elaboration.[3] What the experiences of countries such as Sierra Leone underscore is that successful nation building is invariably predicated upon the legitimation of political power and the construction of effective, durable political institutions.

Precolonial Antecedents

The name Sierra Leone was first coined in the fifteenth century by Portuguese explorers, but Sierra Leone as a political entity did not exist prior to British colonization in the nineteenth century. Following the country's Portuguese "discovery," coastal Sierra Leone was invaded by the Manes, a southern Mande people who may have lived in the hinterland of the Ivory Coast and Gold Coast (Ghana), around the middle of the sixteenth century.[4] The Manes are said to have recruited Sumbas, infamous for their cannibalism, in their conquest of Bulom (referred to as "Sape" in Portuguese records), Temne and Loko country, but were later defeated by the combined forces of the Susus and Fulas. Portuguese slave ships followed the coastal route of the Mane invasion, scooping up hordes of war captives and refugees destined for enslavement in the Americas. A prominent Bulom king is reported to have opted for enslavement by the Portuguese rather than face capture by the Manes and risk being consumed by Sumbas.[5] The Mendes are the contemporary descendants of the Manes, as are the Vais, Konos, and Krims.

The Mendes inhabit much of southeastern Sierra Leone and parts of western Liberia. Roughly 30 percent of Sierra Leone's population is Mende, making it one of the country's two largest ethnic groups alongside the Temne. Most of the ethnic groups in southeastern Sierra Leone have been annexed culturally by the Mendes. The Sherbros of Bonthe, the Krims (related to Sherbro, among whom they are known as Akimas) and Vais of Pujehun, and to a lesser extent the Kissis of Kailahun, have all been assimi-

Table 5.1   Sierra Leone's Major Ethnic Groups

Ethnic Group	Region	Size	Comments	Political Affiliation
Mende	Most of southeastern Sierra Leone and parts of western Liberia	About 30% of Sierra Leone's population	Descendants from the Sudan, Ivory Coast, and Ghana entered coastal Sierra Leone in the mid-16th century	SLPP (Sierra Leone People's Party) NPRC (National Provisional Ruling Council)
Krio	The Freetown Peninsula	About 3 to 10% of Sierra Leone's population	Descendants of freed slaves of various ethnic backgrounds	
Limba	Northern Sierra Leone	About 10% of Sierra Leone's population	One of the country's original inhabitants	APC (All People's Congress) AFRC (Armed Forces Revolutionary Council)
Lokko	Northern Sierra Leone, below Futa Jallon Region	About 3% of Sierra Leone's population	Related to the Mende, but cut off from them by the Temne during 19th-century ethnic wars	
Temne	Northern Sierra Leone (particularly Bombali, Tonkolili & Port Loko)	About 30% of Sierra Leone's population	Closely related to the Landuma and Baga ethnic groups from Guinea	APC (All People's Congress) AFRC (Armed Forces Revolutionary Council) ACRM (Anti-Corruption Revolutionary Movement)

lated culturally and linguistically by the Mendes. Hardly any Sherbro is spoken on Sherbro Island today, which is quite remarkable, given the fact that the Sherbros are believed to have been among the original inhabitants of present-day Sierra Leone. In effect, the Sherbros of Bonthe have been incorporated into the identity of their conquerors, the Manes (now Mendes). The Vais of Pujehun are today largely known as Gallinas Mende, but the Konos of northeastern Sierra Leone, to whom they are related, have escaped assimilation by the Mendes.[6] The Lokos of northern Sierra Leone are also related to the Mendes but were cut off from the latter by the Temne during the ethnic wars of the nineteenth century. Port Loko, a Temne town in northern Sierra Leone, derived its name from Loko slaves who were shipped from its port. Although Loko and Mende are mutually intelligible languages, the Temnes have had a greater cultural influence on the Lokos than the Mendes.

Compared to southern and eastern Sierra Leone, which are largely dominated by Mende, the northern region is the most ethnically fragmented in the country, with the exception, perhaps, of the so-called Western Area (the Freetown peninsula). The largest ethnic group in the north is the Temne, a close relation of the Landuma and Baga ethnic groups of Guinea. The Temne were an inland people up until the late sixteenth century when they reached the Sierra Leone estuary and divided the Bulom, who dominated the coast, into a northern (Bulom) and southern (Sherbro) half. By the end of the sixteenth century, the Temnes were entrenched around Freetown, which later became the seat of British colonial government and the capital of independent Sierra Leone. Today, Temne are the dominant ethnic group in three (Bombali, Tonkolili, Port Loko) of five northern districts. The Susus, another ethnic group in the north, had their own empire in the twelfth century but were defeated by the Mandingos in the thirteenth century, after which many fled to the coast with the Yalunkas, a related ethnic group. The Fulas entered the upper Guinea coast around the fifteenth century, defeating the Mandingos, capturing Futa Djallon and Futa Toro, and displacing the Susus, Yalunkas, and Temnes. The Temnes later found their way into Sierra Leone, while their Baga cousins remained in present-day Guinea. Other ethnic groups in the north are the Limba, the country's third-largest ethnic group and one of its original inhabitants; the Mandingo; and the Koranko and the Loko (called Gbandi by Limbas).[7]

Local wars and waves of migrations in the upper Guinea coast provided rich pickings for slave traders who began making frequent visits to the coast in the second half of the fifteenth century. The Mane invasion not only coincided with the onset of full-blown European slaving, but its aftermath also helped sustain the slave trade in that many Sherbro (Sape) war captives were sold to the Portuguese in exchange for European goods. With the abolition of the slave trade in the latter part of the eighteenth century, and due to the efforts of British abolitionists and philanthropists (Granville Sharp, William Wilberforce, Thomas Clarkson), Freetown was established as a home for freed slaves in 1787. The territory earmarked for the new settlement belonged to the Temnes, one of whose subchiefs, King Tom, bartered the Freetown peninsula to the settlers in exchange for £59 (pounds sterling) worth of European goods. King Naimbana, however, never consented to the treaty signed by his subchief, King Tom, and wanted the settlers out of his jurisdiction. Naimbana later reached an accommodation with the settlers, but this did not prevent King Jimmy (King Tom's successor) from burning down the first settlement.

The settlers, later known as Krios (or Creoles), came from a variety of ethnic backgrounds. Most were captured on slave ships en route to the New World while others came from Jamaica (Maroons), Nova Scotia (black loyalists from the American War of Independence), and England (black poor).[8] In addition to having to deal with the hostility of the local Temne, the settlers were also divided along multiple fault lines that reflected their diverse backgrounds. A total of one hundred distinct African languages, for example, were spoken in the colony of Freetown in the first quarter of the nineteenth century.[9] The most important division at the time pitted liberated Africans against Maroons and Nova Scotians. The latter had been exposed to the West while the former had never left Africa. Christianization and education of liberated Africans later became a means of bridging the social and cultural gap between these two uprooted communities. Under the auspices of the Church Missionary Society, the absorption of liberated Africans into settler society received a boost from the establishment of Fourah Bay College in 1827, the CMS Grammar School in 1845, and the Annie Walsh Memorial School in 1849. The wealth accumulated from trading by some liberated African families also eased their entry into "respectable" settler society.[10]

Aside from education, wealth, and Christianity, other factors facilitated the incorporation of liberated Africans—who had, in the words of Africanus Beale Horton, "landed naked and in a state of abject rudeness and poverty" in Sierra Leone and "without the least knowledge of civilization"—into mainstream settler society.[11] Many liberated Africans adopted European surnames (Williams, Johnson, Jones, Taylor, Metzger, Wright, Lewis) while retaining African first names (Ayodele, Kojo, Femi, Shola, Tokumboh) that signified their places of origin. Others hyphenated their surnames, combining African and European names, such as Caramba-Coker, Shorunkeh-Sawyerr, Awoonor-Gordon, Tuboku-Metzger, Bankole-Jones, Atere-Roberts, Abayomi-Cole, and Adesimi-Davies, to name a few prominent Krio family names. The Kabaslot dress worn by Krio women, which combines African and Western fashion, also came to symbolize the cultural hybridization of Krios.

The customs, rites, and languages of liberated Africans evolved into resourceful and major components of Krio identity. Komojade (otherwise known as *pul na do*—the coming out or naming of a newborn) and Awujoh (feast held in honor of the departed or to celebrate ancestors), which respectively form part of the birth and death rites of the Krios, came from the Yorubas. African secret societies—Ojeh, Geledeh, Gunugu—also form part of the Krio cultural inheritance. Thus, a Krio was likely to be both a Freemason and a member of an African secret society. Even the language, Krio, is inundated with words and expressions borrowed from languages spoken in West Africa. Thus, while the Krios, as Christopher Fyfe wrote, "assumed unquestioningly that the Christian religion and European customs and morality were superior to indigenous African religion, customs and morality, they still retained an African identity."[12] The extent to which an African identity was retained depended on group origin, as liberated Africans and later Aku (Muslim) Krios maintained closer links to African traditions than the descendants of Maroon and Nova Scotian settlers who were exclusively Christian Anglophiles.

By far the most politically conscious group of settlers were the Nova Scotians, who, in the words of P. E. H. Hair, developed a "strain of blanco-phobia" that marked a "first step toward negritude and black African nationalism." By "using the moralistic slogans of the whites—Christian equality, British liberty, the Rights of man—the Nova Scotians claimed power in the Freetown community, power for themselves as civilized Africans in their own continent; and consequent on this, the ultimate exclusion of whites." In contrast to the liberated Africans, "the Nova Scotians knew the whites only as oppressors of their race."[13] But it was a liberated African, James Africanus Beale Horton (1835–1883), who heralded the dawn of nationalism in Africa. Born and raised in Freetown, Horton trained as a doctor in Edinburgh and wrote many books and pamphlets covering a wide variety of topics. He set out to prove that Africans were not biologically inferior to Europeans and maintained that Africans were capable of governing themselves.[14] Regarding self-government in Sierra Leone, Horton had this to say:

> Sierra Leone is, to a certain degree, a place on the coast that the British Government (to carry out their laudable intentions for Africa) could give up to self-government with hope of success. . . . It has a better and more increasing revenue than any other part of the coast; in it are congregated all the blood and sinews of the various tribes in every part of the coast. . . . The inhabitants of the colony have been gradually blending into one race, and a national spirit is being developed.[15]

Horton's Sierra Leone was, however, limited territorially to Freetown and its environs and circumscribed culturally by an emergent Krio identity. The Krios may have begun to develop a common national spirit in the nineteenth century, but the same could not be said about the ethnic groups of the hinterland. The emergence of a distinctive Krio identity in the nineteenth century was in response to both European racism and the migration of "natives" to Freetown. Some Krios saw themselves as Afro-Saxons, capable of the same cultural and intellectual achievements as Europeans, but they displayed some of the same prejudices toward other Africans that they rejected from Europeans. In short, Krio proto-nationalism of the nineteenth century did not include any serious attempt to question the motives of European imperialism. Rather, British imperialism was held up as benevolently paternalistic, a posture that invited critiques of Krios as surrogate imperialists.[16]

Prior to official colonization in 1808, jurisdiction over Sierra Leone was exercised by the Sierra Leone Company; its main task was to facilitate trade with the interior and protect the interests of the settler community. Company rule was necessitated by the inability of settlers to fend off attacks on their new settlement by pirates and indigenous Africans and, having failed at self-government, the settlers considered company rule to be in their best interest, at least in the short term. Company rule, however, did not end attacks on the new settlement by French privateers and local Temne chiefs. While these attacks often leveled and devastated the nascent settlement, they also helped forge unity among an otherwise divided settler community. In the face of extensive financial losses and in order to protect the settlement from being plundered by raiders from French ships and by Temne warriors, the Sierra Leone Company decided to hand over the affairs of the colony to the British Crown.

Freetown was declared a British Crown Colony in 1808, to which was added the Sherbro Island in 1823. Colonialism was justified by the British on the grounds that it would facilitate the diffusion of commerce, civilization, and Christianity. The American Colonization Society had tried unsuccessfully to acquire Bonthe with the assistance of John Kinzell, a former slave from South Carolina who had returned to Bonthe (his original home before enslavement) to start a business.[17] Contact between the colony of Freetown and the hinterland was limited throughout the nineteenth century to European missionary activities and trade by Krio merchants who traveled into the interior. The latter part of the nineteenth century saw a steady influx of Africans from the hinterland into Freetown, a development that alarmed Krios who saw the new arrivals as "unredeemable savages" and "unwashed aborigines." For the Krios, Europeans represented a racial rather than a cultural Other; protectorate Africans, on the other hand, were viewed not as a racial but as a cultural Other. By the time a British protectorate was declared over the Sierra Leone hinterland, relations between the Krios and both native Africans and Europeans had taken a turn for the worse.

Colonialism, State Formation, and Ethnic Identities

Colonial state expansion into the interior required the settlement of border disputes with the Liberian government and the French. Sofa warriors led by Samory Toure threatened the imperial designs of both the British and French; in hot pursuit of the Sofas, British and French forces engaged each other in battle in northern Sierra Leone under the mistaken belief that they were fighting Samory's forces.[18] The British and French established an Anglo-French Boundary Commission to settle competing border claims and in 1895 signed an agreement that delimited the boundary between Sierra Leone and the former French colony of Guinea. The Liberian border settlement was complicated by that country's claim that Prince Mana had ceded the Gallinas (including Turner's Peninsula) to Liberia. The Gallinas chiefs, however, rejected incorporation of their chiefdoms into Liberia and the bulk of their territory remained within Sierra Leone after the initial border settlement in 1891. Prior to this settlement of Sierra Leone's southern border with Liberia, Sierra Leone's eastern border with Liberia was settled in 1886 by an agreement that divided Kailondo's country (home of the Kissis). Liberia gave up parts of Luawa chiefdom in exchange for portions of the Gola forest and £4,000 in cash. By the end of the nineteenth century, Sierra Leone's border with Guinea and Liberia had been agreed upon, although these colonial border settlements have not stopped Guinea and Liberia from making claims to Sierra Leonean territory in the postcolonial period.

Although the protectorate of Sierra Leone did not officially become part of Britain's imperial domain until 1896, it was nonetheless considered to be within its sphere of influence from as early as 1808. The British, prior to 1896, had "established a trading empire in its hinterland whose maintenance was secured by military force, for if Governors were not allowed to acquire territory, they were prepared to interfere in the affairs of their neighbors in the interests of the security of the colony and its trade."[19] The passage of the Foreign Jurisdiction Act in 1890 made it "lawful for Her Majesty the Queen to hold, exercise and enjoy any jurisdiction which Her Majesty now has or may at anytime hereafter have within a foreign country in the same and as ample manner as if Her Majesty had acquired that jurisdiction by the cession of conquest of territory."[20] This legislation, enacted at a time when imperial interests were equated with territorial expansion, provided expansionist-minded colonial governors with a rationale for annexing the Sierra Leone hinterland.

Within this sphere of influence, surplus value (in the form of primary commodities and labor) was routinely extracted from the interior, but British competition with France and the trade wars among chiefs of the hinterland continued to threaten the colony of Freetown, whose economic survival largely depended on the capacity of the colonial government to protect the trade routes of the hinterland, from whence much of its revenue was derived.[21] Traveling commissioners, the precursors of district commissioners, were dispatched inland to sign trade and "friendship" treaties with local chiefs and settle quarrels among them. A frontier police force, some of whose members became notorious for seizing the property of local producers, was also assembled to ensure peace, order, and security. When traders and "big men" refused to conform to customs regulations, militarism in the form of punitive expeditions (the Yoni and Tambi expeditions of 1887 and 1892 come to mind) was the standard colonial response. Designed to ensure a steady flow of revenue to Freetown, these military campaigns set the stage for the proclamation of a British protectorate over the Sierra Leone hinterland.

Colonial annexation of the hinterland did not go uncontested. Creoles in Freetown questioned the forceful annexation of the protectorate. In the view of Sir Samuel Lewis, a Krio member of the legislative council, negotiation, rather than proclamation backed by force, was a less costly way of effecting the territorial incorporation of the protectorate into the colonial state.[22] Favoring annexation but mindful of a possible protectorate backlash, the Krio elite of Freetown could not dissuade colonial authorities from annexing the protectorate by force. This annexation was immediately followed by the imposition of the hut tax, which, in the words of Governor Cardew, was "necessitated by the benefits of police protection and a settled government."[23] Imposing a tax on huts built with mud, wattle, and sticks triggered the most violent confrontation between the colonial state and the people of the protectorate. The anticolonial rebellion sparked by the hut tax has been well documented elsewhere.[24] Suffice it to emphasize, however, that the underlying cause of the anticolonial uprising in the protectorate was not simply the hut tax but the cumulative disruption and subversion by colonialism of traditional institutions and processes. The arrest, deposition, and beating of chiefs, the usurpation of their judicial powers, and the excesses and abuses of the frontier police symbolized, in dramatic fashion, the political subjugation of traditional society to an expansionist colonial state.

The hut tax also highlighted the bifurcated character of colonial rule in Sierra Leone. In contrast to protectorate inhabitants, colony residents were not required to pay taxes on their homes, and this reinforced feelings of injustice associated with the tax. In the words of Sir David Chalmers, the commissioner appointed by the British Crown to investigate the disturbances caused by the hut tax, the hut tax should not have "been imposed in the protectorate until it was also imposed in the colony" because "through the imposition of this direct . . . tax, . . . this newly-formed protectorate, with its inchoate organization, was taxed more heavily than the colony, with all its advantages of protection of persons and property, regular courts of justice, schools, roads and the other advantages that flow from long-settled government."[25]

The main purpose of the hut tax, however, was not to raise revenue but to secure labor for the colony and to provide incentives for cash crop production. Labor was required for portage duties, to construct and maintain roads and the railway, and with the advent of mining in the 1930s, to work in the mines. Construction of a railway route linking Freetown with the northeastern agricultural produce center of Pendembu opened the country to commerce, facilitated the extraction of surplus from the interior, increased colonial revenues, and enhanced state capacity. By 1922, the railway department was the largest single government employer, with 2,274 Africans and 55 Europeans on its payroll.[26] Palm kernels, chrome ore, and rice were transported from the interior to Freetown and imported merchandise was hauled from Freetown to the provinces. Construction of the rail-way enhanced the penetrative capacity of the colonial state but fostered processes of uneven development, since the rudimentary infrastructure (roads, clinics, schools) required to extract surplus were located in export-producing regions, mainly in the south and east.

Traditional authorities were among the chief intermediaries and benefi-ciaries of colonial rule in Sierra Leone. Indirect rule required local chiefs to maintain law and order in their chiefdoms, for which they received annual stipends from the colonial government. By 1930, stipendiary payments and gifts to chiefs accounted for roughly 10 percent of the colonial state's total expenditure on the protectorate or the equivalent of 20 percent of annual hut tax receipts. Between 1949 and 1952, during the early stages of formal colonial disengagement, salary payments to chiefs doubled from £23,070 (sterling) to £42,681.[27] Throughout the colonial period, the salaries of chiefs claimed over half of the revenue of the Native Administrative units established by the colonial government. In addition to annual emoluments, tax rebates, and gifts, traditional authorities were also allowed to retain some of their customary privileges. The Protectorate Native Law Ordinance of 1924 gave paramount chiefs "the same power with respect to obtaining labor for his own benefit as have the other chiefs in the paramount chief-dom"; this meant that "the farms of such chiefs . . . shall be worked by the laborers of such chiefs, and by all the people respectively . . . and such peo-ple . . . shall continue to supply labor sufficient to enable the farms of their chief to be properly worked."[28] By co-opting pliable traditional rulers and creating new sources of wealth for them, the colonial government decen-tralized its despotism at the cost of delegitimating traditional authority.[29] Transforming chiefs into agents of colonial rule undermined the consensual and traditional bases of legitimacy. The abuses and excesses of some of these chiefs were to later trigger rural unrest during the terminal phase of colonial rule.[30]

A cursory glance at colonial finances shows a dramatic increase in colonial revenue following the annexation of the protectorate. Colonial rev-enue in 1901 was £192,138 (sterling), compared to £105,741 in 1896. By 1910, total revenue had climbed to £424,215, with more than half of this amount coming from custom receipts. After custom duties, the railway brought in more revenue than any other service or transaction, contributing £21,394 in 1901 and £99,946 in 1910. While the hut tax in 1901 and 1910 respectively contributed only £34,868 and £49,704 respectively to total colonial government revenue, these figures represented the bulk (90 per-cent) of the protectorate's direct contribution to colonial revenue.[31] As the colonial government expanded its revenue base, it was better able to enforce its rules, routinize its authority, and in some cases provide limited social goods.

Colonialism not only established new political hierarchies and authority

patterns, but it also enclosed sixteen ethnic groups within the same territorial
and political space. Krios, all of a sudden, found themselves sharing the
same political space with people they had long considered savages. But
what the distinction between Krios and natives failed to take into account
was the significant number of Krios who were of native or protectorate origin. The Mende origin of the Browne, Mason, Bowen, and Marke families,
the Temne origin of the Gurney-Nicol family, the Limba origin of the
Meheux family, and the Susu origin of the Sarif-Easmon family have been
documented.[32] Although he considered himself no less Krio, George
Gurney-Nicol, the first African to graduate from Cambridge University in
1879, was actually the son of a "creolized" Temne father.[33] A fair number of
Krios were either descendants of "recaptives" who were originally snatched
from the Sierra Leone hinterland during the waning years of the Atlantic
slave trade, or the early protectorate beneficiaries of Christian missionary
education. Moreover, a "native" fostered in a Krio home became a Krio simply by changing his/her name, acquiring education, and converting to
Christianity.

The distinction between non-natives (Krios) and "natives" ("country-
men") survives to this day. Historically, it formed the basis for the bifurcated administration of colonial society. Krios were classified as British subjects and natives as British protected persons. Politically, Krios were
represented in colonial institutions such as the Legislative Council, while
the protectorate had no such representation until 1924. Colonial administration also reflected this colony/protectorate or Krio/native dichotomy.
Natives were administered indirectly through traditional authorities while
Krios were under the direct jurisdiction of colonial institutions in Freetown.
The colonial legal system reinforced this dual character of colonial rule—
Krios were subject to British law while natives were judged by three types
of courts—the court of the district commissioner, mixed courts involving
district commissioners and paramount chiefs, and the traditional court of
the paramount chief. This political, administrative, and legal dualism
helped shape the contours of ethno-regional mobilization and conflict during the consolidation (1900–1945) and terminal phases (1945–1961) of
colonial rule.

An important event in the early politicization of ethnic identities was
the passage of the Tribal Administration (Freetown) Act of 1905. This act,
which was designed to regulate the ethnic communities of Freetown, officially recognized the institution of tribal headmen in Freetown and sought
"to promote a system of administration by tribal authority among the tribes
settled in Freetown."[34] Under the provisions of this ordinance, the governor
was empowered to recognize as "tribal ruler" any "Chief, Alimamy or
Headman, who with other headmen or representatives of the sections of the
tribe, endeavors to enforce a system of tribal administration for the well-
being of members of the tribe, resident in or temporarily staying in

Freetown."[35] The principal function of tribal rulers was to serve as ethnic intermediaries in the construction and administration of the colonial state. The acting police commissioner underscored the important role played by tribal headmen in Freetown in a 1908 report:

> The tribal ruler adjudicates tribal cases, saving time and giving men an easier hearing than they would otherwise obtain. They are useful as mouthpieces of the Government in conveying orders to the people. They are of the greatest assistance in enquiring into matters for the police when the occasion demands, and in helping to bring fugitives . . . The fact that they are representative men for each tribe, I am sure, is a great factor in the reduction of crime as each headman is naturally anxious to stand well with the Government . . . The tribal leader is also a local agent for members of the tribe who come down from the protectorate and a medium for inter-tribal palavers in Freetown.[36]

The important point to note about tribal headships in Freetown under colonial rule is that they laid the foundation for the mobilization of disparate ethnic groups. Rather than foster integration, the colonial state fetishized cultural differences, giving them institutional expression through the delimitation of political, administrative, judicial, and social boundaries. Reinforcing this political construction of ethnic difference was the segregation of Freetown into ethnic enclaves. Mendes resided in Ginger Hall, Fulas in Fula Town, Madingos in Madungo Town, and Kroos in Kroo Town. Europeans, for their part, lived in segregated quarters at Hill Station. State-urban relations thus came to be racially and ethnically structured, a fact not unconnected to the ethnic politicization of the decolonization process.

Colonial state construction triggered the movement of people from the protectorate to Freetown. This migration dramatically altered the demographic landscape of Freetown. Fifty-eight percent of Freetown's population in 1891 was Krio but this share fell to 36 percent in 1911 and 27 percent in 1947.[37] A direct outcome of the movement of "natives" from the hinterland to Freetown was the rise in ethnic tensions between Krios, who saw Freetown as exclusively theirs, and the immigrant communities. The Krios rejected these new arrivals and urged the colonial government to zone the city and to stem "the swarm of Mendis and other aboriginal tribes, who infest this metropolis . . . [and who] should be apportioned plots of vacant land in one or another of our vacant villages."[38]

Rapid urbanization created administrative problems, reinforced the utility of tribal headmen, and helped arouse strong feelings of cultural differences among urban residents. Capital penetration had led to the establishment of strong commercial links between merchants resident in Freetown and indigenous traders of the interior. These links brought a steady influx of caravan traders from as far away as Timbuctu in present-day Mali, and Futa Djallon in Guinea, to the city of Freetown. As Michael Banton wrote,

Trading expeditions brought many natives to Freetown and small communities grew up there of representatives of the principal trading tribes. In the 1850s the Fula, Mandinka and Serakule came together and elected a joint headman as they wanted to have someone with authority to arrange for the reception of trading caravans. Freetown soon acquired a reputation in the interior as a place where fine clothes could be bought and where people were free. Refugees from tribal wars and chiefdom disputes fled to Freetown.[39]

In addition, the construction of defense fortifications in Freetown, and later the railway, triggered an exodus of laborers from the rural areas to Freetown. The 1890 "Colony Report" noted,

The construction of fortifications for the defense of Freetown harbor and the building of additional barracks at Tower Hill gave constant employment during the dry season to large numbers of the laboring classes. These works, which have been going on for five years, caused an influx of aborigines to the capital . . . In the rainy season, however, when building operations are suspended, this surplus population show no desire to return to their homes in the interior.[40]

Thus, both the revenue and security imperatives of colonial state formation catalyzed the migration of "natives" to Freetown. To the degree that urbanization was tied to processes of state formation, and given the fact that it was in urban settings that ethnicity was first politicized, ethnic mobilization can be understood as a response to processes of state formation.

Education also had the effect of reproducing and sharpening ethnic differences. The American United Brethren in Christ established mission schools in the interior as early as the 1860s, but their activities did not extend beyond Sherbro and Mende country. Given the early Islamization of northern Sierra Leone by Muslim emissaries, most Christian missions stayed away from the north, preferring instead to work among the Mendes and Sherbros who were traditionally animists. Both Harford School for Girls, established by the Evangelical United Brethren missionaries in 1900, and Bo School, established by the colonial government in 1905, were located in Mendeland. Roughly 80 percent of all schools in the protectorate in 1938 were in Mendeland.[41] This educational head start by the Mendes, coupled with the fact that much of the basic colonial infrastructure (roads, railway, clinics) in the protectorate was concentrated in Mendeland, was to later give rise to perceptions of regional deprivation among northern groups. In effect, "European decisions on where to locate schools, plantations, agricultural extension services, railways, and other modern enterprises in African colonies determined which tribal, regional and religious groups would rise to the top of African society."[42]

A major objective of colonial education policy was to "strengthen tribal patriotism" and "to enable . . . boys to acquire a good education without loss of their natural attachment to their respective tribes."[43] At Bo School, for example, Mende students were taught by Mende teachers and Temne students by Temne teachers. The two groups were residentially segregated and recreational sporting events, such as tug-of-war contests, often featured Mende versus Temne teams. Krios, for their part, were prohibited from attending Bo School because of the colonial government's insistence that the sons and nominees of chiefs, who comprised the bulk of Bo School's student body, should retain their "pristine purity free from modernizing tendencies" that the Krios represented.[44]

The cultural divide separating Krios from protectorate Africans played right into the hands of local colonial administrators, who became increasingly resistant to Krio demands and interests around the turn of the nineteenth century. Having identified themselves historically with British imperialism, Krios were disillusioned by what they perceived to be discrimination and betrayal at the hands of the British. Not only were jobs once held by Krios now performed by Europeans, the employment requirement for the West African medical staff stated that "candidates must be of European origin."[45] In 1892, Creoles occupied eighteen of forty senior posts in the civil service, but by 1912 they held only fifteen of the ninety-two senior civil service positions.[46] At the same time that the top echelon of the colonial civil service was being Europeanized, Krios were also losing out to Lebanese traders as *comprador* agents of European commercial houses. European discrimination, Lebanese displacement, and the threat of political marginalization by protectorate Africans coalesced to transform Krios into an "estranged collectivity." Initially, protectorate Africans were dismissed as a social rather than a political threat. By 1924, however, when the British decided to extend representation in the legislative council to protectorate chiefs, the Krios could see the handwriting of their political demise on the wall. Krios were the only Africans allowed representation on the legislative council, but pursuant to its policy of mediating and leveraging its dominance through intermediaries, the colonial government appointed three protectorate paramount chiefs (two from the Mende, one from the Temne) to the legislative council in 1924. These appointments ethnicized protectorate representation and underscored the instrumental value of ethnic mobilization in the political process.

The passage of the 1924 Constitution, which for the first time granted representation to the protectorate in the legislative council, was preceded by the formation of political organizations representing colony and protectorate interests. Two such organizations were the Sierra Leone National Congress (SLNC), whose membership was exclusively Krio, and the Committee of Educated Aborigines (CEA), which was founded by educated protectorate Africans in 1922. The SLNC was a branch of the National Congress of British West Africa (NCBWA) and some of its members held important positions in the colonial government. In contrast to the SLNC's position that any extension of the franchise should be based on educational qualifications, the CEA was opposed to restrictions that would effectively disenfranchise the vast majority of protectorate residents. Education in the protectorate was more important to the CEA than the elective franchise and the organization warned that the franchise must not "be granted to a handful of colony Africans on behalf of protectorate Aborigines" without "the consent of the two hundred ruling houses in the protectorate."[47]

Deep-seated hostility between Krio and protectorate leaders slowed the pace of decolonization and arrested the development of national consciousness in Sierra Leone. Like Africanus Beale Horton in the nineteenth century, the leaders of the Sierra Leone branch of the NCBWA projected themselves as spokespersons for Sierra Leone, a claim that could not be reconciled with the division between Krios and protectorate Africans. The goals of the NCBWA, founded in 1920, included greater African representation in the colonial government, expansion of the franchise, and "the establishment of a British West African university to give British Africans technical and scientific training, and especially the training necessary for the holding of positions in the colonial service."[48] The NCBWA organized rallies and protest marches, in addition to petitioning the colonial office on a wide variety of issues. But to the degree that NCBWA demands were proto-nationalist, they had less to do with the aspirations of the masses than the interests of educated elites. That Krio elites could claim to speak for a country in which most of the inhabitants felt estranged from their leadership highlights an inherent contradiction of early nationalist discourse in Sierra Leone.

Constitutional decolonization gained momentum after World War II as the British sought a soft landing from their colonial adventures. Constitutional proposals introduced in the legislative council in 1947 provided for an African majority in the legislative council, which was to be dominated by protectorate representatives. Increasing protectorate representation in the legislative council angered Krio elites who now faced the real prospect of being ruled by people they had long considered to be inferior. The 1947 proposals, which were not enacted into law until 1951, precipitated the formation of political organizations representing competing Krio and protectorate interests. The National Council of the Colony of Sierra Leone (NCSL) was formed in 1950 after the failure of Krio elites to alter the provisions of the 1947 constitutional proposals. The NCSL was an exclusively Krio organization whose leaders objected to "foreigners [i.e., protectorate Africans] preponponding in our legislative council" and preferred secession of Freetown from the rest of Sierra Leone to sharing power with protectorate Africans. In the words of the NCSL leader, Herbert Bankole-Bright, "We Creoles have been here for 180 years whilst these natives have no education. I talked to Oliver Lyttleton about the subject and told him he was being too autocratic. Why should he permit a minority to rule in East Africa and not here in Sierra Leone."[49]

The separatist demands of Krio elites did not go down well with colonial officials who were determined to hand over power to ethnic majorities rather than educated minorities. The NCSL lost all the colony seats it contested in the 1957 elections (the last election before independence, and the party later dissolved), with some of its leaders joining the SLPP-dominated coalition government of 1960.

In contrast to the separatist NCSL, the SLPP, the party that was formed in 1951 to represent protectorate interests, was broadly inclusionary, albeit dominated by protectorate Africans. The party's motto was and still remains "One Country, One People." Three different organizations—the Sierra Leone Organization Society (SOS), the Protectorate Educational Progressive Union (PEPU), and the People's Party—came together to form the SLPP as a counterweight to the NCSL. Chiefs dominated PEPU while the SOS was led by educated protectorate Africans. E. N. Jones, a Krio committed to integration of the colony and the protectorate, was founding leader the People's Party.[50] The overriding objective of the SLPP was to put an end to Krio dominance in the colonial institutions of rule. But despite bitter differences between Krio and provincial elites, leading elements of both communities came together under the leadership of Sir Milton Margai to form the first government of an independent Sierra Leone. Krios, for example, were overrepresented at the Lancaster House independence conference of 1960, comprising almost half of the twenty delegates at the independence talks.[51]

Postcolonial Patterns and Trends

Sierra Leone was granted political independence by Britain in 1961 after a decade of preparation for self-rule. Anticolonial nationalism in Sierra Leone never assumed the form of a transformative ideology nor did it rise above the minimum requirements of an independence movement. The colony-protectorate schism, the politicization of ethnicity, the role of chiefs, and the exclusionary logic of the terminal colonial state combined to deprive nationalism of its socially emancipatory potential. Independence was neither preceded nor followed by any serious attempt to mobilize the population on the basis of a common national imaginary. Gershon Collier captures the relative lack of euphoria and mass involvement at the time of independence:

> The atmosphere did not exude that excitement and high expectancy one normally associates with such an historic impending event. This was largely because independence did not come as the result of a particularly difficult national struggle. No deep emotions had been aroused and no major battles won, nor had there been any outpouring of national emo-

tions in response to great rallying cries from national leaders. As a matter of fact, the vast majority of the people were totally oblivious of what was happening; they were not in any way personally and individually involved nor did they have strong sentiments for independence.[52]

The institutional bequest of parliamentary democracy lacked the unqualified support of a political class whose commitment to constitutional democratic governance was at best opportunistic. A parliamentary system based on the Westminster model, with a government led by a prime minister and a governor-general serving as titular head of state, was supposed to provide a semblance of continuity with terminal colonial arrangements. The rights and freedoms of the individual were enshrined in the 1961 independence constitution, which also contained provisions for an independent judiciary and a free press. The fragility of these arrangements was underscored in 1967 when supporters of the SLPP in the army intervened in the political process to prevent the orderly transfer of power from the SLPP to the APC. This intervention derailed the country's nascent democratic experiment and heightened the politicization of the military along ethnic lines.

Attempts at reordering state institutions to benefit political incumbents blurred the distinction between state institutions and the government of the day. This was particularly evident after the death of Sir Milton Margai, Sierra Leone's first prime minister, in 1964. As leader of the United Front, a collection of representatives of political organizations in attendance at the 1960 independence conference, Milton Margai managed to co-opt key northern leaders into the first independent government. Margai was a conservative politician allied with paramount chiefs and extremely deferential to the British. Under his patriarchal leadership, a healthy distance was maintained between state institutions and the interests of the SLPP. The financial secretary and the head of the army were British expatriates and only nine out of a total of fifty-seven officers in the army at the time of independence were Africans. Milton Margai simply "left military affairs almost entirely to the British officers at the army headquarters in Murraytown."[53]

Albert Margai succeeded Milton Margai as SLPP leader and prime minister in 1964. Unlike his more conciliatory and accommodating half-brother, Albert Margai was brusque and his abrasive leadership style alienated friend and foe alike. Prominent northern politicians defected from the SLPP and joined the opposition APC after Albert Margai became prime minister. Margai accelerated the pace of Africanization in the civil service, ethnicized the officer corps of the Sierra Leone army, and attempted to transform Sierra Leone into a one-party state. At the time of Milton Margai's death in 1964, fifteen out of the fifty-member officer establishment were British officers. By 1967, however, only three British officers remained, with most of the outgoing officers replaced by Mende officers (Albert Margai's ethnic group). The percentage of Mende officers in the army doubled from 26 percent in 1964 to 52 percent in 1967 and nearly 64 percent of officers commissioned under Albert Margai were Mende.[54] Margai's efforts to centralize and personalize political power backfired and mounting opposition to his leadership led to his party's defeat in the 1967 general elections. Rather than accept electoral defeat, SLPP diehards prevailed upon the army commander to seize power, thereby preventing the orderly transfer of power from the SLPP to the APC.

Brigadier David Lansana justified his 1967 praetorian intervention on the grounds that civil war was imminent because "the results of the elections had reflected not political opinions but tribal differences."[55] Lansana also accused the governor-general of acting unconstitutionally in appointing Siaka Stevens, the APC leader, as prime minister before all the results of the 1967 elections were tallied. But the Dove-Edwin report on the conduct of the 1967 elections found "no tribalism as a result of the elections."[56] According to this report, "The whole of the Government's arrangements for the 1967 elections was rigged and corrupt. At all levels, before, during and after the elections, this corruption was evident. They were determined to use all means, fair or foul, to win and remain in office and if all failed to get Brigadier Lansana to take over."[57]

Although Lansana's attempt to rescue the SLPP from electoral defeat failed, his intervention set in motion a chain of events that destroyed the country's early democratic promise. Since 1967, defeated and opposition politicians have tended to join forces with allies in the military to overthrow governments. Lack of distance between senior army officers and politicians effectively precluded objective methods of controlling the military. Efforts to subjectively rein in the army, on the other hand, did more to invite than prevent coups.

Less than forty-eight hours after he declared martial law, Lansana was removed from the political scene in a countercoup led by three majors (Charles Blake, Sandy Jumu, and Bockarie Kaisamba) who disliked Albert Margai but were sympathetic to the SLPP. Career ambitions, as David Dalby suggested, may have played an important role in this countercoup[58]; indeed, Blake, Jumu, and Kaisamba wasted no time promoting themselves once in office, with Blake assuming the rank of colonel while Jumu and Kaisamba became lieutenant colonels. Anton Bebler also cited "internal tensions in the army, a desire for self-promotion and the influence of the Nigerian and Ghanaian coups of 1966" as factors behind the 1967 countercoup. Lansana never commanded the respect of his immediate subordinates, many of whom regarded him as incompetent and unfit to lead the army. A group of officers had earlier gone so far as to call for his resignation, accusing the brigadier of "nepotism, tribalism, immorality, drunkenness and the inability to administer."[59]

The 1967 countercoup led to the establishment of Sierra Leone's first military government, the National Reformation Council (NRC), led by

Brigadier Andrew Juxon-Smith. The priorities of the NRC, according to Juxon-Smith, were to end tribalism, corruption, and nepotism and to pursue policies of economic austerity and budgetary stability. With no close ties to either the SLPP or APC, Juxon-Smith appeared to be more reformist than his colleagues on the junta. He saw his task in strictly puritanical terms and in his zeal to "bury" and "cremate" tribalism once and for all, the NRC leader banned the institution of tribal headmen in Freetown and ordered the deletion of all ethnic references from government forms. To tackle corruption, the NRC established an anticorruption squad consisting of army and police officers and instituted several commissions of inquiry to probe corruption and nepotism in Albert Margai's government. One of these commissions concluded that "stealing from the government was as common as petty larceny of private property" and ordered Albert Margai, who was thoroughly discredited at the hearings, to pay back to the state the sum of Leones 800,000 (£400,000 at the time).[60]

Juxon-Smith's efforts to restore probity to state institutions and improve the financial solvency of the state were undercut by his draconian leadership style and bizarre flights of visionary fancy. The chairman's leadership style caused considerable unease among his peers and compatriots. In one of his uncompromising rhetorical flourishes, the NRC chairman warned that

> it has come to our notice that people are planning trouble. Let me say this now, that there is martial law in Sierra Leone. Perhaps it wasn't explained to the populace what martial law means. It means that military law is supreme to civil law, and that anybody who does any act or conduct . . . prejudicial to the interests of the state, that person will be immediately court-martialed, the maximum sentence for which is death. And I'll have no scruples whatsoever to confirm the sentence. I will confirm it instantaneously . . . and you will be shot by firing squad. That is what martial law means.[61]

Brazen threats to "obey or else" failed to silence opposition to military rule. On the very day in 1968 that Blake, Jumu, and Kaisamba were planning to arrest Juxon-Smith, northern ranks of the army dislodged the NRC from power. Unlike the leaders of the 1967 coups, who were mostly southerners and Mende, the leaders of the 1968 coup were predominantly northerners and Temne.

A self-styled Anti-Corruption Revolutionary Movement briefly took charge of the state after the 1968 coup. Although this coup was essentially an "amenities coup," ethnoregional considerations shaped its planning, execution, and outcome. Most of the coup participants were northerners sympathetic to the APC. Lieutenant Colonel John Bangura, who had been released earlier from prison by Juxon-Smith, was reportedly in contact with the coup plotters before they struck. Later appointed chairman of an interim governing council, Bangura was "trusted" by the APC "because he was reputed . . . to have the . . . interests of the APC at heart."[62] Needless to say, the 1968 coup was anti-officer, anti-SLPP, and pro-APC.

The 1968 coup was followed a week later by the swearing in of Siaka Stevens as the country's new prime minister. Stevens and the APC moved quickly to restore civilian control over the military by dismissing officers whose loyalties were considered suspect because of their ethnic identity. As Cox wrote, "Throughout 1968 and 1969, the APC eliminated as many Mendes as possible from the officer corps. Apart from those called upon to answer charges of treason, other Mendes were simply pensioned off without explanation. The result was that by the Fall of 1969, there remained a single Mende among the ten most senior army officers."[63] "Retribalization" of the army's officer corps found expression in the clientelization of its officers. Bangura was promoted to the rank of brigadier and appointed force commander of the army in 1969. In that same year, Lieutenant Colonel Joseph Momoh was appointed commander of the army's First Battalion. Both Bangura and Momoh were northerners, as were both general staff officers.

Despite the fact that its leadership was comprised almost entirely of northerners, the APC had campaigned in 1967 as a party of commoners whose election would put an end to the elitism, corruption, and ethnoclientelism of the SLPP. The APC's founding rhetoric was, however, belied by its performance in office. The imposition of one-party rule in 1978 and the subordination of society and the state to the "interests of the recognized party" only succeeded in delegitimizing political institutions, alienating the citizenry, and fostering rebellion against the government. The Internal Security Unit, later renamed Special Security Division, was routinely deployed to harass and terrorize students, workers, peasants, and other opponents of the government. Press freedom was severely curtailed and any discussion of political alternatives to the APC was considered treasonable. Loyalty, opportunism, and sycophancy became qualifications for office at both national and local levels. As one politician observed at the time, "No one will become Chief without the approval of the Pa (Siaka Stevens). Although he may not interfere, he makes his view known. It is subtle. He sends somebody with the word. Here chieftaincy has a high importance for the people and the government."[64] This decentralized despotism foreclosed the democratization of customary power, distanced the state from peasants, and became a major factor in rural rebellions.

Ethnoregional politicization of the army by Siaka Stevens assumed a modicum of solidarity in political outlook among northern ethnic groups. This, however, has seldom been the case. As Magbaily Fyle contends,

The term "northerners" in Sierra Leone politics, sometimes used synonymously with the Temne, does not have the same meaning as southern/

Mende. Most of the ethnic groups in the north do not identify themselves with the Temne or speak Temne as a second language. Thus while a Kissi, Vai, Sherbro from the south could often speak Mende and identify politically with the Mende, the same cannot be said for a Koranko, Yalunka, and Limba from the north, most of whom do not speak Temne. Even with the advent of APC rule, most of these groups, though identifying themselves with the APC, never interpreted this association in terms of a Temne dominated relationship.[65]

As it turned out, disaffection among Temne political elites fractured northern support for the APC. Fragmentation of the APC's northern political base spawned at least two abortive coups in the first five years of APC rule, not to mention defections from the party and the formation of the United Democratic Party (UDP) in 1970. The UDP had a predominantly Temne leadership, which threatened the northern base of the APC. John Bangura, the force commander of the army, was sympathetic to the UDP while Joseph Momoh, the first battalion commander, was aligned with Stevens, his fellow Limba. What began as a civilian conflict between the APC and UDP carried over into the military in the form of a growing rift between Bangura and Momoh. As one observer noted, "Just as an earlier Bangura-Lansana rivalry had been inflamed by struggles between the APC and SLPP, feuding between the UDP and APC was now clearly exacerbating relations between Bangura and Momoh."[66]

In response to the threat posed by the UDP, Siaka Stevens and the APC declared a state of emergency, banned the UDP, and arrested its leaders in 1970. The banning of the UDP and the arrest of officers loyal to Bangura precipitated the failed coup of 1971. Bangura, together with three other officers (Majors Falawa Jawara and S. E. Momoh; Lieutenant J. B. Kolugbonda) were executed on 29 June 1971. Interestingly, most of the low-ranking officers implicated in the 1971 abortive coup were Mendes, demonstrating once again the antipathy among Mende officers remaining in the army toward Siaka Stevens and the APC. Another alleged coup in 1973 resulted in the arrest of two principal UDP leaders, Mohamed Forna and Ibrahim Bash-Taqi, and former brigadier Lansana. All three men were hanged by the state after being tried and convicted on dubious treason charges.

Stevens retired from the presidency in 1985, but not before handpicking Brigadier Joseph Momoh as his successor. Choosing his successor was the ultimate measure of the degree to which Stevens had personalized power. Although the one-party constitution stipulated that the first vice-president should succeed the president in the event of the latter's retirement or indisposition, Stevens arbitrarily amended the constitution and imposed his choice of successor on both his party and the country, much to the chagrin of Sorie Koroma, his erstwhile vice-president. The man Stevens chose as his successor, Brigadier Joseph Momoh, symbolized the politicization of the coercive apparatuses of the state and the clientelization of its top officers. By first appointing Momoh (at the time head of the national army) to parliament in 1978, and in choosing him as his successor in 1985, Siaka Stevens left no doubt about the primacy of one-party government over state institutions.

Momoh inherited a marginalized parliament and judiciary, an executive and bureaucracy steeped in corruption, a politicized army and police, and a repressed civil society. The personalist leadership style of Stevens did not carry over into the Momoh phase of APC rule as the latter clearly lacked his predecessor's stature, and expectations that he would be an improvement over Stevens never materialized. Instead, a parasitic cabal, which came to be known locally as the Binkolo Mafia (most of its members were from Binkolo, Momoh's hometown), replaced the personal rule of Stevens. The members of this inner circle belonged to Ekutay, an organization of Limba politicians, cultural entrepreneurs, and influence peddlers. The political clout of Limbas and descendants of Binkolo was by no means limited to the political realm. Most of the senior and junior officers of the armed forces under Momoh were either Limba or from the north. Membership in Ekutay became such a prized social currency—it provided access to public offices and resources—that even non-Limbas sought membership.

The deflation of state capacities that began under Siaka Stevens accelerated under Momoh. Much of this contraction was due to the unrestrained predations of ruling elites. By the time Momoh was ousted from power in a 1992 coup d'état, the state's extractive and allocative capacity had all but disappeared. Gross domestic product had fallen from US$1.1 billion in 1980 to $857 million in 1990 and international reserves, which stood at a paltry $31 million in 1980, dipped to an all-time low of $5 million under Momoh. Average GDP growth rates in the last five years of the Stevens dictatorship (1980–1985) hovered around 3 percent but dropped to 1.1 percent in the first five years (1985–1990) of the Momoh government. From 1990 to 1995, not a single economic sector or activity registered any growth, with exports showing the sharpest decline (see Table 5.2 below).

Declining exports were due to the informalization of the economy, diamond smuggling by rogue politicians and businessmen, and the pervasive insecurity created by the RUF rebellion. Export revenue, which stood at US$224 million in 1980, plunged to $139 million after five years of the Momoh government. Total government revenue as a percentage of GDP also recorded a sharp decline from 17.0 percent in 1980 to 3.9 percent in 1990 under Momoh, well below the African average of 22.5 percent for the same period.[67] The increased contribution of taxes on domestic goods and services as a percentage of total revenue was the product not of any expansion in domestic economic capacity but of the precipitous drop in export earnings that predated, and could therefore not be blamed on, the RUF insurrection.

Table 5.2   Average Annual Growth Rate of the Economy (in percentages)

Indicators	1980–1990	1990–1995
GCP	1.6	–4.2
Agriculture	4.4	–2.8
Industry	5.7	–2.8
Services	–1.1	–5.9
Exports	2.8	–15.2
Domestic Investment	–6.5	–20.0

Source: World Bank, *World Development Report 1997.*

By all accounts, Momoh was an unmitigated disaster as head of state. More predatory but less repressive under Momoh than Stevens, the state continued to atrophy as informal channels of accessing its offices and resources displaced bureaucratic ones. Like his predecessor, Momoh was not interested in a strong bureaucracy that could function autonomously from the interests of the APC and its leaders. Instead, he crowded state apparatuses with unscrupulous cronies who embarked upon systematically dismantling the state to secure unfettered access to its resources. The scope and magnitude of corruption under Momoh is detailed in the reports of the Beccles-Davies, Lynton Nylander, and Laura Marcus-Jones commissions of inquiry. A Reconciliation Commission established in 1996 to review these reports concluded that "Momoh appeared to treat Sierra Leone as his personal fiefdom and felt that he was at liberty to act as if its finances were at his disposal no matter what contrary advice was tendered."[68]

Failure to legitimize the organization and exercise of political power, combined with the cumulative effects of repression and predatory accumulation on an impoverished population, sowed the seeds of institutional collapse and armed rebellion. Predatory accumulation by the political class impoverished society, lumpenized the country's youth, devalued education, and incapacitated the state. In effect, how political elites exercised power and accumulated wealth helped shape RUF terror. The rapacity of APC elites was inherently incompatible with societal interests and the long-term reproduction of elite dominance.[69] A dysfunctional state increasingly at odds with society and incapable of performing basic tasks could not withstand the deadly struggle for access to the country's diamond resources among elites and lumpens alike.

The RUF insurrection would not have been possible with an effective state machinery in place. Perhaps the most visible symbols of institutional decomposition were the army and police, where recruitment and promotions had been politicized since Albert Margai's tenure as prime minister. As President Kabba noted:

For nearly thirty years now, recruitment into the army . . . has been based on tribal and political patronage. The government of the day regarded the army as an instrument of the ruling party and not as a national institution. . . . To give practical effect to its new-found role, the role of recruitment into the army was altered from that based on qualification to one based on the card system—that is, one based on political, tribal or regional affiliation. . . . The result of this mode of recruitment was that every soldier had a political patron and collectively those patrons belonged to the ruling party, to which the army owed its loyalty and allegiance, and not the nation.[70]

The RUF rebellion, which hastened the collapse of the APC, led to the relaxation of some of these recruitment preferences, making it possible for hordes of urban and rural lumpens to join the national army. As Momoh himself was to acknowledge later in exile, "In the quest to increase numbers, training standards and discipline may have subsided also, because not too much time was given to screening entrants. The result is that a large number of undesirables, waifs, strays, lay-abouts and bandits may now be in the nations's military uniform."[71] Since their recruitment was dictated by desperation rather than ethnicity or patronage, new recruits were not particularly loyal to the APC.

The leaders of the 1992 coup stormed to power vowing to breathe new life into moribund state institutions, to end the war, and return power to an elected civilian government. Captain Valentine Strasser, who emerged as head of state, described the 1992 coup as a clean-up exercise whose main purpose was to eradicate "an oppressive, corrupt, exploitative, tribalistic bunch of crooks and traitors."[72] To run the country, the coup leaders constituted themselves into a National Provisional Ruling Council (NPRC). Next to ending the war, which the NPRC failed to do during four years in office, the eradication of corruption was high on the rhetorical agenda of the new leadership. The assets of key members of Momoh's government were frozen and commissions of enquiry were set up to investigate charges of corruption in the public service and recover state assets that were improperly obtained during the period June 1986 to September 1991. Commissions of enquiry and asset seizures were, however, rendered less meaningful in light of the spectacular display of wealth by previously destitute subalterns. This, in addition to the disastrous handling of the war and the increased involvement of armed regulars in rebel activities, coalesced to transform what had started as a popular coup into an unpopular regime.

As the security situation deteriorated under the NPRC, and with mounting evidence of collaboration between soldiers and rebels, provincial urban communities organized themselves into civil defense militias to defend their towns. Most of these efforts were organized and led by secret-society members and vigilante youth. The most notable of these civil defense forces was the Kamajor militia, a predominantly Mende group with close ethno-region-

The 1992 Coup: A Timeline to Rebellion

1985: President Stevens (APC) retires and appoints General Joseph Saidu Momoh (APC) as his replacement. Mass expulsion of students from Fourah Bay College.

January 1987: Demonstrations and protests against President Momoh and his "Binkolo Mafia."

March 1987: Unsuccessful coup attempted—four conspirators, including former vice-president Francis Minah, are executed in October.

1990: Popular calls for a return to a multiparty political system are dismissed by President Momoh.

Late 1990: Several thousand Liberian Refugees enter Sierra Leone, adding further strain to the country's already unstable economy.

1991: Border fighting erupts between government forces and Charles Taylor's National Patriotic Front of Liberia (NPFL). Foday Sankoh (a Temne) forms the Revolutionary United Front (RUF) that is backed by Taylor's NPFL.

March 1991: President Momoh announces his support for multiparty politics.

April 1991: Momoh sends two thousand troops to combat the NPFL and RUF. Sierra Leone descends into civil war.

May 1991: Fierce fighting has killed at least five thousand civilians and refugees in Sierra Leone.

August 1991: A popular referendum approves the return of a multiparty system.

September 1991: A transitional government is formed.

April 30, 1992: Army Captain Valentine Strasser leads a coup by thirty mutinous soldiers, forcing President Momoh into exile and forming the National Provisional Ruling Council.

al ties to the NPRC leadership. Complementing the services of the Kamajors were mercenaries hired by the NPRC to help prosecute the war. Executive Outcomes, a South African mercenary outfit with ties to the diamond industry, helped turn the tide of the insurrection against the rebels in 1995, thus paving the way for elections to be held a year later.[73] But the fact that the NPRC had to subcontract the primary function of the state to mercenaries underscored the depth of state failure in Sierra Leone.

With the failure of the NPRC to end the war and restore state capacities, a restive public turned its attention to hastening the junta's departure from the political scene. Demonstrations by women's organizations, students, petty traders, and unemployed youth became the order of the day. Unflattering songs depicting NPRC leaders as rebel collaborators enlivened these demonstrations. International pressures also helped convince NPRC leaders to give up power in exchange for study-abroad packages and other exit inducements. Multiparty elections were held in 1996 in which the SLPP and Ahmad Tejan Kabba emerged victorious.

Fourteen months into the second republic, "sobel" elements (soldiers moonlighting as rebels) of the Sierra Leone army closed ranks with the RUF to overthrow the democratically elected government. The main agenda of this sobel-rebel alliance did not rise above the criminal expropriation of public resources and private property. As the country collapsed into criminal terror, the international community imposed sanctions on the new junta and encouraged regional leaders to reinstate President Kabba. Kabba was eventually returned to power in March 1998 by a Nigerian-led West African intervention force but was almost toppled again in January 1999 by the same elements that ousted him in 1997. With no army at his disposal to rely on, the Nigerians were again called upon to rescue the state from marauding gangs of criminal insurgents whose brazen invasion of Freetown cost the lives of over five thousand civilians. In the wake of this brutal invasion, a severely weakened President Kabba signed a peace agreement with the RUF that granted rebels a blanket amnesty and rewarded some of their leaders with ministerial positions. The Lomé Peace Agreement later unraveled after the RUF decided to make another run at invading Freetown in May 2000 and capturing state power.

The hope of many Sierra Leoneans was that the election of Kabba in 1996 would put an end to the war and begin a process of national recovery and renewal. This, however, was not the case as the security situation continued to deteriorate. There were many reasons for this, including the widespread "sobelization" of the army and the failure to disarm RUF combatants prior to the 1996 elections. Compounding these problems was the government's gross mismanagement of the country's security, especially its policy of appeasing criminal insurgents and belligerent warlords.[74] In his effort to restore peace, Kabba signed the Abidjan Accord in 1996 with

Foday Sankoh, the RUF leader. This agreement granted a blanket amnesty to all combatants and called for the encampment and disarmament of RUF combatants. Sankoh's obduracy, intransigence, and delusional flights of grandeur doomed the agreement from the start, but this did not disincline Kabba from signing yet another agreement with the warlord in 1999. As in 1996, the ill-fated 1999 Lomé agreement amnestied all combatants but went further in requiring the government to share power with rebel leaders. Kabba's capitulation to the RUF, especially the president's decision to share power with an unrepentant horde of mass murderers, rapists, and arsonists, was incongruent with public opposition to the very notion of sharing power with rebels. In both instances of reaching out to rebels, Kabba only succeeded in endangering the lives and property of ordinary citizens.

Having inherited a rogue army whose interests were incompatible with society, Kabba could not rely on the national army to provide security. After the first in a series of unsuccessful coups against his government in 1996, the president turned over responsibility for his personal security to a unit of Nigerian soldiers. The Nigerians were also asked to help retrain and restructure the armed forces. This Nigerian involvement, coupled with the presence of Executive Outcomes (a South African mercenary outfit), provided a modest but robust counterweight to a disloyal and unpopular army. But the security provided by Nigerian soldiers and Executive Outcomes did not extend beyond Freetown and a few prized diamond-mining areas of interest to the corporate affiliates of Executive Outcomes. To protect the rest of the country, the government had to rely on army regulars and civil defense militias. Clashes between these militias, especially the Kamajors, and the army inflamed an already volatile situation and helped precipitate the 1997 coup. SLPP ties to the Kamajor militia created the perception among northerners that the SLPP was assembling a parallel military force or, more specifically, a Mende militia.

But it was primarily among political elites that the conflict in Sierra Leone came to have an ethnic overtone. When in power, northern and southern politicians blamed each other for the rebellion, thus making it difficult to mobilize the entire population against the rebellion. The degree to which the RUF insurgency attracted support from opposition politicians cannot be overstated, especially after elements of the army formed an alliance with the RUF following the 1997 coup. As Yusuf Bangura wrote,

> Once elements in the RSLMF formed an alliance with the RUF, and some important elites from the north and Western Area (the Freetown peninsula) decided to support or work with them, geo-ethnic divisions became magnified. . . . Even though the RUF rebellion is not ethnic, and the RUF (more eastern and southern in composition) and AFRC (more northern and Western Area) formed an alliance in pursuing a common goal, the

conflict had strong ethnic overtones among key political elites. . . . Politicians, civil servants, lawyers, businesspersons and other members of the elite who felt alienated from the Kabba government joined or supported the AFRC. A large proportion of these individuals were of northern or Western Area origin.[75]

In effect, political elites superimposed their competing agendas on a conflict created by their untrammeled rapacity. These agendas involved the use of ethnicity as a tool for making political comebacks, especially in the case of discredited politicians who stood no chance of being elected by the people. It came as no surprise, therefore, that among the northern politicians who either joined or supported the RUF rebellion were John Karefa-Smart, the runner-up in the 1996 presidential election, and Abass Bundu, an also-ran in the same presidential contest.

Failure to restore the protective capacity of the state transformed Sierra Leone into a ward of the international community. After a series of false starts, the United Nations deployed over sixteen thousand peacekeepers in Sierra Leone, whose task was to disarm all combatants and help the government restore its presence and authority throughout the country. The British took over the task of retraining the Sierra Leone army from the Nigerians, with the goal of establishing a democratically accountable and efficient military force. British training, equipment, and advice to the Sierra Leone army forced the RUF on the defensive and helped stabilize the security situation in the country. But while the British won kudos from Sierra Leoneans, there are lingering doubts about the reliability and professionalism of the new army, since many of the retrained soldiers are former sobels and rebels who committed horrible atrocities in the past.

A relatively stable security environment made it possible for the 2002 elections to be held, the country's first since the official termination of hostilities in 2001.[76] It was widely expected that these elections would help consolidate a fragile peace and build legitimacy for the political system, but legitimacy does not rest on elections alone and unless government performance can begin to approximate the minimum expectations of citizens, the potential for authoritarian reversal remains. Both the manner in which power is exercised and wealth accumulated are detrimental to institutional legitimation, economic development, and the promotion of national unity. As John Lonsdale observed,

> Modern African regimes, overcrowded at first with power, have used force to narrow the ranks of their collaborators, many have stifled productive effort in the process. They have strangled the ambition of independent capitalists who might become their rivals; they have neglected the peasants on whose labors they depend. Nobody today is being liberated by the process of state formation, save for the growing army of bureaucrats.[77]

Stated differently, the political class bears ultimate responsibility for the collapse of the state in Sierra Leone. It was the predatory mode of accumulation of this class that contracted state capacities, undermined the legitimacy of public institutions, and alienated the vast majority of citizens.

The United Kingdom and the United Nations
In June 1998, the United Nations created the UN Observer Mission in Sierra Leone (UNOMISIL) for an initial period of six months. The purpose of UNOMISIL was to monitor and advise on efforts to disarm combatants and restructure Sierra Leone's military forces. While UNOMISIL personnel had to be evacuated from the country following the December 1998 rebellion, the UN special representative, Francis G. Okelo (Uganda), and the chief military observer continued in their efforts and, in the aftermath of the rebellion, initiated a series of diplomatic efforts to open dialogue with the rebels and negotiate a peace settlement with the government. In July 1999, all parties to the conflict signed the Lomé Agreement to end hostilities and form a government of national unity. An expanded role for UNOMISIL was requested and the UN increased the number of its military observers to 210.

In October 1999, the UN created the Assistance Mission to Sierra Leone (UNAMSIL) with a much larger mission, including 6,000 military personnel and 260 military observers to assist the government and parties in carrying out the provisions of the Lomé Agreement. By March 2001, UNAMSIL was expanded to include up to 17,500 military personnel and had adopted a more expansive role in Sierra Leone's civil affairs and administration.

As the former colonial power in Sierra Leone, the United Kingdom has also played a significant role in attempts to stabilize and rebuild the nation. Since 1995, the U.K. has maintained nonmilitary links with Sierra Leone that have involved more money, more aid, and more political action than that given by the British to any other African state. Between 1998 and 2000, the Labor government in the U.K. committed more than £65 million (sterling) to Sierra Leone, including £14 million from the Department for International Development invested in the Disarmament, Demobilization and Reintegration Program (DDR) being conducted by the Sierra Leone government. The object of DDR is to disarm and reintegrate over 45,000 rebel soldiers back into civilian life. The assistance package provided by the U.K.'s Department of International Development is also aimed at strengthening Sierra Leone's media, supporting the economy, aiding in anticorruption measures, rebuilding the legal system, and restoring the positions of local paramount chiefs in the country.

Rebuilding the State and Reimagining the Nation
State restoration in Sierra Leone is unlikely in the absence of regime transformation. Restoring state capacity and probity will depend on how politi-

cal power is reconstituted. The state in Sierra Leone cannot be restored in a predatory form, as this will preclude both its legitimation and effectiveness in the performance of basic tasks.

How the state is reconstituted is more important than who restores it. The authoritarian model has been discredited by over two decades of dictatorship. Unless democratic rule translates into meaningful improvement in the lives of ordinary citizens, however, the potential for instability, rebellion, and authoritarianism would persist. Regarding alternative models of state restoration, Marina Ottaway has argued that "the authoritarian solution—perhaps more promising in the short run—in the long run is very likely to lead to a new cycle of discontent and collapse. The democratic solution is certainly the most desirable and probably the only viable one in the long run, but it is unfortunately the most difficult to implement in the short run."[78]

While democracy remains the only viable route to state restoration in Sierra Leone, the state can only be put back together if the exercise of political power is legitimized, if autonomous state institutions are created, and if processes of accumulation are distanced from the exercise of state power. Accomplishing these objectives would transform the relationship between state and society.

There is a desperate need to rehabilitate the state, but not along the lines prescribed by multilateral financial institutions. While donor emphasis on fiscal responsibility and transparency are broadly supportive of democratization, the same cannot be said for the privatization schemes and antisubsidy prescriptions of the International Monetary Fund. Privatization has mostly benefited politicians and their business cronies while the removal of government subsidies for basic items such as rice and petrol continues to deepen the misery of ordinary citizens. The reason successive governments failed to build public support for state institutions is not because the state is interventionist; rather, it is because the interventions of the state have done more to enrich political elites and their associates than alleviate the misery of the masses. An interventionist state that is ineffective cannot be rendered effective by simply making it less interventionist. The relevant issue is not whether the state is interventionist but who benefits from its interventions. Ensuring that state interventions do not privilege the affluent few or disadvantage the impoverished majority is a better way of assuring the efficacy and legitimacy of the state.

Arguably, a limited state is not suited to meeting the challenges of societies seeking to develop democracies with effective state institutions. Industrialized democracies can afford a limited state because they have attained high levels of material and human development, along with a politically active bourgeoisie. Before these societies became developed, however, the state was protectionist and interventionist. Even in contemporaneous Western society, governments still bail out and provide subsidies for declining sectors and endangered private businesses. Corporate welfare may be suited to the needs of capitalism in advanced democracies, but for African states like Sierra Leone, it is mass welfare that is most likely to build public support for democracy and the state.

Ending the culture of impunity as it relates to corruption and human rights abuses is critical to state restoration. "Corruption is still stronger than law"[79] and "the tradition of people seeking political office to line their pockets and that of their family, rather than to improve . . . their country, is still widespread and endangers the future."[80] Although elected, the present SLPP government is not fundamentally and operationally different from the APC dictatorship. It is public knowledge, for example, that politicians and their relatives are actively engaged in diamond mining and smuggling. Investigative newspaper reports implicating top public officials (Septimus Kaikai, Prince Harding, and Patrick Kemokai come to mind) in acts of corruption have often been greeted by silence and inaction from the government. An Anti-Corruption Commission established by British funds to help foster transparency in governance has been hampered in its activities by interference from the government. The British government, the country's main external patron, has threatened to withdraw support for the country's reconstruction unless concrete steps are taken to tackle the problem of corruption.

Protection of the basic human rights of the individual is also critical. This requires confronting the issue of impunity, prosecuting individuals who bear the most responsibility for human rights abuses, and restoring the independence of the judiciary. Already, the Special Court, a hybrid court established by the United Nations and the Sierra Leone government, has instituted legal proceedings against individuals who are alleged to bear the greatest responsibility for war crimes and crimes against humanity committed during the country's armed conflict. Among the indictees are Charles Taylor, the former warlord president of Liberia, as well as former rebel and Kamajor leaders. A Truth and Reconciliation Commission, modeled after the South African example, has also been involved in hearing testimonies from perpetrators and victims of war crimes. The outcome of both proceedings, especially the Special Court, should go a long way in restoring respect for the rule of law and the sanctity of human life.

Underdevelopment and poverty remain the greatest threats to the country's security dilemma. Among the main goals of the newly reconstituted state should be the demilitarization of security and the provision of social welfare benefits. Embarking on these tasks would build support and legitimacy for the state. And the state must be reconstructed before the nation can be reimagined. Alleviating mass poverty is critical to restoring the legitimacy of the state and is the surest means of reducing ethnic tensions and promoting national cohesion.

Survey of Views on the State, Ethnicity, and National Identity

Survey Sources and Methods

A total of 1,194 surveys were conducted across various regions of Sierra Leone. While the surveys were administered randomly at a large number of locations, both urban and rural, ultimately some 47 percent of respondents were inhabitants of the capital city, Freetown. (See Table 5.3.) Despite this, the sample did encompass a significant number of rural residents, with almost 19 percent of respondents identifying themselves as village dwellers. In line with the main focus of this study—on nationalism, ethnic identity, and the role of the state—the surveys were partitioned according to the ethnic identities of respondents. The five ethnic groups explicitly identified were those constituting the largest ethnic groups in Sierra Leone: the Mende (34 percent), Temne (32 percent), Krio (3 to 10 percent), Limba (8.4 percent), and Lokko (3 percent). The sample analyzed here roughly approximates this broader population distribution, with 36 percent of respondents identifying themselves as Mende, followed by 24 percent Temne, 11 percent Krio, 7 percent Limba, and 7 percent Lokko; 15 percent of survey respondents identified with ethnic groups other than the five specified (e.g., Bullom, Fulani, Kissi, Kono, and Koranko) and were subsequently categorized as "other."

Since the surveys were administered randomly, it was hoped that the sample would encompass a fair range of respondents in terms of demographic characteristics such as gender, age, income, and education. In fact, analysis of the sample confirms a reasonable demographic distribution. However, with regard to gender, over 62 percent of respondents overall are male, clearly reflecting a slight bias since, in terms of the general population of Sierra Leone, only approximately 48 percent of citizens between the ages of fifteen and sixty-four (99 percent of the survey sample falls into this age category) are male. In terms of education, the modal category is ten to twelve years of school (i.e., completed secondary education), with 77 percent of respondents being educated to the high school level or above. With regard to income, distribution is fairly concentrated, with over 53 percent of respondents declaring monthly household incomes of less than Leones 300,000, and the majority of those (39.9 percent) having incomes less than Leones 100,000 (over one-quarter of respondents actually failed to disclose their income).

Additionally, it should be noted that although the total sample size is 1,194, many respondents either did not identify with any ethnic group, or identified with two or more groups. In order to facilitate less ambiguity in interpreting the survey analyses, these surveys were omitted, leaving a total of 1,029 surveys utilized here.

In the analysis that follows, the survey data is utilized to examine several attitudinal dimensions of ethnic identity in Sierra Leone, including

- The extent and standard of government provisions for basic social services and protections
- The preferred balance between national unity and minority group interests, as well as the proper role for government in determining and maintaining that balance
- Perceptions of own and other ethnic groups with regard to the relationship between ethnic and national identity—namely distinguishing those groups considered "truly" Sierra Leonean.
- The role of foreign countries and international organizations in both sustaining peace and order in Sierra Leone and contributing to war and violence.

Table 5.3   Respondent Demographics

Group	Gender %		Average Age	Average Education	Employment %		Average Income
Krio	M	63	38	13–15 yrs.	E	53	Le 100,000–300,000
	F	33			U	42	
					M	5	
Limba	M	59	34	10–12 yrs.	E	45	Less than 100,000
	F	41			U	51	
					M	4	
Lokko	M	54	37	10–12 yrs.	E	36	Less than 100,000
	F	46			U	63	
					M	1	
Mende	M	65	39	10–12 yrs.	E	49	Less than 100,000
	F	32			U	50	
					M	1	
Temne	M	59	36	10–12 yrs.	E	36	Less than 100,000
	F	41			U	61	
					M	3	
Other	M	66	35	10–12 yrs.	E	47	Le 100,000–300,000
	F	44			U	49	
					M	4	

Note: E = Employed; U = Unemployed; M = Missing.

The Role of Government

Regarding the role of government in Sierra Leone, we asked our respondents who was, in their minds, responsible for protecting them from crime and military violence and providing basic services such as health care and the schooling of children. Table 5.4 shows the results of this survey.

As Table 5.4 indicates, there is clearly some consistency across ethnic groups in terms of perceptions of the government's provision of basic serv-

Table 5.4   The State as Provider and Protector

Group	Sample Size	Crime Protection %		Foreign Violence Protection %		Health Care%		Children's School %		Average
Krio	113	Govt.	81	Govt.	83	Govt.	58	Govt.	41	66
		No One	2	No One	4	No One	3	No One	0	2
		Self	7	Self	2	Self	28	Self	31	17
Limba	76	Govt.	79	Govt.	78	Govt.	46	Govt.	39	61
		No One	0	No One	5	No One	1	No One	1	2
		Self	21	Self	3	Self	41	Self	39	26
Lokko	67	Govt.	85	Govt.	82	Govt.	55	Govt.	40	66
		No One	0	No One	4	No One	3	No One	3	3
		Self	10	Self	3	Self	36	Self	37	22
Mende	371	Govt.	93	Govt.	96	Govt.	74	Govt.	65	82
		No One	1	No One	1	No One	1	No One	1	1
		Self	5	Self	1	Self	19	Self	19	11
Temne	244	Govt.	80	Govt.	83	Govt.	55	Govt.	39	64
		No One	1	No One	2	No One	2	No One	0	1
		Self	16	Self	9	Self	35	Self	34	24
Other	158	Govt.	92	Govt.	91	Govt.	57	Govt.	44	71
		No One	1	No One	1	No One	2	No One	1	1
		Self	6	Self	3	Self	37	Self	34	20
Total	1,029									

Notes: "Govt." includes government, government ministries, the Sierra Leone army, police, armed forces, and the state. "Self" includes myself, relatives (e.g., husband, parents, children, etc.), and private provisions.

ices and national security. Among most ethnic groups, the average percentage of respondents indicating that the government is the primary provider of basic services and protections ranges from 64 percent (Temne) to 71 percent (Other). Clearly, the government is perceived as having its most active role in terms of national security, with a vast majority of respondents perceiving the government to be the primary source of protection from both civil and foreign violence. The perception of government in terms of providing basic health and education services, however, is less positive, as indicated by the significant percentage of respondents claiming personal responsibility for these services. Notably, the obvious outlier in all categories is the Mende, who clearly perceive a more active role for the government, with an average of 82 percent over all categories crediting government with the provision of goods and services.

The more central and active role of government perceived by the Mende is likely due to the fact that the group is closely identified with the incumbent SLPP government. Under colonial rule and in the first few years of independence, Mendes were at the receiving end of government benefits. Mendes felt alienated from the APC government during the 1970s and 1980s but in the 1990s the military government of Valentine Strasser resurrected the practice of "Mende favoritism" in both the government and the military, a trend that has continued under the current SLPP government—a party that traditionally has been supported by the Mende and has subsequently rewarded that support when in office.

The fact that the Temne ethnic group perceives the government to play a less active role in providing basic services and protection is also likely reflective of contemporary circumstances, in particular their current political marginalization. The strong presence of Temne in the ranks of sobel and later rebel irregulars is largely indicative of their lack of identification with the SLPP and NPRC (1992–1996) governments. Since the APC was removed from power in 1992, Temnes have held less positive views of the government, which is not surprising since Mendes had a corresponding negative view of government when their party was out of power. Periodizing Temne and Mende responses on the role of government is likely to show a correlation between the perceptions of these two ethnic groups and the party in power.

The Proficiency of State Provisions

"Part of the role of central government is to provide services and protection to its citizens. We would like to ask you some questions that relate to the adequacy of services and protection that the central government in Sierra Leone provides its citizens. In Sierra Leone, how satisfied or dissatisfied are you with the following?"

As illustrated by Table 5.5, all ethnic groups exhibit general dissatisfaction with the efficiency of the central government in its provision of basic goods and services, with the average distribution of satisfaction across categories fairly concentrated between a low of 34 percent (Lokko) and a high of 49 percent (Mende). It is notable that, in the same way that government is perceived to be most active in its provision of national security, it is also perceived to be most efficient in this area, with a majority of respondents expressing satisfaction with government protection from crime and foreign violence.

In terms of the standard of health, education, and road services provided by the government, it seems likely that perceptions are, to some extent, reflective of regional and local circumstances. For example, the relatively higher rate of satisfaction with road services among the Krio (25 percent) may be a consequence of the fact that 82 percent of Krio respondents are city dwellers; in contrast, the 9 percent satisfaction rate among Temne may

Table 5.5   The Proficiency of State Provisions

Group	Sample Size	Crime Protection		Foreign Violence Protection		Basic Health Care		Education		Roads		Average
Krio	113	Satisfied	53	Satisfied	55	Satisfied	33	Satisfied	34	Satisfied	25	40
		Dissat.	46	Dissat.	44	Dissat.	66	Dissat.	66	Dissat.	74	59
Limba	76	Satisfied	49	Satisfied	64	Satisfied	37	Satisfied	34	Satisfied	16	40
		Dissat.	51	Dissat.	35	Dissat.	62	Dissat.	64	Dissat.	84	59
Lokko	67	Satisfied	49	Satisfied	69	Satisfied	22	Satisfied	19	Satisfied	9	34
		Dissat.	51	Dissat.	31	Dissat.	78	Dissat.	81	Dissat.	91	66
Mende	371	Satisfied	73	Satisfied	71	Satisfied	43	Satisfied	43	Satisfied	14	49
		Dissat.	26	Dissat.	28	Dissat.	56	Dissat.	56	Dissat.	85	50
Temne	244	Satisfied	57	Satisfied	61	Satisfied	30	Satisfied	30	Satisfied	9	38
		Dissat.	42	Dissat.	38	Dissat.	69	Dissat.	69	Dissat.	94	62
Other	158	Satisfied	63	Satisfied	61	Satisfied	42	Satisfied	42	Satisfied	20	45
		Dissat.	36	Dissat.	37	Dissat.	57	Dissat.	57	Dissat.	80	54
Total	1,029											

reflect the fact that only 28 percent of respondents in this group live in cities. This possibility is further reinforced by the rates of satisfaction among the Mende; while the Mende have the highest rates of satisfaction in terms of government provision of health and education services (43 percent), only 14 percent of Mende express satisfaction with road services—clearly reflecting the small proportion of respondents in this group (32 percent) that are city dwellers.

Overall, there appears to be some correlation between the extent to which government is considered as the provider of goods and services, and perceptions of how well those services are actually provided. The Temne for example, do not appear to benefit particularly from the government provision of health and education services (Table 5.4) and, correspondingly, appear to have a generally unfavorable perception of the standard of those services. This, of course, may reflect a normative evaluation in the sense that Temne respondents consider the government responsible for the provision of basic services, and when that responsibility apparently is not met, services are perceived as unsatisfactory. It is notable, however, that the provision of basic services alone does not equate to satisfactory perceptions of such services; while a majority of Mende respondents benefit from government provision of health and education services (74 percent and 65 percent respectively), only a minority are actually satisfied with such services (43 percent in both cases).

Nationalism and Ethnic Identity

National unity versus ethnic self-determination

"One thing that a central government can do is to help the people of a country work toward a feeling of national unity, to bring the people together for common cause and purpose. So that we can understand better how you feel about this, I want to ask you to listen to a few statements and tell me how strongly you agree or disagree with each."

- The unity of Sierra Leone is more important than the interests of any particular group or people in the country.
- The central government of Sierra Leone represents the interests of most of the peoples of Sierra Leone.
- It is more important that individual groups or people have the right to determine their own future than it is for the country to have a sense of unity and common purpose.
- In Sierra Leone, the central government represents the interests of all of the peoples in the country.
- Sierra Leone should remain united even if it requires armed force to do so.
- Do you strongly agree, disagree, or strongly disagree that military force should be used to keep Sierra Leone united?
- In your opinion, how effective has the central government of Sierra Leone been in trying to solve or trying to seek solutions to the problems among the peoples of the country?

As is evident from Table 5.6, a large majority of respondents from every ethnic group perceive national unity to take priority over group or individual interests—over 90 percent of respondents in every case. In contrast, only a minority of each group—ranging from 16 percent of Lokko respondents to 39 percent of Limba respondents—perceived group or individual rights to take precedence over national unity. Clearly, the responses to these two questions demonstrate some degree of overlap that, at first glance, appears to be contradictory. However, the wording of the two questions evidently addresses two separate issues; while the first questions the appropriate balance between national unity and group/individual interests, the second questions the importance of group/individual rights (namely, the right to determine one's own future) relative to national unity. In this sense, the larger proportion of affirmative responses to the latter questions is less ambiguous—arguably, the imprecise and more subjective nature of group interests make them less vital relative to national unity than the more fundamental and thus more indispensable idea of group or individual rights.

In terms of government representation, a large proportion of respondents express the sentiment that the government of Sierra Leone is not rep-

Table 5.6 Nationalism and Ethnic Identity

Group	Sample Size		National Unity More Important Than Group Interests	Government Represents Most People	Individual or Group Rights More Important Than National Unity	Government Represents All People	Armed Forces to Achieve Unity if Necessary	Military Force Should Be Used	Government Is Effective in Seeking Solutions
Krio	113	A	97	53	27	35	69	44	56
		D	2	45	68	64	28	50	42
		M	1	1	5	1	3	6	3
Limba	76	A	92	39	39	24	70	38	46
		D	8	59	61	75	28	61	53
		M	0	1	0	1	3	1	1
Lokko	67	A	96	54	16	18	82	55	45
		D	4	46	82	82	18	45	52
		M	0	0	2	0	0	0	3
Mende	371	A	95	64	34	43	79	43	70
		D	4	35	64	55	20	56	29
		M	1	1	2	2	1	1	1
Temne	244	A	95	41	31	19	76	35	48
		D	4	57	66	77	23	64	50
		M	1	2	3	4	1	1	2
Other	158	A	92	47	36	28	76	35	61
		D	5	48	62	68	22	63	37
		M	3	5	2	4	2	2	2

Note: A = percentage Agree; D = percentage Disagree; M = percentage Missing.

resentative of all, or even most, people in the country. The outlier however is the Mende, with 64 percent of Mende respondents believing that the government represents most people and 43 percent believing it represents all people; this corresponds to some extent with the positive response among Mende (70 percent) regarding the effectiveness of government in seeking solutions to problems among the people of Sierra Leone. Perhaps not surprisingly, the Krio have the second-highest rate of agreement among the named ethnic groups regarding government representation of Sierra Leone's people, and the effectiveness of government in dealing with intergroup issues (56 percent). As the descendents of freed African slaves, the Krio (or Creole) have been members of Sierra Leone's elite since colonial times, benefiting particularly from the acquisition of British education and culture. The Krio are largely educated professionals who traditionally have been influential in both the politics and economy of the country. In this sense, it seems intuitive that this group would have a relatively more positive view of the representational and problem-solving roles of the government in the nation's ethnic problems.

Perhaps more revealing, however, are the responses of the Limba, only 39 percent of whom believe that the government represents most or all of Sierra Leone's people, with only 46 percent perceiving the government to be effective in solving intergroup problems. The third-largest ethnic group in the country, the Limba are considered to be among the oldest inhabitants of present-day Sierra Leone and are traditionally known as palm-wine tappers. The strong perception among Limba respondents that the government is unrepresentative and ineffective is not surprising given the close identification of Limbas with APC rule, especially during the Momoh years (1985–1992). Both APC heads of state, Stevens and Momoh, were Limba, as were many ministers and officials in the APC. Although relations between Temne and Limba were conflictual within the APC, both ethnic groups identified with and were favored by the APC. Additionally, the lumpen military interregnum of 1997–1998 was led by Limbas who felt the incumbent SLPP government was more committed to the Kamajor militia than the national army. Most of the politicians who collaborated with this junta were from the APC, including former president Momoh. Momoh and other APC politicians, mostly northerners (Limba, Temne, etc.), were prosecuted and convicted on treason and other related charges, a process that may have succeeded in further alienating northerners, especially Limbas and Temnes, from the current SLPP government. Also, while the Limba were politically privileged under Momoh's APC government, there is much to suggest that, historically, they have suffered from economic neglect.

In considering the use of force to keep Sierra Leone united, the survey responses appear to be somewhat ambiguous. While a clear majority of all ethnic groups (between 69 percent and 82 percent) agree that armed forces should be used if necessary to maintain national unity, a much smaller proportion of each group (between 35 percent and 55 percent) agree that military force is an acceptable route to unity. Clearly, it seems then that these responses are contradictory. One possibility, however, is that respondents make some distinction between "armed force" and "military force." Arguably, respondents may be more likely to associate military force with government force and, subsequently, with government bias. In contrast, "armed forces" may be more highly associated with international organizations and peacekeeping operations. This possibility is reinforced by the fact that those groups most likely to perceive the government as representative (Mende, Lokko, and Krio) are also more likely to favor the use of "military" force, whereas those groups with less favorable perceptions of the government (Temne and Limba) are more strongly opposed to the use of such force. In terms of the use of "armed" force, the same pattern is not evident, with the Krio being the least supportive of this option. In this sense, while respondents may be willing to maintain national unity through the use of force, they may prefer that such force not be applied by the central government of Sierra Leone.

Identity I: personal perceptions. As is evident from Table 5.7 below, a vast majority of each ethnic group considered themselves to be truly Sierra Leonean: 85 percent of Krio, 99 percent of Limba, 99 percent of Lokko, 89 percent of Mende, and 89 percent of Temne. In terms of both their own and others' perceptions, the Krio are clearly the least likely to be considered as truly Sierra Leonean, a fact that is likely a consequence of their heritage as settlers. This perception is probably reinforced by the fact that, while the Krio intermarried with the indigenous peoples of Sierra Leone, they remained culturally detached from the local majority and became more associated with British practices, including the Christian religion.

At the other end of the spectrum, the Limba, on average, are most strongly perceived as being truly people of Sierra Leone, both by themselves and by other ethnic groups. As with the Krio, such a perception likely has historical roots since the Limba have lived in the northern part of present-day Sierra Leone for hundreds of years and, as mentioned previously, are considered to be, along with the Sherbro, among the country's oldest inhabitants.

Table 5.7 **"Of the Following Peoples, Which Do You Consider to Be Truly Sierra Leonean?"**

Group	Sample Size		Krio	Limba	Lokko	Mende	Temne
Krio	113	Y	85	86	87	75	76
		N	8	2	4	10	10
		M	7	12	9	15	14
Limba	76	Y	71	99	93	78	84
		N	24	0	0	16	9
		M	5	1	7	6	7
Lokko	67	Y	73	93	99	81	82
		N	22	3	0	13	12
		M	5	4	1	6	6
Mende	371	Y	62	85	87	89	81
		N	27	2	4	4	6
		M	11	13	9	7	13
Temne	244	Y	61	96	94	86	89
		N	33	0	4	10	7
		M	6	4	2	4	4
Other	158	Y	61	94	91	87	89
		N	23	1	2	4	3
		M	16	5	7	9	8

Note: Y = percentage Yes; N = percentage No; M = percentage Missing.

After the Krio, the Mende are the group least likely to be considered truly Sierra Leonean by others, and are also the group most likely to consider other groups not to be truly Sierra Leonean. Arguably, these attitudes do not appear reflective of historical circumstances. In fact, not only do the Mende constitute approximately one-third of the country's population, but they have occupied the southern region of Sierra Leone for hundreds of years and are thus considered to be one of the country's older ethnic groups. In this sense, it is less clear why the Mende might not be considered to be truly Sierra Leonean. One possibility may be related to the language spoken by this group—a language belonging to the Mande language group and one that makes the Mende distinct from other ethnic groups in Sierra Leone, providing a permanent reminder of their immigration from the interior centuries ago. Alternatively, such perceptions may be a consequence of conflict rather than culture. The history of the Mende in Sierra Leone is largely distinguished by the group's constant struggle for control of the country, with the result that they have a number of long-standing disputes with other ethnic groups, particularly the Temne. These disputes may have resulted in a heightened sense of hostility toward the Mende, not to mention a stronger sense of ethnic identity within the group itself (possibly explaining why only 89 percent of Mende themselves identify as truly Sierra Leonean).

Identity II: perceiving others. As is evident from Table 5.8 (below), a majority of respondents across all groups believed that they were perceived by other ethnic groups as being truly Sierra Leonean. While the relatively large proportion of respondents across groups that failed to answer this question (between 10 and 20 percent) indicates some uncertainty regarding the feelings of others, there is generally a good degree of congruence in the perceptions of the different ethnic groups.

In fact, with the exception of the Krio who are somewhat overly optimistic—about 72 percent of Krio respondents believe that individuals across the other groups consider them to be truly Sierra Leonean, when on average only 67 percent of respondents from other groups actually do—the other four groups tend to be overly pessimistic regarding the perceptions of others. This is particularly true of the Lokko and Limba groups, where an average of 85 percent and 81 percent of respondents respectively consider that other groups view them as truly Sierra Leonean, when in fact the proportion of respondents from the other ethnic groups that consider these two groups to be truly Sierra Leonean is around 90 percent. The data are also revealing in terms of where the disjunction between perceptions of self and Other occur. For example, while only about 77 percent of Mende perceive that the Temne consider them to be truly Sierra Leonean, 86 percent of Temne respondents actually do consider the Mende to be truly Sierra Leonean; similarly, while only 73 percent of Temne believe that the Mende consider them truly Sierra Leonean, 81 percent of the Mende respondents

Table 5.8 **"Do Any of the Following Peoples See Your People as Being Truly Sierra Leonean?"**

Group	Sample Size		Krio	Limba	Lokko	Mende	Temne
Krio	113	Y	80	74	75	69	69
		N	4	6	6	11	11
		M	16	20	19	20	20
Limba	76	Y	78	92	86	76	83
		N	12	1	3	13	7
		M	10	7	11	11	10
Lokko	67	Y	82	91	94	82	84
		N	7	0	0	7	6
		M	11	9	6	11	10
Mende	371	Y	75	77	82	84	77
		N	9	4	3	3	8
		M	16	19	15	13	15
Temne	244	Y	76	82	82	73	76
		N	14	9	9	18	14
		M	10	9	9	9	10
Other	158	Y	70	84	85	82	80
		N	16	3	3	6	6
		M	14	13	12	12	14

Note: Y = percentage Yes; N = percentage No; M = percentage Missing.

viewed the Temne as truly Sierra Leonean.

Clearly, then, the history of long-standing disputes between the Temne and the Mende ethnic groups seems to have resulted in a sense between both groups that the other views them, at least in terms of national identity, less favorably than is actually the case. While the fact that subjective perceptions between groups appear to change more slowly than objective realities is not at all surprising, these findings may nevertheless be promising for the future dynamics of intergroup relations in Sierra Leone. Arguably, national identity is as much about how one is perceived, as about how one perceives oneself. In this sense, increased congruence between perceptions of self and others within and among the various ethnic groups of Sierra Leone (in particular, recognizing the extent of positive attitudes among other groups) is likely to contribute to a stronger sense of national unity and identity across the nation.

Civil Conflict and International Relations

Peace and order. As Table 5.9 (below) illustrates, a majority of all ethnic groups in Sierra Leone are in agreement regarding those countries contributing to peace in the nation; across groups, a majority of respondents

Table 5.9   "Have Any of the Following Countries Contributed to Creating and Sustaining Peace and Order in Sierra Leone?"

Group	Sample Size		Burkina Faso	Ghana	Guinea	Great Britain	Liberia	Libya	Nigeria	United States
Krio	113	Y	1	90	89	100	4	6	99	88
		N	72	3	3	0	70	62	0	4
		M	27	7	8	0	26	32	1	8
Limba	76	Y	4	88	93	99	3	8	97	88
		N	68	4	4	1	72	67	3	4
		M	28	8	3	0	25	25	0	8
Lokko	67	Y	1	93	94	97	6	12	99	84
		N	75	3	6	1	75	67	1	6
		M	24	4	0	2	19	21	0	10
Mende	371	Y	1	90	95	98	2	5	98	94
		N	57	3	1	1	55	53	1	2
		M	42	7	4	1	43	42	1	4
Temne	244	Y	1	93	92	98	4	9	98	82
		N	76	2	5	1	74	67	1	6
		M	23	5	3	1	22	24	1	12
Other	158	Y	1	92	95	99	1	5	99	91
		N	69	3	3	1	69	63	1	3
		M	30	5	2	0	30	32	0	6

Note: Y = percentage Yes; N = percentage No; M = percentage Missing.

cited Ghana (91 percent), Guinea (93 percent), Great Britain (99 percent), Nigeria (98 percent) and the United States (88 percent), as all contributing to the maintenance of peace in their country, with these perceptions being fairly uniform across groups. Clearly this reflects the activities and involvement of these nations in the training and support of government personnel in Sierra Leone, as well as their aid in rebuilding the nation's shattered infrastructure.

For example, in addition to supporting and offering overseas training facilities to the Sierra Leone police force, the British were also involved in the retraining of the country's army in 2000. Nigeria has also been prominent in its support of Sierra Leone and was responsible for the training of officer cadets for the Sierra Leone army after the invasion of Freetown in 1999, as well as the accommodation of Sierra Leonean refugees displaced by the persistence of civil conflict. Nigeria has also been swift to respond to calls for assistance from the Sierra Leonean government following rebel incursions by the RUF. The United States has also assumed an active role in the securing of peace and the rebuilding of civil society in Sierra Leone. As a major supporter of the Special Court for Sierra Leone, an institution designed to facilitate reconciliation and restore peace in the country, the

U.S. Congress appropriated $20 million in funds for this court in 2003 alone. Meanwhile, both Ghana and Guinea continue in their efforts to aid the government and people of Sierra Leone. While Guinea has provided resettlement programs for refugees from Sierra Leone (particularly those from the northern region of the country), Ghana has been praised by the president of Sierra Leone, Ahmed Tejan Kabbah, for the significant role it has played in bringing peace to his country.

War and violence. Again, as Table 5.10 (below) demonstrates, there appears to be a great deal of congruence across Sierra Leone's ethnic groups in terms of perceptions of those countries that have contributed to the war and violence in the nation; on average, across ethnic lines, respondents over-whelmingly identified Burkina Faso (96 percent), Liberia (99 percent), and Libya (87 percent) as countries that have been instrumental in exacerbating Sierra Leone's civil conflict. Clearly, these perceptions reflect the support of these countries for rebel forces in Sierra Leone. In Liberia, for example, the government has actively supported the Revolutionary United Front (RUF), the main rebel group in Sierra Leone and the one responsible for

Table 5.10   "Have Any of the Following Countries Contributed to War and Violence in Sierra Leone?"

Group	Sample Size		Burkina Faso	Ghana	Guinea	Great Britain	Liberia	Libya	Nigeria	United States
Krio	113	Y	96	66	8	1	98	89	1	4
		N	1	0	58	65	1	8	65	61
		M	3	34	34	34	1	3	34	35
Limba	76	Y	93	3	9	0	100	87	3	0
		N	1	63	57	64	0	3	61	62
		M	6	34	34	36	0	10	36	38
Lokko	67	Y	94	3	13	3	99	81	3	4
		N	1	75	66	76	1	12	76	73
		M	5	22	21	21	0	7	21	23
Mende	371	Y	96	2	4	1	98	89	2	2
		N	1	50	46	49	1	5	48	47
		M	3	48	50	50	1	6	50	51
Temne	244	Y	95	0	8	0	99	85	71	3
		N	0	74	67	74	0.5	8	2	69
		M	5	26	25	26	0.5	7	27	28
Other	158	Y	99	3	9	1	99	92	58	1
		N	0	61	56	62	0	4	4	60
		M	1	36	35	37	1	4	38	39

Note: Y = percentage Yes; N = percentage No; M = percentage Missing.

much of the death and destruction that has plagued the nation during the past decade. In fact, the Special Court of Sierra Leone has recently issued an indictment for the arrest of former Liberian president Charles Taylor for his support of the RUF and the fomenting of conflict in the country.

Burkina Faso has also been a source for concern in terms of promoting civil conflict in Sierra Leone; in particular, it has been criticized by the United Nations for providing a transit route for diamonds being smuggled out of Sierra Leone that have funded rebel activity and subsequently fueled conflict there. In the same vein, while Libya has publicly debated its efforts to settle the conflict in Sierra Leone, it is well known that Libyan president Colonel Muammar Gaddafi provided training grounds, financing, and weapons to the leader of the RUF, Foday Sankoh, who was responsible for the massacre of thousands of innocent Sierra Leoneans.

The United Nations. As Table 5.11 indicates, there is a general consensus across all of Sierra Leone's ethnic groups that the United Nations has successfully worked as an agency of peace rather than conflict in the nation. On average, 96 percent of respondents perceived the UN as contributing to the creating and sustaining of peace and order in Sierra Leone. In fact, the

Table 5.11 **"Has the UN or Any Other International Agency Contributed to Creating and Sustaining Peace and Order/War and Violence in Sierra Leone?"**

Group	Sample Size		UN Peace	UN War
Krio	113	Y	94	4
		N	4	87
		M	2	9
Limba	76	Y	97	4
		N	1	95
		M	2	7
Lokko	67	Y	97	3
		N	3	96
		M	0	1
Mende	371	Y	96	3
		N	1	92
		M	3	5
Temne	244	Y	98	3
		N	0	94
		M	1	3
Other	158	Y	96	3
		N	0	90
		M	4	7

Note: Y = percentage Yes; N = percentage No; M = percentage Missing.

United Nations Mission in Sierra Leone (UNAMSIL), has been working diligently to address some of Sierra Leone's most pressing problems in the wake of its protracted civil conflict, including the plight of ex-combatants and unemployed youth, illegal mining activities, and the extension of government authority across the country. In addition to its humanitarian efforts in local communities, UNAMSIL peacekeepers have been working with government security agencies to conduct patrols to deter civilian aggression and generally reassure the population. UNAMSIL's adjustment, drawdown, and withdrawal plan, which has been designed to transfer responsibility from UNAMSIL to Sierra Leone's own security forces, has also created a mobile Force Reserve that will work with the country's own police and armed forces to respond to crises nationally.

Conclusion

The root causes of state decomposition and war in Sierra Leone can be traced to a rapacious political class whose greed precluded the construction of effective state institutions and the legitimation of political power. Predatory accumulation and its attendant repression laid the groundwork for the violence and terror that convulsed Sierra Leone throughout much of the 1990s. The return of constitutional democracy has simply liberalized a predatory regime rather than alter the basic spoils logic of the political system. Liberalization of a predatory system represents regime persistence rather than change. Regime change can only be realized when the exercise of power is distanced from the accumulation of wealth and when the political class provides the leadership that is required to build accountable state institutions.

Ethnic mobilization in Sierra Leone has disproportionately favored elites rather than ethnic masses who have been called upon to pay the ultimate price in defending against putative threats to their communities that are often contrived. Temne support for the APC is just as solid as Mende support for the SLPP, but it is precisely such unwavering support for competing political parties on the part of the two largest ethnic groups that renders the political process amenable to the interests of ethnic politicians and cultural entrepreneurs who are the least interested in the promotion of national unity. By and large, however, the political allegiances of political elites have been influenced less by considerations of ethnicity than by calculations of personal reward; the political loyalties of the masses, by contrast, continue to be unduly shaped by ethnic sentiments that are frequently at odds with their interests and aspirations. Another way of putting this is to say that the beneficiaries of ethnic mobilization are the least motivated by ethnicity, while those motivated by ethnicity have gained the least from ethnic mobilization. Political elites are united on the basis of a common class interest, but the masses are still wedded to the politics of affect.

Notes

The authors would like to acknowledge Ibrahim Abdullah for his administration of the surveys in Sierra Leone. They would also like to thank Maria Elena Sandovici and Myung-Hee Kim for their assistance in survey analysis.

1. See David Keen, "Incentives and Disincentives for Violence," in *Greed and Grievance: Economic Agendas in Civil Wars,* eds. Mats Berdal and David Malone (Boulder, CO: Lynne Rienner Publishers, 2000), 35.

2. Elizabeth Rubin, "An Army of One's Own: In Africa, Nations Hire a Corporation to Wage War," *Harper's Magazine* (February 1997): 46.

3. For a discussion of nation as cultural elaboration, see Homi Bhabha, ed., *The Nation and Narration* (London: Routledge, 1990), especially Bhabha's chapter on "Narrating the Nation."

4. See Walter Rodney, *History of the Upper Guinea Coast 1545–1800* (Oxford: Oxford University Press, 1970) for a detailed discussion of the Mane invasion.

5. Ibid.

6. See Adam Jones, *From Slaves to Palm Kernels: A History of the Galinhas Country (West Africa), 1730–1890* (Wiesbaden: Franz Steiner Verlag, 1983) for a study of Gallinas country.

7. See Michael Banton, "The Ethnography of the Protectorate: Review Article," *Sierra Leone Studies*, no. 4 (June 1955): 246.

8. For detailed information on the various settler groups, see R. Kuczynski, *A Demographic Survey of the British Colonial Empire, West Africa*, vol. 1 (Oxford: Oxford University Press, 1948).

9. See Sigismund Koelle, *Polyglotta Africana* (London: Church Missionary House, 1854).

10. See Akintola Wyse, *The Krio of Sierra Leone: An Interpretive History* (London: C. Hurst & Co., 1989), 5–6, for an account of how liberated Africans came to be accepted into settler society.

11. See Davidson Nicol, ed., *Africanus Horton: The Dawn of Nationalism in Modern Africa* (London: Longmans, 1969), 28.

12. Christopher Fyfe, cited in Akintola Wyse, *The Krio of Sierrra Leone* (London: C. Hurst & Co., 1989), 14.

13. See P. E. H. Hair's review of Christopher Fyfe's *A History of Sierra Leone,* in *Sierra Leone Studies*, no. 17 (June 1963): 285–286 (281–296).

14. For a sampling of Horton's ideas on African independence, see Robert July, "Africanus Horton and the Idea of Independence in West Africa," *Sierra Leone Studies*, no. 18 (1966): 2–17.

15. See James Africanus Beale Horton, *West Africa: Vindication of the Negro Race* (Edinburgh: Edinburgh University Press, 1868), 89.

16. For one such critique, see E. A. Ayandele, *The Educated Elite in the Nigerian Society* (Ibadan: Ibadan University Press, 1974).

17. See J. Hargreaves, "African Colonization in the Nineteenth Century: Liberia and Sierra Leone," *Sierra Leone Studies*, no. 16 (June 1962): 190–191.

18. For a brief description of this incident, see M. C. F. Easmon, "A Note on the Waima Incident," *Sierra Leone Studies*, no. 18 (1966): 59–61.

19. See Michael Crowder, *West Africa Under Colonial Rule* (London: Hutchinson, 1968), 151.

20. Cited in Cyril P. Foray, *Historical Dictionary of Sierra Leone* (Metuchen, NJ: Scarecrow Press, 1977), 185.

21. For a brief description of some of these precolonial trade routes, see P. K. Mitchell, "Trade Routes of the Early Sierra Leone Protectorate," *Sierra Leone Studies*, no. 16 (1962): 204–217.

22. Frederic Cardew, the governor, who insisted that the show of force was necessary in annexing the protectorate, overruled Lewis.

23. Governor Frederic Cardew, quoted in James Harrison, *"The Twenty Seventh of April: The Sierra Leone Wars of 1898,* master's thesis, City College of the City University, New York, 1972, 54.

24. See *Report by Her Majesty's Commissioner and Correspondence on the Subject of the Insurrection in the Sierra Leone Protectorate* (London: Darling and Son, 1898), hereafter referred to as Chalmers Report; Harrison, "The Twenty Seventh of April"; J. D. Hargreaves, "The Establishment of the Sierra Leone Protectorate and the Insurrection of 1898," *Cambridge Historical Journal* 12 (1956): 56–80.

25. Chalmers Report, 73.

26. J. Ralph Best, *A History of the Sierra Leone Railway, 1899–1949* (Freetown: mimeo, 1949).

27. See *Sierra Leone: Estimates of Revenue and Expenditure* (Freetown: Government Printer, 1930, 1949, 1952).

28. See *Protectorate Native Law Ordinance, 1924* (Freetown: Government Printer, 1924), especially part 1: "Rights of Paramount Chiefs, Chiefs and Headmen to Labor."

29. See Mahmood Mamdani's *Citizen and Subject: Contemporary Africa and the Legacy of Late Colonialism* (Princeton, NJ: Princeton University Press, 1996), for a discussion of "decentralized despotism" and the continued "bifurcation" of power in Africa.

30. See *Reports of the Commissioners of Enquiry into the Conduct of Certain Chiefs and the Government Statement Thereon* (Freetown: Government Printer, 1958).

31. See *Sierra Leone: Estimates of Revenue and Expenditure* (Freetown: Government Printer, 1912).

32. See Akintola Wyse, "Searchlight on the Krio of Sierra Leone," Occasional Paper No. 3, Institute of African Studies, Fourah Bay College (Freetown: 1980).

33. Ibid., 4.

34. Quoted in Michael Banton, *West African City* (London: Oxford University Press, 1957), 14.

35. Ibid.

36. Ibid., 16–17.

37. Ibid., 24.

38. See the *Sierra Leone Weekly News*, 2 October 1900, 4.

39. Banton, *West African City*, 7–8.

40. Cited in Banton, *West African City*, 8.

41. See Martin Kilson, *Political Change in a West African State: A Study of the Modernization Process in Sierra Leone* (New York: Atheneum, 1969), 77.

42. Ibid., 70.

43. See T. S. Alldridge, *A Transformed Colony* (London: Seeley and Co., 1910), 139.

44. Quoted in Richard Corby, "Western Educated Sons of Chiefs, District Commissioners and Chiefdom: The Role of Bo School and Its Graduates in the Local Level Development of Sierra Leone, 1906–1961," Ph.D. dissertation, Indiana University, 1976, 82.

45. Quoted in Leo Spitzer, *The Creoles of Sierra Leone* (Madison: University of Wisconsin Press, 1974), 46.

46. Christopher Fyfe, *A History of Sierra Leone* (Oxford: Oxford University Press, 1962).

47. Quoted in Kilson, *Political Change in a West African State*, 126.

48. Ibid., 90.

49. Quoted in Michael Crowder, "An African Aristocracy," *Geographical Magazine* 31, no. 4 (1958): 183.

50. In an act of symbolic identification with the protectorate, E. N. Jones later changed his name to Lamina Sankoh, a Temne name. What used to be known as Trelawney Street in Freetown is now Lamina Sankoh Street.

51. The nine Creoles in attendance as delegates at the 1960 Lancaster House independence conference were J. A. Nelson-Williams, C. B. Rogers-Wright, J. Barthes Wilson, C. M. A. Thompson, J. C. Dougan, H. R. S. Bultman, H. N. Georgestone, E. Harris, and C. Cummings-John. Two other Creoles, I.T.A. Wallace-Johnson and Gershon Collier, attended the conference as advisers. For details, see *Report of the Sierra Leone Constitutional Conference, 1960* (Freetown: Government Printer, 1960).

52. Gershon Collier, *An Experiment in Democracy in an African Nation* (London: University of London Press, 1970), 97.

53. See Thomas Cox, *Civil-Military Relations in Sierra Leone* (Cambridge, MA: Harvard University Press, 1976), 51.

54. Ibid., 75.

55. See *Report of the Dove-Edwin Commission of Inquiry into the Conduct of the 1967 Elections and the Government Statement Thereon* (Freetown: Government Printer, 1967), 18.

56. Ibid., 17.

57. Ibid., 19.

58. Dalby contends that the "acceleration of their own promotion" could not be discounted as a "subsidiary" motive for the countercoup of 1967. See David Dalby, "The Military Take-over in Sierra Leone," *The World Today* (August 1967): 359.

59. See Cox, *Civil-Military Relations in Sierra Leone*, 85.

60. See *Report of the Forster Commission of Inquiry on the Assets of Ex-Ministers and Ex-Deputy Ministers and the Government Statement Thereon* (Freetown: Government Printer, 1968), 44.

61. Quoted in Humphrey Fisher, "Elections and Coups in Sierra Leone," *Journal of Modern African Studies* 7, no.4 (1969): 635.

62. This was the view of the APC leadership at the time. For details, see APC Secretariat, *The Rising Sun: A History of the All Peoples Congress Party of Sierra Leone* (Freetown: APC Publications, 1982), 96.

63. Cox, *Civil-Military Relations in Sierra Leone*, 85.

64. Quoted in Fred Hayward, "Political Leadership, Power and the State: Generalizations from the Case of Sierra Leone," *African Studies Review* 27, no. 3 (1984): 30.

65. C. Magbaily Fyle, "The Military and Civil Society in Sierra Leone: The 1992 Military Coup d'Etat," *Africa Development* 18, no. 2 (1994): 130.

66. Cox, *Civil-Military Relations in Sierra Leone*, 212.

67. See World Bank, *World Development Report* (Washington, DC: World Bank, 1997).

68. See *Second Report of the National Commission for Unity and Reconciliation* (Freetown: Government Printing Department, 1996), 7–8; otherwise known as the *Cross Report*.

69. See Jimmy D. Kandeh, "Sierra Leone: Contradictory Functionality of the Soft State," *Review of African Political Economy* 55 (1992): 30–43, for a discussion of how the mode of accumulation of Sierra Leone's political class undermined the long-term reproduction of its dominance.

70. See *West Africa* (20–26 October 1997): 1671.

71. See *West Africa* (23 October–3 November 1996): 1676.

72. See "The Sierra Leone Coup," *West Africa* (11–17 May 1992): 788–789.

73. For accounts of the role of Executive Outcomes in Sierra Leone, see Jeremy Harding, "The Mercenary Business: Executive Outcomes," *Review of African Political Economy* 71 (1997): 87–97; Rubin, "An Army of One's Own," 44–55.

74. See Yusuf Bangura's "Strategic Policy Failure and Governance in Sierra Leone," *Journal of Modern African Studies* 38, no. 4 (2000): 551–577, for a discussion of some of the miscues of the government in its handling of the country's security.

75. Ibid., 552–553, 555.

76. For an analysis of this election, see Jimmy Kandeh, "Sierra Leone's Post-Conflict Elections of 2002," *Journal of Modern African Studies* 41, no. 2 (2003): 189–216.

77. John Lonsdale, "Political Accountability in African History," in *Political Domination in Africa: Reflections on the Limits of Power,* ed. Patrick Cabal (Cambridge: Cambridge University Press, 1986), 155.

78. Marina Ottaway, "Democratization in Collapsed States," in *Collapsed States,* ed. William Zartman (Boulder, CO: Lynne Rienner Publishers, 1995), 235.

79. See Richard Dowden, "Sierra Leone Locked in Shackles of Corruption," *Daily Guardian* (London), 12 October 2002. Dowden, among other things, reports that the present "government is thwarting attempts to clean up and rebuild the country."

80. These are the words of Clare Short, then British development secretary, as quoted in Dowden, ibid.

6

Ethnic Grievance or Material Greed?

Ricardo René Larémont & Robert L. Ostergard Jr.

Thus far in this study we have concentrated on the relationships among state boundaries, state performance, national identity formation, and civil conflict in four African states, with a particular focus on perceived ethnic grievances and the persistent possibilities of transethnic nationalism within the boundaries of postcolonial states. In this chapter we examine a different question. Do explanatory relationships exist among the presence of natural resources, the access and competition for those resources, arms purchases, and civil conflict in Sudan, Ethiopia, the Democratic Republic of Congo (DRC), and Sierra Leone?

Exploring the role of natural resources in sustaining conflict and civil wars, we address, first, the specific natural resources at play in Sudan, Ethiopia, the DRC, and Sierra Leone; and, second, how these resources aggravate civil conflict, specifically engaging the debate engendered by Mats Berdal and David Malone in their edited book *Greed and Grievance: Economic Agendas in Civil Wars*.[1]

In our four cases of alleged ethnic competition, the existence of natural resources and the scramble for them, the artificiality of borders, and the weakness of states converge. To varying degrees in our case studies, the weakness or the implosion of the state has pushed the leaders of ethnic or racial groups to compete for natural resources that can be sold so that profits can be used to purchase small arms. In our cases, the states are weak and unable to engage in adequate internal policing; this allows ethnic conflict, where it exists, to mushroom into more serious civil conflict or warfare. Because the state is particularly weak in Sierra Leone, the DRC, and Sudan, conflicts that initially may be "internal" in character quickly become regionalized, affecting neighboring states and the international community.

This chapter and the subsequent chapter by William G. Martin provide economic contexts for our analysis of conflict, warfare, and the possible collapse of the state. Historically, civil wars and civil conflict in Africa have not been fueled just by primordial "ancient hatreds." When examining the role of either ethnicity or economics and their relationship with conflict, we need to focus on the relationships among these factors and the following issues: (1) the onset of conflict; (2) the duration of conflict; and, (3) the termination of conflict. This typology has been recognized explicitly or implicitly in recent literature that analyzes civil conflict.[2] These distinctions become clear in our case studies. For instance, civil conflict in Sudan has been linked to ethnic and religious differences, but the recent discovery of oil in the country has changed the strategic targeting of violence and the pattern of conflict, ultimately affecting the conditions for ending the war. All sides in civil conflicts need resource bases to sustain their efforts. There are two particular challenges for understanding the processes for attaining and maintaining peace: first, the nexus between natural resources and arms purchases must be understood, addressed, and confronted; second, the global incentives that prolong warfare (for example, the demand for "conflict diamonds") must be examined. Without addressing these two issues, lasting solutions will be elusive and peace will not be attained.

For centuries, states have needed to obtain economic resources to establish or to consolidate institutions and to conduct warfare.[3] During periods of civil conflict, governments and rebels both need resources. Governments need resources to maintain their primary and secondary institutions and to combat rebel forces. Rebels need resources to mount resistance to the state and to address the needs of their local constituencies. In the sections that follow, we detail the precise natural-resource bases at stake in Sudan, Ethiopia, the DRC, and Sierra Leone and how these resources sustain conflict and warfare. Furthermore, we claim that not all types of natural resources are equivalent: The type of resource and the market for that resource significantly affect the nature of conflict.

In two of our four cases (Sierra Leone and the DRC) the porosity and frequent indefensibility of borders merge with the particular dynamics of trading in alluvial diamonds to create new types of political instability. Our observations lead us to conclude that the presence of alluvial in contrast to deep-shaft kimberlite diamonds creates critical differences in the understanding and analysis of warfare in Africa.[4] Both alluvial and deep-shaft diamonds, when extracted from the earth, are lightweight and easily transportable (like heroin and cocaine in Peru and Colombia). Because of their light weight and high value they provide rebels with an easy means to finance warfare, because in addition to being easily transportable, diamonds are valuable and quickly sold. Alluvial diamonds, however, are more destabilizing than deep-shaft diamonds because deep-shaft diamonds can be excavated only by corporate, capital-intensive, deep-mining processes, whereas alluvial diamonds are obtained by independent artisanal miners using manual labor and the most basic of technologies—a pan and water. Although various commodities sustain warfare, diamonds—and especially alluvial diamonds—are extremely advantageous to combatants as an export commodity. In addition to the factors mentioned above, their transport is less easily detected and monitored. Arguably, diamonds operate to destabilize African societies in the same way that coca or cocaine play destabilizing roles in Latin America. Opium poppies play the same role in Southeast and Southwest Asia. Lightweight, high-value commodities such as diamonds, coca, and opium enhance the potential for funding rebel movements and for destabilizing the state.

While analysis of the diamond trade applies particularly to the DRC and Sierra Leone, we see that the discovery of petroleum in southern Sudan has extended and even changed the nature of warfare in that state. The discovery of petroleum and the potential windfall from petroleum has provided additional incentives for the government in Khartoum to commit itself to the territorial integration of the south and to the continued prosecution of a war of national "integration." Our least-conflicted case, Ethiopia, involves an analysis of access to navigable harbors and the socioeconomics of coffee farming and coffee marketing.

Greed or Grievance: A Critical Perspective

Research regarding the relationship between natural resources and civil conflict is extensive, but the state of the literature still reveals that theoretical inconsistencies remain in understanding the relationship between these variables. Recent studies from the social science discipline of economics have challenged conventional theories that link civil conflict to grievances, especially those grievances centered around ethnic issues. In the forefront of this new research has been Paul Collier and others at the World Bank's Development Research Group. Collier and his colleagues have brought quantitative methodologies to bear on two important questions regarding civil conflicts: the factors that contribute to the onset of civil wars and the factors that contribute to the duration of civil wars. Collier reaches conclusions that by his own admission, are counterintuitive: "inequality, political repression, and ethnic and religious divisions . . . provide no explanatory power in predicting [the onset] of rebellion."[5] He claims that "economic characteristics—dependence on primary commodity exports, low average incomes, slow [economic] growth, and large diasporas, [which can provide financial support to rebellions]—are significant and powerful predictors of civil war."[6]

With regard to the duration of these conflicts, Collier, Hoeffler, and Söderbom argue that "the duration of conflict is determined by a substantially different set of variables from those that determine the initiation of conflict. Notably, the duration of a conflict is substantially increased if the society is composed of a few large ethnic groups, if there is extensive forest cover, and if it commenced since 1980."[7]

In the specific case of Africa, Collier and Hoeffler conclude that "Africa's economic characteristics generated an atypically high risk of conflict, but this was offset by its social characteristics which generated an atypically low risk."[8] Africa's civil wars are due, according to a significant portion of their argument, to its poor economic performance. Again, these findings are counterintuitive to the large base of political science and historical research that generally finds the reverse of Collier et al.'s conclusions, namely that ethnic cleavages are intricately related to the onset of civil conflict, while the presence of natural resources, particularly in the post–Cold War period, tends to prolong it.

A crucial factor in understanding the results obtained by Collier and his colleagues involves the theoretical framework used for their models. Their framework uses four principal assumptions:

- Rebellion involves the large-scale predation of productive economic activities.
- Any sense of grievance in warfare is deliberately generated by rebel leaders; recruits who join these organizations and who agree to accept these grievances have been duped by their leadership.
- Motivation for conflict is unimportant; it only matters whether the organization conducting the rebellion can sustain itself financially.
- Predatory behavior may not be the objective of the rebel organization but it is a means of financing it.[9]

Hence, for Collier rebellion has nothing to do with the objective circumstances of ethnic grievance; the feasibility of predation or plundering for the continuation of warfare is what really matters. Collier's macro perception is that the activities of rebel organizations are tantamount to a form of organized crime in which ethnic grievances do not seem to matter. One way of understanding Collier's epistemology involves an analysis of the cause-and-effect mechanism that he assumes.

As an economist, Collier is concerned with individual choices and the costs and benefits of those choices. From his disciplinary perspective, Collier's understanding of the mechanisms that spur civil war and rebellion are consistent. The problem, however, is that the approach often overlooks critical theoretical and methodological issues that are relevant, leading to conclusions that are questionable. From a theoretical perspective, his approach tries to explain civil war through individual choice behavior (choosing to rebel against an established state authority), which focuses strictly on an individual cost-benefit approach as displayed in Figure 6.1.

By itself, the model is elegant—it narrows rebellion down to a question of feasibility. But elegance does not guarantee explanatory power; such a narrow field of analysis leads to both theoretical and practical problems, particularly in the context of Africa and the settlement of civil conflict.

While not dismissing the economic interpretation of civil conflict, David Keen has argued that most often ethnic groups may be subject to exploitation or violence.[10] Either the government or rebels may exploit civilians in order to fight a war, or they may fight a war in order to exploit

Figure 6.1   Economic Analysis of Civil War Onset Mechanism

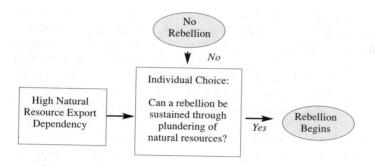

civilians. As Keen argues, this type of violence against groups can take place in peace and in war, but it can also precipitate, as well as shape, outright conflict.[11] Hence, Keen argues convincingly, our approach to civil conflict must examine the interplay between greed and grievance, understanding how greed may generate grievance and rebellion, further legitimizing greed as a response.

Greed on the part of the state can lead to grievance by populations. William Reno, in part, sheds light on this issue by focusing on leaders' preferences for weak institutions in Africa. Reno argues that in "shadow states" (the concept of personal rule within the façade of the sovereign state), patrimonial leaders are not interested in creating and sustaining viable, effective, impartially administered state systems. Rather, their key to power lies in creating systems of patronage in which they become the preeminent patron, making "clients" reliant primarily upon their largess. The formation of effective, stable states potentially undermines these systems of patronage and, consequently, their bases for power.[12]

Because of the patrimonial structure of African state politics, greed is certainly an issue in the power structures of African states because it helps to bolster support for the state's rulers. However, other elites that control successful government institutions may eventually pose challenges to the state's rulers. By providing needed and effective public goods, such as security and protection, these elites may acquire the allegiance of the beneficiaries of such public goods, causing a decrease in support for the state's rulers. Such climates of shifting allegiance may promote coups and revolutionary movements in an attempt to oust the state's arguably ineffective rulers. The logical conclusion of Reno's analysis is that it is not in the interest of the state's rulers to provide effective institutions that can provide public goods. To do so would create a climate for grievances that would challenge the power and prerogatives of the state's rulers. When war commences under this scenario, it may be difficult to stop because economic interests remain that allow combatants to create and maintain privileges for their ethnic group.[13]

Both Keen and Reno provide insight into some of the theoretical problems associated with Collier's conclusions. The origins of conflict in Africa cannot be associated just with "greed"; rather, grievances in pursuit of greed may not only provide the explanation for the onset of conflict; they may explain the duration of conflict as well.[14] If this is the case, why did Collier find such a strong basis for the greed thesis? The answer to that question can be found in the methodology that Collier used to test his hypotheses.

The purpose of Collier's studies in this area was to test the strength of the greed and grievance hypotheses that explain civil war. Rebellions occur either as a result of grievance (ethnic or religious divisions, extreme inequality, lack of political rights, etc.) or as a result of greed, which manifests in other reasons for building a rebel organization. The opportunity to build such a rebel organization may depend on access to finance in the form of natural resources or donations from a diasporic community. If we examine Collier's variables and their measurement, we can begin to understand why Collier's results proved to be so strong (see Table 6.1).

Collier's methodological problem emanates from the measurement of the variables and the behavior that is being tested. The hypotheses that Collier tests with these variables are centered on individual and group issues or behavior. The grievance hypothesis revolves mostly around the issues of political, social, and economic inequality between ethnic and religious groups. The onset of civil conflict, however, is a substate-level problem. Collier's measures are aggregated mostly at the state level, which mask substate issues. A clear example of this problem can be seen in the inequality measures Collier employs in his analysis.

The inequality measures—income and land ownership inequality—are measured at the state level. Inequality in income and land ownership is measured across the entire state population. At best, these measures represent a relationship between upper and lower classes within a given state. Fundamentally, the measure does not capture the issues associated with grievance, which is inequality between ethnic and religious groups rather than between the richest and poorest classes within a society. Most often African states are fractured across two or more ethnic groups. Importantly, Collier's income and land inequality measures do not capture the differences between ethnic groups that constitute the basis for grievances.

Although it was likely not intended by Collier, the inequality measures hold an underlying assumption of class conflict within the state, as they measure relationships between the "haves and the have-nots" purely on an income or property basis. The use of state-level inequality measures also assumes a particular social relationship or structure that is in place within a state. As we have shown, however, the actual phenomenon of interest is between substate-level ethnic groups. For African states in particular, the

Table 6.1   Collier's Variables for the Greed and Grievance Tests

Concept Measured	Variable Measurement	Hypothesis Being Tested
Extortion of natural resources	The ratio of primary commodity exports to GDP	Greed—Opportunity
Funding from diasporas	Emigrants living in the United States as a proportion of the population in the country of origin	Greed—Opportunity
Funding from hostile governments	Dummy variable for post–Cold War conflicts	Greed—Opportunity
Low cost of recruits—what do recruits give up in income by joining a rebellion?	Mean income per capita	Greed—Opportunity associated with low costs; possibly associated with economic grievance
Low cost of recruits—income and changing attitudes	Male secondary school enrollment	Greed—Opportunity associated with low costs; possibly associated with economic grievance
Low cost of recruits—potential loss of new income opportunities	Growth rate of the economy	Greed—Opportunity associated with low costs; possibly associated with economic grievance
Cost of conflict—specific capital	The length of time since the most recent conflict	Greed—Opportunity associated with cost of equipment for rebellion
Weak government military capability, proxied by the favorability of terrain to rebels	The proportion of the country's terrain that is forested; proportion of country's terrain that is mountainous	Greed—Opportunity associated with weak government capacity
Weak government capacity, proxied by the dispersion of populations	Gini coefficient of population dispersion, measured by population data per 400 km^2	Greed—Opportunity associated with weak government capacity
Social cohesion, ethnic and religious diversity reduces functional capacity	Index of ethno-linguistic fractionalization	Greed—Opportunity associated with a cohesive rebel group; Grievance— conflict between ethnic and religious groups
Ethnic and religious hatreds	Ethnic polarization measurements	Grievance—Ethnic and religious conflict
Political repression	Political rights variable from Polity III dataset	Grievance—Political rights violations and repression
Political repression	Autocracy score from Polity III dataset	Grievance—Political rights violations and repression
Political openness	Gastil Index from Freedom House	Grievance—Political rights violations and repression
Ethnic majority dominance	Ethnic dominance, occurring if the largest ethnic group constitutes 45–90% of the Population	Grievance—Group exclusion or minority exploitation
Inequality	Income inequality measured by the Gini coefficient (the ratio of the top-to-bottom quintiles of income groups in the country)	Grievance—Inequality of resource distribution
Inequality	Land ownership inequaltiy, measured by the Gini coefficient of land ownership	Grievance—Inequality of resource distribution

Source: Information has been extracted from Paul Collier and Anke Hoeffler, "Greed and Grievance in Civil War," Washington, DC: World Bank, 21 October 2001.

use of such highly aggregated variables at the state level reveals an ahistorical bias in his analysis because class development and class consciousness in Africa have been incomplete, at best. On the other hand, it may be true that class and ethnicity are interrelated, and that colonial policies did produce class-related inequalities between identity groups or geographic subregions.[15] The issue of inequality still remains a substate-level issue, however, escaping detection by aggregate state-level measures.[16] In contrast to Collier, Donald Horowitz's research addresses this critical point.

According to Horowitz, the relationship between social classes and ethnicity has been greatly misunderstood. As he has pointed out, where ethnicity and class coincide or are synonymous, ranked groups emerge; when ethnic groups cross class lines, unranked groups surface.[17] The two structures are depicted in Figure 6.2.

In societies that are hierarchically ordered, the structure supposes some level of subordination between ethnic groups (A and B). Hence one group is privileged over the other. In societies that have a parallel ordering, the structure between ethnic groups is not definitively ranked, though it is probable that a hierarchical structure exists within each of the groups individually. In other words, a class structure exists that most likely transcends ethnic groups. In the case of most African societies, the dominant, though not exclusive, framework of reference is the hierarchical ordering of ranked groups, which further calls into question the significance of Collier's model in explaining the onset and duration of Africa's civil conflicts.

While we do not dismiss the potential influence of the greed hypothesis in explaining Africa's civil conflicts, on theoretical, methodological,

Figure 6.2   Horowitz's Ranked and Unranked Ethnic Systems

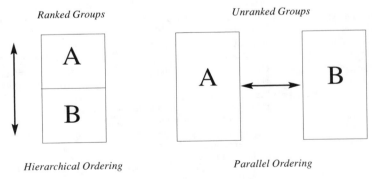

Source: Donald Horowitz, *Ethnic Groups in Conflict* (Berkeley: University of California, 2000), 22.

and historical grounds we cannot accept the significant explanatory power that Collier associates with his findings. Instead, we argue that the case studies analyzed in our study support the position that Keen takes, namely that an explanation of civil conflict must entail a thorough examination of the relationship between the greed and grievance hypotheses. Moreover, as we would expect, our findings reinforce the notion that ethnic and religious cleavages are correlated with the onset of civil war, while natural resources play a significant role in determining the conflict's duration by providing both the government and rebel groups with capital for arms purchases that sustain their warmaking efforts.

Sudan: From Ethnic Division to Resource Collision

The discovery of petroleum reserves in southern Sudan has complicated the process of national unification in that war-torn country. Since finding significant oil reserves in 1980, the Khartoum government has focused on controlling this valuable asset. Controlling that asset, however, remains problematic because the inhabitants of the South have sustained a rebel war against the North for decades. As Francis Deng explained in Chapter 2, the relationship between southern and northern peoples is an extraordinarily complex one riven by profound racial, ethnic, cultural, and religious differences. The fear of the continuation of these historic inequalities between the North and South helped provoke the 1955–1972 Sudanese civil war in which the South sought full secession from the North. After almost ten years of peace, the civil war resumed in 1983.[18] The discovery of significant, valuable petroleum reserves in 1980, and the subsequent discovery of additional reserves during the 1990s, slowly transformed the war between the North and South and accelerated the relevance of natural resources in warfare.

Background: Petroleum and the Unity of the Sudanese State

Although petroleum reserves were originally discovered in Sudan during the 1950s, the amounts found were relatively small. In 1980, Chevron, the U.S. oil company, announced that it had found oil in the Upper Nile region and that reserves there could produce more than twenty thousand barrels per day. The discovery was good news for President Gaafar al-Nimeiry, whose ambitious but underfunded development plans had increased Sudan's foreign debt and dependence on aid. The petroleum discovery also signaled the need to begin a tremendous structural shift in Sudan's economy from agriculture to natural-resource exploitation.

As the second-largest cotton producer and exporter in the world, Sudan's agriculture-based economy provided earnings for about 80 percent of its population, employment for 70 percent of the labor force, 40 percent of Sudan's GNP, and 95 percent of its foreign exchange earnings.[19] Before the government could make any progress toward integrating the oil discoveries into the economy, however, civil war broke out in 1983 when al-Nimeiry attempted to shore up his weakening regime by aligning with the Muslim Brotherhood. After al-Nimeiry introduced the *sharia* (Islamic law), the South rebelled, endangering further oil exploration.[20] Although Chevron had been active in the country since 1974 and had discovered the oil reserves at the Heglig and Unity oil fields near the towns of Bentiu, Melut, and Muglad, it halted oil exploration in southern Sudan after rebel attacks on their sites killed several of their workers.[21]

Since 1992 the Khartoum government has been engaged in a process to renew the development of its oil production. After government forces captured the oil fields in the western Upper Nile area, Bashir's government entertained offers from European, Asian, and Arab investors seeking to fund the development of Sudan's oil resources. Following the 1996 discovery of significant oil reserves in the Unity areas of Toma South, El Toor, and El Nar, Arakis Energy of Canada, which had earlier purchased Chevron's concessions in Sudan, entered into a consortium, the Greater Nile Petroleum Operating Company, which comprised Arakis, China National Petroleum Corporation, Petronas of Malaysia, and the Sudanese national oil firm Sudapet. The purpose of the consortium was to engage in further exploration and development of Sudan's oil reserves, particularly the Unity and Heglig fields in the South.[22]

By 1998, the government had signed contracts with a Malaysian consultancy firm to oversee the construction by Chinese, British, and Argentine oil companies of a 1,610-kilometer oil pipeline to link Port Sudan on the Red Sea to the oil fields in southern Sudan. The number of firms investing in Sudan's oil development also increased substantially. New investors in petroleum exploration in the Sudan included Lundin Oil (Sweden), Gulf Petroleum Company (a Qatari-Sudanese partnership), National Iranian Gas Company (Iran), OMV (Austria), Royal Dutch Shell (Netherlands), and Talisman (Canada), which had bought out Arakis Energy and its interests in Sudan. Refining and distribution contracts were issued to AGIP (Italy), Mobil, Nile Petroleum (Sudan), and Royal Dutch Shell.[23]

In April 1999, a 1,610-kilometer pipeline from the Unity and Heglig oil fields to the Al-Basha'ir Red Sea terminal was completed, making the processing and export of petroleum for Sudan much more feasible. Annual capacity for the pipeline is expected at 2.5 million tons per year. The location of petroleum reserves in the South obviously makes their capture and sale valuable to the government and the rebel groups. However, the rebel groups have had little capital that can be expended to exploit the petroleum reserves. Hence, their strategy has been to view the pipeline as a logical military target that it attacks regularly to disrupt the government's attempt to exploit the reserves. Since opening in 1999, Sudan's oil pipeline has been attacked and crippled by rebel forces several times.

The social and political fallout of Sudan's newfound wealth cannot be

Map 6.1 Sites of Oil Production in Sudan

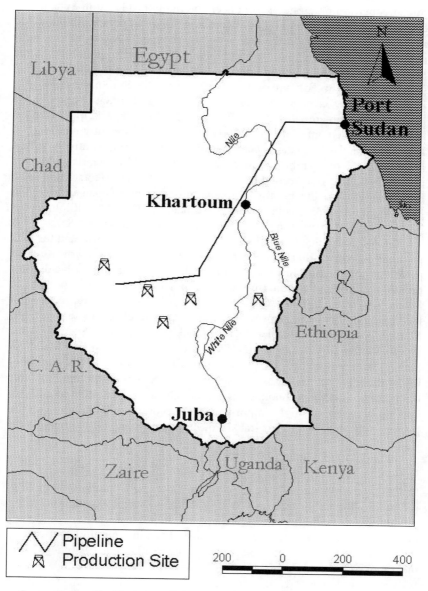

Pipeline
Production Site

200   0   200   400

Source: Produced by Binghamton University GIS Core Facility.

overlooked. In those areas where petroleum resources have been found, it has been alleged that the government has been actively involved in military attacks on local ethnic groups (principally Dinka and Nuer) so that they can be removed from the land, making petroleum exploration and drilling easier.[24] According to at least one estimate, 4.3 million people have been forced either to immigrate or have been internally displaced in Sudan. It is claimed that one of every eight refugees and displaced persons in the world is Sudanese.[25] Because of the interaction of geography and racial discrimination, it is very likely that the geographical placement of petroleum in the South will sustain civil war in both the short term and medium term.

The discovery of petroleum reserves in the Sudan significantly increased its presence and leverage in global energy markets. Presently, the government estimates that there may be 3.2 billion barrels of proven oil reserves in the country, of which 900 million barrels are fully recoverable. By world standards, Sudan's petroleum reserves are comparatively paltry. For example, Saudi Arabia has an estimated 261.7 billion barrels of petroleum reserves. Iraq (the second-largest petroleum reserve country) has 112.5 billion barrels.[26] In 2001, daily petroleum production in Sudan amounted to 185,000 barrels a day, with revenues estimated at US$400 million yearly. The government expects to produce 450,000 barrels per day by 2005.[27]

For a country that has suffered from both a protracted war and the lack of other resources that can contribute to its economic growth, Sudan's petroleum production has significance. The following table reveals how recently petroleum production and exports have become important in Sudan. As Table 6.2 shows, Sudan was a net petroleum importer for most of the time period covered; however, with the opening of its pipeline in 1999, Sudan's petroleum import dependence quickly disappeared. Sudan became a net exporter of petroleum in 1999, which has proven to be critical for Sudan's economy and for the prosecution of the civil war. Before the opening of the pipeline, Sudan experienced general economic decline. As Table 6.3 shows, however, economic growth stabilized around 1998 as oil production grew increasingly important in the economy. Economic stability from petroleum revenues has transformed the government's approach to the war.

Sudan's Civil War: The New Chapter

In 1992, government military expenditures increased sharply to over $530 million. In 1993 expenditures fell after the government experienced reversals during its military campaign that year. In 1994 military expenditures increased again in order to take advantage of the internal divisions emerging within the ranks of southern resistance forces. During 1994 the government moved militarily against the oil fields in the Nuer region and successfully captured them. After capturing these fields, government military expenditures remained high. Because of the completion of the pipeline in 1999, we can expect the government's military expenditures to remain level and perhaps increase.

What is most startling is the extent of military expenditures relative to the government's overall budget. Figure 6.4 shows that from 1991 until

Table 6.2   Sudan: Petroleum Data

Year	Crude Oil Production (1,000 Tonnes)	Crude Oil Imports (1,000 Tonnes)	Crude Oil Exports (1,000 Tonnes)
1980	0	964	0
1981	0	813	0
1982	0	736	0
1983	0	740	0
1984	0	617	0
1985	0	639	0
1986	0	811	.
1987	0	480	0
1988	0	798	0
1989	0	557	0
1990	0	837	0
1991	0	1,013	0
1992	0	750	0
1993	0	327	0
1994	0	641	0
1995	0	761	0
1996	102	712	0
1997	254	630	0
1998	329	258	0
1999	3,450	0	1,672
2000	9,300	0	3,556

Source: Organization for Economic Cooperation and Development, *IEA Oil Information, Database Edition,* 2002.

Table 6.3   Sudan: Macroeconomic Performance Indicators

Year	GDP (US$ millions)	GDP per capita	GDP Growth (%)
1980	4,271	221	2
1981	4,588	230	7
1982	4,912	239	7
1983	4,838	229	−2
1984	4,566	210	−6
1985	4,505	201	−1
1986	4,642	202	3
1987	4,591	196	−1
1988	4,656	195	1
1989	4,784	196	3
1990	4,763	192	0
1991	5,049	199	6
1992	5,298	205	5
1993	5,525	208	4
1994	5,748	211	4
1995	7,194	257	25
1996	7,482	261	4
1997	8,208	280	10
1998	8,709	290	6
1999	9,161	300	5
2000	9,922	319	8

Sources: World Bank, *World Economic Indicators 2002.*

Figure 6.3   Sudan's Military Expenditures, 1989–1999 (Millions US$, 1999=100)

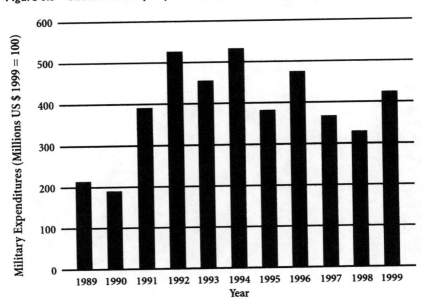

Source: U.S. Department of State, United States Arms Control and Disarmament Agency, "World Military Expenditures and Arms Transfers," www.state.gov, accessed 22 May 2004.

1993 military expenditures equaled or exceeded 60 percent of Sudan's central government expenditures. That percentage dropped substantially in 1995 (to under 40 percent) when Sudan experienced a temporary 25 percent rise in its GDP, the result of a large one-year transfer of foreign aid. With increasing economic performance, the percentage of the government's budget dedicated to military expenditures crossed the 50 percent line for the following two years, then fell under 50 percent for both 1998 and 1999. What the data indicate is an effort on the government's part to maintain a level of military spending in the $300 to $400 million range without regard to budgetary or economic restrictions.

The government's increased capacity for weapons purchases has drawn attention from the international community, illustrating the diverse interests at play in the country. First, arms suppliers have had a keen interest in meeting the government's increasing demand, particularly those that had a dual interest in Sudan's potential oil wealth. For example, China has been a major supplier of weaponry to Sudan's government, irrespective of Sudan's use of the weapons or its international politics, as long as Sudan gave China favorable concessions in Sudan's oil explorations.[28] In 1994, France provided assistance and satellite imagery of Sudan People's Liberation Army (SPLA) positions to the government in exchange for the extradition

Figure 6.4 **Sudan's Military Expenditures as a Percentage of Central Government Expenditures, 1991–1999 (1999=100)**

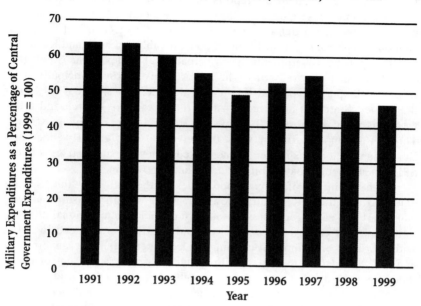

Source: U.S. Department of State, United States Arms Control and Disarmament Agency, "World Military Expenditures and Arms Transfers," www.state.gov, accessed 22 May 2004.

of "Carlos the Jackal," an international terrorist wanted for carrying out attacks in France and other countries.

In 1994 the European Union imposed an arms embargo on Sudan, forcing Sudan to purchase armaments elsewhere. Since then, the former Soviet-bloc states, South Africa, Iran, Malaysia, Libya, Slovakia, Jordan, Qatar, and Yemen have replaced Europe as sources for armaments for the Sudanese government.[29] From these suppliers, the government has acquired light and medium arms and munitions, tanks, artillery, and aircraft.[30] In particular, the government has purchased Antonov-26 transport planes, MiG-24 helicopter gunships, and MiG fighter-bombers for bombing raids against the South. Furthermore, the government has acquired substantial numbers of Chinese T-59 tanks (which are a modified version of the Soviet T-54 tank) and Polish T-55 tanks, which were first shipped to Yemen before being sent on to Sudan.[31]

Land mines have also played an important role in the ongoing civil war. According to the United Nations, there are between 500,000 and 2 million land mines in Sudan.[32] A diplomat who defected in 1997 claimed that the Sudanese government had acquired Scud missiles. This information would concur with intelligence provided by the Egyptian government, which claimed that Iraq had transferred Scud missiles to Sudan in 1990 and 1991.[33] Additionally, there are reports that the government of the Sudan has obtained chemical weapons. To substantiate this claim, Norwegian doctors working in southern Sudan have reported the use of chemical weapons, including mustard gas, in 1990 and in 2000, notably in Lanya and Kana.[34]

To fight the government, the principal rebel group in the South (the SPLA) has also acquired arms. The SPLA receives arms principally from Eritrea, Ethiopia, Egypt, and Uganda. It also receives arms covertly from the United States. It acquired most of its tanks from Eritrea and other weapons from surplus U.S., Russian, and Eastern European stocks. Through a complex arms network that involved supplying Rwandan and Burundian Hutu rebels in Kenya, the United States has supplied arms to the SPLA in an attempt to destabilize the Sudanese government.[35]

With the influx of arms to both sides of the civil war, the fighting extended into the new century. However, with Western pressure building and Khartoum eager for access to southern oil fields, international negotiations aimed at ending the twenty-year-old conflict commenced in 2002, with a critical breakthrough coming in December 2003. The government and SPLA leaders agreed to an oil-revenue-sharing arrangement that provided for an equitable division of oil revenues between the two sides.[36] Key provisions for the South in the agreement include special funds set aside by the Khartoum government to rebuild the war-torn southern region and to bring the South's living conditions on par with those in the North.

Ethiopia: Ranked Ethnicities and Grievances

In Ethiopia, intrastate ethnic conflict and interstate warfare revolve around two important factors: ethnic and socioeconomic structures that affect the production and marketing of coffee and access to navigable harbors. The historically tense and hostile relationship between the principal farmers of coffee, the Oromo peoples, and the principal coffee-purchasing intermediary agents, the Amhara and Tigray peoples, has deeply affected the volatile market for coffee, Ethiopia's principal export crop. On the other hand, Ethiopia's need for access to navigable harbors in the Red Sea has provoked conflict between Ethiopia and Eritrea. After Eritrea obtained independence from Ethiopia, a border war broke out near a sparsely populated town called Badme, which lies near the Ethiopian-Eritrean border. While it has been alleged that this has been a "border war," we contend that the underlying economic cause for warfare between Ethiopia and Eritrea remains Ethiopia's lack of access to the sea.

To understand the ethnic and socioeconomic sources of conflict within Ethiopia, it is useful to employ the framework established earlier in the discussion about greed and grievance. Ethiopia's society, in Horowitz's scheme, would be classified as having ranked groups with a hierarchical ordering. As Edmond Keller pointed out in Chapter 3, the origins of Ethiopia's ethnic and class problems date back to the period between the late nineteenth century and the early 1930s when Amhara colonialism was extended southward to include the Oromo people. The extension of Amhara colonialism fundamentally restructured social relations among the Oromo. The Oromo never truly functioned as a single ethnic group, as Keller has pointed out. The Oromo traditionally consisted of multiple clans that lived independently of each other. Any basis they had for identifying with each other came through aspects of language and customs.[37] When Ethiopia colonized the southern region, the relatively sophisticated social and political institutions that the Oromo had in place were systematically destroyed and replaced with what would evolve into an ethnically based class system. The structure of the colonized area is depicted in Figure 6.5. The majority of the people in the emerging class system were Oromo southerners, and as Keller notes,

> Most significant about this emerging class system was that it developed simultaneously with the development of a sense of ethnic consciousness among those groups being colonized. This new form of identity transcended local neighborhoods and kin groups. There emerged a broadened sense of ethnic affiliations based on the language and culture of a people juxtaposed against the language and culture of the forces of oppression.[38]

Figure 6.5   Southern Ethnic Class System Under Ethiopian Colonialism

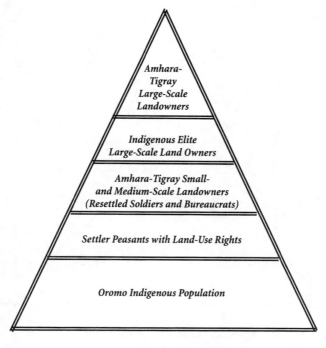

Source: Adapted from Edmond Keller, *Revolutionary Ethiopia: From Empire to People's Republic* (Bloomington: Indiana University Press, 1988), p. 62.

It was this structure that laid the foundation for the emergence of ethnic nationalism. Since their colonization during the nineteenth century, the Oromo, who comprise the largest ethnic group within Ethiopia, have been relegated to a secondary socioeconomic and cultural status by the Amhara and Tigray.[39]

Ethnicity, Class, and Ethiopia's Coffee Industry

Coffee is vital to Ethiopia's economy, comprising 60 percent of the country's total exports. The principal regions for the growing of coffee are Sidamo, Kefa, Welega, Illubabor, and Harerge.[40] All of these regions lie within what is called Oromia by Oromo nationalists.[41] The first three regions account for more than 70 percent of the coffee grown in Ethiopia.[42] But, as Figure 6.6 reveals, Ethiopia's coffee exports (and the income derived from these exports) fluctuate wildly. This fluctuation in production and prices has meant that coffee exports do not provide either sufficient profitability for farmers or predictability for government tax coffers.

Map 6.2 Areas of Coffee Production in Ethiopia

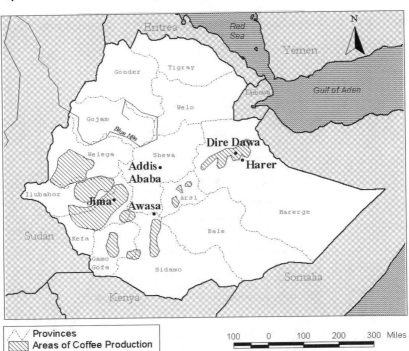

Source: Produced by Binghamton University GIS Core Facility.

Moreover, the history of Ethiopia's ethnic classes has laid a foundation that provides volatility to the inherent problems of coffee marketing.

Coffee is grown principally by Oromo farmers who then sell their goods to Tigray and Amhara intermediaries at auction at Addis Ababa and Dire Dawa.[43] The Tigray and Amhara purchasing intermediaries average profits of 26 percent or more from their purchase and sale of coffee while Oromo coffee farmers have experienced declining income for extended periods of time.[44] Because Oromo peoples are not well represented in coffee brokering and because Tigray and Amhara peoples tend to dominate that business, the socioeconomics of coffee buying and selling mean that class antagonisms merge with ethnic differences to spark conflict. Table 6.4 illustrates the average differential between the price paid to coffee farmers in Jimma and Sidamo and the price obtained at auction in Addis Ababa. Analyses of these data reveal that the markup can be as high as 100 percent (the difference between the prices paid to farmers and the amount obtained at auction in Addis Ababa). These markups, which may seem reasonable in a competitive business environment, nevertheless ineluctably provoke class and ethnic tension.

The distinctive ethnic and class bias in Ethiopia's coffee industry, and

Figure 6.6   Total Coffee Export Amounts and Value, 1984–2002

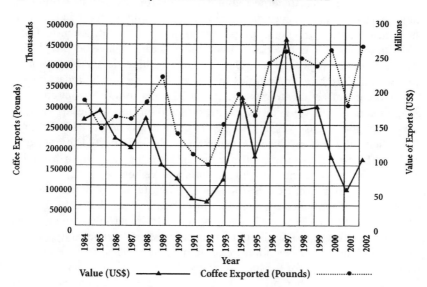

Value (US$) ——▲—— Coffee Exported (Pounds) ·········●·········

Source: Data obtained from the International Coffee Organization, http://www.ico.org/index.htm.

Table 6.4   Farmers' Price and Auction Price for Coffee (in Jimma and Sidama), 1997–1998 Growing Season

Month	Farmers' Price (Birrs/kg)	Auction Price (Birrs/kg)
October	7.0–8.6	14.9–15.4
November	7.3–8.6	15.4–15.8
December	10.1–10.9	17.7–18
January	9.8–10.1	17.9–18.1
February	8.4–9.2	15.5–16.7
March	8.9–9.8	14.6–15.8
April	9.6	14.5–15.2
May	9.5–9.8	14.4–15.1
June	9.1–9.2	13.3–15.9

Source: Roy Love, Sheffield Hollam University, "A Note on Farmers' Share of Coffee Prices in Ethiopia and Their Relative Volatility," eea.ethiopiaonline.net/Econ-foc/ef3-5/royL3-5.htm (accessed 11 April 2003).

the collapse of global coffee prices due to overproduction in recent years have established fertile ground for a major shift in agricultural production in the country. Though little attention has been given to the issue in recent research, Ethiopia—and Africa as a whole—have become major focal points in the global drug trade. European governments and the United States have become concerned about Africa's role as a transit point for major narcotics such as cocaine, heroin, mandrax, and others.[45] In Ethiopia, the concern is with the domestic production of *qat*, a mild, green-leaf narcotic. In an unstable coffee price environment, farmers have been replacing their coffee plantings with qat. Qat, which is in high demand in Somalia, Yemen, and diaspora communities in the West, pays a much higher price to farmers than coffee, creating a logic for the farmer to move from coffee to qat production.[46] In 1999, of the estimated $900 million wholesale value of qat production in East Africa, about $500 million was produced in Ethiopia alone, with the rest produced in Kenya and Somaliland.[47] Ethiopia used perhaps half of its output while exporting the remainder to Somalia, Somaliland, Djibouti, the United Kingdom, and Yemen.

Like all drug crops, qat distorts local agricultural economies. Farmers enjoy the short-term gain of the higher price paid for qat, but in the medium term and long term the "easy" money obtained from qat sales produces two deleterious effects: first, easily obtained qat money creates local hyperinflationary pressures; and second, the shift to qat discourages the production of necessary food crops for the local markets. Farmers become rich temporarily, but they pay higher prices for goods that are not produced locally. Further "advantages" for changing crops include qat's being more drought-resistant than coffee—a serious consideration, given Ethiopia's susceptibility to drought—plus qat is also easier to harvest than coffee. Despite what may be perceived as local benefits by Ethiopian farmers, growing qat may actually produce results similar to those already observed with coca production in Columbia and Peru. The shift to the planting and production of narcotic drugs destabilizes local agricultural economies and societies in the long term.

The Ethiopian—Eritrean War

In 1999 a war broke out between Ethiopia and Eritrea over an arid and remote region between both countries near the town of Badme. While it has been claimed that this was a border war, the conflict more likely was provoked because Ethiopia ceased to have reliable outlets to harbors for its agricultural products after Eritrea seceded from Ethiopia.[48] Quite plausibly, the Ethiopia-Eritrea war came to an end after Ethiopia was assured alternate port access by neighboring Djibouti. The arrangement between Ethiopia and Djibouti may also explain Eritrea's attempts to destabilize Djibouti's government during the war.

Despite the poverty of each of their countries, both Ethiopia and Eritrea found funds to launch one of the most destructive wars ever fought in the Horn of Africa. While Western and Eastern European governments had called for the fighting to stop, data clearly show that these governments supplied both Ethiopia and Eritrea with armaments to fight the war. Following Eritrea's independence in 1993, major arms shipments began to both countries, as Figures 6.7 and 6.8 demonstrate. Financial support for Eritrea is reported to have come from Libya through direct assistance and an annual $50 million oil allotment.[49] Among the hardware purchased by Eritrea during the 1999–2000 war were attack helicopters from Italy, MiG-29 fighter jets from Russia, SU-25 jets from Georgia, and multibarreled rocket launchers from Bulgaria.[50] For its part, Ethiopia reinforced itself with Sukhoi-26 fighter jets and helicopters from Russia, small arms from China (including AK-47s), and over a hundred T-55 tanks from Bulgaria. This infusion of arms led to more than a hundred thousand deaths of Ethiopians and Eritreans.[51] When the war was finally settled, instability within Ethiopia among the Oromo and Somali populations, tense border conditions with Somalia and Eritrea, and Ethiopia's reemerging support for the SPLA in Sudan made Ethiopia a potential tinderbox of ethnic grievances that may take decades to sort out.

The Democratic Republic of Congo: From Grievance to Greed

The Democratic Republic of Congo (DRC) is a fractured, disunited country. The political unification of the country has been difficult because its porous and difficult-to-defend borders make it vulnerable to neighboring states that have political and economic interests and combatants within the

Figure 6.7   Country Armament Transfers to Eritrea, 1993–2000[52]

Source: SIPRI data.

Figure 6.8   Country Armament Transfers to Ethiopia, 1993–2000[53]

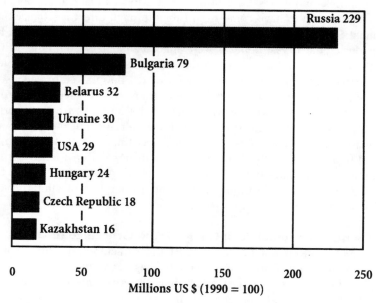

Source: SIPRI data.

DRC. These neighboring states include Uganda, Rwanda, and Burundi to the east and Angola and Zimbabwe to the south and southwest. These same states have played and most likely will continue to play active military roles in the DRC for three reasons: first, ethnic conflicts in border regions between the DRC and many of these states remain unresolved; second, these states have economic incentives to seize valuable mineral resources found in the DRC; and third, the DRC's government and military forces are comparatively weak and foreign governments can emplace themselves with relative ease in the DRC. For these reasons, these "external" actors will continue to play "internal" roles in the DRC for the foreseeable future.

The current problems of the DRC have ethnic and economic origins. The DRC's more recent descent into political chaos began after Laurent Kabila and his Alliance of Democratic Forces for the Liberation of Congo-Zaire (ADFL) overthrew Zaire's long-standing dictator, Mobutu Sese Seko, in 1997. During the summer of 1998, Kabila ordered Rwandan military forces that had helped him overthrow Mobutu to leave the country. However, the Rwandan military remained in the eastern DRC, left there to protect Rwanda, Burundi, and Uganda from incursions by armed nongovernmental forces operating in the area. Amongst these nongovernment groups were the Interahamwe militia of ethnic Hutus who had fought the Tutsi-led Rwandan government, Hutu members of the former Rwandan military forces accused of involvement in the 1994 genocide of Tutsis in Rwanda, traditional Congolese defense forces called the Mai Mai who had fought to keep out the influx of Rwandan immigrants from the DRC, members of the Alliance of Democratic Forces who were supported by Sudan and fought against the government of Uganda, and Hutu groups accused of fighting against the Tutsi government of Burundi. Rwanda, Uganda and Burundi began support for the Rally for Democracy (RCD), a Tutsi-dominated group that began a revolt against Kabila's government. In the civil war that erupted, armed forces from Rwanda, Burundi, and Uganda took up positions within the eastern part of the DRC, while forces from Namibia, Angola, Zimbabwe, and Chad assisted the government and the nongovernmental groups in the DRC. Uganda, Rwanda, and Burundi initially viewed the conflict as a security issue, each trying to prevent attacks from groups based from within the DRC borders. At the same time, these governments and the governments and groups supporting Kabila have also added another dimension to the conflict—they covet the country's natural resources.

The DRC has some of the richest deposits of mineral resources in the world. It is the leading source of cobalt, holds the world's largest diamond and coltan reserves, and is the world's fifth-leading source for copper.[54] Its principal export commodities are diamonds, copper, cobalt, coltan, petroleum, and coffee. While having tremendous potential wealth, the country

remains mired in poverty because warfare inhibits the productive exploitation by the government of these resources. Business mismanagement practices in the DRC have also inhibited the productivity and profitability of
mines and petroleum-drilling sites that are already in operation. Warfare,
however, constitutes the primary obstacle to the development of the DRC's
mineral resources.

The ongoing war has caused both internal and external investments in
the DRC's mining industries to decline. Those who choose to invest in the
DRC do so at considerable risk. Ongoing warfare has pushed those who
have remained interested in investing in the DRC to focus primarily on diamond mining and secondarily on gold and coltan mining as opposed to
other possible investment ventures. In this unstable security environment,
diamond mining is more profitable than other forms of investment because
the light weight, small size, and easy transportability of diamonds facilitate
their sale (and their being smuggled). This contrasts with the problems of
transporting heavy metals such as copper and cobalt to market.

Because of chronic political instability and the weakness of the government in the DRC, diamond mining and to a smaller extent gold and
coltan mining have been seized by independent entrepreneurs and agents of
foreign governments because they can make them profitable activities,
despite the war. Among these ventures, diamond mining has become the
most attractive. The DRC remains one of the world's principal sources for
diamonds. Although the average value of diamonds found in the DRC is
considerably less (at $15 to $38 a carat) than the value of diamonds found
in Sierra Leone (where diamonds sell for an average of $230 a carat),
incentives remain in place for diamond entrepreneurs to engage in business
there.[55]

In the DRC, diamonds are mined by two methods: capital-intensive,
deep-shaft mining methods undertaken by multinational corporations and
labor-intensive artisanal mining methods undertaken by manual laborers.
Deep-shaft diamond companies use more expensive, capital-intensive techniques to extract diamonds, while "artisanal" miners rely upon their labor,
luck, and access to rivers and dam systems where alluvial diamonds can be
found. In the DRC, given the significant geological prevalence of diamonds
in deep-shaft mines, incentives will remain for multinational mining companies to pursue their capital-intensive methods for diamond extraction in
the country. Diamond extraction processes adopted by these multinational
diamond mining companies, however, employ fewer workers than the artisanal mining sector. A critical result of this difference is that mining activities in the DRC do not create a pool of itinerant independent miners who
can be organized by warlords into militia or who can be preyed upon by
middlemen intermediaries.

The social organization of mining labor in the DRC contrasts in part
with Sierra Leone, where we find a greater prevalence of artisanal miners

as opposed to laborers employed at capital-intensive mining companies. This difference has created considerable local incentives in Sierra Leone that entice underemployed men to take a chance in the hope that they will make a lot of money as artisanal miners. These men, however, are paid lower wages than laborers in the deep-shaft mining sector, and because artisanal miners operate either independently or semi-independently, they must rely upon and therefore are often exploited or intimidated by diamond-purchasing intermediaries or warlords.

Returning to the analysis of the DRC, this mix of artisanal mining and traditional mining companies, when combined with extensive black market smuggling, means that actual diamond production figures for the DRC are not precise. Complicating matters further, deals have been struck between the government of the DRC and foreign governments wherein foreign governments are paid in diamonds rather than cash for their provision of police or military protection in regions of the DRC that cannot be safeguarded by the government in Kinshasa. In Mbuji-Mayi in Eastern Kasai Province, for example, the government of the DRC has negotiated an arrangement with the government of Zimbabwe for the Zimbabwean National Defence Force to provide security within the province. In that province the DRC government and the government of Zimbabwe have created a joint venture called the Mineral Business Company that controls mining and access to mining in the area. The profits from the Mineral Business Company are then used to pay for the costs of sustaining the Zimbabwean military in the area and to buy armaments from Eastern Europe.[56] As part of this arrangement, first Ridgepointe (a Zimbabwean mining firm) and then Oryx Natural Resources (another Zimbabwean firm) took over substantial segments of the government's mines of Eastern Kasai province.[57] Further implicated in this arrangement are Lebanese merchant families (the Ahmads, the Nassours, and the Khnafers) who serve as diamond-purchasing intermediaries and who help transport diamonds first to Dubai and then to Antwerp. Moreover, it has been alleged that some members of these families have ties to Amal, Hizbollah, and Al-Qaida.[58]

Diamonds mined in Eastern Kasai province are shipped by charter airplane to Dubai where they are transshipped to Antwerp for processing. According to the United Nations Security Council, this smuggling arrangement accounts for the increase in Dubai's shipments of diamonds to Antwerp from $5.5 million in 1998 to $149.5 million in 2001.[59] Because of this arrangement, much of the revenue derived from diamond sales flows to foreign governments and independent entrepreneurs rather than the government of the DRC. Consequently, the government is deprived of needed income. Evidence of the redirection of diamonds is evident from the import records of the High Diamond Council in Antwerp, which reveal dramatic increases in diamond exports not only from the United Arab Emirates (UAE) but also Hong Kong.

Table 6.5   Diamond Exports from United Arab Emirates and Hong Kong Toward Belgium (in US$ millions)

Country	1997	1998	1999	2000	2001
UAE	2.5	5.5	14.9	108.1	149.5
Hong Kong	90	46.4	71	170.6	170.4

Source: Dutch High Diamond Council (HRD), Diamond Intelligence Briefs.

Map 6.3   Mineral Resources in the Democratic Republic of Congo

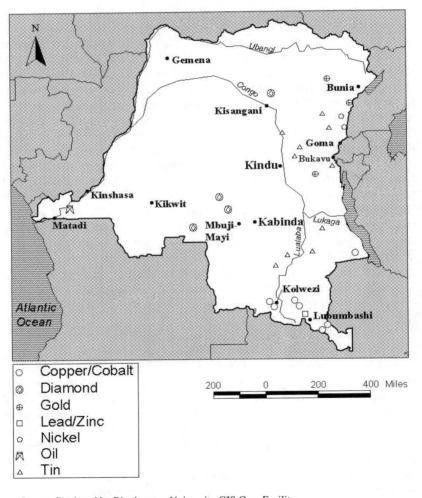

Source: Produced by Binghamton University GIS Core Facility.

Although substantial quantities of diamonds are being smuggled from Eastern Kasai province to the UAE and Hong Kong, the DRC government continues its official mining activities through a consortium known as Minière de Bakwange.[60] This consortium involves the government, De Beers (South Africa), and SIBEKA (Belgium). Production figures from this consortium have been down consistently. This downturn can be attributed to the ongoing civil war, local mismanagement of the mines, and smuggling.

Beyond diamond activity in Eastern Kasai province, diamond, gold, and coltan production has increased in the northeast of the DRC. Uncut diamonds, gold, and coltan are being transported from this area to Uganda, Rwanda, and Tanzania for overseas export as part of an illicit, clandestine network.[61] As evidence of diamond exploitation from this area, the Dutch High Diamond Council (HRD) has reported that diamond exports from Rwanda leaped from 13,000 carats in 1997 to 30,491 carats in 2000. The value of diamond exports increased from $720,455 to $1,788,036 during the same period.[62] As evidence of gold exploitation from this area, it has been reported that "the Bank of Uganda, which controls all gold exports, show that Uganda's gold exports shot up from $12.4 million in 1994 to

Table 6.6   Uganda: Mineral Exports, 1994–2000

Year	Gold (tons)	Coltan (tons)	Cobalt (tons)
1994	.22	—	—
1995	3.09	—	—
1996	5.07	—	—
1997	6.82	2.57	—
1998	5.03	18.57	—
1999	11.45	69.5	67.48
2000	10.83	—	275.98

Source: Uganda, Ministry of Energy and Mineral Development.

Table 6.7   Uganda: Mineral Production, 1994–2000

Year	Gold (tons)	Coltan (tons)	Cobalt (tons)
1994	.0016	.0435	—
1995	.0015	1.824	—
1996	.003	—	—
1997	.0064	—	—
1998	.0082	—	—
1999	.0047	—	76.74
2000	.0044	—	287.51

Source: Uganda, Ministry of Energy and Mineral Development.

$110 million in 1996."[63] The following data were released by Uganda's Ministry of Energy and Mineral Development in 2000. They reflect substantial increases in gold and coltan exports from 1994 to 2000, even though mineral production for those same materials decreased during the same period. These data lead logically to the conclusion that the sources for these exports originate elsewhere, most probably in areas of the eastern DRC that are under Ugandan and Rwandan military control.

In the area of diamonds, since 1997 Uganda has become a major exporter. This increase in diamond exports coincides exactly with the moment that Ugandan military forces emplaced themselves on DRC territory. The following figures are from the High Diamond Council in Antwerp.

The same trends that were observable for Uganda were also observable

Table 6.8   Uganda: Rough Diamond Exports, 1997–October 2000

Year	Volume (carats)	Value (US$)
1997	1,511.34	198,302
1998	11,303.86	1,440,000
1999	11,024.46	1,813,500
2000	9,387.51	1,263,385

Source: HRD, Diamond Intelligence Briefs.

Table 6.9   Rwanda: Mineral Production, 1995–2000

Year	Gold (tons)	Coltan (tons)
1995	1	54
1996	1	97
1997	10	224
1998	17	224
1999	10	122
2000	10	84

Source: Rwanda Official Statistics (No. 227/01/10/MIN).

Table 6.10   Rwanda: Rough Diamond Exports

Year	Volume (carats)	Value (US$)
1997	13,060.39	720,425
1998	166.07	16,606
1999	2,500.83	439,347
2000	30,491.22	1,788,036

Source: HRD, Diamond Intelligence Briefs.

for Rwanda, yet another country that has placed their troops upon DRC territory.

Rwanda has become the primary beneficiary from coltan extraction in the DRC, with the Rwandese army seriously implicated in its smuggling. Profits from coltan sales sustain the 40,000-member RCD army.[64] Coltan is mined in the eastern DRC, transported to Rwanda in Rwandese military vehicles, and then sent to Thailand, Germany, the United States, and Kazakhstan for final processing.[65]

The government of the DRC remains nominally active in gold mining in northeastern DRC. Because of Ugandan and Rwandan involvement in the area, however, the government has attempted to keep only two mines in operation. These mines are managed by Bonro Resource Corporation and an Anglo-American/Berrick joint venture. The mines run erratically because of the war. As the government in Kinshasa does not have the military capacity to impose its control, Rwanda, Uganda, and Burundi have taken advantage of the situation to expropriate the minerals.[66]

Moving to the southwest of the DRC, the story repeats itself. Angola and Namibia have troops in the area, supporting the government in maintaining peace and order. Angolan troops in particular provide security in regions where the DRC military does not have the capacity to deploy its troops. In exchange for this security arrangement, the government of the DRC has conceded petroleum rights to the government of Angola and its parastatal petroleum company known as SONANGOL.[67] This concession has enlarged Angola's stake in petroleum markets.

Because of these various activities, the DRC government's official mining activities have suffered. The state-owned mining company, Gécamines, officially controls most of the copper and cobalt mines in the DRC, but because of its failure to maintain mining equipment since 1993, it has had to sell portions of its inventories and mines to foreign investors. Gécamines's only other competitor in the copper industry, SODIMCO, has also experienced declining production and productivity in its mines. Because of declining native Congolese productivity, OMG (United States), Forrest Group (Luxembourg), and First Quantum (Canada) have been willing to step in with investments to improve the infrastructure of the DRC's copper-mining industries, especially at Lubumbashi.[68] According to a United Nations Security Council Report, in at least one joint venture in Lubumbashi, OMB and Forrest Group have skimmed off all the profits from copper, cobalt, and germanium sales, excluding their state-run coinvestor (Gécamines) from sharing in the profits.[69] First Quantum has invested considerable sums at the Lonshi mines at the Zambian border.[70] The Lonshi mines are located a mere thirty kilometers from First Quantum's other copper mines across the border in Zambia. American Mineral Fields and Anglo-American PLC have also taken interest in Gécamines. American Mineral Fields and Anglo-American are also expanding and renovating copper mines in Katanga Province in southeast DRC.[71] American Mineral Fields and Anglo-American expect the Katanga mines to be among the lowest-cost producers of copper in the world when renovated. A consortium involving Anglo-American (South Africa), Billiton (Canada), Iscor (South Africa), Union Minière (Belgium), and CNNC (China) have also signed an agreement to develop mines in Kolwesi. Furthermore, in January 2001, the government created the Kababankola Mining Company, which is a joint venture undertaken by Tremalt Ltd. (a Zimbabwean company that controls 80 percent of the venture) and Gécamines (20 percent). Within the profits distribution scheme of this consortium, Tremalt receives 32 percent of net profits, the DRC receives 34 percent, and the government of Zimbabwe receives 34 percent. This contract provides one more example of entrenched Zimbabwean economic interests in the DRC.[72] Despite these numerous initiatives, copper and cobalt yields in the DRC continue to decline.[73] Tables 6.11–6.13 reveal how diamond, copper, cobalt, coltan, and petroleum production have fared in the Democratic Republic of Congo for the years 1983 to 2000.

These data reveal sporadic production patterns during Mobutu's reign.

Table 6.11   Democratic Republic of Congo: Diamond Data

Year	Government Production Carats	Government Production US$	Government Production US$/carat	Artisanal Production Carats	Artisanal Production US$	Artisanal Production US$/carat
1983	5,538,110	47,789,332	8.63	6,174,620	91,129,628	14.76
1984	6,566,807	56,662,573	8.63	11,562,880	159,852,768	13.82
1985	6,619,142	54,089,605	8.17	12,998,029	145,362,062	11.18
1986	7,910,900	64,996,879	8.22	14,541,128	160,211,379	11.02
1987	7,719,927	66,393,062	8.60	11,600,792	129,327,369	11.15
1988	7,999,902	72,391,218	9.05	10,226,870	206,235,257	20.17
1989	8,911,220	91,796,991	10.30	8,740,985	159,057,133	18.20
1990	9,560,479	102,573,619	10.63	9,770,072	155,125,266	15.88
1991	7,215,970	76,981,768	10.67	10,598,159	135,212,089	12.76
1992	4,345,016	46,319,911	10.66	8.934,164	185,091,516	20.71
1993	4,710,324	52,175,187	11.08	10,616,768	259,782,433	24.47
1994	4,878,410	53,321,776	10.93	11,376.742	243,178,171	21.38
1995	5,507,050	62,690,410	11.38	16,344,807	314,783,138	19.26
1996	6,506,815	75,924,114	11.67	15,436,905	312,973,482	21.27
1997	6,167,811	78,096,666	12.66	15,580,462	308,059,805	19.77
1998	6,831,000	93,963,800	13.76	19,252,000	356,839,000	18.53
1999	4,788,000	97,261,900	20.31	15,327,000	192,635,000	12.57
2000	4,640,000	76,603,665	17.98	11,366,000	162,800,000	14.32

Sources: Christian Dietrich, "Hard Currency: The Criminalized Diamond Economy of the Democratic Republic of the Congo and Its Neighbours," The Diamonds and Human Security Project, Occasional Paper No. 4, (Ottawa, Canada: Partnership Africa Canada, 2002), 52; Banque Centrale du Congo Condensé d'Informations Statistiques 31/2001; Observatoire Gouvernance Transparence, Centre National d'Expertise, 1998 and 1999 annual reports.

Table 6.12   Democratic Republic of Congo: Copper, Cobalt, and Coltan Production

Year	Copper (thousands of tons)	Cobalt (thousands of tons)	Coltan (thousands of tons)
1980	460	14	*
1981	505	11	*
1982	503	6	*
1983	502	5.3	*
1984	501	10	*
1985	491	10.6	*
1986	503	14.4	*
1987	500	12	*
1988	471	10	*
1989	440.6	9.3	*
1990	355.5	10	*
1991	291.5	8.8	*
1992	144.3	6.6	*
1993	60	2.2	*
1994	40.6	3.3	*
1995	34.9	3.9	*
1996	40.1	6	*
1997	37.7	3	*
1998	38.2	4	*
1999	31.2	2	*
2000	30.5	3	*

Sources: Mining Journal, Annual Survey, 1980–2000; International Monetary Fund, *Democratic Republic of the Congo: Selected Issues and Statistical Appendix,* July 2001, IMF Country Report No. 01/123, p. 51.

* = Figures for coltan are sketchy because coltan began to be important for the telecommunications industry in approximately 1997. *Mining Journal,* the best source for mining data, is beginning to collect data re coltan.

Clearly, the production of minerals and petroleum has been declining since the start of the major war in 1998. The DRC's overall macroeconomic performance has been declining steadily, as Table 6.14 reveals. Even under the stability of Mobutu's reign, the country's economic performance dwindled through inept management and corruption. After his overthrow, the country's economic performance continued to decline, with economic growth reaching negative levels again due to the ensuing war.

Because the DRC government does not have adequate state resources to fund police control of its territory, arms smuggling has become endemic. Small arms are most often purchased because large armament contracts are beyond the fiscal means of warring groups. The increased availability of inexpensive pistols, rifles, and grenades has increased mortalities in the DRC. The most popular arm imported is the Chinese-made AK-47, which can be purchased for approximately US$20. According to governmental and nonprofit agencies, most of the small arms are trafficked into the east-

Table 6.13   Democratic Republic of Congo: Petroleum Data

Year	Petroleum Crude Exports per year (millions of barrels)	Spot Price Petroleum	Petroleum Exports (US$ millions)
1980	7.32	—	—
1981	7.30	—	—
1982	8.39	—	—
1983	9.12	29.1	268.01
1984	11.71	30.17	353.29
1985	12.04	28.1	338.32
1986	10.15	14.9	151.23
1987	10.94	18.6	203.48
1988	10.43	15.65	163.22
1989	10.16	19.55	198.62
1990	11.71	17.4	203.75
1991	8.01	18.4	147.38
1992	11.47	19.5	223.66
1993	7.40	19.3	142.82
1994	8.21	14.83	121.75
1995	8.51	18.75	159.56
1996	10.7	19	203.3
1997	10.1	17	171.7
1998	9.4	12	112.8
1999	8.7	13	113.1
2000	8.3	17	141.1

Sources: United States Department of Energy, Energy Information Administration, International Energy Database, April 2002; International Monetary Fund, *Democratic Republic of the Congo: Selected Issues and Statistical Appendix,* July 2001, IMF Country Report No. 01/123, p. 51.

ern DRC, principally Eastern Kasai, North Kivu, South Kivu, and Katanga. Perhaps not coincidentally, these are areas controlled by Uganda, Rwanda, Burundi, and Zimbabwe. According to agency reports, most of the small arms that arrive in the DRC originate in China, France, North Korea, South Africa, Russia, and the United States.[74] Given the weakness of the state, the availability of small arms in the black market, and the interests of foreign governments in exploiting the DRC's mineral resources, warfare and the chronic instability it brings to the DRC will continue for the short and medium terms.

Sierra Leone: Ethnic Manipulation and Personal Gain in War

The war in Sierra Leone was one of the first to turn the world's attention to the trade in natural resources for the purpose of continuing war. It is also the primary case that is often cited for evidence of the "greed" motivation in civil war. However, as Jimmy Kandeh illustrated in Chapter 5, such characterizations are not so clear-cut. As Kandeh explained, the origins of Sierra Leone's conflict are partly rooted in the country's ethnic problems,

Table 6.14   Democratic Republic of Congo: Macroeconomic Data

Year	GDP (US$ millions)	GDP per capita	GDP Growth (%)
1980	7,531	280	2
1981	7,708	278	2
1982	7,673	269	0
1983	7,781	264	1
1984	8,213	270	6
1985	8,251	263	0
1986	8,640	267	5
1987	8,871	265	3
1988	8,913	258	0
1989	8,800	246	−1
1990	8,222	222	−7
1991	7,530	197	−8
1992	6,379	170	−11
1993	5,831	142	−13
1994	5,604	132	−4
1995	5,643	129	1
1996	5,592	123	−1
1997	5,274	113	−6
1998	5,432	113	3
1999	5,330	113	8
2000	4,990	112	−6

Sources: World Bank, World Economic Indicators 2002; International Monetary Fund, *Democratic Republic of the Congo: Selected Issues and Statistical Appendix,* July 2001, IMF Country Report No. 01/123.

but a rapacious political class that had little interest in building effective and legitimate state institutions manipulated ethnicity to perpetuate the war. Furthermore, strong ethnic identities with political parties made it easy for Temne and Mende ethnic leaders to manipulate constituent loyalties for their own personal gain. The result has been the pillaging of Sierra Leone by ethnic politicians who have used ethnic identity as the weapon of choice against each other.

Diamonds have been the major issue in the natural-resources area. However, at the outset of the civil war, rebels utilized Sierra Leone's agricultural base as a means of support for warfare, particularly coffee. When the war started, rebel forces attacked and held the coffee-producing regions of Sierra Leone.[75] Coffee was smuggled out of the country through a number of different land and sea avenues. Figure 6.9 shows the impact of the civil war on Sierra Leone's coffee exports. After the onset of the civil war in 1991, official exports declined sharply. However, coffee exports certainly did not stop; they continued through illicit smuggling operations.[76]

In Sierra Leone, control of diamond mines and diamond trafficking has been the key to wealth, power, and political control. For decades, diamonds have been the most valuable export commodity. Diamond mining and dia-

Figure 6.9   Sierra Leone's Exports of Coffee, 1983–2000

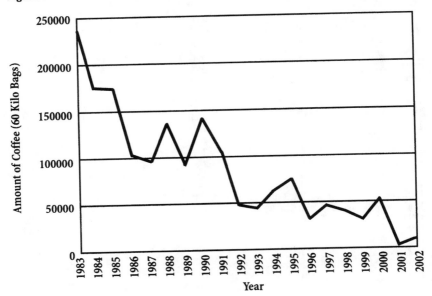

Source: International Coffee Organization, "Historical Statistical Data," www.ICO.org, accessed 2 May 2004.

mond sales have not benefited the Sierra Leone government, however, because most diamonds are smuggled across the border to Monrovia, Liberia, where De Beers and other diamond purchasers have set up offices. Diamond smuggling across the Liberian border began during the 1950s and has continued since then.[77] Since the onset of civil war in 1991 (which came to a tenuous end in January 2002), smuggling has accelerated, expanding to Guinea and Gambia.[78] The magnitude of smuggling seriously deprives the Sierra Leone government of needed income. Profits obtained from smuggling are used to purchase small arms that sustain warfare. Since the civil war began in 1991, more than seventy-five thousand persons have perished in Sierra Leone's civil war. Despite the declaration of a truly chimerical January 2002 peace accord, the resource bases that have exacerbated ethnic fractionalization and warfare in Sierra Leone are still there, threatening the prospects for peace.

Diamonds were discovered in Sierra Leone in 1930 in Yengema (Kono district), which lies in eastern Sierra Leone near the Guinean border.[79] During the period from the 1930s through the 1950s, most of the diamonds in Kono district were mined by a British company connected to De Beers, the Sierra Leone Selection Trust.[80] In 1956 British colonial authorities decided to limit Sierra Leone Selection Trust's monopoly access to Sierra

Leone's diamonds by circumscribing their mining activities to the Yengema field (in Kono district) and Tongo field (in Kenema district). This decision opened the market to other participants in the diamond trade, specifically African manual laborers and Lebanese middlemen.[81]

In the diamond trade, mining done by manual laborers is known as "artisanal" mining. Under British policy, an estimated seventy-five thousand independent artisanal miners were mining diamonds in Kono district by 1956.[82] From the 1960s through the 1990s (when De Beers eventually withdrew from diamond mining in Sierra Leone), diamond mining eventually became an activity of substantial numbers of these independent artisanal miners who sold their uncut diamonds to Lebanese intermediaries in Sierra Leone. These Lebanese (and occasionally their Liberian, Guinean, or Senegalese counterparts) then arranged for the transfer of these uncut diamonds to "gray" markets, principally in Monrovia, Liberia, where De Beers had set up a purchasing office. Diamonds have also been diverted to Burkina Faso, Guinea, and Gambia.[83]

To provide one example of the effects of these diversions, in 1999 Liberia reported $290 million in diamond exports, even though it is well understood that there are relatively few diamond mines in Liberia.[84] Diamonds exported from Liberia originate in eastern and southeastern Sierra Leone and then are smuggled into Liberia. This smuggling network has provided personal enrichment to various members of Sierra Leone's and Liberia's political and economic elites. It has profited various prime ministers and their associates and deprived both states of needed revenue.[85]

Official government-sanctioned diamond production in Sierra Leone peaked at 2 million carats per annum during the 1970s.[86] Between 1992 and 1996, exports dropped to an average of 250,000 carats yearly. Between 1997 and 1999, the situation deteriorated further. During those years only 36,384 carats were exported subject to governmental supervision.[87] In 1999, only 9,320 carats were officially exported from Sierra Leone.[88]

The diamonds data listed in Table 6.15 should be correlated with Sierra Leone's macroeconomic performance (Table 6.16). When these data are analyzed together, the substantial decline of Sierra Leone's economy becomes apparent, showing negative economic growth during the civil war. The implications, of course, are quite grim for Sierra Leone's people and the government.

In this context of declining official diamond exports and increasing contraband trade, we need to understand further how the extraordinary value of Sierra Leone's diamonds fits within the world market; control of Sierra Leone's diamond mines are critical for wealth and power. According to the *Mining Journal*, Sierra Leone's diamonds (as well as diamonds from Namibia) are among the most valuable in the world, averaging $250 a carat. This high value enhances the importance of controlling access to these diamonds.[89]

Table 6.15   Sierra Leone: Diamond Data

Year	Sierra Leone Exports (carats)	Liberia Exports (carats)	Total Exports (carats)
1980	625,000	310,000	935,000
1981	410,000	300,000	710,000
1982	175,000	375,000	550,000
1983	160,000	410,000	570,000
1984	250,000	375,000	625,000
1985	75,000	225,000	300,000
1986	225,000	150,000	375,000
1987	230,000	225,000	455,000
1988	225,000	300,000	425,000
1989	25,000	180,000	205,000
1990	78,000	280,000	358,000
1991	251,534	280,000	531,534
1992	334,081	280,000	614,081
1993	200,200	280,000	480,200
1194	255,000	280,000	535,000
1995	60,000	280,000	340,000
1996	270,092	250,000	520,092
1997	104,000	230,000	334,000
1998	7,919	200,000	207,919
1999	9,320	200,000	209,320
2000	450,000	155,000	605,000

Sources: Mining Journal Annual Review, 1980–2000; HRD, *Diamond Intelligence Brief;*
Note: Figures from 1980 to 1989 are approximate, from John Williams, Donald
Sutherland, Kimberley Cartwright, and Martin Byrnes, *Sierra Leone Diamond Policy Study,
January 2002,* available at www.dfid.gov.uk.

Within Sierra Leone we find diamond mining undertaken by the same
two processes as in the DRC: technology-intensive, corporate-sponsored
deep-shaft mining, and labor-intensive, individual artisanal mining.
Artisanal miners use the most rudimentary technologies (manual labor, a
pan, a sieve, and water) and these miners sell their diamonds to intermediaries—often Sierra Leone–born Lebanese, Liberians, Guineans, or
Senegalese—who transport them for sale in Liberia, Guinea, Gambia, and
Burkina Faso. The artisanal miners who pan for diamonds in rivers and
dike systems are sometimes called "tributors" who are sustained financially
by their intermediaries until they discover diamonds. Needless to say, most
of the artisanal miners are paid meagerly, with the intermediaries retaining
the lion's share of profits. Most artisanal miners are young, impoverished,
underemployed males.

The three principal locations for diamond mining are Koidu-Yengema
(Kono), Tongo, and Zimmi. Koidu-Yengema is the largest and oldest of
Sierra Leone's diamond fields. It is mined mostly by traditional deep-mining techniques and secondarily by artisanal miners. It is a prize for the government and rebels alike. More recently it has been mined and protected by

Table 6.16   Sierra Leone: Macroeconomic Data

Year	GDP (US$ millions)	GDP per capita	GDP Growth (%)
1980	949	293	5
1981	969	294	2
1982	1,016	302	5
1983	985	287	–3
1984	1,007	287	2
1985	949	265	–6
1986	959	262	1
1987	1,003	268	5
1988	1,022	267	2
1989	1,083	277	6
1990	1,135	284	5
1991	1,044	255	–8
1992	943	225	–10
1993	944	220	0
1194	1,007	229	7
1995	901	200	–11
1996	916	198	2
1997	760	161	–17
1998	782	162	3
1999	693	141	–11
2000	741	147	7

Sources: World Bank, *World Economic Indicators 2002.*

international mining companies, including Diamond Works and Rex Diamonds.[90] The Tongo deposit southwest of Kono is a rich deposit mined by alluvial mining rather than corporate deep-mining techniques. Because it is a site of alluvial mining, it attracts independent artisanal miners and is beyond corporate or state control. The deposit is rich, estimated to hold 20 million carats at a value of $3.3 billion. Yet another field, the Zimmi field, runs south of the town of Zimmi, along the Moro River, and down the Liberian border. It has the potential to be mined with both traditional deep-mining methods and alluvial techniques. The Tongo and Zimmi fields have been the principal targets for competition and seizure by government and rebels alike: the fields can be mined by low-cost labor rather than higher-cost industrial methods; they are of high value; access to the Liberian trans-shipment market is easy; and the Sierra Leonean government is unable to assert control over these areas.

As late as 2002, diamonds were still being mined in southern and southeastern Sierra Leone and transshipped to the Burkina Faso, Guinean, and Gambian diamond markets. After sales of uncut diamonds have been completed there, arms are purchased—primarily from arms brokers in Liberia and Burkina Faso—to supply rebel soldiers.[91] The former Liberian government of Charles Taylor was active in this arrangement from 1991

Map 6.4   Diamond Resources in Sierra Leone

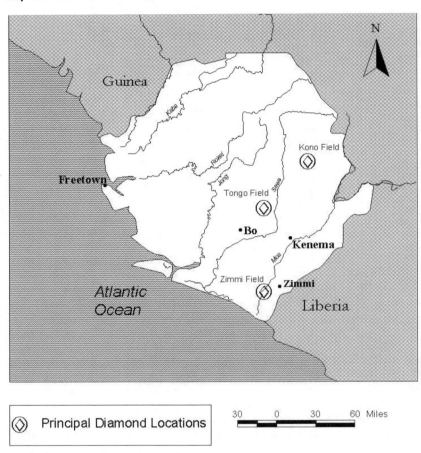

Source: Produced by Binghamton University GIS Core Facility

until 2003. Blaise Campaore's government in Burkina Faso has also been implicated in these arms-trading arrangements.[92] For Charles Taylor's regime in Liberia, trafficking in Sierra Leone's diamonds was critical for survival. Because of Taylor's active support for warfare in West Africa, he was accused of being a war criminal and blocked from receiving aid from the European Union. After the denial of European financial aid, Taylor became more reliant upon sales of illicitly smuggled Sierra Leone diamonds to sustain his regime. According to U.S. government sources, Taylor and his allies among the Sierra Leone rebels garnered $30 million to $125 million a year from illicit diamond sales.[93]

Arms smuggled to Sierra Leonean rebels originate primarily in Eastern Europe, especially Ukraine, Bulgaria, and Slovakia.[94] However, surplus weaponry from the Cold War has been found in the country. For instance, small arms and ammunition used in Nicaragua's *contra* civil war of the 1980s have been found in Sierra Leone.[95] After shipment from Eastern Europe, intermediate points of transport include Libya, Côte d'Ivoire, Chad, Burkina Faso, Guinea, and Liberia.[96] After their arrival at these locations, the end-user certificates are often altered or forged, making it possible for the arms to be shipped to Liberia or Sierra Leone. On the government side, arms purchases also continue. Government purchases are made principally in the United Kingdom, Nigeria, China, Russia, Ukraine, and Bulgaria.[97] The government's arms of preference include U.K.-made G-3 rifles, Chinese-made chrome-plated AK-47s, machine guns, grenades, and grenade launchers. Because of easy access to low-cost small arms and because plentiful, illicit diamond sales continue in Sierra Leone and neighboring countries, the arms trade will continue, with predictable carnage for Sierra Leone (and Liberia) for the short and medium terms.

Conclusion

The recent research concerning the "greed" or "grievance" arguments about the origins of civil wars provides a limited basis for the analysis of the complex interactions in many conflicts. The turn toward quantitative macroeconomic analyses of substate-level ethnic conflicts only serves to cloud the issues, making practical solutions to the issues more obscure. While we discount the significance of the macroeconomic findings reviewed earlier in this chapter, we do not dismiss the importance of the greed argument as part of the motivation in understanding civil wars. We emphasize, however, that the greed argument should not be utilized as *the* definitive source for answers on the origins of civil wars. Such arguments are misleading and dangerous because the settlement of disputes based solely on the greed hypothesis would have policymakers deal exclusively with the market conditions that perpetuate greed conditions. To resolve conflict in Africa, both greed and grievance need to be addressed.

In analyzing the issue of grievance, we have focused on the issues present in the four case studies—Sudan, Ethiopia, the DRC, and Sierra Leone—elaborating on the work previously addressed in this book by Francis Deng, Edmund Keller, Herbert Weiss, and Jimmy Kandeh. All four of their studies have illustrated the important role that ethnic or religious divisions have played in the conflicts in each country. Our findings illustrate that ethnic or religious grievances were the dominant factor contributing to the onset of conflict in all four cases. Natural resources have played an important role of sustaining and perpetuating war in Sudan, the DRC, and Sierra Leone. In the case of Ethiopia, natural resources did not play a direct role in sustaining its war with Eritrea. Lack of access to the Red Sea for its exports, however, did provide motivation for the initiation of warfare. Furthermore, Ethiopia illustrates the relevance of economic issues (greed) in perpetuating ethnic grievances. In conclusion, as we noted in the beginning of this chapter, our case studies provide significant evidence that allows us to concur with Keen's assessment: grievance and greed need to be taken into account to understand the origins of civil wars in the African context.

Notes

1. Mats Berdal and David Malone, eds., *Greed and Grievance: Economic Agendas in Civil Wars* (Boulder, CO: Lynne Rienner Publishers, 2000).

2. See for instance Paul Collier and Anke Hoeffler, "Greed and Grievance in Civil War" (Washington, DC: World Bank, 2001); Ibrahim Elbadawi and Nicholas Sambanis, "Why Are There So Many Civil Wars in Africa? Understanding and Preventing Violent Conflict" (Washington, DC: World Bank, DECRG, 2000); Paul Collier, "Economic Causes of Civil Conflict and Their Implications for Policy" (Washington, DC: World Bank Development Research Group, 2000); Paul Collier and Anke Hoeffler, "On Economic Causes of Civil War," Oxford Economic Papers, No. 50 (1998), 563–573; Patrick M. Regan, "Third Party Interventions and the Duration of Intrastate Conflicts" (Washington, DC: World Bank, 2000).

3. See, for example, Charles Tilly, *Coercion, Capital, and European States, A.D. 990–1992* (Oxford: Blackwell, 1992).

4. There are two basic types of diamond deposits: primary (kimberlite and lamproite pipe sources) and secondary (alluvial) sources. Kimberlite and lamproite pipes raise diamonds from the earth where they originate. Alluvial sources are created by erosion from kimberlite or lamproite pipes that concentrate in river channels, riverbeds, sand, or gravel.

5. Paul Collier, "Economic Causes of Civil Conflict and Their Implications for Policy," World Bank Development Research Group, 15 June 2000, 21.

6. Ibid.

7. Paul Collier, Anke Hoeffler, and Måns Söderbom, "On the Duration of War," presented at the World Bank, Development Research Group and University of California, Irvine, Center for Global Peace and Conflict Studies, Workshop on Civil Wars and Post-Conflict Transitions, 18–20 May 2001 (available at http://econ.worldbank.org/files/12204_CHS_Duration.pdf; accessed 20 November 2003), p. 17.

8. Paul Collier and Anke Hoeffler, "On the Incidence of Civil War in Africa," World Bank Development Research Group, August 16, 2004, 17.

9. Paul Collier, "Economic Causes of Civil Conflict and Their Implications for Policy," World Bank, 15 June 2000, 3.

10. David Keen, "Incentives and Disincentives for Violence," in *Greed and Grievance: Economic Agendas in Civil Wars,* eds. Mats Berdal and David Malone (Boulder, CO: Lynne Rienner Publishers, 2000), 32–33.

11. Ibid., 31.

12. William Reno, "Shadow States and the Political Economy of Civil Wars," in *Greed and Grievance: Economic Agendas in Civil Wars,* eds. Mats Berdal and David Malone (Boulder, CO: Lynne Rienner Publishers, 2000), 43–68; see also William Reno, *Warlord Politics and African States* (Boulder, CO: Lynne Rienner Publishers, 1998).

13. Reno, "Shadow States and the Political Economy of Civil Wars," 43–68.

14. In a similar vein Stathis Kalyvas has argued that greed, or looting, as a cause of civil wars is analytically problematic because it is unclear if the looting is the cause of the war or the motivation of the combatants (or both). The implications are theoretically significant, though not critical for our line of argument here. See Stathis N. Kalyvas, "'New' and 'Old' Civil Wars: A Valid Distinction?" *World Politics* 54 (October 2001): 99–118.

15. On this point, see Naomi Chazan, Robert Mortimer, John Ravenhill, and Donald Rothchild, *Politics and Society in Contemporary Africa*, 2d ed. (Boulder, CO: Lynne Rienner Publishers, 1992), 105–130; Nelson Kasfir, "Relating Class to State in Africa," *Journal of Commonwealth and Comparative Politics* 21, no. 3 (November 1983).

16. International relations scholars addressed the methodological issue of the "levels of analysis" over four decades ago. In that line of scholarship, they contended that consistency in the level of analysis had to be maintained in research and that crossing these levels of analyses would defy theoretical integration (see J. David Singer, "The Levels of Analysis Problem" in *The International System: Theoretical Essays*, eds. Klaus Knorr and Sidney Verba (Princeton, NJ: Princeton University Press, 1961). In a similar sense, comparative political scientists confront a levels-of-analysis problem in trying to explain a substate-level phenomena with state-level evidence. Of course, international relations scholars conveniently did away with the levels-of-analysis issue to accommodate the recent "theories" on the democratic peace; comparative political scientists will probably not be able to find a convenient solution to their levels-of-analysis problem.

17. Donald L. Horowitz, *Ethnic Groups in Conflict* (Berkeley: University of California Press, 2000), 20–22.

18. The prolonged second civil war has resulted in at least 1.5 million deaths and has displaced more than 3 million people thus far; see "The Oil Industry Fueling Civil War in Sudan," *Global Dialogue* 4, no. 3 (December 1999).

19. "Sudan Pushing Cotton Exports," *New York Times*, 12 July 1980.

20. One interesting side note to the 1983 outbreak of conflict concerns the potential role of water as a dominant factor in the SPLA's decision to launch the war. After hostilities broke out, the SPLA successfully stopped the construction of the Joglei Canal project, which Sudan and Egypt began jointly in 1978. The purpose of the canal was to supply water from the Sudd swamplands, providing water that Sudan and Egypt could share equally. The SPLA launched successful military attacks against the project, halting construction. According to Kukk and Deese, "One of the major reasons that the SPLA and the majority of the southern Christian Sudanese wanted the project stopped was that it was carrying water from their 'homes' to the Arab north, whether in Sudan or Egypt, without any concern for their needs." The government stopped the project because of the war. See Christopher L. Kukk and David A. Deese, "At the Water's Edge: Regional Conflict and Cooperation over Fresh Water," *UCLA Journal of International Law and Foreign Affairs* 1, no. 21 (Spring 1996): 21–64.

21. It was probably no coincidence that Chevron's departure from Sudan also came with the collapse of world oil prices, which would have decreased Chevron's financial capacity for exploration and development.

22. "Sudan: Oil and Gas Industry," www.mbendi.co.za (accessed 8 December 2002).

23. Ibid.

24. Leon P. Spenser, "Key Points Related to Sudan and Oil," Washington Office on Africa, www.woafrica.org (accessed 18 May 2001).

25. U.S. Committee on Refugees, USCR World Refugee Survey, 9 September 1999, www.refugees.org (accessed 7 December 2002).

26. *BP Statistical Review of World Energy* (London: BP p.l.c., 2002) 4.

27. CIA, The World Factbook, Sudan, www.cia.gov; IRW, "Sudan: Ministry Plans to Double Oil Output," www.africaonline.com, August 2001 (accessed 7 December 2002); Spenser, "Key Points Related to Sudan and Oil."

28. Human Rights Watch, "Sudan Global Trade Local Impact: Arms Transfers to All Sides in the Civil War in Sudan," http://www.hrw.org/pubweb/arms.html (accessed 30 November 2003).

29. www.smallarmssurvey.org (accessed 8 May 2003); *SIPRI Yearbook 2000*.

30. Human Rights Watch, www.hrw.org/reports98/sudan/sudarm988-02.htm (accessed 8 May 2003).

31. *SIPRI Yearbook 2000*, 354.

32. United Nations Department of Humanitarian Affairs, Mine Clearance and Policy Unit, "The Landmine Situation in Sudan: Assessment Situation, Mission Report," August 1997, 10.

33. *SIPRI Yearbook 1991*.

34. *SIPRI Yearbook 2000; SIPRI Yearbook 1990*, 109.

35. Human Rights Watch, "Sudan Global Trade Local Impact: Arms Transfers to all Sides in the Civil War in Sudan," http://www.hrw.org/pubweb/arms.html (accessed 30 November 2003); Lora Lumpe, ed., *Running Guns: The Global Black Market in Small Arms* (London: Zed Books, 2000).

36. Subsequent negotiations settled the issues of national power sharing and the status of Abyei, the Nuba Mountains, and the Blue Nile states. The texts, memoranda, addenda, and protocols of the Inter-Governmental Authority on Development (IGAD) Peace Process that ended Sudan's 1983–2004 civil war can be found at the United States website http://www.usip.org/library/pa/sudan/pa_sudan.html.

37. Edmond Keller, *Revolutionary Ethiopia: From Empire to People's Republic* (Bloomington: Indiana University Press, 1988), 64.

38. Ibid., 63.

39. Asafa Jalata, *Oromia and Ethiopia: State Formation and Ethnonational Conflict, 1868–1992* (Boulder, CO: Lynne Rienner Publishers, 1993), 47–114; Keller, *Revolutionary Ethiopia*, 158–163.

40. Haile-Mariam Teketel, "The Production, Marketing, and Economic Impact of Coffee in Ethiopia," Ph.D. dissertation, Stanford University, 1973, 27.

41. Jalata, *Oromia and Ethiopia*, 22–25.

42. Stefan Dercon and Lullseged Ayalew, "Smuggling and Supply Response: Coffee in Ethiopia," *World Development* 31 (1995): 1798.

43. Teketel, "The Production, Marketing, and Economic Impact," 27.

44. United Nations Office for the Coordination of Humanitarian Affairs, "Ethiopia: Feature—The High Cost of Coffee," http://www.irinnews.org (accessed 11 April 2003).

45. Chris Allen, "Africa and the Drugs Trade," *Review of African Political Economy* 26, no. 79 (March 1999): 5–11.

46. Yves Guinand, *Mission Report—East and West Hararghe (20–28 April 1999)* (Addis Ababa: United Nations Development Programme, Emergencies Unit for Ethiopia UNDP-EUE, 1999).

47. Reginald Herbold Green, "Khatt and the Realities of Somalis: Historic, Social, Household, Political and Economic," *Review of African Political Economy* 26, no. 79 (March 1999): 33–48.

48. Fiona Flintan and Imeru Tamrat, "Spilling Blood over Water? The Case of Ethiopia," in *Scarcity and Surfeit*, eds. Jeremy Lind and Kathryn Sturman (Pretoria, South Africa: ISS, 2002).

49. Libya's oil allotment was cancelled in 2003, contributing to Eritrea's economic slide.

50. The British Broadcasting Corporation, News.bbc.uk/1/hi/world/ Africa.280273.stm (accessed 15 November 2003); web.amnesty.org/web\web.nsf/ printpages/tt3_Russian (accessed 25 June 2003).

51. Amnesty International, web.amnesty.org/web\web.nsf/printpages/tt3_ Russian (accessed 25 June 2003); http://www.foreignpolicy-infocus.org/briefs/ vol5/v5n25eritethiop_body.html (accessed 25 June 2003).

52. The Swedish International Peace Research Institute (SIPRI) cautions that its arms transfers data refer to actual deliveries of major conventional weapons. To permit comparison between the data on such deliveries of different weapons and identification of general trends, SIPRI uses a trend-indicator value. The SIPRI values are therefore only an indicator of the volume of international arms transfers and not of the actual financial values of such transfers. Thus they are not comparable to economic statistics such as gross domestic product or export/import figures.

53. Ibid.

54. Christian Dietrich, "Hard Currency: The Criminalized Diamond Economy of the Democratic Republic of the Congo and Its Neighbors," The Diamonds and Security Project, Occasional Paper No. 4 (Ottawa: June 2002), 7; Dena Montague, "Coltan and Conflict in the Democratic Republic of Congo," *SAIS Review* 22, no. 1 (winter-spring 2002): 105; "Democratic Republic of the Congo—Copper Mining," http://www.mbendi.co.za (accessed 24 February 2003).

55. "Precious Metals/Diamonds/Development and Exploration," *Mining Journal*, Mining Annual Review 2000.

56. "Report of the Panel of Experts on the Illegal Exploitation of Natural Resources and Other Forms of Wealth of the Democratic Republic of the Congo," United Nations Security Council S/2002/1146 (8 October 2002), 13.

57. International Crisis Group (ICG), "Scramble for the Congo: Anatomy of an Ugly War," ICG Report No. 26 (20 December 2000): 60; "Democratic Republic of the Congo—Diamond Mining": www.mbendi.co.za (accessed 22 February 2003); Yenga Mabiola, "Democratic Republic of Congo," *Mining Journal*, Mining Annual Review 2001; "Report of the Panel of Experts on the Illegal Exploitation of Natural Resources and Other Forms of Wealth of the Democratic Republic of the Congo," United Nations Security Council S/2001/357 (12 April 2001), 9.

58. "Report of the Panel of Experts on the Illegal Exploitation," United Nations Security Council S/2002/1146 (8 October 2002): 19.

59. "Report of the Panel of Experts on the Illegal Exploitation," United Nations Security Council S/2001/357 (12 April 2001): 26.

60. "Democratic Republic of the Congo—Diamond Mining": http://www. mbendi.co.za (accessed 22 February 2003).

61. Yenga Mabiola, "Democratic Republic of Congo," *Mining Journal*, Mining Annual Review 2001; "Scramble for the Congo," ICG Report No. 26 (20 December 2000): 31; "Report of the Panel of Experts on the Illegal Exploitation," United Nations Security Council S/2002/1146 (8 October 2002), 32.

62. "Report of the Panel of Experts on the Illegal Exploitation," United Nations Security Council S/2001/357 (12 April 2001), 25.

63. "Scramble for the Congo," ICG Report No. 26 (20 December 2000), 31.

64. Celine Mayroud and John Kalinga, "Coltan Exploration in Eastern Democratic Republic of the Congo (DRC)," in *Scarcity and Surfeit*, eds. Jeremy Lind and Kathryn Sturman (Pretoria, South Africa: ISS, 2002), 177.

65. Ibid., 176–177.

66. Ingrid J. Tamm, *Diamonds in Peace and War: Severing the Conflict-Diamond Connection* (Cambridge, MA: World Peace Foundation, 2002).

67. "Report of the Panel of Experts on the Illegal Exploitation," United Nations Security Council S/2001/357 (12 April 2001), 36.

68. Mabiola, "Democratic Republic of Congo," 2.

69. "Report of the Panel of Experts on the Illegal Exploitation," United Nations Security Council S/2002/1146 (8 October 2002): 10.

70. "Democratic Republic of the Congo—Diamond Mining": http://www. mbendi.co.za (accessed 21 February 2003).

71. Ibid.

72. "Report of the Panel of Experts on the Illegal Exploitation," United Nations Security Council S/2002/1146 (8 October 2002), 10.

73. Mabiola, "Democratic Republic of Congo"; "Report of the Panel of Experts on the Illegal Exploitation," United Nations Security Council S/2002/1146 (8 October 2002), 10.

74. U.S. Arms Control and Disarmament Agency, *World Military Expenditures and Arms Transfers 1997* (Washington, DC: ACDA, 1999), table III; Richard F. Grimmett, *Conventional Arms Transfers to Developing Nations, 1991–1998* (Washington, DC: CRS, 4 August 1999), 88; http://www.worldpolicy.org/projects/ arms/links/dollarsandsense.html (accessed 29 May 2003); http://www. Una-uk.org/disarmament/smallarms/scourge.congo.html (accessed 29 May 2003).

75. Interview, Ambassador Joseph Melrose, former U.S. ambassador to Sierra Leone, 17 October, 2003.

76. While agriculture, and coffee in particular, provided substantial "upstart" funding for Charles Taylor's protracted conflict in Liberia and Sierra Leone, timber proved to be one of the most consistent sources of funding. Because of the United Nations' inability to impose timber sanctions against Taylor (France and China being substantial importers of Liberian timber), Taylor was able to rely on West Africa's last rain forest as a reliable funding source. Though reports vary, estimates of Taylor's annual income from the timber trade range from $66 million to $100 million. Carola Hoyos, "UN Urged to Put Sanctions on Liberia's Timber Exports," *Financial Times* (London), 6 September 2001, 4; see also the series of reports produced by Global Witness at their website: http://www.globalwitness.org/reports/ index.php?section=liberia.

77. H. L. van der Laan, *The Sierra Leone Diamonds* (Oxford: Oxford University Press, 1965), 128; Alfred Zack-Williams, *Tributors, Supporters, and Merchant Capital: Mining and Underdevelopment in Sierra Leone* (Aldershot, England: Avebury, 1995), 50.

78. Lansan Gberie, "War and Peace in Sierra Leone: Diamonds, Corruption, and the Lebanese Connection," The Diamonds and Human Security Project, Occasional Paper No. 6 (Ottawa: Partnership Africa Canada, 2002), 9.

79. John L. Hirsch, *Sierra Leone: Diamonds and the Struggle for Democracy* (Boulder, CO: Lynne Rienner Publishers, 2000), 26.

80. Ibid., 27.

81. Zack-Williams, *Tributors, Supporters, and Merchant Capital*, 139.

82. Ian Smillie, Lansana Gberie, and Ralph Hazelton, *The Heart of the Matter: Sierra Leone, Diamonds, and Human Security* (Ottawa: Partnership Africa Canada, 2000), 3–4; van der Laan, *The Sierra Leone Diamonds*, 65.

83. "Report of the Panel of Experts on Sierra Leone Diamonds and Arms," United Nations Security Council, S/2000/1195 (14 December 2000), 16.

84. www.american.edu/projects/mandala/ted/ice.diamond.htm (accessed 26 January 2003).

85. Smillie, Gberie, and Hazelton, *The Heart of the Matter*, 3–4.

86. "Report of the Panel of Experts on Sierra Leone Diamonds and Arms," United Nations Security Council, S/2000/1195 (14 December 2000), 16.

87. Ibid., 16; J. Anyu Ndumbe, "Diamonds, Ethnicity, and Power," *Mediterranean Quarterly* 12, no. 4 (Fall 2001): 92 (90–105).

88. "Report of the Panel of Experts on Sierra Leone Diamonds and Arms," United Nations Security Council, S/2000/1195 (14 December 2000), 21.

89. http://www.c-r.org/pubs/occ_papers/briefing3.htm (accessed 26 January 2003).

90. Ibid.

91. "Report of the Panel of Experts on Sierra Leone Diamonds and Arms," United Nations Security Council, S/2000/1195 (14 December 2000), 10; Eric G. Berman, "Re-Armament in Sierra Leone: One Year After the Lomé Peace Agreement," *Small Arms Survey, Occasional Paper No. 1* (December 2000), 13.

92. Berman, "Re-Armament in Sierra Leone," iv, 13.

93. Richard Holbrooke, Permanent Representative of the United States to the United Nations Mission in New York, "Statement Before the United Nations Security Council's Exploratory Hearing on Sierra Leone Diamonds," 3 July 2000, U.S. UN Press Release #102 (00).

94. Berman, "Re-Armament in Sierra Leone," 16–17.

95. Ambassador Joseph Melrose interview, 82.

96. Ibid., 16–18, 82.

97. Ibid., 18–24.

7

The World Economy and the African State

William G. Martin

While each of our case studies is rich in local detail and causes, they nevertheless share common determinants and dilemmas. Indeed, these shared attributes make possible the hope for a richer and more peaceful future across many cases, and thus drive us to search for common patterns, explanations, and policy projections. The task set for this chapter is to analyze one of these critical shared domains: the long-term location and role of African states within world economic relationships.

Since international factors are by formal definition beyond the boundaries of the state, they are most often introduced as "external" elements, to be noted at key moments but rarely explained. This is understandable: We do not want to introduce, much less attempt to resolve, long debates over the origins and legacies of colonialism, the Cold War, unequal exchange in commodity markets, the debt crisis, international financial institutions, etc. Yet, as this list drawn from discussions in this book about the Democratic Republic of Congo, Ethiopia, Sierra Leone, and Sudan suggests, the dilemmas African states face have for a very long time been tied to the cycles, rhythms, and vicissitudes of the world economy. This chapter seeks to unravel these long-term patterns, with particular emphasis on addressing the dilemma, posed by all our case studies, of the long-term decline in state resources, institutional capacities, and legitimacy.

Frameworks: State Formation in World Historical Perspective

As the 1980s came to a close, hopes for democratic revival and development blossomed across Africa and indeed much of the Eastern and Southern Hemispheres. As popular uprisings proliferated, dictatorships, single-party states, and white minority regimes were toppled. Activists and analysts alike looked forward to a second independence era, marked by popular participation and stable, responsive states. The predictions were bold: Economic globalization and democratization in Africa, when coupled with similar trends in Eastern Europe and Asia, would cement the triumph of modernity and liberalism on a world scale.

By the beginning of the new millennium these expectations and analyses were subverted by more brutal facts. On the one hand, endemic political instability, war, and even the disappearance of some states were undeniable, while a condition of permanent economic crisis for the majority of the continent's people existed on the other. The cases of Ethiopia, the DRC, Sudan, and Sierra Leone are all good examples, in very different ways, of these processes. Neither rising official GNP statistics nor regular elections in many states could deny these disheartening, seemingly long-term trends. What had been perceived in the early 1990s as the beginning of a transition from rigid regimes and economies to more open and efficient governments and economies had failed to cohere.

At the center of this dilemma stood the African state, the pivotal institution that had managed the economy for almost two generations, and upon which the hopes for a more democratic and prosperous future had been focused. Political scientists and economists in particular strived to chart and explain the dilemmas of the 1990s. By applying methodological and historical criteria, their work may be broken into two groups. The first is the oldest tradition, conceptualizing African political activity through models of states in a developing, international state system. Seen through a comparative-politics or international-relations lens, African states remained young states, following in the footsteps of European or Latin American states—and continue to do so in the radical context of twenty-first-century globalization. Thus a "third wave" of democratization in Latin America and southern Europe in the 1980s was seen as spreading to Africa in the 1990s.[1] For these writers the tasks of constructing viable institutional structures and a national identity are still in their infancy—and often hobbled by "traditional African values." The collapse rather than transition of many states, however, has subverted earlier, optimistic theories, generating new notions such as an enduring condition of "complex political emergencies."[2]

A focus upon local attributes distinguishes a second approach, one that emphasizes not comparison and the universal attributes of state formation and development, but rather locality and the uniqueness of African political processes, particularly ethnicity and identity formation. Given the focus on the most striking phenomena of the 1990s—state breakdown, war, and genocide—it is hardly surprising that scholars and policymakers in the North severely criticized African states, their governing classes, and, for most, local political culture. Here African states were neither simply young states, nor even imploding, collapsing, or fragmenting states, but inherently incapable states due to traditional African political processes or cultural attributes. Thus, for example, if southern Europe or Latin America have been marked by corporatist cultures and regimes, Africa has been marked by "neopatrimonial" regimes, whereby "the chief executive maintains authority through personal patronage, rather than through ideology or law . . . relationships of loyalty and dependence pervade a formal political and administrative system and leaders occupy bureaucratic offices less to perform public service than to acquire personal wealth and status."[3] Personal rule is then quite easily linked to local culture, especially ethnic or tribal rule and violence. Conflict in Africa thus becomes, for example, "a function of leaders trying to stay in power in systems where institutions are weak. Because the struggle for power takes place in a context where the resources most easily at hand to be mobilized are ethnic ones, conflict is often ethnic conflict."[4]

Whatever their conclusions, these two master approaches share a common assumption: that states, like the societies they purportedly bound, possess sovereignty, autonomy, and are thus relatively self-contained units of analysis that may be studied in isolation and compared. This is a fatal flaw that has worked against placing states and local actors within transnational networks and processes. The most critical defect is the exclusion of interstate relationships from the conception of the state, leaving only "internal" or national factors to explain local expressions of state formation or failure. These deficiencies define the literature on the African state in the 1970s right through the 1990s. As Adebayo Olukoshi has stressed, even in the numerous studies of state failures in the 1990s one finds that "analytic attention was focused exclusively on the internal sources of the African crisis; the role of external factors was completely downplayed or totally discounted."[5]

A first corrective might be to unearth and conceptualize the role of the most obvious international factors as they impinge on the African state—and here the potential list is long, including the impact of debt crises, structural adjustment, falling commodity prices, falling levels of aid and capital investment, etc. These are important factors that we consider below. The challenge is, however, more substantive: to abandon the study of the state as an isolated, sovereign institution, and to see state formation as inherently a relational, transnational process. Writers on neoliberalism and the state in the age of "globalization" appreciate this process, and indeed herald its appearance.[6]

Yet these relationships are neither novel nor recent. Indeed, they are older than even the imposition of colonialism in the late nineteenth century. Nor are these one-way dependency relationships; the rise of rich, deeply institutionalized and often democratic states in Europe and North America was dependent upon the creation of weakly institutionalized, nondemocratic states, economies, and colonial territories in the South. Our central, orienting claim is this: Throughout the history of modern capitalism, state formation and *de*formation in core and peripheral areas have moved hand-in-hand as part of the evolution of an interstate system.

Africa provides ample examples of this process, from the rise of slave states to the Fante confederation during the seventeenth, eighteenth, and mid-nineteenth centuries; through the imposition of colonial territories and settler states in the late nineteenth and early twentieth centuries; to the emergence of independent, majority-ruled states in the last half of the twentieth century. As our chapters chart in each of our cases, even for Ethiopia, the colonial period set in place current state boundaries, key institutions of the state, and enduring ethnic and racial identities. More recent postcolonial developments have shaken these patterns; it remains uncertain whether they will hold much longer. As these comments suggest, any assessment of global factors in African state formation must be both historically and place-specific. Our task here is to sketch, within a state-relational framework, the key world relationships that have commonly impacted African states.[7] It is to this task that we now turn, first examining common claims regarding determinants of state success and failure in the most recent period, and then setting these against long-term trends of African states' world economic relationships.

Historic Globalization and the African State: Empirical Measures and Trends

No state escapes its economic environment. Indeed, state legitimacy and capacity are closely related to prevailing economic conditions, although the relationship is hardly unidirectional. Economic crisis, for example, may propel and sustain challenges to dictatorial rule, as it did in the 1980s and 1990s in Africa, or it may just as easily undermine support for democratic states as in the opening years of the new millennium. The impact on state capacity is more direct: Long periods of severe economic decline clearly undermine the fiscal, monetary, and institutional resources necessary to sustain strong, stable states.

Over the course of the last half-century, two long periods have marked the world economy: the post–World War II boom that lasted until the mid-1970s, and a subsequent period of crisis, stagnation, and attempted recovery through increasing waves of innovation. These periods do have clear political markers in Africa, as each of our cases documents. Boom conditions could and did underwrite stable and wealthy—if corrupt—states across the continent, as is most explicitly argued by Herbert Weiss and Tatiana Caryannis for Mobutu's Congo. The early and mid-1970s economic crises are also clearly reflected in the coups, attempted coups, and radically new, often Marxist, state policies in Ethiopia, Sudan, Sierra Leone, and the Congo. The last two decades bear particular scrutiny, given the enduring conflict that has wracked the continent and the disastrous economic performance of all but a few African states.

Economists, policymakers, and Africanists alike offer a common explanation for the continent's downward economic spiral: Africa has become increasingly irrelevant to the world economy. One of the most cited authors is political economist Manuel Castells, who in his multivolume study writes at length of the "marginalization of Africa in the global economy," pinpointing "the destructive role of African nation-states on their economies and societies."[8] The governor of the Central Bank of Tunisia is equally blunt: "The marginalization of these [African] countries is reflected in their small share of world trade (barely 2 percent), output (not much higher), and foreign investment (1 percent)."[9] As a senior African economist stated the consensus, in a special issue of the IMF journal *Finance and Trade Review* dedicated to Africa: "Africa's economic marginalization, the result of its relatively isolationist policies and closed economies, explains why economic prosperity has eluded most of the continent."[10]

Seen from a longer, world-economic perspective these views are simply unsustainable. First, Africa's difficulties are part of a shared, long-term trend faced by all the states and peoples along the periphery of the world economy: a steadily unequal distribution of income worldwide. The gap between the rich North and poorer South has been accelerating, and Africa is hardly alone in suffering from this as several recent studies chart.[11] This becomes clear if we plot Africa's annual GDP per capita against that of the continent's main colonial and postcolonial partners in the North (see Figure 7.1).[12]

Returns from Global Production and Trade

Income disparities may of course have little to do with world economic relationships. Indeed, many would retort: Is not Africa's falling share of world income a sign of African states' withdrawal from the world economy?

Figure 7.1   Africa's GDP Per Capita as a Percentage of Former Colonial Partners, 1960–2000

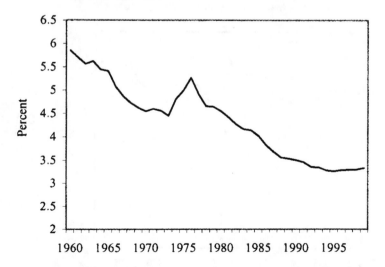

Source: World Bank, "GDP per capita (constant 1995 USD)," *World Development Indicators,* CD-ROM, 2002.

Has not the collapse of private and state incomes been a result of this withdrawal? Have not African states, wedded to nationalist programs, been bypassed by the globalization of finance, trade, and production in the 1980s and 1990s?

Examining trade or investment flows in a relational framework demonstrates otherwise. While Africa's share of world trade has indeed been declining, this does not indicate withdrawal. Indeed, of all continents, Africa has historically been *more engaged* and *more dependent* upon trade than any major region of the world—both core and peripheral—throughout the 1970–2000 period. Only East Asia surpasses Africa in the 1990s, and even then Africa's dependence on trade increased rather than waned in the 1990s.[13] Africa's rising dependence is notably higher than the Organization for Economic Co-operation and Development countries, as the relationship of trade as a percentage of GDP in Figure 7.2 demonstrates.

What has changed is the *value* of Africa's exports. Here the legacy of colonial rule is telling: A heavy and continuing dependence on primary products—particularly in the face of the European and U.S. oligopolies that control processing and marketing worldwide—has been disastrous. With over 80 percent of Africa's exports consisting of primary products and raw materials (including petroleum), African states are particularly susceptible to commodity price fluctuations. Recent research sustains the Prebisch-Singer hypothesis of a steady downward trend, as revealed in the following chart of commodity prices in Figure 7.3 (food, nonfood agricul-

Figure 7.2   Africa's Relative Trade Dependence, 1960–2000

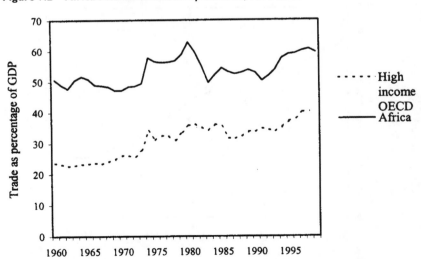

Source: World Bank, "Trade (% of GDP)," *World Development Indicators*, CD-ROM, 2002.

tural products, and minerals)[14] over the course of the entire twentieth century.

The sharp decline since 1970 is particularly notable, driving prices well below the historical lows reached after World War I and the crash of 1929. Examining key commodity prices against an index for Africa's major imports, manufactures, reveals this in detail in Figure 7.4. Even a slight

Figure 7.3   Aggregate Commodity Price Index, 1900–1990 (1970=100)

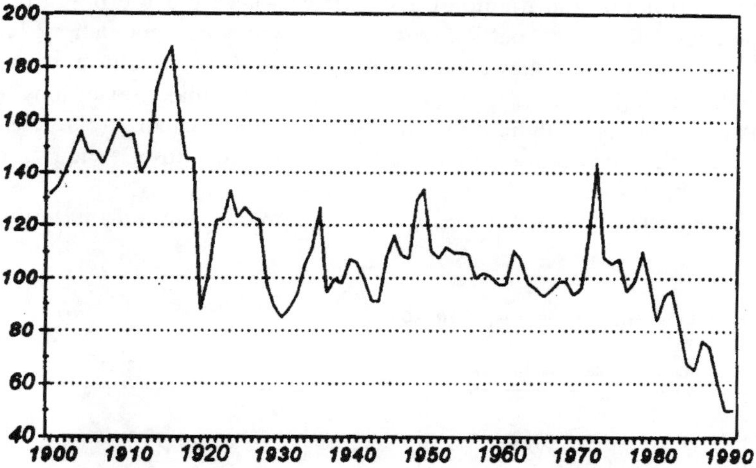

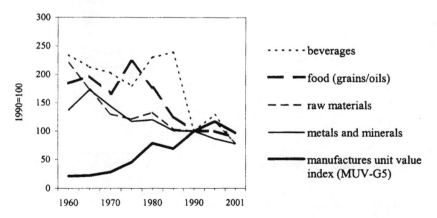

Source: Javier León and Raimundo Soto, "Structural Breaks and Long-Run Trends in Commodity Prices," *Journal of International Development* 9 (1997): 347–366, data from p. 350.

Figure 7.4   Commodity Prices and Manufactures Unit Index, 1960–2001

······ beverages

— — food (grains/oils)

– – – raw materials

—— metals and minerals

—— manufactures unit value index (MUV-G5)

1990=100

Source: World Bank, table 6.4: Primary Commodity Prices, *World Development Report,* various years (Washington, D.C.: World Bank, 2001, 2002).

upturn in the mid-1990s did not reverse these trends; no amount of increased export volumes could offset plunging prices.

These trends are well illustrated by the data for several of the major export commodities of our case study states, the DRC (diamonds, copper), Ethiopia (coffee), and Sudan (cotton, petroleum after 1999; see Figure 7.5).[15]

As can be seen, price increases during the mid-1970s world economic crisis have been rolled well back—even in the case of petroleum. Discovery of new natural-resource deposits has in selected cases—as in recent petroleum and diamond discoveries—held out the potential to expand state capacities, particularly in states with small populations (e.g., Botswana). As argued, however, in Chapter 6, and specifically in the case of Sudan, rising incomes from oil or minerals may, under conditions of a weakened state and ethnic divisions, only serve to sustain and accelerate war. Here the long-term data chart a bleak future for those relying on primary products.

When set against the price of imports from core areas, as in terms of

Figure 7.5 Commodity Prices, 1960–2001

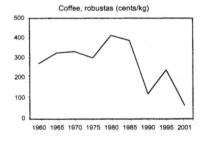

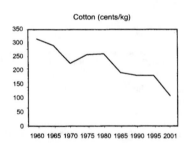

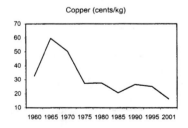

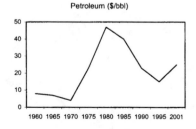

Source: World Bank, table 6.4: Primary Commodity Prices, *World Development Report,* various years (Washington, DC: World Bank, 2001, 2002).

trade data, the cost of Africa's high degree of colonial integration into the world economy are even more starkly revealed (see Figure 7.6).

As the United Nations Conference on Trade and Development (UNC-TAD) recently summarized, "If the terms of trade had stayed at 1980 levels, Africa's share of world exports would be double today's figure. Furthermore, African growth per annum could have been 1.4 percentage points higher, raising per capita income to a level 50% above the current figure."[16] The decline in the terms of trade for three of our four country studies (figures for Sudan being absent in the World Bank database) illustrates this well (see Figure 7.7).

The charts indicate, moreover, a radical shift during the early 1980s as the terms of trade moved decisively against Africa's traditional exports, and African producers and states were unable to promote more value-added manufactured exports.[17] Successful new export products, such as clothing and cut flowers shipped to the European Union or the United States, may well hold the best hope for export promotion. But they are few in number, and mark a return to production and trade patterns of the colonial period, with European firms and large-scale, usually settler farms dominating both production and trade.[18] Indeed, most African states may more properly be said to be experiencing deindustrialization as tariffs have fallen as part of structural adjustment programs, and state industries have been sold or closed and private industries have shuttered their doors. In short, far

Figure 7.6   Africa's Terms of Trade, 1960–1999 (1995=100)

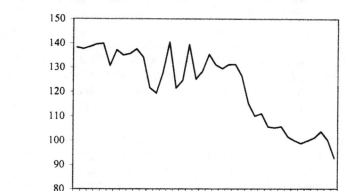

Source: William Easterly and Mirvat Sewadeh, "Terms of Trade, Goods and Services (1995 = 100)," *Global Development Network Growth Database,* http://www.worldbank.org/research/growth/GDNdata.htm.

Figure 7.7   Terms of Trade: DRC, Ethiopia, Sierra Leone (1995=100)

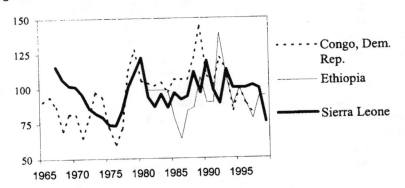

Source: William Easterly and Mirvat Sewadeh, "Terms of Trade, Goods and Services (1995 = 100)," *Global Development Network Growth Database,* http://www.worldbank.org/research/growth/GDNdata.htm.

from Africa's withdrawing from the world trading system, the world trading system has continued to draw upon the primary-product production system put in place in the colonial period—while the prices paid for these products have been falling and prices for Africa's imports have been rising.

Capital Flows

If trade liberalization and export growth is one leg of the recent globalization wave, finance is the other. The evidence for the charge that globalization has bypassed Africa is stronger here. As is well known, there was a sharp, radical shift to increasingly heavy debt loads during the late 1970s. As Figure 7.8 shows, this was a common pattern all along the periphery of the world economy. As campaigners for debt cancellation have argued, debt repayments leave few funds for local investment or state services. Africa's debt burden has been further compounded as demonstrated above by falling prices for Africa's exports and worsening terms of trade, as well as sharply falling overseas aid.

Many policymakers in the 1990s expected that foreign direct investment would offset rising debt and reliance on commodity prices, and thus strongly advocated tariff reductions, open exchange regimes, and the privatization of state firms and activities. As Figure 7.9 shows, however, Africa's share of foreign direct investment (FDI) has nevertheless suffered during the 1990s and the beginning of the twenty-first century.

Again, Africa is not alone in being bypassed by the growing flow of investment capital. Taking World Bank categories of "developed" and

Figure 7.8 Global Debt by Region, 1980–2003

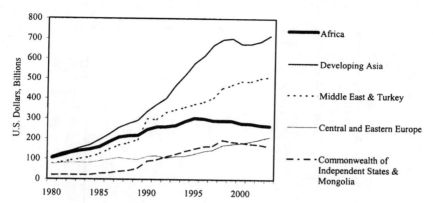

Source: International Monetary Fund, *World Economic Outlook Database,* April 2002, available at http://www.imf.org/external/pubs/ft/weo/2002/01/data/index.htm.

Figure 7.9 Africa's Share of World Foreign Direct Investment, 1970–2000

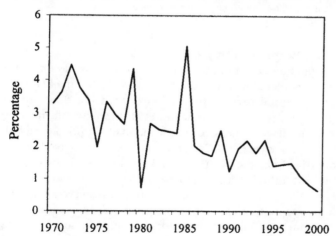

Source: United Nations Conference on Trade and Development (UNCTAD), *UNCTAD Handbook of Statistics Online,* available at http://stats.unctad.org/public.

"developing areas," current data show a remarkable polarization, as Figure 7.10 demonstrates. Still, unsustainable debt loads and falling capital inflows have, for most analysts, only served to confirm Africa's marginal role in the world economy.

Figure 7.10   Comparing "Developed" and "Developing" FDI per Capita, 1970–2000

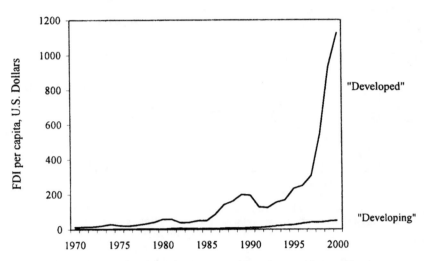

Source: United Nations Conference on Trade and Development (UNCTAD), *UNCTAD Handbook of Statistics Online,* http://stats.unctad.org/public.

Opening Africa's Markets and Shrinking African States

Despite this common depiction, a strong case can be made that Africa is not a net debtor but a net world creditor. For as with commodity trade, the examination of capital reveals significant flows from South to North. Surprisingly, as recent studies indicate, even the poorest, most highly indebted countries have witnessed significant levels of private capital outflows in the last thirty years.[19] "Capital flight" for twenty-five low-income African countries over the period from 1970 to 1996 is estimated, for example, at $285 billion (in accumulated stock in 1996 dollars), while debt stood at $178 billion.[20] These are not insignificant sums as "annual capital flight was equivalent, on average, to 3.8 per cent of GDP."[21] Estimates for our four case studies, for example, stand as outlined in Figure 7.1.

Moreover, rising public debt across Africa in the late 1970s and 1980s matched rising capital flight: The countries with the largest external debts were precisely those with the largest capital flight.[22] One must stress here that while governments are severely indebted (as indicated by the tables in several sections above), capital flight and investment abroad is carried out by private actors. Put another way, states may be severely indebted, but countries may not be—private actors have actually invested African funds heavily overseas.

Table 7.1   Total Real Capital Flight[23]
(adjusted for trade misinvoicing, in million 1996 dollars)

	Real Capital Flight	With Imputed Interest Earnings	As % of 1996 GDP
DRC	13,388	22,991	392
Ethiopia	5,523	8,018	133
Sierra Leone	1,473	2,278	257
Sudan	6,983	11,614	161

Source: James K. Boyce and Léonce Ndikumana, "Is Africa a Net Creditor?" *Journal of Development Studies* 38, no. 2 (December 2001): table 4, p. 43; table 5, p. 44.

The inclusion of private human capital accentuates these observations, for it is quite evident that African professionals fled the continent throughout the 1980s, a trend that accelerated into the 1990s. No reliable, long-term statistics on the "brain drain" exist, but by any measure the numbers are large, affecting not only public-sector employment in higher education and health sectors, but also professional and technological labor supply for the private sector. A 2002 World Bank report noted, for example, that "about 30,000 Africans who hold Ph.D. degrees live outside the continent, and 130,000 Africans study in higher learning institutions outside Africa. Many of these who find employment abroad never turn."[24] A recent Economic Commission on Africa workshop similarly noted that by 1993 over 21,000 Nigerian doctors were practicing in the United States alone, 60 percent of all Ghanaian doctors trained locally in the 1980s had left the country, and in Sudan, 17 percent of doctors and dentists, 20 percent of university lecturers, and 30 percent of engineers in 1978 alone had gone to work abroad.[25] Yet another recent study estimates that Africa lost 60,000 middle- and high-level managers between 1985 and 1990, with currently 23,000 professionals leaving every year for new jobs in Europe and the United States, costing Africa as much as $4 billion a year.[26] South Africa, with its advanced and deep labor market, has been especially affected in the postapartheid period.[27]

Summarizing Capital, Migration, and Trade Engagements

Across all of key sectors driving globalization—trade, finance, capital, or migration—it is demonstrably evident that Africa has never comprised a set of isolated, national economies and nation-states. The cost of Africa's embeddedness in the world economy has, however, varied significantly. It was the global depression after 1975 that marked a clear sharp shift—as it did for other primary producing areas along the periphery of the world economy. The years following 1975 also led to a radical policy shift in the

North and South, from Keynesian and socialist support for national economic planning and development, to the aggressive pursuit by core states of neoliberal policies that stressed the removal of the state from direct economic activity and, for the South, the end of the developmentalist, modernizing state.

Falling prices for Africa's goods, rising debt, shrinking capital inflows and rising outflows, and the loss of skilled labor intersect these new processes and policies of the 1990s. The cost of structural adjustment policies and International Monetary Fund (IMF) and World Bank conditionalities have been increasingly recognized, even if most analyses still see Africa as marginally engaged in world economic networks. What remains less noted is the impact of these developments on state capacities and legitimacy, and how these have been shaped by the relationship with northern states and institutions. We now turn to explore this area.

State Capacities:
Central Government Expenditures, Health, Education
All states draw legitimacy from providing basic human needs and the climate within which they can be delivered. These range from the need to secure territory and the legal regimes, to the provision of basic services, most notably health and education. Colonial rule established Western schools and health services, under either missionary or government auspices. Still, these efforts were minimal; very little of the colonial state's budget was spent on public education or health for Africans: the colonial state was racially formed at its core. One of the great achievements of the early postindependence governments was to deracialize the state and correspondingly expand education and health services (although the colonial bias for urban elites and particular ethnic and racial groups remained, as our cases explicitly argue for Ethiopia (e.g., Addis Ababa and Amharas, Tigrayans), Sierra Leone (Krio), Sudan (the Arab North), and, in part, the Congo (Kinshasa, and, on more recent evidence, enmity toward Rwandaphone populations). These efforts were central pillars of establishing the state's legitimacy and the nation-building effort.

State Expenditure Patterns
The post-1975 global economic crisis, the globalization of production and finance, and structural adjustment have reversed these trends. While rates of growth of government expenditure fell off even in core states, African state expenditure as a percentage of GDP fell off in absolute terms. And when core state spending rose in the 1990s, African expenditure per capita fell off sharply, as Figure 7.11 illustrates. If neoliberalism has been applied to all states, it clearly has not forced state forms or expenditures into a single pattern or trend line.

Figure 7.11   Government Expenditures as Percentage of GDP, 1960–2000

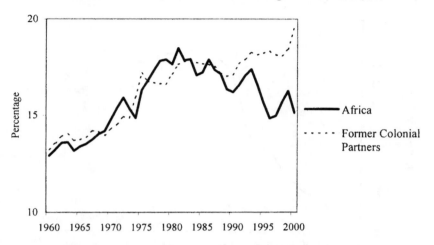

Source: World Bank, "General Government Final Consumption Expenditure (% of GDP)," *World Development Indicators*, CD-ROM, 2002.

If states seem to be spending equivalent shares of GDP per capita, African states' much lower national income means that per capita spending has been far less than rich states to the north. Per capita spending in constant 1995 U.S. dollars rose sharply after independence, from US$80 to over twice that level two decades later—a growth rate that was quickly and sharply curtailed as the debt crisis hit (see Figure 7.12).

Comparable data for our four case studies is less available, especially during extended war years. Yet the trends are similar, as Figure 7.13 illustrates.[28]

The result of these trends was that African states fell farther and farther behind the ability of rich northern states to provide for their citizens. As the income gap grew, as Figure 7.1 above demonstrated, the gap in actual state spending grew as well. African states never spent much by comparison to European colonial powers. Still, as the figure below documents, African states began to close the gap in the 1960s, from a ratio of 3 percent of the ex–colonial powers' per capita income to over 4 percent by the late 1970s—only to see these efforts fall sharply thereafter (see Figure 7.14).

The cause of the widening gap between the expenditures of core and African states is directly traceable to falling incomes that made African states susceptible to the imposition of neoliberal policies designed to "shrink the state" through the privatization of services, the selling of parastatal enterprises, and the removal of restrictions on foreign exchange and capital flows. While these policies were adopted and African states

Figure 7.12   State Expenditure Per Capita, Africa, 1960–1999

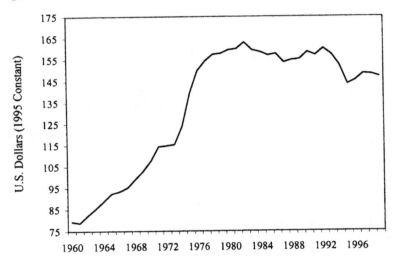

Source: World Bank, "General Government Final Consumption Expenditure (% of GDP)," *World Development Indicators,* CD-ROM, 2002.

Figure 7.13   Public Expenditure per Capita

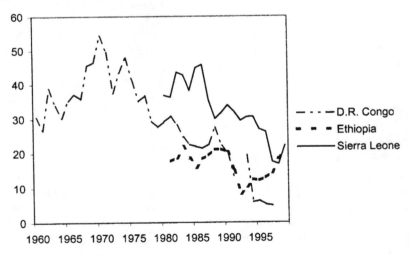

Source: World Bank, "General Government Final Consumption Expenditure (% of GDP)," *World Development Indicators,* CD-ROM, 2002.

became smaller and weaker, larger and more firmly bounded economic and political institutions emerged in the North (North American Free Trade Agreement [NAFTA], European Union [EU], World Trade Organization [WTO], etc.).

Figure 7.14   Africa's Government Expenditure per Capita as Percentage of Former Colonial Partners' Expenditures, 1960–1998

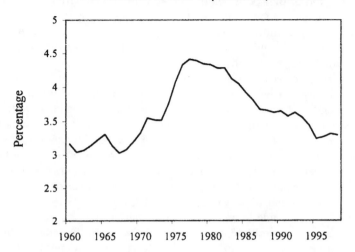

Source: World Bank, "General Government Final Consumption Expenditure (Constant 1995 U.S. dollars)" *World Development Indicators,* CD-ROM, 2002.

Data on state-sponsored employment and the size of state bureaucracies demonstrate these trends, peaking in the 1990s. Yet at no point can African states be termed bloated or swollen, as was so often charged in the 1980s and 1990s. As one recent study of available data concluded,

> The data show instead three unexpected things about bureaucracy and growth in Africa. First, regarding their size, African public bureaucracies are not as large as often imagined. To the contrary, relative to other states, African states deploy a small stock of personnel to manage their territories and populations. Second, as to the trend in public employment, the number of bureaucrats has been falling rather than rising in much of [sub-Saharan Africa] since about 1980. Africa's small state bureaucracies for the most part have been getting smaller. Third, with respect to larger bureaucracies being associated with lagging national incomes, the inverse comes closer to the truth. At least two countries with higher levels of public employment have had superior economic records.[29]

As World Bank and other studies reveal, public-sector employment in Africa is about average for low-income states; on a per capita basis Africa actually has fewer government workers than any other developing region.[30]

Health and Education
Falling state expenditures and falling public employment inexorably undermined the key services that underpin the legitimacy of the state: basic human welfare services, most notably education and health. This is evident

in the survey data of our case studies, where levels of dissatisfaction with the state provision of transport, health, and education were strikingly high. While national identity may remain high—as is again evident in our cases, even across the vast, multiethnic, and war-torn DRC—state legitimacy inevitably is low (we would need, of course, longer-term survey data to establish a more precise relationship).

World economic crisis has not, it must be noted, had a universal effect on state capacities and resources. Over the course of the last twenty-five years, as several authors have shown, core states have expanded welfare spending, while it has declined for Latin America and most poor states.[31] As one author puts it, "From 1972 to 1995, globalization increased in both developed and developing countries, yet trends in government spending for social welfare [central government expenditure on social security and welfare services as a percentage of GDP] diverged during this period: spending rose in rich countries and slightly declined in LDCs."[32]

While we lack reliable long-term data on health or education spending by African states, the trend line clearly follows that of overall state spending marked above, and in many cases health services accounted for a falling share of a falling state budget. As Meredeth Turshen argues, the austerity and structural adjustment programs of the early 1980s ushered in a downward spiral in public spending on health care all across the continent:

> Real disbursements per person dropped. In Madagascar, expenditures fell 24 percent between 1977 and 1985; they fell 14 percent in Central African Republic between 1982 and 1991, and 13 percent in Congo between 1980 and 1987. In Senegal, a reduction in the proportion of public expenditure on health led to shortages in hospitals and public health centers, the introduction of payment for consultations and medical care even for the destitute, and a freeze on the recruitment of doctors. In southern Africa during the 1980s, real per capita government expenditure fell in Malawi, Mozambique, Swaziland, and Zambia.[33]

The downward spiral held, moreover, regardless of macroeconomic policies: "average health expenditure as a percentage of gross domestic product declined in countries with large and small improvements in macroeconomic policies. The decline was more drastic in strong reformers such as Tanzania and Gambia, countries that had most faithfully followed prescriptions for economic adjustment."[34] With per capita health care spending stagnating in the 1990s at a continental average of $25 to $35, African spending never approached even 1.5 percent of the level spent by rich states in the North.[35]

The trajectory of state spending on education parallels the narrative for health services, rising sharply after independence in the 1960s, only to suffer reverses in the 1980s and 1990s. As one recent summary put it, during the 1970s and 1980s "per capita expenditure on education was drastically cut in real terms in most countries. The average annual growth rate of public expenditure on education between 1970–1980 was 4.4%, but between 1980–1983, the average annual growth rate was –9.2% . . . Within higher education, public recurrent expenditure per tertiary student fell from $6,461 in 1975 to $2,365 in 1983."[36] World Bank estimates of sub-Saharan African education expenditures, expressed in public spending per capita, reveal similar trends (see Figure 7.15). Africa's share of total world spending on education, never more than 3 percent, fell steadily as well across the 1980 and 1990s.[37]

The Shifting Balance of North/South Political Power
Data can document poverty and shrinking resources, and even chart the rise and fall of state legitimacy and capacities. What remains undetermined, however, is whether the phenomena of the current conjuncture mark a fundamental shift in the structural foundations of institutional and political power. To answer this question requires placing empirical trends within a long-term, interstate framework in order to see if current patterns mark a new age of state formation and deformation across the world economy.

One outcome is clear: It is unlikely there will be a return to the strong developmentalist states of the 1960s and 1970s. When African movements in the late 1970s and 1980s overthrew dictatorships and minority rule, a return to development was expected but did not materialize. As we have seen above, world-economic forces became a key element in the subsequent weakening of most African and third-world states in the 1980s and 1990s. In many key areas African governments had little role in formulat-

Figure 7.15   Africa: Per Capita Education Spending (in 1995 US$)

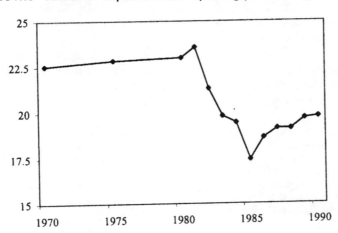

Source: World Bank, "Public Spending on Education, total (% of GDP)" and "GDP per capita (constant 1995 USD)," *World Development Indicators* CD-ROM, 2002.

ing the policies and programs that undermined state institutions and power: Africans have had little if any influence on market power and prices, debt repayment policies, the evisceration and sale of state enterprises and marketing boards, the collapse of university education and elite health care facilities, and the imposition of user fees for primary health care and schooling.

The evaporation of state institutions and power is often termed the collapse, fragmentation, or even disappearance of the state. What this limited vision fails to appreciate is not simply the role of "external" forces (the World Bank, IMF, etc.) in this outcome, but the actual transfer of key state functions to Northern states and international institutions. Basic policymaking processes, and increasingly the previous basic security and welfare functions of African states, have been steadily moved North to core states, international financial institutions, and foreign private-sector aid agencies, charities, and NGOs. Any significant degree of state sovereignty or relative autonomy, to the degree that they existed in the 1960s, is increasingly absent and unlikely to be retrieved. Seen in long-term perspective, the often rhetorical charge that Africa is being "recolonized" thus captures a truth: a post-1975 stripping away of state power and activities toward the core states of the interstate system.

This is easiest to demonstrate in the fields of capital and finance. As Thandika Mkandawire has pointed out,[38] financial liberalization directed by the IMF and World Bank in the 1990s not only impoverished the state and severed elected officials' control over financial and economic policy institutions, but also relocated power and policy elsewhere. Planning and policymaking by African bureaucrats were steadily eroded in favor of planning and policymaking conducted in Washington—and imposed by a growing number of staff in the relevant bureaus of the IMF, World Bank, and WTO. Misplaced reliance upon the "private" sector was also evident: private banks failed to replace previous state lending, while policies designed to attract foreign investors failed to attract productive capital. Meanwhile, national capital flowed out free of controls, as documented above.

The forced creation of central banks free of state control illustrates these dynamics at work. As Mkandawire summarizes,

> For all their self-perception of being independent and apolitical technocrats, most African central banks relate to international financial institutions in a totally dependent manner and are completely beholden to these institutions both ideologically and institutionally. Their dependence on foreign institutions is deepened by the poor shape of their economies and by the fact that independence from local centers of power has been earned on their behalf by foreign international institutions.[39]

Nothing illustrates better the bypassing of the state and the maintenance of foreign control than the IMF's and World Bank's open veto of governments' appointments to central banks and national ministries. In the case of very weak states, elected officials act as conduits to bypass state bureaucracies, through facilitating linkages between foreign institutions and new local commercial operations. As William Reno has argued, in extreme cases foreign firms may benefit from the collapse of central state bureaucracies and the rise of local warlords, who under current conditions can control territories containing mines or plantations.[40]

Similar processes are at work in the educational and health fields as well, where the attack on state revenues and activities has dictated the privatization of state functions—often under the control of foreign donors and NGOs. The key policy transition for education took place in the 1980s, on the heels of a succession of influential World Bank reports that attacked the overexpansion of education, especially at higher levels, and advocated cost-cutting and cost-recovery via fee-paying schemes to private institutions.[41] As the editors of a special issue of the *CODESRIA Bulletin* on higher education in Africa summarized, "what has prevailed [since the early 1980s], is the trend towards the privatization and marketization of the system." This means not simply turning existing state universities into commercial institutions, but the replacement of the state by "the phenomenon of the private university, whether owned by religious or secular organizations."[42] The result of these trends is that higher education has been transformed:

> From centers of excellence and sites of contestation and renewal of ideas, the universities have been largely reduced to centers of mediocrity and sites of stagnation and subsistence, including the pursuit by students and staff alike of multiple modes of survival that distract from concentrated academic work. The infrastructure and environment of learning have also continued to suffer declines even as the brain drain intensifies.[43]

These patterns extend, moreover, to primary and secondary education, where the underfunding of books, facilities, and salaries has been matched to the introduction of fee-paying schemes. Private schools, often supported by religious orders and foreign NGOs, have been expanding rapidly.[44] Even where funding for education has been sustained, increased foreign funding and influence have inexorably worked against national policy dialogue.[45]

This pattern of the relocation of state capacities in the domains of finance and education extends to health services. Behind the raw figures on falling expenditures outlined above stand not only the closure of public health services and the rise of private facilities, but also the displacement of health care policy and financing into the hands of overseas financial institutions, states, aid agencies, and NGOs. Increasingly, the state is being "bypassed" as new relationships are forged between local health care providers and overseas policymakers and funders. This need not imply the growth of new supranational institutions. As with the case of education and

UNESCO, in the area of health care the leading international organization that promoted the substantive expansion of primary health care service in postcolonial Africa and Asia—the World Health Organization—has seen its role decline as the privatization of health care has been put in place following policy mandates from the newly empowered World Bank.

Indeed, as the pressure for privatization exerted by the IMF, World Bank, and core states increased in the 1980s, "some third world governments virtually abandoned their historic role in the health sector, and many African governments renounced their commitment to free health care."[46] As is forcefully argued above in the Sierra Leone chapter, the implementation of IMF recommendations to privatize state services, impose user fees, and remove subsidies has all too often benefited politicians and local elites, while impoverishing ordinary citizens and their view of the state. By the end of the century most African states were spending approximately $14 per person on health care per year. Foreign aid funds and NGOs began to take over health care, accounting for more than half to between 80 and 90 percent of total health-sector investments.[47] As state health care budgets fell, states closed clinics and hospitals, fired state health care workers, and instituted rising user fees for even the most basic health care. As Turshen documents at length,[48] states have lost their funding and policy roles as well as their control of facilities and services. Those pursuing advanced curative care now fly north, while those needing primary care must increasingly pay for it in the private sector. For many citizens, the state has become increasingly irrelevant as a health care provider. Little remains of the postindependence, statist model of basic health care as a public good.

The Long Durée:
Cycle, Secular Trend, or New Interstate System?
As the data and these examples suggest, it is implausible to maintain that Africa's economic and political crises derive from the continent's economic isolation or neopatrimonial and ethnically driven politics. The long-term evidence demonstrates quite otherwise, namely that the collapse of some African states, and the diminished capacity of almost all, are part of long-term global processes and trends. At issue is thus not integrating Africa further into the world economy to resolve its difficulties, but rather changing the nature and terms of Africa's engagement within the world economy. As the argument above has sought to illuminate, this requires an assessment of interstate relations and how they have altered as the world economy has changed.

The timing of these transitions is evident in the times-series data on trade, finance, and migration, which reveal a radical decline during the 1980s and 1990s in the income and resources available to Africa's peoples and states. The examination of state expenditures and services such as education and health has shown, moreover, not simply declining funding or adverse market forces, but a relocation of state decisionmaking and institutional capabilities to overseas states and financial institutions, and, to a lesser degree, nongovernmental organizations operating in the country. If African states are collapsing, this is taking place as many of their activities and powers pass into the arms of other, arguably less democratic, organizations and institutions.

Discussions of African leaders' use of overseas partners (as in Jean François Bayart's discussion of strategies of "extraversion"),[49] or, more substantively, "transboundary" relationships in the age of "globalization,"[50] begin to address the intertwined processes of state *deformation* in Africa and state *formation* elsewhere. We need to ask, however, if contemporary phenomena mark a fundamental rupture and reordering of state relationships within the world economy. Are the changes of the last two decades, for example, marking simply a long-term trend of global polarization between rich and poor states? Or is this a cyclical phenomenon, a typical product of any period of financial speculation and a global economic crisis? Or are the changing relationships among African states and rich states to the north signs of the birth of a new global governance structure?

It is here that the study of African states' relationship with other states and political institutions may be particularly useful in our analysis of Africa's dilemmas and the global process of state formation. Seen from the African side of these relationships, one may discern successive world epochs of core and African state formation. These are not recent products of globalization, but reach back to at least the seventeenth and eighteenth centuries, to the interdependent creation of militarized states in Africa, planter colonies in the Americas, and urbanizing core states in northwestern Europe. The end of Atlantic slavery undermined this configuration of strong and weak states, opening the door to attempts to create modern bureaucratic states such as the Fante Confederation in mid-nineteenth-century West Africa. The expansion of the boundaries of European states through formal colonial conquest in the late nineteenth century put an end to this process, creating in Africa and Asia—as in Latin America much earlier—the highly skewed foundations of the postcolonial state that emerged in the 1950s. Independence gave us, however, a new matrix for interstate forms and relations, as the U.S.-led liberal world order matched independence to Keynesianism and national development. This implied fixing the territorial boundaries of the state—and expanding state institutions, resources, and power—and trying to obtain legitimacy through state activity.

The new interstate system also dissolved many of the economic borders imposed by past colonial empires and instituted new, more open boundaries for the flow of commodities and foreign direct investment. Regulating these new exchanges required new institutions in core areas— the Bretton Woods institutions in particular—and developmentalist, nationalist states along the periphery of the world economy. The data and analysis

in previous sections strongly suggests that the post–World War II epoch—
which generated and sustained the notion of independent, sovereign state
formation everywhere—has collapsed and cannot be revived. The territorial, economic, and cultural boundaries of African states, which seemed so
fixed and legitimate in the post–World War II period, now appear to be
irrevocably weakening.

In large part the attack on liberal forms of the state came from below,
as rebellions in the late 1960s shattered the Keynesian state in Europe and
the United States and propelled more radical movements in Africa that
protested authoritarian rule and economic underdevelopment. Rising commodity prices and then foreign loans, however, did keep afloat the African
state during the late 1970s. Indeed, the call by states in Africa and Asia for
a new international economic order grew stronger in the wake of OPEC's
price rises.

By the mid-1980s, however, mounting debt and popular protest
stripped away such hopes from Africa's elites, while core states and institutions responded by enforcing, as detailed above, structural adjustment policies and the demise of the central activities, policies, and social services of
the developmentalist, nationalist-born, African state. This transition was
particularly detrimental for Africa, layered as it was over Africa's enduring
colonial role in the international division of labor. Wedded to primary-product production regulated by the state and the preservation of colonial ethnic
and territorial boundaries, African states were ill placed, even in contrast to
Asia and Latin America, to benefit from the displacement of high-wage
manufacturing from core zones of the world economy to lower-wage zones.
Unlike Northeast Asia, African states had not been given privileged access
to U.S. markets for their manufactures during the 1960s and 1970s, and in
the 1980s and 1990s lacked the infrastructure and authoritarian regimes
required—as so evident in Northeast Asia and China—to attract the newer
forms of industrial subcontracting flowing from a second wave of deindustrialization from core zones during the 1990s. While core capital thus
launched waves of innovation, and semiperipheral states benefited from
deindustrialization in Europe and North America, peripheral areas with
strong democratizing movements suffered severely—and Africa was at the
forefront of this group.[51]

In short, the conjuncture after 1975 of a long-term global market shift
against primary products, a global economic crisis, popular uprisings
against corrupt rulers and states, and the emergence of neoliberal policies
and institutions were particularly lethal for African states and terminated
almost fifty years of twinning state development in the South to a liberal
interstate system. While Northern states and economic blocs subsequently
strengthened their capabilities and tightened their new regional borders
(e.g., the rise of NAFTA, the EU, and the WTO), the coherence and bound-
ary-setting capacities of African states were seriously undermined.

These conditions rebounded on state legitimacy and the cultural conditions of citizenship. Where states became unable to provide employment, basic security, and economic and social services, alternative social networks and groups emerged. Few have proven more powerful than the reemergence of ethnic and tribal identities forged during the colonial period, and suppressed during the postindependence period by states that achieved the deracialization but not the detribalization of society, to use Mamdani's formulation.[52] Under current conditions, the lack of state legitimacy and the weakness of a common citizenship endowed by the state has been starkly revealed in many countries. This too works seriously against any return to the state form that existed for the last half of the twentieth century—as the results of successive democratic elections have revealed. Meanwhile, core states have moved to restrict citizenship rights ever more narrowly, while tightening borders—especially those facing Africa and her descendants.

Under these conditions, the meaning of democracy or the possibility of legally protected civil rights becomes uncertain. As Mkandawire has put it, African states are becoming "choiceless democracies,"[53] where elections may take place and political parties may rotate in power, but where the government has been stripped of authority over the most basic of state functions. States may not simply lose legitimacy, but cease for many to be a focal point of political life. And this rebounds back on the colonial tribal legacy. As Olukoshi argues, "The decline of social citizenship and of the role of the state in social provisioning has, in many cases, been paralleled by the creation or revival of ethnic, communal, and religious networks and structures as individuals and groups seek alternative means of producing their own social welfare needs in a process that also challenges the postcolonial, national-territorial secular state project of independence."[54] Yet it is difficult even to imagine a revival of the territorial, developmentalist state, given the continuing insistence on neoliberal policies of core states and international financial institutions. The present epoch is not simply one of weakened states that might be revived in more prosperous times, but of the demise of the old pattern of state formation and legitimacy.

Looking Forward:
State Formation, Neoliberalism, and Regional Power

These observations suggest that the phenomena of the last two decades may indeed mark a significant transition in the interstate system, rather than simply a linear trend of polarization between core and peripheral states (as might be suggested by economic and inequality data), or a cyclical moment of protected markets and colonial relations that are common in great depressions (as in the 1930s or 1880s).

Two observations suggest a new pattern of interstate relations is emerging. First, wholly new networks, political institutions, and relationships have been forged between forces above and below national states— most notably for African states, between international agencies and local civil society groups. The explosion in the number and reach of international NGOs, and the power and knowledge of the World Bank and the WTO, signal these new institutional networks' being formed. To be sure, these networks are no less hierarchical than the older interstate-system patterns, with domination assured by core states matched to vertical power relationships across the interstate system. These networks also operate outside the formal control of elected governments, as is stressed by avid proponents purporting to represent "civil society."

Second, state-centered allegiances and struggles are giving way to new forms of accommodation and resistance that more directly challenge the new institutions to which political power has been relocated. Social movements—which since the late eighteenth century have been focused on the capture of state power as their ultimate objective, and were so instrumental in creating new states through antislavery and anticolonial struggles—now increasingly view the state as not a target to capture, but to oppose through transnational alliances. This is most evident in the networks that link the world's new indigenous, land, reparations, and antiglobalization movements. Movements increasingly realize that "choiceless" states no longer can assure self-determination and prosperity—the world-relational constraints on sovereignty, citizenship, and state power are now all too evident. Similarly, governing classes (including past state officials transmuted into commercial entrepreneurs in the wake of structural adjustment and privatization) have moved to consolidate their position by linking with transnational political and financial institutions such as the World Bank, WTO, and the IMF.

As each of the chapters in this book illustrates, specific countries have experienced and responded to these changes in very diverse ways. Like all other African states, the DRC, Ethiopia, Sierra Leone, and Sudan have been subject to falling primary products, pressure from international financial institutions, the rise of new civic and NGO actors, and the demise of developmental state planning as institutionalized in the 1950s and 1960s. Local factors beyond our purview here, such as the impact of the discovery of oil wealth in Sudan, or the character of the new political movements that destabilized old regimes as in the DRC, Ethiopia, and Sierra Leone, have similarly shaped how each state has charted its own course amidst the general patterns outlined above.

Our focus on individual states misses, however, a set of relationships central to the new epoch of state formation we have outlined above: relations among African states themselves and particularly between stronger and weaker states. Deteriorating state borders and capacities have created counter-opportunities for even small and moderate powers, as Uganda's interventions in the DRC and Rwanda illustrate well. As previous chapters have shown, Museveni's relatively stable regime has been able to significantly determine the course of regime change in surrounding states, as well as enrich a number of Ugandan politicians, generals, and businessmen through the illicit diamond, gold, and coltan trade in the war-torn DRC.

Still, there are sharp limits to the regional power and designs of Uganda, given its relatively small territory, population, and resources.[55] Museveni has failed to put in place a compliant regime in Kinshasa, or eliminate anti-Museveni insurgent groups in the DRC (or Sudan)—while the cost to the Congolese has been hundreds of thousands of deaths, especially in the northeast Ituri region occupied by Uganda. Uganda's international standing appears higher than its size would warrant; it was one of only five African states President Bush visited in July 2003 (albeit for a four-day visit only). This visibility rests, however, on its continuous role as a compliant state, from adopting strict structural adjustment programs, through supporting U.S. attacks on Sudan, to backing the U.S. invasion of Iraq (as did its neighbors Eritrea and Ethiopia), and joining the "coalition of the willing." In revealing Uganda's dependence on the North and its separation from other African states' positions, these actions undermine any serious bid for regional or continental leadership. The vast majority of African states, led by the continent's strongest states and the African Union, firmly opposed, for example, the U.S. actions in Iraq.

It is to these stronger states and supranational institutions to which many look for significant attempts to counter regional conflict and economic decline amidst the fading power of individual African states. Africa's dominant states and the regional organizations they dominate are not, however, among our case studies. Yet they deserve at least brief comment given the new opportunities for both African organizations and Africa's few stronger states to expand as older forms of governance and territoriality fade away.

Among Africa's states, two stand out: Nigeria and South Africa. Neither in the last fifty years has been truly "hegemonic" in its regions, if by that term we mean domination, with consent in the Gramscian sense, across commercial, financial, and ideological relationships. Yet both have dominated their regions through their economic weight and military power for a considerable time, even as they have remained subordinate to powers to the north. In this sense they are "subhegemonic," as events in West Africa, including Sierra Leone, and in southern and central Africa, including the DRC, have recently shown.

South Africa and Nigeria have also been consistently targeted by policymakers in the North as being "pivotal states" to the West, due to their size, influence, and economic power that potentially extends beyond their region.[56] Of particular concern to Western policymakers is the ability of trusted African states to take over declining commitments from the West, especially in the area of peacekeeping. This is a clear priority for the

United States, which failed so dismally in Somalia in 1993, and for France and Europe, which blundered so badly in Rwanda and the Congo in the 1990s. As the Atlanticist and realist Henry Kissinger recently put it, "No state except Nigeria or South Africa is in a position to play a major role outside its immediate region," while "African security issues . . . should be left largely to African nations, with South Africa and Nigeria playing the principal roles."[57]

While other states such as Algeria, Egypt, Kenya, Senegal, Uganda, or Zimbabwe have from time to time been candidates for "pivotal" status, Nigeria and South Africa remain the most enduring cases for obvious reasons. Nigeria's importance arises from its population of 130 million, oil wealth, and military resources, while South Africa's smaller population of 43 million is offset by its industrial economy, which is the largest by far in Africa. The contrast between the two in terms of economic power and infrastructure, however, is sharp: South Africa's GDP (2001) of $122 billion is over three times Nigeria's GDP of $37 billion, giving South Africa a GDP per capita figure of $2,850 in contrast to Nigeria's $290 GDP per capita.[58] Nigeria's and South Africa's population or GDP and GDP figures (for 2001) similarly stand out from other candidates for "pivotal" status, particularly in sub-Saharan Africa, as Table 7.2, which includes our case studies, shows. As can be seen from Nigeria's interventions in Sierra Leone

Table 7.2 Economic and Military Profiles: Pivotal State Candidates and Case Study States

	Population (millions)	GDP ($ billions)	GDP per capita $	Military Expenditure ($ millions)
Nigeria	130	37	290	1,560
South Africa	43	122	2,820	1,960
Algeria	31	51	1,650	1,830
Egypt	65	100	1,530	2,390
Kenya	31	11	350	200
Uganda	23	6	260	140
Zimbabwe	13	62	480	263
DRC	52	4	80	69
Ethiopia	66	7	100	533
Sierra Leone	5	1	140	20
Sudan	32	11	340	424

Sources: GDP and population figures for 2001 from World Bank, *World Development Indicators 2003*, table 1.1, "Size of the Economy," 14–16, online at http://www.worldbank. org/data/wdi2003/tables/table1-1.pdf. Military expenditure figures for 1999, from U.S. Department of State, *World Military Expenditures 2003*, online at http://www.state.gov/documents/organization/18739.pdf; figures for Kenya and Sudan are estimated.

and Liberia in the 1990s, its regional strength has been exercised through its military power, which is in turn based upon a military-dominated state able to divert petroleum profits toward authoritarian ends. Its domination of the regional organization of Economic Community of West African States (ECOWAS) is illustrated in these interventions, which despite a claimed cost of $8 billion must be considered failures. In both cases Nigeria was forced to rely on the UN or EU for military and relief operations.

By the end of the 1990s and the emergence of an elected government in Nigeria, such interventions had run their course; troop strength fell almost 30 percent during the decade, while expenditures rose but slightly (7 percent).[59] In 1998 Nigeria refused to commit troops to Guinea-Bissau, while withdrawing its troops from Sierra Leone. Under elected General Olusegun Obasanjo, Nigeria seemed set to move away from unpopular foreign military engagements and toward the use of more diplomatic and institutional forms of conflict resolution.

Nigeria's financial and military weaknesses, driven in part by falling oil prices and a rising external debt, stand in sharp contrast to South Africa's position. Unlike Nigeria, it has long dominated its region economically since at least the interwar period.[60] It is now the major source of capital investment for central and southern Africa, just as southern Africa is the major buyer for South Africa's more advanced manufactures. To many in the region South African domination remains a constant, even in the postapartheid period, resting as it does on highly unequal trade, financial, and military relationships.

Yet the Mandela and Mbeki governments have, if anything, been more hesitant to exercise military power than many expected or, in the case of peacekeeping, have wanted. Its disastrous military intervention in Lesotho in September 1998 led to more careful diplomatic efforts, as in the DRC, and a far greater wariness in the early years of the Mbeki presidency to commit resources, much less troops, to quell regional conflicts. Like Nigeria, a democratic South Africa has seen a shrinking of its military in the 1990s, with expenditures falling almost 60 percent over the course of the 1990s, and troop strength falling by a third.[61] Current spending is heavily committed to new naval equipment, rendering the state even less capable of deploying troops over long distances. As the new century opened, the new government was both less capable and less interested in performing expensive peacekeeping commitments. As one comparison of the two states' hegemonic ambitions puts it, "During the 1990s, Nigeria was willing but unable to carry out swift and decisive military interventions in West Africa. South Africa was more able but largely unwilling to undertake such military actions in southern Africa."[62]

Where innovation has truly taken place is in the South African government's attempt to insert itself as a mediator between the new neoliberal institutions and policies in the North and the continent as a whole. This is a far different matter than regional military power, the central issue in most regional studies, and far more central to the changing forms of state formation we have charted above in the postliberal period. At issue is not the South African government's full acceptance of privatization and structural adjustment policies: Mandela accepted this very early on, followed by Mbeki's even more ardent agreement with the IMF and World Bank; in this, South Africa appears like any other African state. What is new is Mbeki's avid pursuit of a leading institutional and ideological role in cementing Africa's future within the polarizing interstate order. The flurry of activity ranges widely at the highest level, from Mbeki's leadership of the neoliberal African Union (in the wake of the collapse of the OAU and continental autonomy), through his formulation and promotion of the New Partnership for Africa's Development (NEPAD), which incorporated previous proposals by Nigeria and Senegal (the OMEGA plan), to the proclamation and pursuit of a continental "African Renaissance" under its leadership.

Proclamations of a renaissance of good governance and peace have led South Africa to engage in diplomatic and peacekeeping efforts on a much wider scale than ever envisioned in the 1990s. By August 2003, South Africa had three thousand troops stationed across Africa versus almost none just three years before—a significant number given that its armed forces had been cut to seventy thousand, less than half the number during the apartheid years. Such commitments operate under not just hesitant UN auspices, but increasingly through African Union initiatives. Nigeria has similarly moved to recommit troops to West African peacekeeping efforts, most notably in Liberia. Both the DRC and Liberia are, however, testing the real limits of Nigerian and South African military—not to mention financial—resources. In the wake of 9/11, the U.S. government's search for reliable partners for its antiterrorist campaigns, as well as for peacekeeping duties outside Europe, is likely to buttress considerably such abilities. Such combined efforts nevertheless reveal how far Africa's leading states have moved away from the past OAU's principle of noninterference in fellow African states' affairs, and toward openly asserting their political and war-making/settling powers across their regions and indeed the continent.

Mbeki's determination to lead this process has been most visible in South Africa's relations with international financial institutions and agencies. Here his key ministers have been deployed across the board, as in his finance minister's chairmanship of the IMF/World Bank board of governors in 1999–2000, and his trade and industry minister's presidency of the UN Conference on Trade and Development between 1996 and 2000 and chairmanship of the World Bank's Development Committee.[63] Launched in Abuja in October 2001, NEPAD provides the concrete vehicle for promoting South Africa's leading role, promising to achieve prosperity and democracy for Africa by reversing the continent's "marginalization from the globalization process."[64] To achieve this, NEPAD argues quite forceful-ly for an end of national development policies of the past, and a fuller, quicker integration into world capital, financial, and technological markets, with South Africa leading the way. As the former director of the UN Economic Commission for Africa, Adebayo Adedeji, has pointed out stark-ly, NEPAD is thus a radical break with recent African development strate-gies from the Lagos Plan of Action (1980) to the UN Plan of Action for the Development of Africa (1991).[65]

NEPAD thus carries us very far from long-standing calls for strength-ening continental autonomy and self-determination.[66] It does recognize and address the fall of the developmentalist state and the rise of neoliberalism, factors which have so fatally undermined past paradigms of national eco-nomic planning. Yet NEPAD as currently composed also indicates the extreme difficulty of securing peace, minimal levels of well-being, and democracy across the continent under these new interstate and international financial relationships. While South Africa might enhance its power by becoming the regional or even sub-Saharan center of neoliberal institutions and multinational corporations, it is likely to do so only by exacerbating inequalities and protest centering around the lack of land, jobs, and basic human services. As Brazil under Lula illustrates, alternative and moderate paths toward regional power do exist, ranging from promoting intraregional and intracontinental trade to harsh bargaining with core powers and espe-cially with the WTO (as in the Group of 21 stance against European and U.S. farm subsidies at the Cancun WTO meetings). For the moment, how-ever, South Africa under Mbeki remains committed to soliciting bilateral relationships with the North, at the cost of forging more collaborative efforts with African states and the South in general.

Given these conditions, the prospect for stronger forms of state power emerging in Africa are not good. Hopes of returning to the era of develop-mentalist states and national economic planning remain but fond memories of the postcolonial state; neither socialist nor capitalist national planning states seem capable of revival in the twenty-first century. Expectations of regional powers leading Africa to its own renaissance continue to founder on their proponents' far too easy compliance with inappropriate neoliberal policies, and the North's willingness to ignore the poisonous fruits of its own African involvement and heritage.

The future seems to portend the continued isolation of the state, pres-sured from above to devolve its responsibilities and powers, and pressured from below to meet the basic needs of its citizens. To the extent that these pressures converge, far more transnational alliances may emerge over the medium term from below as well as above. Here the thrust of movements against globalization, privatization, debt repayment, and neoracism—so evident even in the new land, anti-WTO, anti-IMF, basic services and reparations movements—may indeed serve to put pressure not only on weak local states but also on the powers that have eviscerated them. This has the potential to increase Africa's returns from its participation in global markets and, indirectly, strengthen African states, as new global movements—in this case, anti-WTO movements—lend strength to African complaints over the international terms of trade in primary products. No one doubts that it has been movement pressures, including from Africa, that have legitimized an assault on the WTO and IMF, and directly led to the collapse of WTO talks in Cancun in 2003 amidst North-South acrimony. This in turn has opened up the real prospect of African cotton producers, for example, winning their demand that the U.S. stop subsidizing its cotton farmers and seriously depressing world cotton prices (a demand bolstered by Brazil's suit in the WTO against the U.S. on this issue, which stands, again, in contrast to the South Africa government's timidity in this field as noted above).

Such developments indicate the possibility and potential gains of African actors—including more powerful African states, organizations, and movements—cooperating across past boundaries as they confront the deadly policies of the past quarter century. The future of Africa may thus not depend upon its states as they have been constructed over the past half century, but in the future of movements that reach across and beyond them.

Notes

Comments from Ricardo Larémont and the project's coauthors are gratefully acknowledged. Assistance from Caleb Bush was invaluable in compiling the data series and is deeply appreciated.

    1. The obvious reference here is Samuel Huntington's *Third Wave* (Norman: University of Oklahoma Press, 1991), which was accompanied by numerous works on the "theory of political transitions"—something that failed to cohere, as we point out below, in the poorer regions of the world economy including, but not only limited to, Africa.

    2. See for example Lionel Cliffe and Robin Luckham, "Complex Political Emergencies and the State: Failure and the Fate of the State," *Third World Quarterly* 20, no. 1 (1999): 27–50.

    3. Michael Bratton and Nicolas Van de Walle, "Neo-Patrimonial Regions and Political Transitions in Africa," *World Politics* 46 (July 1994): 458.

    4. Henry Bienen, "Leaders, Violence, and the Absence of Change in Africa," *Political Science Quarterly* 108, no. 2 (1993): 271.

    5. Adebayo Olukoshi, "State, Conflict and Democracy in Africa: The Complex Process of Renewal," in *State, Conflict and Democracy in Africa,* ed. Richard Joseph (Boulder, CO: Lynne Rienner, 1999), 453. Indeed, Olukoshi's inability to escape the internal/external dichotomy demonstrates the difficulty of seeing states as integral parts of a larger world economy.

    6. See for example David Moore, "'Sail On, O Ship of State': Neo-Liberalism, Globalisation and the Governance of Africa," *Journal of Peasant Studies* 27, no. 1 (1999): 61–96, or David Held, "Democracy, the Nation-State and the Global System," *Economy and Society* 20, no. 2 (May 1991): 138–172.

    7. We cannot pursue the theoretical and historical implications of such a perspective here; see for example William G. Martin and Mark Beittel, "Toward a

Global Sociology: Evaluating Current Conceptions, Methods, and Practices," *The Sociological Quarterly* 39, no. 1 (1998) 139–161.

8. Manuel Castells, *The End of Millennium* (Oxford: Blackwell, 1998), 88, 96 passim.

9. Mohamed Daouas, "Africa Faces the Challenge of Globalization," *Finance and Trade Review* (December 2001): 38, 4, online at: http://www.imf.org/external/pubs/ft/fandd/2001/12/daouas.htm, accessed 29 July 2002.

10. S. Ibi Ajayi, "What African Needs to Do to Benefit from Globalization," *Finance and Trade Review* (December 2001): 38, 4, online at: http://www.imf.org/external/pubs/ft/fandd/2001/12/ajayi.htm, accessed 29 July 2002.

11. There is a considerable literature on rising world inequality, with studies by the UN Development Program and a variety of scholars being challenged by others. For the debate among sociologists see Roberto Korzeniewicz and Timothy Moran, "World-Economic Trends in the Distribution of Income, 1965–1992," *American Journal of Sociology* 102, no. 4 (January 1997): 1000–1039; Glenn Firebaugh, "Empirics of World Income Inequality," *American Journal of Sociology* 104, no. 6 (May 1999): 1597–1630, and Korzeniewicz's and Moran's response "Measuring World Income Inequalities," *American Journal of Sociology* 106 (July 2000): 209–214; and Brian Goesling, "Changing Income Inequalities Within and Between Nations: New Evidence," *American Sociological Review* 66 (October 2001): 745–761. We cannot adequately summarize the debate here. Central to the debate over long-term trends, however, is the adequacy and coverage of measures of GNP/GDP and the use of either market or "purchasing power parity" exchange rates; for purposes here of the long-term analysis of state capacity and world market power, we agree with those who utilize market exchange rages; see in this regard Robert Wade, "The Rising Inequality of World Income Distribution," *Finance and Development* 38, no. 4 (December 2001), online at: http://www.imf.org/external/pubs/ft/fandd/2001/12/wade.hm.

12. Former colonial powers here and elsewhere include Belgium, France, Japan, United Kingdom, United States, and Germany. For more extensive GNP comparisons by region, see Giovanni Arrighi, "The African Crisis," *New Left Review* 15 (May-June 2002): 5–38, especially p. 15. Arrighi uses GNP data by comparative world regions, representing Africa as part of a global whole; here we have chosen a more relational representation, pairing Africa with the states that have historically dominated economic and political relationships.

13. See World Bank, "Trade (% of GDP)," *World Development Indicators*, CD-ROM, 2002.

14. The twenty-four commodities included in this series were aluminum, bananas, beef, coffee, cocoa, copper, cotton, hides, jute, lamb, lead, maize, palm oil, rice, rubber, silver, sugar, tea, timber, tin, tobacco, wheat, wool, and zinc.

15. We exclude here Sierra Leone's major export, as well as a significant commodity for the DRC: gem diamonds. Long-term, world price series for gem diamonds—versus industrial diamonds—are unavailable and inapplicable here, due to, among other factors, the monopoly practices imposed by De Beers' Central Selling organization, the vast differences in local diamond quality and sizes, and, especially, the irregularity of local pricing and returns under war conditions. More recent diamond prices for the products of Sierra Leone and the DRC are treated extensively in Chapter 6 by Ricardo Larémont and Robert Ostergard.

16. See also UNCTAD, "From Rhetoric to Reality of African Development: UNCTAD Calls for Major Policy Shift," 11 September 2001, online at: http://www.unctad.org/en/press/pr0120en.htm; see pp. 34–40 in the full report, UNCTAD, *Economic Development in Africa: Performance, Prospects and Policy*

Issues (Geneva: UNCTAD, 2001), 7; online at: http://www.unctad.org/en/docs/pogdsafricad1.en.pdf.

17. A short-lived upturn in commodity prices in the mid-1990s was not sustained.

18. See especially the conclusion in Peter Gibbon, "Present-Day Capitalism, the New International Trade Regime and Africa," *Review of African Political Economy* 29, no. 91 (March 2002): 95–112; as well as Philip Raikes and Peter Gibbon, "'Globalisation' and African Export Crop Agriculture," *Journal of Peasant Studies* 27, no. 2 (January 2000): 50–93.

19. Ibi S. Ajayi, "An Analysis of External Debt and Capital Flight in the Severely Indebted Low Income Countries in sub-Saharan Africa," IMF Working Paper WP/97/68, 1997; Akorlie A. Nyatepe-Coo, "Capital Flight in Low-Income sub-Saharan Africa: The Effects of Political Climate and Macroeconomic Policies," *Scandinavian Journal of Development Alternatives* (December 1994): 59–78; and James K. Boyce and Léonce Ndikumana, "Is Africa a Net Creditor? New Estimates of Capital Flight from Severely Indebted sub-Saharan Countries, 1970–96," *Journal of Development Studies* 38, no. 2 (December 2001): 27–56.

20. Boyce and Ndikumana, "Is Africa a Net Creditor."

21. Ibid., 44.

22. Boyce and Ndikumana, "Is Africa A Net Creditor," 47–48. It should be noted that North Africa and middle-income countries such as South Africa (which has experienced high levels of capital flight during and after the struggle against apartheid) are excluded from this study.

23. These estimates of privately held external assets and capital flight, based on omissions and errors in official statistics, follow methods constructed by the World Bank in the mid-1980s and subsequently developed by others. On these methods, including exchange and interest rate calculations (e.g., the use of the U.S. producer price index and rates on short-term U.S. treasury bills), see Boyce and Ndikumana, "Is Africa A Net Creditor," especially pp. 28–29, 34–40.

24. World Bank, *A Chance to Learn: Knowledge and Finance for Education in sub-Saharan Africa* (Washington, DC: World Bank, 2001), 18.

25. Economic Commission on Africa, conference report on "Sharing Knowledge to Enrich Research, Training and Policy Making" (16 August 2000) in Addis Ababa, online at: http//www.un.org/Depts/renyo/newsletter/n19/acteca.htm, accessed 3 August 2002.

26. Dejene Aredo, "The International Migration and the Brain Drain from Africa," Addis Ababa University, paper presented at OSSREA workshop, "The Ethiopian Educational and Training Policy and Its Implications: Challenges and Opportunities," Addis Ababa, as reported in the press; see AllAfrica.com, "Africa's Brain Drain Reportedly Costing $4 Billion a Year," online at http://www.allafrica.com/stories/200204300167.html (accessed 3 August 2002); see also "Brain Drain Costs Africa Billions," BBC News, online at http://news.bbc.co.uk/1/hi/world/Africa/1605242.stm (accessed 2 August 2002). These are surely rough estimates, but they indicate the magnitude of the outflow.

27. A recent study for South Africa shows that official South African statistics recorded as emigrants only 35 percent of the South Africans who appeared as immigrants, over the course of 1989–1997, in the immigration statistics of the United States, United Kingdom, Canada, New Zealand, and Australia—over 233,000 left in this period to these four countries alone; see Mercy Brown, David Kaplan, and Jean-Baptiste Meyer, "Counting Brains: Measuring Emigration from South Africa" (Development Policy Research Unit, University of Cape Town, 2001), 3–4, online at http://www.queensu.ca/samp/publications/policybriefs/brief5.pdf; Brown et al.

estimate that emigration of professionals accelerated in the 1990s while immigration declined.

28. See individual chapters for details, e.g., on Ethiopian figures in particular.

29. Arthur Goldsmith, "Africa's Overgrown State Reconsidered: Bureaucracy and Economic Growth, *World Politics* 51, no. 4 (1999): 520.

30. Ibid., table 2, 527–529.

31. Nita Rudra, "Globalization and the Decline of the Welfare State in Less-Developed Countries," *International Organization* 56, no. 2 (spring 2002): 411–445; and for Latin America, Robert Kaufman and Alex Segura-Ubiergo, "Globalization, Domestic Politics, and Social Spending in Latin America: A Time-Series Cross-Section Analysis, 1973–1997," *World Politics* 53, no. 4 (2001): 553–587.

32. Nita Rudra, "Globalization and the Decline of the Welfare State in Less-Developed Countries," *International Organization* 56, no. 2 (spring 2002): 416.

33. Meredeth Turshen, *Privatizing Health Services in Africa* (New Brunswick, NJ: Rutgers University Press, 1999), 16; for longer-term examples, see her table 1.2, 14.

34. Ibid., 16.

35. Calculated from World Bank, "Health Expenditure, Total (% of GDP)" and "GDP per capita (constant 1995 USD)," *World Development Indicators*, CD-ROM, 2002.

36. Joel Samoff and Bidemi Carrol, "The Promise of Partnership and Continuities of Dependence: External Support to Higher Education in Africa," paper presented at the 45th Annual Meeting of the African Studies Association, 5–8 December 2002, Washington, D.C., 11–12.

37. Calculated from estimates by UNESCO in *World Education Report 1991* (Paris: UNESCO, 1991), table 2.9, 36, which shows Africa's share of total public expenditure on education rising from 0.8 percent in 1970, to 1.78 in 1980, only to then fall steadily to less than 1 percent by the closing years of the decade. Subsequent estimates in the *World Education Report 2000* (table 12, 118) show a similar trend for the 1990s.

38. Thandika Mkandawire, "The Political Economy of Financial Reform in Africa," *Journal of International Development* 11, no. 3 (1999): 321–342, see especially pp. 322–323, 337–339.

39. Ibid., 338.

40. See William Reno, "How Sovereignty Matters: International Markets and the Political Economy of Local Politics in Weak States," in *Intervention and Transnationalism in Africa,* eds. Thomas Callaghy, Ronald Kassimir, and Robert Lathan (New York: Cambridge University Press, 2001), 197–215.

41. See Samoff and Carrol, "The Promise of Partnership," 12–14.

42. Adebayo Olukoshi and Felicia Oyekanmi, "Editorial," *CODESRIA Bulletin*, nos. 1–2 (2001): 2; see also the discussion, data and extensive examples in Akilagpa Sawyer, "Challenges Facing African Universities," paper presented at the 45th Annual Meeting of the African Studies Association, 5–8 December 2002, Washington, D.C., 13–14.

43. Olukoshi and Oyekanmi, "Editorial," 2.

44. See for example the case studies in Joel Samoff, ed., *Coping with Crisis: Austerity, Adjustment, and Human Resources* (Chicago: University of Chicago Press, 1994).

45. See Joel Samoff, "Responses to Crisis: (Re)Setting the Education and Training Policy Agenda," in *Coping with Crisis: Austerity, Adjustment, and Human*

Resources, ed. Joel Samoff (Chicago: Chicago University Press, 1994), 219–253, especially 249–250.

46. Turshen, *Privatizing Health Services in Africa*, 16.

47. Ibid., 16.

48. Ibid., chap. 1, "The Collapse of Public Health" (1–22), and the case studies in chapter 2, "Restructuring Health Care in Southern Africa" (23–40).

49. Jean-François Bayart, *The State in Africa: the Politics of the Belly* (New York: Longmans, 1993).

50. See the useful discussion in Robert Lathan, Ronald Kassimir, and Thomas Callaghy, "Introduction: Transboundary Formations, Intervention, Order, and Authority," in *Intervention and Transnationalism in Africa,* eds. Callaghy, Kassimir, and Lathan (New York: Cambridge University Press, 2001), 1–22.

51. As we have argued above, the lack of capital investment cannot alone explain Africa's economic difficulties (as Arrighi tends to stress in "The African Crisis," for example), for the continent remains heavily dependent upon trade and investment flows, while other zones such as Russia and Eastern Europe face similar difficulties.

52. See Mahmood Mamdani, *Citizen and Subject, Contemporary Africa and the Legacy of Late Colonialism* (Princeton, NJ: Princeton University Press, 1996).

53. Thandika Mkandawire, "Crisis Management and the Making of 'Choiceless Democracies'," in *State Conflict and Democracy in Africa*, ed. Richard Joseph (Boulder, CO: Lynne Rienner, 1999), 119–136.

54. Olukoshi, "State, Conflict and Democracy in Africa," 458–459.

55. For comparisons of basic economic and demographic indicators, see the next section and the next table. Recent oil discoveries in Uganda (by Canada's Heritage Oil) might change these calculations in the distant future.

56. See for example the central article by Robert S. Chase, Emily B. Hill, and Paul Kennedy, "Pivotal States and U.S. Strategy," *Foreign Affairs* 75, no. 1 (1996): 33–51, where a "pivotal state" was defined not simply by their relations with neighbors, but also their importance to the United States and Europe, namely as "a hot spot that could not only determine the fate of its region but also affect international stability" (p. 33). Thus in this article Algeria, Egypt, and South Africa were the only African candidates, although one could clearly find other states that dominate their immediate region. Algeria was valued for its importance to the Western Mediterranean and Europe (see pp. 46–47); Egypt's relevance was its relation to Israel and U.S. Middle East interests (see pp. 40–41), not Africa. As for the DRC (Zaire at the time): "Physical size is a necessary but not sufficient condition: Zaire comprises an extensive tract, but its fate is not vital to the United States. What really defines a pivotal state is its capacity to affect regional and international stability" (p. 37).

57. Henry Kissinger, *Does America Need a Foreign Policy? Toward a Diplomacy for the Twenty-First Century* (New York: Simon and Schuster, 2001), 207–209—cited in Adekeye Adebajo and Christopher Landsberg, "South Africa and Nigeria as Regional Hegemons," in *From Cape to Congo: Southern Africa's Evolving Security Challenges,* eds. Mwesiga Baregu and Christopher Landsberg (Boulder, CO: Lynne Rienner Publisheres, 2003), 175.

58. All figures from World Bank, *World Development Indicators 2003*, table 1.1, "Size of the Economy," 14–16, online at: http://www.worldbank.org/data/wdi2003/tables/table1-1.pdf, accessed 25 April 2003.

59. U.S. Department of State, *World Military Expenditures 2003*, online at: http://www.state.gov/documents/organization/18739.pdf, 87; figures are for 1989–1999, with expenditures in constant 1999 dollars.

60. See William G. Martin, "Region Formation Under Crisis Conditions: South vs. Southern Africa in the Interwar Period," *Journal of Southern African Studies* 16, no. 1 (March 1990): 112–138.

61. U.S. Department of State, *World Military Expenditures 2003*, online at: http://www.state.gov/documents/organization/18739.pdf, 93; figures are for 1989–99, with expenditures in constant 1999 dollars.

62. Adebajo and Landsberg, "South Africa and Nigeria as Regional Hegemons," 172.

63. Not all African governments of course have been pleased with South Africa's position and concessions at international meetings, most notably South Africa's attempt to accept on behalf of Africa WTO trade rules; NGOs and social movements have been especially dismissive. See Patrick Bond, ed., *Fanon's Warning: A Civil Society Reader on the New Partnership for Africa's Development* (Trenton, NJ: Africa World Press, 2002).

64. NEPAD mission statement, "The New Partnership for Africa's Development (NEPAD)," Abuja, October 2001, p. iv; http://www.un.org/esa/africa/nepad/engversion.pdf.

65. Adebayo Adedeji, "From Lagos to Nepad," *New Agenda* 8 (2002): 32–47.

66. See Thandika Mkandawire and Charles C. Soludo, *Our Continent, Our Future: African Perspectives on Structural Adjustment* (Trenton, NJ: Africa World Press, 1999).

8

Conclusion

Ricardo René Larémont

Sorting out the relationships among borders, state formation, and nationalism in Sudan, Ethiopia, the DRC, and Sierra Leone was a challenge. In our approach we used historical analysis and public opinion surveys to understand whether there was citizen support for these states and to ascertain whether these states were considered to be effective. We also tried to discern whether the state was deemed to be the legitimate source of authority within different regions of the four countries studied. We identified the extent of ethnic collaboration or animosity, and we arrived at conclusions regarding the prospects for the future of borders, the status of states, and the future of nations. Our analyses inform and, occasionally, startle. By wedding historical analysis to public opinion surveys, we obtained an understanding of the direction in which these four states and inchoate nations were developing.

Specifically, we found that in Sudan we have arrived at a moment in history in which there appears to be a fundamental change among many northern Sudanese concerning their definition of what it means to be Sudanese. The survey data reveal that significant numbers of northern Sudanese (many of whom heretofore defined themselves as Arabs) are now beginning to embrace Africanity into the definition of what it means to be Sudanese. This new revelation, if it were to continue, would create a cultural matrix for rapprochement between so-called northern Arabs and so-called southern Africans. This finding is indeed promising for the prospects for peace because one of the principal causes for the breach in the North-South divide—the racial division between Arab and African—may, at least as the data reveal, be ameliorating. On the other hand, our data also reveal that there is considerable public sentiment among southerners toward separation and partition. If this hardening of public attitudes toward the territorial integrity of Sudan continues in the South, possibilities for unification will dim.

In Ethiopia we learned that members of the Tigray ethnic group generally approved of the Ethiopian government's performance, whereas members of the Amhara, Oromo, and Sidama ethnic groups were generally more critical. On the question of Ethiopian identity versus identification with one's ethnic group, the surveys revealed that majorities within the Amhara and Sidama communities placed greater value upon Ethiopian identity rather than subnational ethnic identities. In contrast, the data reveal that majorities within the Tigray and Oromo communities value their identification with the ethnic group rather than their affiliation with an Ethiopian identity. There is a significant divide on the question of identity. Follow-up surveys with ancillary questions will be needed to explain whether this divide can be bridged in the foreseeable future.

The data from the Democratic Republic of Congo provided surprising results. Whereas most modernization theorists from Karl Deutsch onwards have argued that national cohesion would become more likely with the increased capacity and effectiveness of the state, in the DRC we learned that despite the fact that the state rarely provides basic services (including public security), the data reveal an extraordinary commitment on the part of most respondents to the territorial integrity of the DRC and the maintenance of its borders. This surprising result demands more research. Our next set of surveys in the DRC needs to try to explain why this high degree of allegiance to the idea of the geographical state persists despite state nonexistence or nonperformance.

We must recognize that geopolitical actors (principally from Uganda, Rwanda, and Zimbabwe) have emplaced themselves on DRC territory and will continue to be there for as long as occupying forces remain focused on capturing and exploiting the substantial mineral interests remaining in the DRC. This complicating factor of foreign intervention in the DRC, coupled with state weakness in Kinshasa, means that Zimbabwe, Uganda, and Rwanda will continue to play profound roles in the DRC. If the DRC's state capacity (especially regarding the military and police) remains weak, the borders of the DRC will remain porous and the state based in Kinshasa will not be able to extend its governmental authority.

In Sierra Leone, the data reveal serious rifts between the Mende and Temne ethnic groups. This is an interesting finding. It provides the opportunity for a shift in political analysis regarding conflict and warfare because heretofore political power in Sierra Leone was wielded by Krios. With struggles for power now shifting from Krio dominance to a dyadic tension between the Mende and the Temne, the situation changes and becomes more unstable. This situation will have to be monitored closely to assure that the newly established peace accord endures.

Borders, Nationalism, and the State

In our four case studies, the phenomena observed—i.e., colonially created borders, multiethnic societies, and comparatively weak states—are present not only in Africa but also in many states and societies throughout the developing world. Throughout these regions we observe states with weak institutions and multiethnic societies with low levels of interethnic integration. These two conditions have been exacerbated by the international legal principle of *uti possidetis* that has reified, validated, and often made immutable the colonial boundaries of these states. From the 1960s until the 1990s in Africa, the existence of multiethnic societies within colonially created yet inviolable borders was assumed; secession or irredentism was considered unacceptable. Beginning during the 1990s with the de jure secession of Eritrea from Ethiopia, the de facto secession of Somaliland from Somalia, the horrific genocide within Rwanda, the tensions between Berbers and Arabs in North Africa, and the considerable social and political instability in West Africa, most of us have been forced to reconsider how peace and stability can be nurtured within the conditions that have been presented to us: unstable multiethnic societies operating within weak states with questionable borders that are recognized by international law.

During the postcolonial period most political leaders have attempted to enforce the allegiance of diverse ethnic groups to the postcolonial state while maintaining the state's colonially crafted boundaries. This strategy of enforced allegiance partly replicated European political and cultural models of coercion and repression of subnationalisms. For postcolonial leaders in the developing world, the future of the multiethnic nation was expected to fit within the geopolitical realities of the colonially demarcated state. This strategy of coercion very often has been unsuccessful. As an alternative to the politics of coercion, the simultaneous strategies of building effective and legitimate state institutions and political tolerance of ethnic differences should have been pursued. This was not done. The state was not built due to a lack of financial and political resources, and social strategies of ethnic pluralism were not pursued because most leaders attempted to craft new nationalisms without reference to ethnicity.

Building effective and legitimate states takes both time and resources. For the most part, Africa and most of the rest of the developing world has had little time (only four decades for almost all of Africa) and few resources—or squandered resources—to realize these goals. The review of the creation of European states in Chapter 1 revealed that the processes of state creation involved the development of taxation and fiscal systems, the building of effective and responsive state bureaucracies, the development of judicial and police systems, and the creation of professional armies. This process required two to four centuries in Europe. The length of time for state building in the developing world, in contrast, has been compressed. To realize these state goals in this short period of time is daunting. Despite our recognition of the need for both adequate time and resources to build responsive, effective, and legitimate state institutions, this particular task must nevertheless be accomplished. We now turn to that discussion.

Questions of both time and international economic context play roles in the definition and building of state authority and institutions. Most of Africa, having been independent only since 1960, has had merely four decades to develop effective governments. Not only have they had a short time to create such states, but they also have had to operate in an internationalized, "globalized" economic context that placed real inhibitions upon their range of options. African leaders (and most political leaders in the developing world) are placed on the periphery of the world economy, and their opportunity to maneuver politically is limited by the constraints of international finance, international economic institutions, and international political instability.

The second factor involves the juridical support given by bodies of international law that validate the maintenance of colonially created borders and that discourage political movements of self-determination by sub-nationalist ethnic groups. The international law doctrine of *uti possidetis* and resolutions promulgated by the United Nations and the Organization of African States support both these policies. United Nations General Assembly Resolutions 1514 (14 December 1960) and 1541 (15 December 1960) disapprove of movements of self-determination by ethnic minorities in the developing world unless such movements are undertaken in regions "geographically separate" from the established state and by peoples "distinct ethnically and or culturally from the country administering it." The burden of proof on these two points is difficult to discharge; these two resolutions effectively condemn most movements of self-determination despite other UN resolutions claiming to approve the right to self-determination.

These two resolutions have the twin effects of juridically recognizing the boundaries of postcolonial states and empowering political elites within those postcolonial states to further their efforts either to capture or to maintain power. The ultimate outcome is that poorly functioning states become legitimized and ameliorative border reform becomes close to impossible. The borders and sovereignty of European and North American states have been tied to the effectiveness of governments. Twentieth-century international law has in effect not only stabilized the borders of African states, it has by stabilizing these borders also played a role in the legitimation of dysfunctional or weak states.

Governments exist and operate within geographic spaces. The most enigmatic aspect of our work during this research has been that the territorial notion of the state and the operations of the state itself are often irrelevant for most of the citizen-respondents or resident-respondents in our surveys. For states to operate and exist, however, state capacity within definable and protected borders must be addressed eventually by the state's political leaders. From the viewpoint of the building of state capacity, certainty about the demarcation of borders and certainty about the protection and policing of borders must be addressed before the state's leaders will be able first to define and then broadcast governmental authority over an understandable area. Given that Africa's borders are artificial colonial creations that are poorly policed and given that most of Africa's rural residents disregard their state's borders and the state itself, we are left with the conclusion that the political leadership still needs both to define and police its territory so that adequate state institutions can eventually be constructed. In many cases in Africa, these issues have not been squarely addressed. They will need to be addressed, however, if effective governance is ever to be created.

While the building of legitimate and effective states remains unrequited and while effective strategies for multiethnic integration are in many places still under study, we must at this moment express our opinion that the proliferation of ethnic subnationalisms in either Africa or most of the rest of the developing world does not serve any economic logic. The creation of ethnically controlled ministates would be economically inefficient, for those states would most often not have the necessary resource bases to be viable in the world economy. It can also be argued that the creation of "ethnic nations" may be close to impossible: Very few "pure ethnic homelands" remain. Taking one example from northern Nigeria, Igbo families from the southeast of the country have migrated to the north in sufficient numbers that they constitute a real and recognizable minority within a predominantly Hausa-controlled north. Short of systematic genocide, segregating or eliminating non-Hausa in the north would be impracticable. Taking a second example from southwest Asia, the creation of a pure Kurdish state may be similarly problematic because of the significant existence of Arabs who live within the Kurdish "homeland." These examples emerging from voluntary or involuntary migration can be replicated throughout the developing world and prove that creating pure ethnic homelands may be a chimera.

Given the objective realities of ethnic diversity in the developing world, three political options seem available: federalism (see, for example, India and Malaysia), state efforts to assimilate ethnic and religious minorities into the dominant nation (see, for example, the Kurds in Turkey or the Malays in Thailand), or annihilation (the Muslims in Bosnia, the Hutu in Rwanda).[1] Since annihilation is morally reprehensible and state assimilation is fraught with difficulty, federalism must be considered as the most viable option.

The Borders/Nationalism/State Conundrum: Federalism as a Solution?

During the nineteenth century, repression of ethnic minorities was considered a requisite for nation building (as in the repression of the Basques and Bretons in France and the Québecois in Canada). During the late twentieth century, however, the development of federalist, confederalist, or decentralized political structures has become normatively preferred as a way of incorporating ethnic minorities into the nation-state. During the late twentieth century, the developed states of Spain, Belgium, Britain, and Canada have experimented with federalism to incorporate ethnic or linguistic minorities. These approaches were undertaken in developed states after leaders concluded that attempts to suppress minority nationalisms were unworkable, counterproductive, and morally unacceptable.

Spain provides an important example of a developed state's usage of federalism to incorporate ethnic and linguistic minorities. Because of Spain's need to deal with potential irredentist movements in Cataluña and in the Basque Provinces, the authors of the post-Franco 1978 Constitution permitted the promulgation of autonomy statutes that enabled provinces to opt for autonomy. According to these statutes, provinces that wished to assert autonomy could obtain sovereignty over local governance, local civil law, natural resources, energy, urban planning, public works, water resources, roadways and infrastructure, and culture. Within this federalist arrangement, the national government retained exclusive jurisdiction over immigration, foreign relations, defense, the administration of justice, customs, penal and labor legislation, international trade, monetary policy, general economic planning, and intellectual property rights. This arrangement has led to the stabilization of relations between the national government and Cataluña. Despite this success in Cataluña, the Basque Provinces remain unsettled. The southern Basque provinces of Navarra and Álava have achieved considerable integration into Spain; majorities in the northern provinces of Guipúzcoa and Vizcaya remain committed to independence.[2]

In Belgium, the situation is different. From the 1830s onward social cleavages have existed between Dutch-speaking Flemings and French-speaking Walloons. The Flemings have felt threatened by the economically, politically, and culturally dominant Walloons, and these perceived threats have created considerable tension in the society and polity. To reconcile these ethnic tensions, the 1970 Constitution and the 1980 constitutional revisions were proposed. The constitution and the revisions created a governmental system that has divided the society and polity into three linguistic communities (Dutch, French, and German) and four regions (Dutch-, French-, and German-speaking, and bilingual Brussels). Legislative powers have been divided in the House of Representatives and the Senate between a French-language group and a Dutch-language group. In both houses of the legislature, proposed legislation can be held in abeyance for thirty days whenever three-fourths of either language group objects to the content of legislation.[3] After the casting of this language-group objection, an opportunity for amendment of the legislation is provided. Upon the second submission of the legislation, proposed bills can become enacted by a simple majority vote of the entire legislature. The three-fourths language-group "quasi-veto" protects ethnic rights while the majority/second-round vote prevents stalemate in the legislative system.

In Britain, in order to counter emergent nationalisms, Prime Minister

Tony Blair introduced local parliamentary rule in Scotland and Wales (known as devolution) in 1999. During the 1990s local nationalisms were represented by the Scottish Nationalist Party and the Welsh Plaid Cymru. Since the introduction of Blair's devolution initiatives, the ardor of Scottish and Welsh nationalist movements has diminished. At the same time—and partly as a result of devolution—Blair's Labor Party has performed well in elections to these local parliaments (defeating the Scottish Nationalist Party in Scotland and the Plaid Cymru in Wales). The results of the Blair innovations have led to the weakening of Scottish and Welsh subnationalisms and the empowerment of the Labor Party.

In Canada the federalist experiment has been less successful. The Canadian constitution permits for enactment of a constitutional amendment to permit secession by a province. In Québec, where most of Canada's French speakers reside, there have been episodic movements advocating secession. When secession was put to an electoral test in 1995 and 1998, however, Québec's voters rejected that option. Québec's voters belong to two camps: a separatist camp represented by the Parti Quebécois and a Liberal Party. The Liberal Party has been committed to remaining within Canada on a federated basis. Despite Parti Québecois efforts to push for sovereignty, voters in Québec twice rejected their entreaties. They did so for two reasons: first, voters assessed the cost of underwriting separate armed forces, diplomatic services, and customs for Québec and deemed these costs to be excessive; second, because Québec has profitable trade relations with Anglophone Canada, voters in Québec understood that commerce would suffer as a result of secession. Canadian federalism will remain problem-ridden because of the asymmetrical terms of financial power between Québec and the central government: It simply costs too much for Québec to secede. Despite this financial reality, many French-speaking cultural nationalists continue to advocate for secession. This tendency will persist until financial and cultural relations between Québec and Canada are modified to remove French/Québecois animus toward the central state.

In Africa, Nigeria, Ethiopia, Ghana, Tanzania, and Uganda have undertaken experiments with federalism with varying degrees of success. Nigeria and Ethiopia will be discussed briefly before principles for successful federalism are outlined.

Nigeria's experience with federalism has been both dynamic and extreme with regard to the devolution of power. It is this author's belief that Nigeria's national government has subdivided Nigeria into what may be an excessive number of provinces for two reasons: First, the creation of a large number of provinces facilitates the creation of patron-client relationships with local officials that inure to the benefit of the national government; second, the creation of a large number of provinces minimizes their capabilities for creating viable, local, independent financial resources that could compete with the fiscal resources of the national government. By creating such a large number of provinces, the national government in Nigeria has afforded itself an opportunity to assure that it maintains this asymmetrical relationship of power with the provinces. This federalist recipe in Nigeria provides for the weakening of the provinces or states and the aggrandizement of the national government. This arrangement brings into question whether the correct balance of power between the central government and the provinces/states has been attained.

In Ethiopia, as Edmond Keller explains in Chapter 3, attempts to create a system of "ethnic federalism" have substantially failed because the provinces in Ethiopia do not have the opportunity to obtain fiscal independence from the national government. The national government either collects the majority of taxes or receives the lion's share of foreign aid. The national government then distributes its income to the provinces. As in Nigeria, an asymmetrical power relationship exists between the national government and the provinces. This asymmetrical power relationship, observable in Nigeria and Ethiopia, contrasts notably with Spain, for example, where both the Basque Provinces and Cataluña have the opportunities to obtain their own fiscal resources.

When federalism is considered as an option, success or failure depends upon the specifics of the devolution of power from the central state to the autonomous unit. Issues to be negotiated for devolution include

- Demarcation of borders of the autonomous unit
- The specifics regarding the sharing of governmental authority between the central government and the autonomous province
- Whether the autonomous province shall have a separate legislature and how legal conflicts between the provincial legislature and the national legislature will be resolved
- Whether the autonomous province will have a separate judiciary and how legal conflicts between the provincial judiciary and the national judiciary will be resolved
- Whether policing and internal security will be controlled by the province or the national government and, if there is overlap between the two, how jurisdictional and coordination questions will be resolved
- Whether local economic development will be controlled and directed by the province or by the national government and, if there is overlap between the two, how cooperation and coordination will be enhanced
- If natural resources are to be found within the province, critical economic issues may arise between the national government and the province concerning the exploitation of these valuable resources
- Taxation—who will tax residents and keep the receipts?

- Cultural matters, especially concerning education and language policy, will have to be resolved. The national government and the autonomous provinces will have to negotiate control of schools and policies toward the use of local languages.

The negotiation of the specifics of these issues determines success or failure of federalist arrangements.

In addition to specifics of the federal arrangement, federalist agreements succeed when two other factors are operative: first, when there is a commitment of political elites on all sides to negotiate, honor, and fulfill the terms of the autonomy agreement; and, second, when the the central state and the autonomous province have the governmental capacity to implement or enforce the agreement.

Future Research Agenda

The strength of this study emerges from the combination of historical analysis, public opinion research, and, where possible, elite interviews. The joining of historical analysis with the empirical data obtained from public opinion surveys has provided a new way of understanding the relationships among borders, state capacity, and nationalism. The public opinion surveys helped us understand attitudes toward the evolution of borders, the state, and the nation in the contemporaneous context; the historical approach explained changes in these factors diachronically.

The results of this study have proved to us that substantial additional investments are needed to extend the use of public opinion research throughout Africa and the rest of the world where these issues are relevant. With additional funding, more robust results will be obtained. We also need to contemplate going beyond the African continent; ethnic conflicts emerging from unstable borders are not peculiar to Africa, but are also present in Europe and Asia. Immediately promising areas for comparative research would include the Balkans, Pakistan/India/Kashmir, the Caucusus, and the Philippines, for example. Ethnic conflict, the effectiveness of the state, the meaning of nationalism, and the legitimacy of states will remain semipermanent issues within security analyses for the foreseeable future. By continuing to focus on these issues, policy-oriented researchers may play an important supporting role in preventive diplomacy and peacemaking.

Civil War and Genocide: Preventive Diplomacy and Peacemaking

Since the fall of the Berlin Wall in 1989, the nature of warfare has transformed fundamentally. It is empirically verifiable that intrastate ethnic warfare has replaced interstate warfare as the dominant form of warfare in the world. Most of these intrastate wars have occurred in the developing world where borders were formed by colonial powers, where state institutions are weak, and where rival ethnic or religious groups often contest for power.

Since the data trends reveal that intrastate ethnic warfare will remain prevalent and will increase, academic researchers need to work on developing quick and timely methods of public opinion data collection that can be used to create and implement strategies to prevent warfare. In our view, this should be part of the twenty-first-century agenda for peace.

This type of research provides data for decisionmaking that may lead to preventive diplomacy and peacemaking. Public opinion studies such as the work produced in this volume can form the basis of "early detection systems" that can help trigger preventive diplomacy and peacemaking that may prevent conflict, warfare, and perhaps genocide. It is the linkage of academic research to preventive diplomacy and peacemaking that makes this work important.

Academic analyses are important. Yet even after academic analyses have been made and diplomatic and military resources have been deployed, in most conflict situations we will still be faced with on-the-ground situations in which, more often than not, needed state institutions such as regular police forces and judiciaries will rarely be present. In these war zones, critical state functions will still have to be built up over the territory. This requirement returns us again to questions of state borders and sovereignty. Without clarity about borders and state capacity to control borders, state jurisdiction will be difficult to define, the institutions of the state will be a challenge to create, and peace and order will remain elusive.

Notes

1. Mohammed Ayoob, *The Third World Security Predicament* (Boulder, CO: Lynne Rienner Publishers, 1995), 169.

2. Hurst Hannum, *Autonomy, Sovereignty, and Self-Determination* (Philadelphia: University of Pennsylvania Press, 1990), 268.

3. Ibid., 408–409.

Acronyms and Abbreviations

ABAKO	Association de Bakongo (Congo)
AFDL	Alliance des forces Démocratiques pour la Libération du Congo
ANC	Armée Nationale Congolaise
APC	All People's Congress (Sierra Leone)
BERCI	Bureau d'Études, de Recherches et de Consulting International
CNS	Conference Nationale Souveraine (Congo)
DRC	Democratic Republic of Congo
EPLF	Eritrean People's Liberation Front
EPRDF	Ethiopian Peoples' Revolutionary Democratic Front
EU	European Union
FAC	Force Armée Congolaise
FAR	Forces Armées Rwandaises (Congo)
FDD	Forces nationales pour la défense de la democratie (Congo)
FDI	foreign direct investment
GDP	gross domestic product
GNP	gross national product
IGAD	Inter-Governmental Authority on Development (Sudan)
IMF	International Monetary Fund
LDC	less developed country
MLC	Mouvement de Libération du Congo
MPC	Military Provisional Council (Sudan)
MPR	Mouvement Populaire de la Republique (Congo)
MONUC	Mission de l'Organization des Nations Unies en République Démocratique du Congo (United Nations Observer Mission in the Democratic Republic of Congo)
NAFTA	North American Free Trade Agreement
NCBWA	National Congress of British West Africa (Sierra Leone)
NCSL	National Council of the Colony of Sierra Leone
NEPAD	New Partnership for Africa's Development
NRC	National Reformation Council (Sierra Leone)
NPRC	National Provisional Ruling Council (Sierra Leone)

325

OAU	Organization for African Unity
OLF	Oromo Liberation Front (Ethiopia)
PDRE	People's Democratic Republic of Ethiopia
RCD	Rassemblement Congolais pour la Démocratie
RUF	Revolutionary United Front (Sierra Leone)
SADC	Southern Africa Development Community
SIPRI	Swedish International Peace Research Institute
SLPP	Sierra Leone People's Party
SNNP	Southern Nations, Nationalities and Peoples (Ethiopia)
SPLA	Sudan People's Liberation Army
SPLM	Sudan People's Liberation Movement
SSLM	Southern Sudanese Liberation Movement
TPLF	Tigray People's Liberation Front
UDP	United Democratic Party (Sierra Leone)
UDPS	Union pour la Démocratie et le Progrès Social (Congo)
U.K.	United Kingdom
UN	United Nations
UNAMIR	UN Assistance Mission for Rwanda
UNCTAD	United Nations Conference on Trade and Development
UNHCR	UN High Commissioner for Refugees
UNAMSIL	United Nations Assistance Mission in Sierra Leone
UNOMISIL	United Nations Observer Mission in Sierra Leone
WPE	Workers' Party of Ethiopia
WSLF	Western Somali Liberation Front
WTO	World Trade Organization

Bibliography

Aadland, Oyvind. "The Process of Democratization in Ethiopia: An Expression of Popular Participation or Political Resistance." *Human Rights Report,* no. 5. Oslo, Norway: Norwegian Institute of Human Rights (1995): 22–47.

Aberra, Worku. "Tribalism Rules in Ethiopia." *New African* (September 1993): 9–22.

Abir, Mordechai. *Ethiopia: The Era of the Princes.* London: Longman, 1968.

Adebajo, Adekeye, and Christopher Landsberg. "South Africa and Nigeria as Regional Hegemons." In *From Cape to Congo: Southern Africa's Evolving Security Challenges.* Edited by Mwesiga Baregu and Christopher Landsberg, pp. 171–203. Boulder, CO: Lynne Rienner, 2003.

Adedeji, Adebayo. "From Lagos to Nepad." *New Agenda* 8 (2002): 31–47.

Ajayi, S. Ibi. "An Analysis of External Debt and Capital Flight in the Severely Indebted Low Income Countries in Sub-Saharan Africa." *IMF Working Paper* (1997): 68–97.

———. "What Africa Needs to Do to Benefit from Globalization." *Finance and Trade Review* (December 2001): 38–52.

Alldridge, T. S. *A Transformed Colony.* London: Clarendon Press, 1910.

Allen, Chris. Review of *Africa and the Drugs Trade. African Political Economy* 26, no.79 (March 1999): 5–22.

Amnesty International Website. http://www.foreignpolicy-infocus.org/briefs/vol5. 25 June 2003.

Anderson, Benedict. *Imagined Communities: Reflections on the Origin and Spread of Nationalism.* New York: New Left Books, 1991.

Anderson, Eugene. *Nationalism and Cultural Crisis in Prussia, 1806–1815.* New York: Octagon Books, 1939.

Anderson, Perry. *Lineages of the Absolutist State.* London: Verso, 1979.

An-Na'im, Abdullahi A. "Islam and National Integration in Sudan: Regional and National Integration." In *Africa: Islam, Christianity and Politics in the Sudan and Nigeria.* Edited by John O. Hunwick. Chicago, IL: Northwestern University Press, 1992.

Anstey, Roger. *King Leopold's Possessive Legacy.* London: Oxford University Press, 1966.

APC Inc. *The Rising Sun: A History of the All Peoples Congress Party of Sierra Leone.* Freetown, Sierra Leone: APC Publications, 1982.

Ardant, Gabriel. *Histoire l'impôt,* vol. 1. Paris: Fayard, 1971.

Arrighi, Giovanni. "The African Crisis." *New Left Review* 15 (May–June 2002): 5–38.

Atiyah, Edward. *An Arab Tells His Story: A Study in Loyalties.* London: John Murray, 1946.

Ayandele, E. A. *The Educated Elite in the Nigerian Society*. Ibadan, Nigeria: 1974.
Ayoob, Mohammed. *The Third World Security Predicament*. Boulder, CO: Lynne Rienner, 1995.
Balandier, Georges. *Sociologie des Brazzavilles noires*. Paris: Librarie Armand Colin, 1955.
Balsvik, Randi R. *Haile Selassie's Students: The Intellectual and Social Background to Revolution, 1952–1977*. East Lansing: African Studies Center, Michigan State University Press, 1985.
Bangura, Yusuf. "Strategic Policy Failure and Governance in Sierra Leone." *Journal of Modern African Studies* 38, no. 4 (2000): 551–577.
Banton, Michael. "The Ethnography of the Protectorate: Review Articles." *Sierra Leone Studies*, no. 4 (June 1955): 246–284.
———. *West African City*. London: Oxford University Press, 1957.
Baqir, Muktar al-Afif, Al-. "The Crisis of Identity in the Northern Sudan: A Dilemma of a Black People with a White Culture." CODESRIA African Humanities Institute, Northwestern University: 13–36.
Barnard, F. M. *Herder's Social and Political Thought*. Oxford: Clarendon Press, 1965.
Bayart, Jean-François. *The State in Africa: The Politics of the Belly*. New York: Longman, 1993.
BBC News online. "Brain Drain Costs Africa Billions." http://news.bbc.co.uk/1/hi/world/Africa/1605242.stm. 2 August 2003.
Beale Horton, James Africanus. *West African: Vindication of the Negro Race*. London: Oxford University Press, 1868.
Beales, Derek. *The Resorgimento and the Unification of Italy*. London: Longman, 1971.
Berdal, Mats, and David Malone. *Greed and Grievance: Economic Agendas in Civil Wars*. Boulder, CO: Lynne Rienner, 2000.
Berlin, Isaiah. *Vico and Herder*. New York: Viking, 1976.
Berman, Eric G. "Re-Armament in Sierra Leone: One Year After the Lomé Peace Agreement." *Small Arms Survey, Occasional Paper No. 1* (December 2000): 3–21.
Beshir, Muhammad Omar. *The Southern Sudan: Background to Conflict*. London: C. Hurst and Co., 1969.
Best, J. Ralph. *A History of the Sierra Leone Railway, 1899–1949*. Freetown, Sierra Leone: Mimeo, 1949.
Bhabha, Homi. "Narrating the Nation." In *The Nation and Narration*. Edited by Homi Bhaba. London: Routledge, 1990.
Bienen, Henry. "Leaders, Violence, and the Absence of Change in Africa." *Political Science Quarterly* 108, no. 2 (1993): 271–282.
Bond, Patrick. *Fanon's Warning: A Civil Society Reader on the New Partnership for Africa's Development*. Trenton, NJ: Africa World Press, 2002.
Bonney, Richard. *The King's Debts: Finance and Politics in France 1589–1566*. Oxford: Clarendon Press, 1981.
———. *Political Change in France Under Richelieu and Mazarin*. Oxford: Oxford University Press, 1978.
———. *The Rise and Fall of the Fiscal State in Europe*. Oxford: Oxford University Press, 1999.
Boyce, James K., and Leonce Ndikumana. "Is African a Net Creditor? New Estimates of Capital Flight from Severely Indebted sub-Saharan Countries." *Journal of Development Studies* 38, no. 2 (December 2001): 27–56.
BP Corporation. *BP Statistical Review of World Energy*, vol. 4 (June 2001).

Bratton, Michael, and Nicolas Van de Walle. "Neo-Patrimonial Regions and Political Transitions in Africa." *World Politics* 46, no. 4 (July 1994): 453–489.

Breuilly, John. *Nationalism and the State.* Chicago, IL: University of Chicago Press, 1993.

Brietzke, Paul. "Ethiopia's 'Leap into the Dark': Feudalism and Self-Determination in the New Constitution." *Journal of African Law* 40 (1995): 44–75.

Brown, Mercy, David Kaplan, and Jean Baptiste Meyer. "Counting Brains: Measuring Emigration from South Africa." Development Policy Research Unit, University of Cape Town. http://www.queensu.ca/samp/publications/policybriefs/brief5.pdf. 2001.

Brubaker, Rogers. *Nationalism Reframed: Nationhood and the National Question in the New Europe.* Cambridge: Cambridge University Press, 1996.

Bureau d'Études, de Recherches et de Consulting International (BERCI) Survey Report, April 1998: *La Confusion des Sentiments.*

———, May 1998: *Kinshasa Report.*

———, November 1998: *Survey.*

Callaghy, Thomas M. *The State Society Struggle: Zaire in Comparative Perspective.* New York: Columbia University Press, 1984.

Carayannis, Tatiana, and Herbert F. Weiss. "Seeking the Peace in the Congo: The Role of the UN and Regional Organizations." In *Dealing with Conflict in Africa: The Role of the United Nations and Regional Organizations.* Edited by Jane Boulden. London: Palgrave Macmillan, 2003.

Castells, Manuel. *The End of Millennium.* Oxford: Blackwell, 1998.

Chandaman, C. D. *The English Public Revenue, 1660–1680.* Oxford: Clarendon Press,1975.

Chase, Robert S., Emily B. Hill, and Paul Kennedy. "Pivotal States and U.S. Strategy." *Foreign Affairs* 75, no. 1 (1996): 33–75.

Chaunau, Pierre. "Le État de Finance." In *Histoire Economique et Sociale de la France, Tome I: De 1450 á 1660.* Edited by Fernand Braudel and Ernest Labrousse. Paris: Presses Universitaires de France, 1982.

Chazan, Naomi, Robert Mortimer, John Ravenhill, and Donald Rothchild. *Politics and Society in Contemporary Africa.* 2d ed. Boulder, CO: Lynne Rienner, 1992.

CIA. *The World Factbook–Sudan;* IRW. "Sudan: Ministry Plans to Double Oil Output." http://www.africaonline.com. August 2001.

Clapham, Christopher. *Haile Selassie's Government.* New York: Praeger, 1969.

Clark, G. N. *The Seventeenth Century.* Oxford: Clarendon Press, 1953.

Cliffe, Lionel, and Robin Luckham. "Complex Political Emergencies and the State: Failure and the Fate of the State." *Third World Quarterly* 20, no.1 (1999): 17–50.

Cohen, John M., and Stephen B. Peterson. *Administrative Decentralization: Strategies for Developing Countries.* West Hartford, CT: Kumarian Press, 1999.

Colley, Linda. "Whose Nation? Class and National Consciousness in Britain, 1750–1830." *Past and Present*, no. 113 (November 1986): 90–117.

Collier, Gershon. *An Experiment in Democracy in an African Nation.* London: University of London Press, 1970.

Collier, Paul. "Economic Causes of Civil Conflict and Their Implications for Policy." World Bank Development Research Group (15 June 2001).

Collier, Paul, and Anke Hoeffler, "On the Incidence of Civil War in Africa." Washington, DC: World Bank Development Research Group.

———. "Greed and Grievance in Civil War." Washington, DC: World Bank, 2001.

Collier, Paul, Anke Hoeffler, and Måns Söderbom. "On the Duration of War." Presented at the World Bank Development Research Group and University of California. Center for Global Peace and Conflict (18–21 May 2001), 17.

Collier, Paul, V. L. Elliott, Harvard Hegre, Anke Hoeffler, Marta Reynal-Querol, and Nicholas Sambanis. *Breaking the Conflict Trap: Civil War and Development Policy.* Washington, DC: World Bank, 2003.

Collins, Robert. *The Waters of the Nile.* Oxford: Clarendon Press, 1990.

Coquery-Vidrovitch, Catherine, Alan Forest, and Herbert Weiss. *Rebellions-Révolution au Zaire: 1963–1965.* Paris: Editions L'Harmattan, 1987.

Corby, Richard. "Western Educated Sons of Chiefs, District Commissioners and Chiefdom: The Role of Bo School and Its Graduates in the Local Level Development of Sierra Leone, 1906–1961." Ph.D. dissertation, Indiana University, 1976.

Cox, Thomas. *Civil-Military Relations in Sierra Leone.* Cambridge, MA: Harvard University Press, 1976.

Crowder, Michael. "An African Aristocracy." *Geographical Magazine* 31, no. 4 (1958): 183–221.

———. *West Africa Under Colonial Rule.* London: Hutchinson, 1968.

Daily Star Online. "War and Peace: Egypt's Stakes in the Future of Sudan." http://www.dailystar.com. 18 November 2002.

Dalby, David. "The Military Take-over in Sierra Leone." *The World Today* (August 1967): 359–390.

Daouas, Mohamed. "Africa Faces the Challenge of Globalization." *Finance and Trade Review* (December 2001): 38–79.

Democratic Republic of the Congo—Diamond Mining." http://www.mbendi.co.za.

Deng, Francis Mading. *Tradition and Modernization: A Challenge for Law Among the Dinka of the Sudan.* New Haven, CT: Yale University Press, 1971.

———. *Africans of Two Worlds.* New Haven, CT: Yale University Press, 1978.

———. *Dinka Cosmology.* London: Ithaca Press, 1980.

———. *Dynamics of Identification.* Washington, DC: Brookings Institution, 1995.

———. *War of Visions.* Washington, DC: Brookings Institution, 1995.

Deng, Francis M., et al., *Sovereignty as Responsibility: Conflict Management in Africa.* Washington, DC: Brookings Institution, 1966.

Deng, Francis M., and M. W. Daly. *Bonds of Silk, The Human Factor in the British Administration of the Sudan.* East Lansing: Michigan State University Press, 1989.

Deng, Francis Mading, and J. Stephen Morrison. *U.S. Policy to End Sudan's War: Report of the CSIS Task Force on U.S. Sudan Policy.* Washington, DC: CSIS (February 2001).

Dercon, Stefan, and Lullseged Ayalew. "Smuggling and Supply Response: Coffee in Ethiopia." *World Development* 31 (1995): 17–98.

Deutsch, Karl. *Nationalism and Social Communication.* Cambridge, MA: MIT Press, 1953.

Diamond, Larry. "Prospect for Democratic Development in Africa." In *Hoover Institution Essays in Public Policy,* No. 7. Stanford, CA: Hoover Institution, Stanford University Press, 1997.

Dietrich, Christian. "Hard Currency: The Criminalized Diamond Economy of the Democratic Republic of the Congo and Its Neighbors." *The Diamonds and Security Project, Occasional Paper No. 4* (June 2002): 3–24.

Dowden, Richard. "Sierra Leone Locked in Shackles of Corruption." *Daily Guardian* (12 October 2002): 15–22.

Dunn, Kevin C. *Imagining the Congo: The International Relations of Identity.* New York: Palgrave Macmillan, 2003.

Easmon, M.C.F. "A Note on the Waima Incident." *Sierra Leone Studies,* no. 18 (1966): 59–91.

Economic Commission on Africa. Conference Report on "Sharing Knowledge to Enrich Research, Training and Policy Making." Addis Ababa, Ethiopia (August 2000).

Egziabher, Tegegne Gebre. "The Influences of Decentralization on Some Aspects of Local and Regional Planning in Ethiopia." *Eastern Africa Social Science Research Review* 14, no. 1 (January 1998): 136–155.

Eisenstadt, S. N. *The Political System of Empires.* London: Free Press of Glencoe, 1963.

Emerson, Rupert. *From Empire to Nation: The Rise to Self-Assertion of Asian and African Peoples.* Cambridge, MA: Harvard University Press, 1960.

Engedayehu, Walle. "Ethiopia: Democracy and the Politics of Ethnicity." *Africa Today,* 2d quarter (1993): 19–30.

EPRDF Fourth Congress Report. Addis Ababa. (August 2001).

Ethiopian Herald. "Forum Discusses Decentralization Affirmative Actions." (6 August 2002): 12–34.

Ethiopian Peoples' Revolutionary Democratic Front. "EPRDF's Five-Year Program of Development, Peace, and Democracy." Addis Ababa, Ethiopia (August 2000).

Finer, Samuel E. "State and Nation Building in Europe: The Role of the Military." In *The Formation of National States in Western Europe.* Edited by Charles Tilly. Princeton, NJ: Princeton University Press, 1988.

———. "State Building, State Boundaries, and Border Control." *Social Science Information* 13, no. 4 (August–September 1974–1979): 78–115.

———. *The History of Government, Volume III.* Oxford: Oxford University Press, 1997.

Firebaugh, Glenn. "Empirics of World Income Inequality." *American Journal of Sociology* 104, no. 5 (May 1999): 1597–1630.

Fisher, Humphrey. "Elections and Coups in Sierra Leone." *Journal of Modern African Studies* 7, no. 4 (1969): 635–687.

Flintan, Fiona, and Imeru Tamrat. "Spilling Blood over Water? The Case of Ethiopia." In *Scarcity and Surfeit.* Edited by Jeremy Lind and Kathryn Sturman. Pretoria, South Africa: ISS, 2002.

Foray, Cyril P. *Historical Dictionary of Sierra Leone.* Metuchen, NJ: Scarecrow Press, 1977.

French, Howard W. "Zaire Rebels Blocking Aid, UN Says." *New York Times* (23 April 1997): 18–35.

Fyle, C. Magbaily. "The Military and Civil Society in Sierra Leone: The 1992 Military Coup d'Etat." *Africa Development* 18, no. 2 (1994): 3–130.

Gabre-Selassie, Zewde. *Yohannes IV of Ethiopia.* London: Oxford University Press, 1975.

Gberie, Lansan. "War and Peace in Sierra Leone: Diamonds, Corruption, and the Lebanese Connection." *The Diamonds and Human Security Project,* Occasional Paper No. 6 (2002): 9–29.

Gibbon, Peter. "Present-Day Capitalism, the New International Trade Regime and Africa." *Review of African Political Economy* 29 (March 2002): 85–112.

Gilkes, Patrick. *The Dying Lion: Feudalism and Modernization in Ethiopia.* London: Julian Friedmann, 1975.

Glenny, Misha. *The Balkans: Nationalism, War, and the Great Powers, 1804–1999.* Harmondsworth, U.K.: Penguin, 1999.

Global Dialogue. "The Oil Industry Fueling Civil War in Sudan," vol. 4.3 (December 1999).

Goesling, Brian. "Changing Income Inequalities Within and Between Nations: New Evidence." *American Sociological Review* 66 (October 2001): 730–761.

Goldsmith, Arthur. "Africa's Overgrown State Reconsidered: Bureaucracy and Economic Growth." *World Politics* 51 (1999): 503–546.

Gourevitch, Philip. *We Wish to Inform You That Tomorrow We Will Be Killed with Our Families: Stories from Rwanda.* New York: Farrar, Straus, and Giroux, 1998.

Government of Sudan. *The Commission of Enquiry*, vol. 31.

Green, Reginald Herbold. "Khatt and the Realities of Somalis: Historic, Social, Household, Political and Economic." *Review of African Political Economy* 26, no. 79 (March 1999): 30–48.

Greenfield, Richard. *Ethiopia: A New Political History.* London: Pall Mall Press, 1965.

Grimmett, Richard F. *Conventional Arms Transfers to Developing Nations, 1991–1998.* Washington, DC: CRS, 1999.

Gudina, Merere. "The New Directions of Ethiopian Politics." *New Trends in Ethiopian Studies* (1994): 3–16.

Guttman, E. "The Reception of Common Law in The Sudan." *Common Law Quarterly* 61 (1957): 390–417.

Hair, P. E. H. "Review of *A History of Sierra Leone.*" *Sierra Leone Studies*, no. 17 (June 1963): 243–286.

Hannum, Hurst, *Autonomy, Sovereignty, and Self-Determination.* Philadelphia: University of Pennsylvania Press, 1990.

Harding, Jeremy. "The Mercenary Business: Executive Outcomes." *Review of African Political Economy* 71 (1997): 67–97.

Hargreaves, J. "African Colonization in the Nineteenth Century: Liberia and Sierra Leone." *Sierra Leone Studies*, no. 16 (June 1962): 190–221.

Harir, Sharif. "Racism in Islamic Disguise? Retreating Nationalism and Upsurging Ethnicity in Darfur, Sudan." In *Historical Discord in the Nile Valley.* Edited by G. Warburg. London: C. Hurst, 1992.

Harrison, James. *The Twenty-Seventh of April: The Sierra Leone Wars of 1898.* New York: City College, 1972.

Hasan, Yusuf Fadl. *The Arabs and The Sudan.* Edinburgh, Scotland: Edinburgh University Press, 1967.

Hassen, Mohammed. "The Macha-Tulama Association and the Development of Oromo Nationalism." In *Oromo Nationalism and the Ethiopian Discourse.* Edited by A. Jalata. Lawrenceville, NJ: Red Sea Press, 1998.

———. *The Oromo of Ethiopia: A History 1570–1860.* Cambridge: Cambridge University Press, 1990.

Hayward, Fred. "Political Leadership, Power, and the State: Generalizations from the Case of Sierra Leone." *African Studies Review* 27, no. 3 (1984): 30–62.

Hearder, Harry. *Italy in the Age of the Risorgimento.* London: Longman, 1983.

Held, David. "Democracy, the Nation State and the Global System." *Economy and Society* 20 (May 1991): 123–172.

Henneman, John Bell, Jr. "France in the Middle Ages." In *The Rise of the Fiscal State in Europe.* Edited by Richard Bonney. Oxford: Oxford University Press, 1999.

Her Majesty's Commissioner and Correspondence on the Subject of the Insurrection in the Sierra Leone Protectorate. London: Darling and Sons, 1898.

Hirsch, John L. *Sierra Leone: Diamonds and the Struggle for Democracy.* Boulder, CO: Lynne Rienner, 2000.

Hobsbawm, Eric. *Nations and Nationalism Since 1780: Programme, Myth, and Reality.* Cambridge: Cambridge University Press, 1990.

Hochschild, Adam. *King Leopold's Ghost: A Story of Greed, Terror, and Heroism in Central Africa.* New York: Houghton Mifflin, 1998.

Holbrooke, Richard. "Statement Before the United Nations Security Council's Exploratory Hearing on Sierra Leone Diamonds," U.S. Mission to the UN, USUN Press Release #194 (00), November 30, 2000.

Horowitz, Donald L. *Ethnic Groups in Conflict.* Berkeley: University of California Press, 1985, 2000.

Human Rights Watch. "Sudan Global Trade Local Impact: Arms Transfers to All Sides in the Civil War in Sudan." http://www.hrw.org/pubweb/arms.html. 30 November 2003.

Huntington, Samuel P. *Political Order in Changing Societies.* New Haven, CT: Yale University Press, 1968.

———. *The Third Wave.* Norman: University of Oklahoma Press, 1991.

ICG Report. "Scramble for the Congo: Anatomy of an Ugly War." *ICG Report* 26 (December 2000).

International Rescue Committee. *Mortality in the Eastern Democratic Republic of Congo* (available online at www.reliefweb.int/library/documents/2001/irc_drc_08may.pdf) (8 May 2001).

Iyob, Ruth. *The Eritrean Struggle for Independence: Domination, Resistance, Nationalism, 1941–1993.* Cambridge: Cambridge University Press, 1995.

Jalata, Asafa. "The Cultural Roots of Oromo Nationalism." In *Oromo Nationalism and the Ethiopian Discourse.* Edited by Asafa Jalata. Lawrenceville, NJ: Red Sea Press, 1998.

———. *Oromia and Ethiopia: State Formation and Ethnonational Conflict, 1868–1992.* Boulder, CO: Lynne Rienner, 1993.

Joireman, Sandra Fullerton. "Opposition Politics and Ethnicity in Ethiopia: We Will All Go Down Together." *Journal of Modern African Studies* 35, no. 3 (1997): 301–398.

Jones, A. H. M., and E. Monroe. *A History of Abyssinia.* New York: Negro University Press, 1969.

Jones, Adam. *From Slaves to Palm Kernals: A History of the Galinhas Country, 1730–1890.* Wiesbaden, Germany: Franz Steiner Verlag, 1983.

Jones, Bruce D. *Peacemaking in Rwanda: The Dynamics of Failure.* Boulder, CO: Lynne Rienner, 2001.

July, Robert. "Africanus Horton and the Idea of Independence in West Africa." *Sierra Leone Studies,* no. 18 (1966): 2–39.

Kalyvas, Stathis N. "'New' and 'Old' Civil Wars: A Valid Distinction?" *World Politics* 54 (October 2001): 80–118.

Kandeh, Jimmy D. "Sierra Leone: Contradictory Functionality of the Soft State." *Review of African Political Economy* 55 (1992): 20–43.

———. "Sierra Leone's Post-Conflict Elections of 2002." *Journal of Modern African Studies* 41, no. 2 (2003): 183–216.

Kasfir, Nelson. "Peace Making and Social Cleavages in Sudan." In *Conflict and Peace Making in Multiethnic Societies.* Edited by Nelson Kasfir. Lexington, MA: DC Heath, 1990.

———. "Relating Class to State in Africa." *Journal of Commonwealth and Comparative Politics* 21, no. 3 (November 1983): 105–130.

Kaufman, Robert, and Alex Segura-Ubiergo. "Globalization, Domestic Politics, and Social Spending in Latin America: A Time-Series Cross-Section Analysis, 1973–1997." *World Politics* 53 (1997): 521–587.

Keen, David. "Incentives and Disincentives for Violence." In *Greed and Grievance: Economic Agendas in Civil Wars*. Edited by Mats Berdal and David Malone. Boulder, CO: Lynne Rienner, 2000.

Keller, Edmond J. "Drought, War, and the Politics of Famine in Ethiopia and Eritrea." *Journal of Modern African Studies* 30, no. 4 (1992): 609–684.

———. "Remaking the Ethiopian State." In *Collapsed States: The Disintegration and Restoration of Legitimate Authority*. Edited by I. William Zartman. Boulder, CO: Lynne Rienner, 1995.

———. *Revolutionary Ethiopia: From Empire to People's Republic*. Bloomington: Indiana University Press, 1988.

Khalid, Mansour. "External Factors in Sudanese Conflict." In *The Search for Peace and Unity in the Sudan*. Edited by Francis Mading Deng and Prosser Gifford. Washington, DC: The Wilson Center Press, 1987.

———. *The Government They Deserve: The Role of the Elite in Sudan's Political Economy*. New York: Kegan Paul Institute, 1990.

Kissinger, Henry. *Does America Need a Foreign Policy? Toward a Diplomacy for the Twenty-First Century*. New York: Simon and Schuster, 2001.

Koelle, Sigismund. *Polyglotta Africana*. London: Oxford University Press, 1854.

Kohn, Hans. *Prelude to Nation States: The French and German Experience, 1789–1815*. Princeton, NJ: Van Nostrand, 1967.

Korzeniewicz, Roberto, and Timothy Moran. "World Economic Trends in the Distribution of Income." *American Journal of Sociology* 102, no. 4 (1997): 1000–1092.

Kuczynski, R. *A Demographic Study of the British Colonial Empire, West Africa*. London: Oxford University Press, 1948.

Kukk, Christopher L., and David A. Deese. "At the Water's Edge: Regional Conflict and Cooperation over Fresh Water." *UCLA Journal of International Law and Foreign Affairs* 1, no. 21 (spring 1996): 21–64.

Laan, H. L. van der. *The Sierra Leone Diamonds*. Oxford: Oxford University Press, 1965.

Lampe, John R. *Yugoslavia as History*. 2d ed. Cambridge: Cambridge University Press, 2000.

Lederer, Ivo J. "Nationalism and the Yugoslavs." In *Nationalism in Eastern Europe*. Edited by Ivo J. Lederer and Peter F. Sugar. Seattle: University of Washington Press, 1969.

Legesse, Asmarom. *Gada: Three Approaches to the Study of African Society*. New York: Free Press, 1973.

Lesch, Ann Mosely. *Sudan: Contested National Identities*. Indianapolis: Indiana University Press, 1998.

Levine, Donald. *Greater Ethiopia: The Evolution of a Multiethnic Society*. Chicago, IL: University of Chicago Press, 1974.

Lienhardt, Godfrey. *Divinity and Experience, Religion Among the Dinka*. Oxford: Clarendon Press, 1961.

Lonsdale John. "Political Accountability in African History." In *Political Domination in Africa: Reflections on the Limits of Power*. Edited by Patrick Cabal. Cambridge: Cambridge University Press, 1986.

Lumpe, Lora, and Lucy Mathiak. *Government Gun-Running to Guerrillas*. New York: St. Martin's Press, 2000.

Lusaka Agreement. http://www.monuc.org/english/geninfo/documents/asp. 24 May 2002; http://www.usip.org/library/pa/index/pa_drc.html. 1 February 2003.

Mabiola, Yenga. "Democratic Republic of the Congo." *Mining Annual Review* (2001): 22–65.

MacGaffey, Janet. *The Real Economy of Zaire: The Contribution of Smuggling and Other Unofficial Activities to National Wealth*. Philadelphia: University of Pennsylvania Press, 1991.

Majoub, Muhammad Ahmed. *Democracy on Trial: Reflections on Arab and African Politics*. London: Andre Deutsch, 1974.

Malcolm, Noel. *Bosnia: A Short History*. New York: New York University Press, 1994.

Mamdani, Mahmood. *Citizen and Subject: Contemporary Africa and the Legacy of Late Colonialism*. Princeton, NJ: Princeton University Press, 1996.

Markakis, John, and Nega Ayele. *Class and Revolution in Ethiopia*. London: Spokesman, 1978.

Martin, William G. "Region Formation Under Crisis Conditions: South vs. Southern Africa in the Interwar Period." *Journal of Southern African Studies* 16 (March 1990): 112–133.

Martin, William G., and Mark Beittel. "Toward a Global Sociology: Evaluating Current Conceptions, Methods, and Practices." *Sociological Quarterly* 39 (1998): 139–181.

Mayroud, Celine, and John Kalinga. "Coltan Exploration in Eastern Democratic of the Congo." In *Scarcity and Surfeit*. Edited by Jeremy Lind and Kathryn Sturman. Pretoria, South Africa: ISS, 2002.

Mazrui, Ali A. "The Black Arabs in Comparative Perspective: The Political Sociology of Race Mixture." In *The Southern Sudan: The Problem of National Integration*. Edited by Dunstan Wai. London: Frank Cass, 1973.

———. *The African Condition*. Cambridge: Cambridge University Press, 1980.

Meinecke, Friedrich. *Cosmopolitanism and the National State*. Translated by Robert Kimber. Princeton, NJ: Princeton University Press, 1970.

———. *The Age of German Liberation*. Translated by Peter Paret and Helmut Fischer. Berkeley: University of California Press, 1977.

Melvern, Linda. *A People Betrayed: The Role of the West in Rwanda's Genocide*. New York: Zed Books, 2000.

Mendelsohn, Jack. *God, Allah, and JuJu: Religion in Africa Today*. New York: Thomas Mendelsohn & Sons, 1962.

Miller, Edward. "War, Taxation, and the English Economy in the Late Thirteenth and Fourteenth Centuries." In *Warfare and Economic Development*. Edited by J. M. Winter. Cambridge: Cambridge University Press, 1975.

Mining Journal. "Precious Metals/Diamonds/Development and Exploration." *Mining Annual Review* (2000): 12–27.

Mitchell, P. K. "Trade Routes of the Early Sierra Leone Protectorate." *Sierra Leone Studies*, no. 16 (1962): 200–227.

Mkandawire, Thandika. "Crisis Management and the Making of 'Choiceless Democracies.'" In *State Conflict and Democracy in Africa*. Edited by Richard Joseph. Boulder, CO: Lynne Rienner, 1999.

———. "The Political Economy of Financial Reform in Africa." *Journal of International Development* 11 (1999): 321–342.

Mkandawire, Thandika, and Charles C. Soludo. *Our Continent, Our Future: African Perspectives on Structural Adjustment*. Trenton, NJ: Africa World Press, 1999.

Montague, Dena, "Coltan and Conflict in the Democratic Republic of Congo." *SAIS Review* 22, no. 1 (Winter-Spring 2002): 103–118.

Moore, David. "Sail on, O Ship of State: Neo-Liberalism, Globalization and the Governance of Africa." *Journal of Peasant Studies* (1999): 61–96.

Mustafa, Zaki. *The Common Law in The Sudan: An Account of the Justice, Equity and Good Conscience Provision*. Oxford: Clarendon Press, 1971.

Ndumbe, Anyu. "Diamonds, Ethnicity, and Power." *Mediterranean Quarterly* 12, no. 4 (Fall 2001): 90–115.

Negaret Gazeta of the Transitional Government of Ethiopia. Proclamation no. 33/1992: A Proclamation to Define the Sharing of Revenue Between the Central Government and the National/Regional Self-Governments, no. 7 (20 October 1992).

New York Times. "Sudan Pushing Cotton Exports," section 2 (12 July 1980): 23–54.

Ngonga, Alphonse Maindo Monga. *Voter en temps de Guerre: Kisangani (RD-Congo) 1997*. Paris: L'Harmattan, 2001.

Niblock, Tim. *Class and Power in The Sudan: The Dynamics of Sudanese Politics, 1898–1985*. Albany: State University of New York Press, 1987.

Nicol, Davidson. *Africanus Horton: The Dawn of Nationalism in Modern Africa*. London: Longman, 1969.

Nyatepe-Coo, Akorlie A. "Capital Flight in Low-Income sub-Saharan Africa: The Effects of Political Climate and Macroeconomic Policies." *Scandinavian Journal of Development Alternatives* (December 1994): 59–98.

O'Brien, Patrick K., and Philip A. Hunt. "England, 1485–1815." In *The Rise and Fall of the Fiscal State in Europe*. Edited by Richard Bonney. Oxford: Oxford University Press, 1999.

Ofscansky, Thomas P. "Warfare and Instability Along the Sudan-Uganda Border: A Look at the Twentieth Century." In *White Nile Black Blood*. Edited by Jay Spaulding and Stephanie Beswick. Lawrenceville, NJ: Red Sea Press, 2000.

Olukoshi, Adebayo. "State, Conflict, and Democracy in Africa: The Complex Process of Renewal." In *State, Conflict, and Democracy in Africa*. Edited by Richard Joseph, pp. 451–465. Boulder, CO: Lynne Rienner, 1999.

Olukoshi, Adebayo, and Felicia Oyekanmi. "Editorial." *CODESRIA Bulletin*, no. 1–2 (2001): 2–16.

Ormond, W. M. "England in the Middle Ages." In *The Rise and Fall of the Fiscal State in Europe*. Edited by Richard Bonney. Oxford: Oxford University Press, 1999.

"Oromia Speaks: An Interview with a Member of the Central Committee of the Oromo Liberation Front." *Horn of Africa* 3 (1980): 24–42.

OSSREA workshop. Addis Ababa. http://www.allAfrica.com. May–July 2003.

Ottaway, Marina. "Democratization in Collapsed States." In *Collapsed States*. Edited by I. William Zartman. Boulder, CO: Lynne Rienner, 1995.

Pakenham, Thomas. *The Scramble for Africa*. New York: Random House, 1991.

Pavkovic, Aleksandar. *The Fragmentation of Yugoslavia: Origins, History, Politics*. 2d ed. London: Macmillan, 2000.

Peemans, Jean-Phillippe. "Accumulation and Underdevelopment in Zaire: General Aspects in Relation to the Evolution of the Agrarian Crisis." In *The Crisis in Zaire*. Edited by Georges Nzongola-Ntalaja. Trenton, NJ: Africa World Press, 1986.

Peterson, Scott. *Me Against My Brother: At War in Somalia, Sudan, and Rwanda*. New York: Routledge, 2000.

Petrovich, Michael Boro. *A History of Modern Serbia*, vol. II. New York: Harcourt Brace Jovanovich, 1976.

Political Parties Registration Proclamation. *Negarit Gazeta*, no. 46. Addis Ababa (15 April 1993).

Prime Minister of the Federal Democratic Republic of Ethiopia. *The System of Regional Administration in Ethiopia*. Addis Ababa (1994).

Protectorate Native Law Ordinance, 1924. Freetown, Sierra Leone: Government Printer (1924).

Prunier, Gerard. *The Rwanda Crisis: History of a Genocide.* New York: Columbia University Press, 1995.

Rahim, Muddathir 'Abd, Al. *Imperialism and Nationalism in the Sudan: A Study in Constitutional and Political Development 1899–1956.* Oxford: Clarendon Press, 1969.

Raikes, Philip, and Peter Gibbon. "Globalization and African Export Crop Agriculture." *Journal of Peasant Studies* 27 (January 2000): 50–93.

Reno, William. "Shadow States and the Political Economy of Civil Wars." In *Greed and Grievance: Economic Agendas in Civil Wars.* Edited by Mats Berdal and David Malone. Boulder, CO: Lynne Rienner, 2000.

———. *Warlord Politics and African States.* Boulder, CO: Lynne Rienner, 2000.

———. "How Sovereignty Matters: International Markets and the Political Economy of Local Politics in Weak States." In *Intervention and Transnationalism in Africa.* Edited by Thomas Callaghy, Ronald Kassimir, and Robert Lathan. New York: Cambridge University Press, 2001.

Report of the Dove-Edwin Commission of Inquiry into the Conduct of the 1967 Elections and the Government Statement Thereon. Freetown, Sierra Leone: Government Printer, 1967.

Report of the Forster Commission of Inquiry on the Assets of Ex-Ministers and Ex-Deputy Ministers and the Government Statement Thereon. Freetown, Sierra Leone: Government Printer, 1968.

Report of the Panel of Experts on Sierra Leone Diamonds and Arms. United Nations Security Council, S/2000/1195 (14 December 2000): 16

Report of the Sierra Leone Constitutional Conference, 1960. Freetown, Sierra Leone: Government Printer, 1960.

Reports of the Commissioners of Enquiry into the Conduct of Certain Chiefs and Government Statement Thereon. Freetown, Sierra Leone: Government Printer, 1958.

Republic of Sudan. *Report of The Commission of Inquiry into the Disturbances in the Southern Sudan During August, 1955.* Khartoum: McCorquedale & Co. Ltd., 1955.

Rodney, Walter. *History of the Upper Guinea Coast 1545–1800.* Oxford: Oxford University Press, 1970.

Rubenson, Sven. *Wichale XVII.* Addis Ababa: Haile Selassie University Press, 1964.

Rubin, Elizabeth. "An Army of One's Own: In Africa, Nations Hire a Corporation to Wage War." *Harpers* (February 1997): 46–65.

Rudra, Nita. "Globalization and the Decline of the Welfare State in Less Developed Countries." *International Organization* 56 (Spring 2002): 411–435.

Rule, John C. "Louis XIV, Roi Bureaucrate." In *Louis XIV and the Craft of Kingship.* Edited by John C. Rule. Columbus: Ohio State University Press, 1969.

Samoff, Joel, ed. *Coping with Crisis: Austerity, Adjustment, and Human Resources.* Chicago, IL: Chicago University Press, 1994.

Samoff, Joel, and Bidemi Carrol. "The Promise of Partnership and Continuities of Dependence: External Support to Higher Education in Africa." Presented at the 45th Annual Meeting of the African Studies Association in Washington, D.C. (December 2002).

Sawyer, Akilagpa. "Challenges Facing African Universities." Presented at the 45th Annual Meeting of the African Studies Association in Washington, D.C. (December 2002).

Schwab, Peter. *Decision-Making in Ethiopia: A Study of the Political Process.* Rutherford, NJ: Fairleigh Dickinson University Press, 1972.

Second Report of the National Commission for Unity and Reconciliation. Freetown, Sierra Leone: Government Printing Department, 1996.

Selassie, Haile I. *The Autobiography of Emperor Haile Selassie I: My Life and Ethiopia's Progress, 1892–1937.* London: Oxford University Press, 1976.

Shahi, Ahmed S., Al-. "Arabism, Africanism, and Self-Identification in the Sudan." In *The Southern Sudan.* Edited by Dunstan Wai. London: Minority Rights Group, 1971.

―――. "Proverbs and Social Values in a Northern Sudanese Village." In *Essays in Sudan Ethnography.* Edited by Ian Cunnison and Wendy James. London: Hurst, 1972.

Sheehan, James J. "What Is German History?" *Journal of Modern History* 53, no. 1 (March 1981): 4–25.

Shin, A. S. *National Democratic Revolutions: Some Questions of Theory and Practice.* Moscow: Nauka, 1982.

Sierra Leone: Estimates of Revenue and Expenditure. Freetown, Sierra Leone: Government Printer 1930, 1949, 1952.

Sieyès, Emmanuel Joseph. *What Is the Third Estate?* Translated by M. Blondel. New York: Frederick A. Praeger, 1963.

Singer, J. David. "The Levels of Analysis Problem." In *The International System: Theoretical Essays.* Edited by Klaus Knorr and Sidney Verba. Princeton, NJ: Princeton University Press, 1961.

SIPRI Yearbook. http://www.smallarmssurvey.org. 8 May 2001.

Smillie, Ian, Lansana Gberie, and Ralph Hazleton. *The Heart of the Matter: Sierra Leone, Diamonds and Human Security.* Ottawa: Partnership African Canada, 2000.

Smith, Anthony D. *Nationalism and Modernism.* New York: Routledge, 1998.

Spencer, John H. *Ethiopia, the Horn of Africa, and U.S. Policy.* Cambridge, MA: Institute of Foreign Policy Analysis, 1977.

Spenser, Leon P., "Key Points Related to Sudan and Oil," Washington Office on Africa, www.woafrica.org/sudoil.htm, 18 May 2001.

Spitzer, Leo. *The Creoles of Sierra Leone.* Madison: University of Wisconsin Press, 1974.

Stepan, Alfred. *Arguing Comparative Politics.* New York: Oxford University Press, 2001.

"Sudan: Oil and Gas Industry." http://mbendi.co.za. 8 December 2002.

Sugar, Peter F. "Roots of Eastern European Nationalism." In *Nationalism in Eastern Europe.* Edited by Peter Sugar and Ivo J. Lederer. Seattle: University of Washington Press, 1969.

Tamm, Ingrid J. *Diamonds in Peace and War: Severing the Conflict-Diamond Connection.* Cambridge, MA: World Peace Foundation, 2002.

Tamrat, Tadesse. *Church and State in Ethiopia, 1270–1527.* London: Oxford University Press, 1972.

Teketel, Haile-Mariam. *The Production, Marketing, and Economic Impact of Coffee in Ethiopia.* Stanford, CA: Stanford University Press, 1973.

Tilly, Charles. *The Formation of National States in Western Europe.* Princeton, NJ: Princeton University Press, 1975.

―――. *Coercion, Capital, and European States.* Cambridge: Basil Blackwell, 1990.

Touval, Saadia. "Partitioned Groups and Inter-State Relations." In *Partitioned Africans.* Edited by A. I. Asiwaju. London: C. Hurst & Company, 1985.

Treasure, G. R. R. *Seventeenth Century France.* London: John Murray, 1966, 1981.

Turshen, Meredith. *Privatizing Health Services in Africa.* New Brunswick, NJ: Rutgers University Press, 1999.

Twinning, W. "Some Aspects of Reception." *Sudan Law Journal and Report* (1957): 229–252.

U.S. Arms Control and Disarmament Agency. *World Military Expenditures and Arms Transfers*. (Washington, DC: U.S. Arms Control and Disarmament Agency, 1999)

U.S. Committee on Refugees. *USCR World Refugee Survey* (September 1999).

U.S. Department of State. *World Military Expenditures 2003*. http://www.state.gov/documents/organization/18739.pdf. 2003.

U.S. State Department, Bureau of Democracy, Human Rights, and Labor. *1999 Country Reports on Human Rights Practices: Ethiopia* (www.state.gov/www/global/humanrights/1999/ethiopia.html).

UNCTAD. "From Rhetoric to Reality of African Development: UNCTAD Calls for a Major Policy Shift." http://www.unctad.org (11 September 2001): 34–46.

———. *Economic Development in Africa: Performance, Prospects, and Policy Issues*. Geneva: UNCTAD, 2001.

UNESCO. *World Education Report 1991*. Paris: UNESCO, 1991.

———. *World Education Report 2000*. Paris: UNESCO, 2000.

United Nations. "UN Report of the Independent Inquiry into the Actions of the United Nation During the 1994 Genocide in Rwanda" (15 December 1999).

United Nations Department of Humanitarian Affairs, Mine Clearance and Policy Unit. "The Landmine Situation in Sudan: Assessment Situation, Mission Report." (August 1997).

United Nations Office for the Coordination of Humanitarian Affairs, "Ethiopia: Feature—The High Cost of Coffee." http://www.irinnews.org (11 April 2003).

United Nations Security Council S/2002/1146. "Report of the Panel of Experts on the Illegal Exploitation of Natural Resources and Other Forms of Wealth of the Democratic Republic of the Congo." (October 2002).

Uwalaka, Emanuel. "Conducting Survey Research in an African Country: Suggestions for Other Researchers." In *Research Methodology and African Studies*, vol. 1. Edited by Abdul Karim Bangura. Lanham, MD: University Press of America, 1994.

Vaccaro, J. Mathew. "The Politics of Genocide: Peacekeeping and Disaster Relief in Rwanda." In *UN Peacekeeping, American Policy, and the Uncivil Wars of the 1990s*. Edited by William K. Durch. New York: St. Martin's Press, 1996.

Verhaegen, Benoit. *Rebellions au Congo*. Brussels: Les Etudes du CRISP, 1969.

Wade, Robert. "The Rising Inequality of World Income Distribution." *Finance and Development* 38 (December 2001): 38–57.

Wai, Dunstan M. "Revolution, Rhetoric and Reality in the Sudan." *Journal of Modern African Studies* 17, no. 1 (March 1979): 74–108.

———. *The African American Conflict in The Sudan*. New York, London: Africana Publishing Company, 1981.

Warburg, Gabriel R. "The Nile Waters, Border Issues and Radical Islam in Egyptian Sudanese Relations: 1956–1995." In *White Nile Black Blood*. Edited by Jay Spaulding and Stephanie Boswick. Lawrenceville, NJ: Red Sea Press, 2000.

Weber, Eugen. *Peasants into Frenchmen*. Stanford, CA: Stanford University Press, 1976.

Weber, Max. "Politics as a Vocation." In *From Max Weber: Essays in Sociology*. Edited by H. H. Gerth and C. Wright Mills. New York: Oxford University Press, 1958.

Weiss, F. Herbert. *War and Peace in the Democratic Republic of Congo* (Uppsala, Sweden: Nordiska Afrikaninstitutet, 2000).

———. "Comparisons in the Evolution of Pre-Independence Elites in French-Speaking West Africa and the Congo." In *French Speaking Africa: The Search for Identity*. Edited by William H. Lewis. New York: Walker and Company, 1965.

Wolfers, Michael. "Race and Class in Sudan." *Race and Class* 23, no. 1 (Summer 1981): 65–89.

Woodward, Peter. *Sudan (1898–1889), The Unstable State*. Boulder, CO: Lynne Rienner, 1990.

Woolf, S. J. *A History of Italy, 1700–1860*. London: Methuen, 1979.

World Bank. "Health Expenditure, Total (% of GDP)." *World Development Indicators*. CD-ROM, 2002.

———. "Size of the Economy." *World Development Indicators*. http://www.worldbank.org/data/wdi2003/tables/table1-1.pdf. 2003.

———. "Trade (% of GDP)." *World Development Indicators*. CD-ROM, 2002.

———. *A Chance to Learn: Knowledge and Finance for Education in sub-Saharan Africa*. Washington, DC: World Bank, 2001.

———. *Ethiopia: Regionalization Study Report*, no. 18898 (February 1999).

———. *Ethiopia: Review of Public Finances*, vol 1, report no. 18369 (30 December 1998).

Wyse, Akintola. *The Krio of Sierra Leone: An Interpretive History*. London: C. Hurst and Co., 1989.

Young, Crawford. *The African Colonial State in a Comparative Perspective*. New Haven, CT: Yale University Press, 1997.

———. *Politics in the Congo: Decolonization and Independence*. Princeton, NJ: Princeton University Press, 1965.

———. *The Politics of Cultural Pluralism*. Madison: University of Wisconsin Press, 1976.

Young, Crawford, and Thomas Turner. *The Rise and Decline of the Zairian State*. Madison: University of Wisconsin Press, 1985.

Young, John. "Along Ethiopia's Western Frontier: Gambella and Benishangul in Transition." *Journal of Modern African Studies* 37, no. 2 (1999): 37–55.

———. "Development and Change in Post–Revolutionary Tigray." *Journal of Modern African Studies* 35, no. 1 (1997): 83–102.

Zack-Williams, Alfred. *Tributors, Supporters, and Merchant Capital: Mining and Underdevelopment in Sierra Leone*. Aldershot, England: Avebury, 1995.

The Contributors

Tatiana Carayannis manages the publication and oral history research of the United Nations Intellectual History Project. Her articles and chapters have appeared in the *Journal of Asian and African Studies,* the *Journal of International Affairs, Dealing with Conflict in Africa: The Role of the United Nations and Regional Organizations* (edited by Jane Boulden), and *UN Voices: The Struggle for Development and Social Justice.* She is currently completing a doctoral dissertation on conflict networks, multilateral institutions, and the Congo wars.

Rachel Cremona is assistant professor of political science at Flagler College.

Francis M. Deng is research professor of international politics, law, and society and the director of the Center for Displacement Studies at the Johns Hopkins University Paul H. Nitze School of Advanced International Studies (SAIS) in Washington, DC. Among other distinguished positions, he most recently served as representative of the United Nations Secretary-General on Internally Displaced Persons from 1992 until 2004. He is a member of the Council on Foreign Relations and winner of the 2004 Distinguished Africanist Award, given by the African Studies Association for lifetime achievement in the field. He has authored or coauthored over twenty books and numerous book chapters and articles in the fields of law, conflict resolution, internal displacement, human rights, anthropology, folklore, history, and politics. He has also written two novels on the theme of the crisis of identity in the Sudan.

Jimmy D. Kandeh is associate professor of political science at the University of Richmond. He has published *Coups from Below: Armed Subalterns and State Power in West Africa,* as well as numerous articles.

Edmond J. Keller is professor of political science, director of the UCLA Globalization Research Center–Africa, and former director of the James S. Coleman African Studies Center at the University of California–Los

Angeles. Keller is the author of two monographs: *Education, Manpower and Development: The Impact of Educational Policy in Kenya* and *Revolutionary Ethiopia: From Empire to People's Republic.* Professor Keller has also written more than 50 articles on African and African American politics, and has coedited three books: *Afro-Marxist Regimes Ideology and Public Policy* (with Donald Rothchild); *South Africa in Southern Africa: Domestic Change and International Conflict* (with Louis Picard), and *Africa in the New International Order: Rethinking State Sovereignty and Regional Security* (with Donald Rothchild). His present research focus is on issues of political transitions in Africa, cultural pluralism and nationalism, and conflict and conflict management in Africa.

Ricardo René Larémont is associate professor of political science, sociology, and Africana Studies at SUNY Binghamton. His research focuses upon ethnic and religious conflict, civil wars, conflict resolution, civil/military relations, and democratization. His publications include, among others, *Islam and the Politics of Resistance in Algeria, 1783–1992* and *The Causes of War and the Consequences of Peacekeeping in Africa.*

William G. Martin is professor of sociology at Binghamton University, State University of New York. He has published widely on Africa, the modern world-system, and the sociology of knowledge, including most recently *Out of One Many Africas* (with Michael West).

Robert L. Ostergard Jr. is associate director of the Institute of Global Cultural Studies, assistant professor of political science, and research fellow at the Center on Democratic Performance, Binghamton University, State University of New York. He also serves as a consultant for the United Nations Commission on HIV/AIDS and Governance in Africa. He is the author of *The Development Dilemma: The Political Economy of Intellectual Property Rights in the International System*, and is editor of *HIV/AIDS and the Threat to National and International Security.* His current research focuses on conflict and the HIV/AIDS epidemic in Africa.

Herbert F. Weiss is emeritus professor of political science at City University of New York, senior policy scholar at the Woodrow Wilson International Center for Scholars, and senior fellow at the Ralph Bunche Institute for International Studies, CUNY. The main focus of his research has been nationalism and independence struggles, mass mobilization, democratization, elections, and militia demobilization. He has been a consultant with the World Bank, the UN, the U.S. government, and various U.S. and international NGOs.

Index

About the Book

Tackling a fundamental question in the study of contemporary African politics, *Borders, Nationalism, and the African State* systematically and comparatively examines the impact of colonial borders on the intertwined trajectories of ethnic conflict and state development.

The authors combine case studies (Democratic Republic of Congo, Ethiopia, Sierra Leone, and Sudan) with thematic chapters to provide a vivid story of state weakness and conflict on the continent. Their richly detailed analysis and often surprising findings offer an insightful reexamination of the prospects for peace in Africa—and prompt a fresh consideration of the nature of the African state.

Ricardo Réne Larémont is associate professor of political science, sociology, and Africana studies at the State University of New York at Binghamton. His previous publications include *The Causes of War and the Consequences of Peacekeeping in Africa* and *Islam and the Politics of Resistance in Algeria*.